National Party Organizations and Party Brands in American Politics

National Party Organizations and Party Brands in American Politics

The Democratic and Republican National Committees, 1912–2016

BORIS HEERSINK

OXFORD
UNIVERSITY PRESS

OXFORD
UNIVERSITY PRESS

Oxford University Press is a department of the University of Oxford. It furthers
the University's objective of excellence in research, scholarship, and education
by publishing worldwide. Oxford is a registered trade mark of Oxford University
Press in the UK and certain other countries.

Published in the United States of America by Oxford University Press
198 Madison Avenue, New York, NY 10016, United States of America.

© Oxford University Press 2023

Library of Congress Cataloging-in-Publication Data
Names: Heersink, Boris, 1984– author.
Title: National party organizations and party brands in American politics :
the Democratic and Republican National Committees, 1912–2016 / Boris Heersink.
Description: New York, NY : Oxford University Press, 2023. |
Includes bibliographical references and index.
Identifiers: LCCN 2023004934 (print) | LCCN 2023004935 (ebook) |
ISBN 9780197695111 (paperback) | ISBN 9780197695104 (hardback) |
ISBN 9780197695128 (epub)
Subjects: LCSH: Democratic National Committee (U.S.)—History |
Republican National Committee (U.S.)—History. | Democratic Party (U.S.)—History. |
Republican Party (U.S. : 1854–)—History. | Political party organization—United States—History. |
United States—Politics and government—20th century. |
United States—Politics and government—21st century.
Classification: LCC JK2316 .H44 2023 (print) | LCC JK2316 (ebook) |
DDC 324.27309/04—dc23/eng/20230216
LC record available at https://lccn.loc.gov/2023004934
LC ebook record available at https://lccn.loc.gov/2023004935

DOI: 10.1093/oso/9780197695104.001.0001

Paperback printed by Marquis Book Printing, Canada
Hardback printed by Bridgeport National Bindery, Inc., United States of America

In memory of Jan Buijs and Sophia Buijs-Houweling

CONTENTS

FIGURES

TABLES

ACKNOWLEDGMENTS

This book has been a work in progress for a while, and, as a result, the list of people I am indebted to is both lengthy and (unfortunately) likely still incomplete. This project started as a dissertation at the University of Virginia (UVA), and I am forever grateful to the members of my committee—Jeff Jenkins, Sid Milkis, Paul Freedman, and Craig Volden—for their support and guidance. I am especially thankful to Sid and Jeff who served as co-chairs. Sid—as one of the founders of the American political development research area—has a deep belief in, and love for, the study of American political history, and in this regard he was essential to making UVA a home for me from my first semester there. Jeff was the best mentor anybody could hope for: loyal, supportive, appropriately critical whenever necessary (especially when it concerned my use of the passive voice), and now a good friend and collaborator. I was also fortunate to receive feedback, pushback, and suggestions from other members of the UVA community, including Andrew Clarke, Thomas Gray, David Klein, Verlan Lewis, Carol Mershon, Kal Munis, Emily Pears, Rachel Potter, Michael Poznansky, Lynn Sanders, Anthony Sparacino, David Waldner, and Nicholas Winter. I am especially grateful to Brenton Peterson and Jon Kropko for their extensive feedback and advice regarding the quantitative sections in this book.

While working on this project I was able to spend a year in residency as a Miller Center fellow, and I am particularly appreciative of Brian Balogh, the director of the program, for his support. Being part of the 2015–2016 fellowship cohort—a remarkable community of historians and political scientists—was a privilege, and I am particularly thankful to my office mates Judge Glock and Lizzie Ingleson. Most importantly, the Miller Center fellowship allowed me to work with Rick Valelly, who agreed to serve as my "dream mentor" in the program. As anybody who knows Rick is surely unsurprised to find out, he lived up to this description in every way possible, and I am forever grateful for his advice, encouragement, and enthusiastic support.

At Fordham University it has been a thrill to join a great department and to receive feedback from Bob Hume, Ida Bastiaens, Monika McDermott, Rich Fleisher, and Bruce Berg. Paul Alongi Jr. and Christian Decker served as my research assistants and are two of the best examples of the kind of incredibly gifted undergraduate student that make the Fordham community special. I am particularly grateful to Jeff Cohen for his friendship and for taking the time to read an early draft of the full manuscript, being appropriately critical about it, and providing helpful suggestions on how to improve it.

Over the years, I have presented this project at a number of conferences and invited talks. I am deeply appreciative of anybody who has provided comments, including John Aldrich, Julia Azari, David Bateman, Richard Bensel, Sarah Binder, Sean Cain, Jordan Carr Peterson, Jeff Grynaviski, Michael Hankinson, Hans Hassell, Nicole Hemmer, Alexander Hertel-Fernandez, Adam Hilton, David Karol, Kate Krimmel, Michael Malbin, Seth Masket, Rob Mickey, Mike Miller, Nico Napolio, Hans Noel, Julie Novkov, Costas Panagopoulos, Sam Rosenfeld, Elizabeth Sanders, John Sides, Yamil Velez, Tim Weaver, and Christina Wolbrecht. I am grateful for the New York political science community—particularly Heath Brown, Anna Law, and Matt Lacombe—for friendship, writing days, and shared meals. Most importantly, I have been incredibly fortunate to have been able to check in regularly with Dan Galvin for feedback on different components of this book. Dan—with consistent generosity and kindness—provided detailed and insightful responses, which have been a major influence on the book. At Oxford University Press, Dave McBride was the perfect editor: supportive of the project from the moment I reached out to him, and clear and consistent in his communications from then on out. I am thankful to him and the anonymous reviewers for their insightful and detailed comments and suggestions.

Finally, I owe thanks to many people for friendship and support over the years, including Emily Sydnor, Paromita Sen, Ellie Kaknes, Abby Post, Matt Scroggs and Suparna Chaudhry, Colin Kielty, Chelsea Goforth and James Stimpson, Earl Pendleton, Merel Miedema, Merel Kuperus, Jorkeell Echeverria, Becky Reuse Hopkinson, Wendy Reuse, Kathie Allen, Jari Mäkeläinen, Todd Yang, Tre Florez and Julio Villarman, Gabrielle Kelly, Jonathan Meier, Michael Mastroianni, Daniel Rommens, Patrick van den Hanenberg, Eduard van de Bilt, and David Plotke. I am also deeply grateful to my family, particularly Mia, Jan, and Sophie; Anne, Peter, and Guido; my sister Marleen; my dad Rien; and most of all, my mom Ria (you are the best and I love you). Last, but not least, I would be remiss not to mention that James never failed to take seriously the important task of forcing me to take writing breaks by regularly blocking my laptop screen when he decided it was nap time (he's a cat).

1

Introduction

National Committees and Party Brands

The Democratic and Republican National Committees (known, respectively, as the DNC and RNC) are the sole truly national organizations in both major American political parties. While other intra-party organizations—such as congressional caucuses and campaign committees or partisan gubernatorial organizations—by definition consist of representatives from those parts of the country where the party has managed to win the most recent elections, national committees exist to represent their parties in each and every state in the union. Originally founded in the 19th century to organize their parties' quadrennial national conventions, over time both committees have expanded their activities to include organizing presidential and midterm election campaigns, raising money for the party and its candidates, providing campaign advice and support, and engaging in major publicity campaigns on behalf of their parties.

Traditionally, political scientists have argued that the DNC and RNC are best understood as "service providers": organizations that engage in activities aimed at helping their parties' candidates win elections and managing the party as an institution. While such activities are appreciated by the candidates, framing the DNC and RNC as service providers has also set an image of these organizations as having a subservient role within the party. Indeed, the first major work on national committees as organizations concluded that the DNC and RNC engage in *Politics without Power*.[1]

In this book I argue that the role national committees play in American politics is considerably more complex and important than previously thought.

[1] Cornelius P. Cotter and Bernard C. Hennessy, *Politics without Power: The National Party Committees* (New York: Transaction Publishers, 1964; republished by Routledge in 2017).

National Party Organizations and Party Brands in American Politics. Boris Heersink, Oxford University Press.
© Oxford University Press 2023. DOI: 10.1093/oso/9780197695104.003.0001

I argue that partisan political actors see national committees as influential organizations because they believe the DNC and RNC have a clear and (to them) important role: helping shape their party's national brand. A party brand provides voters with crucial information about the parties' policies and priorities at a given moment in time. National committees use their publicity divisions to try to promote a brand they believe will help the party win future elections. In trying to communicate this information to voters, national committees rely on a broad (and changing) array of political communication tools—including advertisements in all forms of media, magazines and other party publications, radio and TV shows, press releases, media appearances by national committee chairs, and websites and online programs. Additionally, both committees regularly create sub-organizations with the stated intent of setting policy positions on behalf of their party as a national institution—policies that the committees then promote through their publicity tools. In doing so, the committees often take sides in major intra-party conflicts over what voters the party should target, what ideological message it should promulgate, and what policies it should embrace—including on fundamental issues such as Prohibition, the role of America in foreign affairs after World War II, civil rights, the role and size of government, and abortion.

I argue that focusing on the committees' branding role helps us better understand their role and influence in American political parties. First and foremost, centering the DNC and RNC's branding role further explains why politicians think the committees are important party institutions and why they are often the site of major intra-party conflicts. Put simply, politicians care about party brands, believe the national committees are central in shaping them, and therefore believe the organizations are valuable. Looking at the national committee branding role also spotlights the fact that the DNC and RNC are often controversial within their parties. After all, if the national committees believe it to be their business to shape a party's brand, they must also determine *what* brand to promote. In doing so, the committees inevitably take sides in intra-party conflicts over what policies the party should support or what voting groups it needs to target. Their branding activities thus placed the national committees in the center of nearly every major intra-party debate in the 20th century and beyond.

Second, concentrating on the committees' branding role helps explain why the committees see differentiation in their activity over time. Previous research has shown that the DNC and RNC sometimes decrease their activities dramatically, often when their party is in the White House. I argue that we can explain this change in activity by considering the relevant political actors' preferences as to when a national committee should engage in major branding efforts. If a party is "out" of the White House, its national committee chairs nearly always have a strong incentive to engage in major branding efforts in the hope of improving their party's electoral performance in future elections. When a party is "in" the White House, control of national committees lies with the incumbent president. Some presidents see value in using their national committee to produce major branding operations in support of legislative proposals, their re-election, or a broader rebranding of the party in their image. But other presidents interpret outright partisan branding as a disadvantage to their own political goals. As a result, "in-party" national committees often find themselves on the sidelines and, as a result, decline dramatically as organizations.

Finally, focusing on DNC and RNC branding teaches us about the difficulties American political parties face in the process of trying to produce an appealing party brand. Indeed, much of this book is not just about when national committees are *successful* in reshaping their party, but about the limits to their ability to achieve this. While the committees try to use their publicity role to push their party to embrace specific policies or form new electoral coalitions, they inherently lack the power to force politicians in their party to comply. Without the ability to force party members to embrace specific policies or broader strategic goals, the only thing the DNC and RNC can do is use their publicity role to send signals to voters and hope they pick them up. But in doing so, they are not alone, as other actors within the party can engage in similar attempts. As a result, national committees can often find themselves on the losing side of such arguments, particularly in recent years when, because of the rise of long presidential primaries and easier access to political communication tools in the era of talk radio, ideological news networks, and the Internet, the national committees' ability to dominate national branding efforts on behalf of their party has almost entirely disappeared.

To summarize, the goal of this book is to reposition our understanding of the DNC and RNC as political institutions. Both committees do indeed engage in service activities on behalf of their parties, and these activities are important and meaningful to the candidates that receive them. But providing voters with information about what policies the party supports and what voting groups it prioritizes is a core national committee activity thus far unexplored. In engaging in these activities, the DNC and RNC have a clear goal: shaping voters' understanding of their party's brand with the hope of convincing them to turn out and vote for the party in future elections. And this is an important role: in laying out the history of the DNC and RNC across more than a century of American politics, I show that politicians are consistently concerned with trying to produce an appealing party brand and believe the national committees have a core role in achieving this. I also show that because of their branding role, both national committees are often in the center of major debates within their parties about how to adjust the party's strategy to ensure future political success. Finally,

I show that the process of (re)shaping or controlling a party's brand has always been difficult but has become even more complicated over time.

In the remainder of this chapter I will lay out the existing political science perspective on the DNC and RNC as political institutions and how it has missed a crucial component of the committees' activity in their parties. Next, I discuss the concept of party brands—what they are, why they are important to parties, and how the need for creating or updating these brands creates a role for the committees. I subsequently discuss how national committees came to take on a branding role within their parties, how they can use this role to push the party in specific policy directions, and why we would expect out-parties to have particular agency and incentive to act in this way. Then, I focus on the role of presidents as party leaders, and the role of political development in determining national committee branding opportunity. Finally, I conclude by discussing the methodological approaches I rely on in this book and by presenting an outline of the remaining chapters.

National Committees as Service Providers

While American parties began to organize in the 1790s, it took several decades for them to create permanent national party organizations. Initially, major intra-party decisions—such as the selection of presidential candidates—were made by a select group of political actors at the federal level through the "King Caucus" system.[2] The limited size of these groups meant that an independent national party organization was not yet necessary for managing the party. This changed when parties began to hold quadrennial national conventions in the 1830s. From then on, representatives from each state gathered as delegates to select the presidential ticket and produce a platform for the national party. Such conventions eventually introduced the need for permanent national party organizations, as they required planning, fundraising, and decisions about the design and execution of the meetings. At the 1848 Democratic National Convention, delegates voted to create a national party organization—which would become known as the DNC.[3] Four years later, the Whigs followed suit, and when Republicans gathered at their first national convention in February 1856, they too created a Committee on National Organization—later renamed the RNC.[4]

[2] See James W. Ceaser, *Presidential Selection: Theory and Development* (Princeton, NJ: Princeton University Press, 1979) 123–169.

[3] *The Proceedings of the Democratic National Convention, Held at Baltimore, May 22, 1848* (Washington, DC: Blair and Rives, 1848) 1.

[4] Ralph M. Goldman, *The National Party Chairmen and Committees: Factionalism at the Top* (Armonk, NY: M.E. Sharpe, 1990), 46; *Official Proceedings of the Republican National*

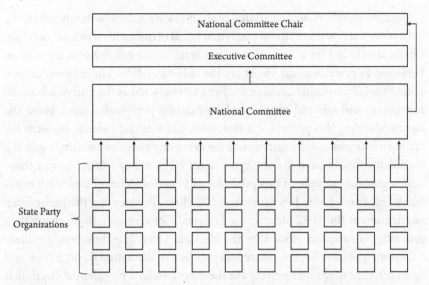

Figure 1.1. Institutional design of the DNC and RNC.

The national committees are made up of representatives of the party organizations from each state in the country (see Figure 1.1). The members are selected by their state party organizations through different approaches—including votes at state conventions or selection by a state party committee.[5] Collectively, the members of the national committee control the institution: they vote to elect the committee's chair, approve budgets, and make decisions on all other crucial decisions that the committee as an institution faces. However, the influence of these members as a collective is limited in practice because the committee does not meet frequently. In no small part this is because of the organizational hassle of gathering individual members from every state in the country in one location. Indeed, in the 19th and early 20th centuries, the DNC and RNC rarely met outside of presidential election years. Starting after 1912, both committees began meeting at least once a year, but even in recent decades the full national committees only meet a few times a year. As a result, committee members are generally not directly involved in day-to-day party management. Those members elected to the DNC or RNC executive committees—which represent a smaller group of committee members—are more involved, but committee membership is still not a full-time engagement.

Convention Convened in the City of Pittsburgh, Pennsylvania, on the Twenty-Second of February, 1856 (New York: New York Republican Committee, 1856), 4–5.

[5] For a more detailed discussion see Cotter and Hennessy, *Politics without Power*, 22–33.

Because members of the national committees are not consistently active, the most powerful position in the organization is that of the national committee chair. Chairs are elected for a two- or four-year term by the full national committee. However, in practice many chairs are the sole candidates under consideration as traditionally, national committee chairs were elected at the end of a national convention and selected by the newly nominated presidential candidates. The logic underlying this process was that, since the national committees were the main party organizations responsible for executing presidential campaigns, the candidates should have the ability to select a chair they trusted to run those campaigns. An example of this process was Franklin Delano Roosevelt's selection of his trusted aide Jim Farley as DNC chair after winning the presidential nomination at the 1932 Democratic National Convention.[6] These chairs then generally remained in office after the election. Over time, however, presidential campaigns have become more independent of the national committee, and new chairs are now usually elected in the months after a presidential election. If a party won that election, the new president selects the committee's chair. But in the losing party, the national committee elects the chair from among party leaders willing to run for the office. For example, after the 2016 presidential election Donald Trump selected Michigan party chair Ronna Romney McDaniel as the next RNC chair, while the DNC saw a competition between multiple candidates culminating in the election of Tom Perez by the committee in 2017.[7]

In the assessment of Hugh A. Bone, chairs "set the tone for their committees, for their headquarters staff, and for the national party in general"[8] but there is no clearly defined job description for what national committee chairs are expected to do. Instead, Cornelius Cotter and Bernard Hennessy note that "the only clear objective of the national chairman is the sweeping command to advance the fortunes of his party."[9] This lack of a clear job description means chairs often have considerable freedom in how to execute their role. And, as they are responsible for hiring and firing committee staff, proposing programs and budgets, and setting the agenda for committee meetings, the chairs generally have considerable agency in determining what their committee does under their leadership.

---

[6] "Roosevelt Nominated on Fourth Ballot," New York Times, July 2, 1932.

[7] "Donald Trump Names Top Michigan Official to Senior G.O.P. Committee Post," New York Times, December 14, 2016; "Democrats Elect Thomas Perez, Establishment Favorite, as Party Chairman," New York Times, February 25, 2017. Note that while outgoing incumbent presidents (like Barack Obama after the 2016 election) can endorse committee chair candidates, they no longer have the power to select the chair.

[8] Hugh A. Bone, Party Committees and National Politics (Seattle: University of Washington Press, 1958), 9.

[9] Cotter and Hennessy, Politics without Power, 61.

However, this agency only applies to chairs that serve when their party has lost the most recent presidential election. National committee chairs of parties that are "out" of the White House can be removed from office through a vote of the full national committee, but this is a relatively rare occurrence.[10] In contrast, "in-party" chairs have considerably less job security since the incumbent president—as the party's leader—can replace them at will. For example, during the presidency of George W. Bush, the RNC had six different RNC chairs, each appointed by Bush and serving on average less than a year and a half. In contrast, during the same eight-year period the out-party DNC had just two chairs who each served a full four-year term. As a result of this presidential control, chairs that serve under an incumbent president generally are understood to be serving as the president's agent.[11]

While the DNC and RNC have been permanent fixtures in American politics since the mid-19th century, a subset of political scientists have been skeptical of their importance. The basis of this sentiment can be traced to two pieces of scholarship: Cotter and Hennessy's book *Politics without Power* and a subsequent article written by Cotter and John F. Bibby. Combined, these studies introduced the view of national committees as "service providers." In this perspective, the DNC and RNC are organizations that help candidates by raising money, providing campaign support, and organizing national conventions. But, as the national committees do not select candidates and cannot force nominees or elected officials to take on specific policy positions, they are otherwise presented as being powerless in American politics. Indeed, Cotter and Hennessy (themselves at one point employed by the RNC and DNC) argued that individual members of the committees are

> large groups of people variously selected, representing different amounts and kinds of local political interests, who come together now and then to vote on matters of undifferentiated triviality or importance, about which they are largely uninformed and in which they are often uninterested.[12]

[10] In no small part because chairs also have at least some power over when and where to hold meetings for the full committee. See Boris Heersink, "Trump and the Party-in-Organization: Presidential Control of National Party Organizations," *The Journal of Politics* 80, no. 4 (October 2018): 1474–1482.

[11] Daniel J. Galvin, "Party Domination and Base Mobilization: Donald Trump and Republican Party Building in a Polarized Era," *The Forum* 18, no. 2 (2020): 135–168; Heersink, "Trump and the Party-in-Organization."

[12] Cotter and Hennessy, *Politics without Power*, 3.

Similarly, Cotter and Hennessy downplayed the influence of national committee chairs, writing that "it is difficult to say what a national party chairman should do. It is even hard to say what he does do."[13]

In later work, Cotter and Bibby concluded that modern national party organizations were largely focused on "rule enforcement, campaign and organizational services, and administrative activities."[14] While they credited the national committees with pushing parties to embrace a more homogenous set of policy positions, Cotter and Bibby's thesis centered on national committees providing services to candidates, while lacking control over those candidates. John Aldrich in his classic book *Why Parties?* describes this shift toward service provision, as "parties as organizations [having] adapted to the changing circumstances," and creating a "new form of party [. . .] one that is 'in service' to its ambitious politicians but not 'in control' of them as the mass party sought to be."[15] The services the national committee provides include raising and distributing money, polling, training of candidates and campaign workers, and publicity. Since candidates are likely pleased to receive such services—as it saves them the trouble of having to invest their own resources in producing them—a service-providing national committee remains relevant within the parties.

In this perspective, candidates over time freed themselves from local party machine politics and effectively took control away from party organizations. This left party organizations—now centered at the national level—with only service provision as a viable political activity. As a result, modern national committees "now play a supportive role, offering resources and services to candidates who seek their help."[16] To be sure, this description of national party organizations as service providers that lack direct control over candidates is fundamentally correct: national committees cannot select candidates, nor can they force elected officials to follow their orders. National committees also clearly do engage in providing a variety of service activities—which candidates (presumably) appreciate. Indeed, a myriad of influential political actors—including presidents, presidential candidates, congressional leaders, governors, other elected officials,

---

[13] Ibid., 67

[14] Cornelius P. Cotter and John F. Bibby, "Institutional Development of Parties and the Thesis of Party Decline," *Political Science Quarterly* 95, no. 1 (1980): 2.

[15] John H. Aldrich, *Why Parties? A Second Look* (Chicago, IL: University of Chicago Press, 2011), 285.

[16] Daniel J. Galvin, "The Transformation of Political Institutions: Investments in Institutional Resources and Gradual Change in the National Party Committees," *Studies in American Political Development* 26, no. 1 (2012): 57. See also: Paul S. Herrnson, *Party Campaigning in the 1980s* (Cambridge, MA: Harvard University Press, 1988); Paul S. Herrnson, "The Evolution of National Party Organizations," in *The Oxford Handbook of American Political Parties and Interest Groups*, ed. Louis Sandy Maisel and Jeffrey M. Berry (New York: Oxford University Press), 57.

and party activists—often pay considerable attention to what their national committees are doing. These political actors are often involved in their national committees: they attend meetings, serve on subcommittees, and publicly and privately discuss their assessments of what the committees are doing and how successful they are at it. These actors also often show considerable interest in (and, at times, concern about) who is in charge of their party's national committee, and they can engage in active competition to gain leadership control of it.[17]

But while the centering of service may be one way to explain why national committees remain relevant in modern American parties, it also presents an image of the DNC and RNC that is still largely in line with Cotter and Hennessy's assessment of national committees as engaging in politics but lacking meaningful power within their parties as they do so. Indeed, in David Karol's more recent assessment "the formal leadership of national, state, and local party chairs" has only "limited importance"[18] in American politics.

Party Brands in American Politics

I argue that existing research has thus far missed an important and influential type of activity the DNC and RNC engage in that transcends service provision: providing publicity on behalf of the national party with the goal of creating a party brand. Political scientists have long argued that party brands—the basic understanding voters have at a given moment in time of a party's policies and general quality of performance in office—are vital in electoral politics. In elections, voters try to find a candidate best suited to their own preferences. Gathering this information for all potential candidates on a ballot is time consuming and lowers the probability of voters participating in elections. Political parties present a solution because they provide voters with an easy heuristic or informational shortcut. If voters have a good sense of what they can expect from a political party (rather than from each individual candidate on a ballot by themselves), they can lower the cost of electoral participation by simply voting with "their" party.

[17] Philip A, Klinkner, *The Losing Parties: Out-Party National Committees, 1956–1993* (New Haven, CT: Yale University Press, 1994); Daniel J. Galvin, *Presidential Party Building: Dwight D. Eisenhower to George W. Bush* (Princeton, NJ: Princeton University Press, 2010); Brian M. Conley, "The Politics of Party Renewal: The 'Service Party' and the Origins of the Post-Goldwater Republican Right," *Studies in American Political Development* 27, no. 1 (2013): 51–67; Sam Rosenfeld, *The Polarizers: Postwar Architects of Our Partisan Era* (Chicago, IL: University of Chicago Press, 2018).

[18] David Karol, "Parties and Leadership in American Politics," in *Leadership in American Politics*, ed. Jeffery A. Jenkins and Craig Volden (Lawrence: University Press of Kansas, 2018), 143.

But for voters to be able to rely on partisanship as a heuristic in elections, the party must have meaning to them: voters must have some understanding of what they are likely to "get" if they vote for a Democrat rather than a Republican. To achieve this, the parties need to produce brands. Anthony Downs, in his 1957 book *An Economic Theory of Democracy*, was one of the first social scientists to acknowledge the importance of such brands (though, as the early case studies in this book will show, politicians relied on this understanding far earlier than that).[19] Subsequently, Donald Stokes, writing in 1963, was the first to identify two components to a party's brand: positional and valance, in which the latter reflects "nonideological actions"[20] such as basic competence in governing or the presence of scandals, and the former represents voters' understanding of a party's ideological and issue positions.[21] Voters combine their understanding of the party's competence and issue positions into a judgment of whether the party is worth voting for.

But how do voters form such an understanding? In part, voters can build knowledge of the parties and their performances by following the news or having their own experiences with political events and outcomes, and this side of the creation of the party brand may be mostly out of the control of political parties as institutions. But parties do not simply sit on the sidelines waiting for voters to come up with an interpretation of their brand: they actively try to shape this understanding by providing voters with information about the party. And they try to do so in a way that they believe is most likely to help the party win future elections. Of course, this is easier said than done, as voters do not simply take in whatever signal a political party sends to them. Instead, what parties try to do is provide voters with informational cues and hope voters will incorporate them in their understanding of the brand.

In doing so, however, parties face a problem: the informational cues they sent to voters must be relatively consistent. If voters receive many conflicting signals from within the same party on issues important to them, the value of party as a heuristic declines, as it does not help voters navigate the political system. Unfortunately for its leaders, American political parties have no easy way to prevent mixed signals being sent toward voters, as parties have no strict control over party membership. Additionally, in a two-party system, both parties often must try to represent relatively broad interests to be electorally successful. As a result, American parties are nearly always "big-tent" coalitions reflecting (sometimes,

[19] Anthony Downs, *An Economic Theory of Democracy* (New York: Harper, 1957).

[20] Daniel M. Butler and Eleanor Neff Powell, "Understanding the Party Brand: Experimental Evidence on the Role of Valence," *The Journal of Politics* 76, no. 2 (April 2014): 492.

[21] Donald E. Stokes, "Spatial Models of Party Competition," *American Political Science Review* 57, no. 2 (1963): 368–377.

very) different ideological and issue preferences. As a result, both parties frequently see major intra-party debates about policy issues or what voting groups the party should prioritize.

While such disagreements are perhaps inevitable, they are also potentially costly. Political scientist Jeffrey Grynaviski has summarized the problem parties face in an insightful metaphor, comparing party attempts at appealing to voters to major corporations' reliance on brands. In the free market, brands are supposed to provide consumers with a level of certainty about the product they are purchasing, regardless of when or where the item is bought. For example, a consumer can go into any McDonalds franchise in the country, buy the same advertised product, and expect the same general quality. At times, though, a specific franchise may present the consumer with something that falls short of that expectation. Such an experience may affect the likelihood that the consumer will return to that specific restaurant, but it also affects the consumer's view of the *brand*:

> [T]he reputation of McDonalds suffers if too many of its local stores offer cold French fries and poor customer service. Similarly, the reputation of a party suffers if it throws its support to too many candidates at odds with their organization on key issues. In both cases, the brand name no longer reduces the public's uncertainty about product or candidate quality, and "brand equity" is lost, with people now more open to sampling new "products" rather than remaining loyal to an existing brand.[22]

Consumers receiving cold fries at a single McDonalds may not be a huge problem for the corporate brand. But more regular negative experiences can result in consumers adjusting their understanding of the chain's brand and making different choices in the future. When they do, the consumers may not just stay away from the restaurants at which they had a poor experience: they may choose to avoid taking the risk of visiting any other franchisees of the corporation as well. Members of a political party run a similar risk. The crucial consideration here is that individual members are affected by the broader sense voters have of their party. As Gary Cox and Mathew McCubbins argue,

> all [caucus members] are hurt by scandal or helped by perceptions of competence, honesty and integrity; all or nearly all are helped by the

---

[22] Jeffrey D. Grynaviski, *Partisan Bonds. Political Reputations and Legislative Accountability* (Cambridge: Cambridge University Press, 2010) 51.

party's platform, when taken as a package. Thus, party records often can be changed in ways that affect the vast majority of party members' reelection probabilities in the same way.[23]

This represents a real problem in the management of American political parties. On the one hand, parties must produce an appealing brand to convince voters to turn out and vote for their candidates in elections. On the other hand, American parties as organizations have no way to control this brand: they cannot ensure that voters will accept favorable information about the party when it is provided to them, but they also cannot control what type of partisan information voters are sent in the first place.

While there are no easy solutions to this problem, parties do try to coordinate their branding as best they can. One solution is partisan control of the congressional agenda.[24] Majority parties in Congress use negative agenda control to prevent the minority party from passing legislation, and they internally agree to try to pass bills the majority of the majority approves of. In doing so, the party tries to provide voters with a set of legislative achievements it can then reward or punish the party for in the next election. There is considerable evidence that parties can indeed constrain their members in Congress with the goal of providing voters with such a legislative record.[25] But while producing a legislative record can help provide voters with informational cues, it is only part of a solution to the branding problem. For starters, it requires that a party have a majority in Congress, since minority parties can only respond to the bills proposed by the majority. Additionally, congressional legislation is hardly the only component of

[23] Gary Cox and Mathew D. McCubbins, *Legislative Leviathan: Party Government in the House* (Berkeley: University of California Press, 1993), 103.

[24] See among others: D. Roderick Kiewiet and Mathew D. McCubbins, *The Logic of Delegation: Congressional Parties and the Appropriations Process* (Chicago: University of Chicago Press, 1991); Cox and McCubbins, *Legislative Leviathan*, 103; Gary Cox and Mathew D. McCubbins, *Setting the Agenda: Responsible Party Government in the U.S. House of Representatives* (New York: Cambridge University Press, 2005); Aldrich, *Why Parties*; John H. Aldrich, and David W. Rohde, "The Logic of Conditional Party Government: Revisiting the Electoral Connection," 2001, accessed at https://themonkeycage.org/wp-content/uploads/2011/07/aldrich-and-rohde.pdf.

[25] See, for example: Jeffery A. Jenkins, "Examining the Robustness of Ideological Voting: Evidence from the Confederate House of Representatives," *American Journal of Political Science* 44, No. 4 (October 2000): 811–822; James M. Snyder and Tim Groseclose, "Estimating Party Influence in Congressional Roll-Call Voting," *American Journal of Political Science* 44 (2000): 193–211; James M. Snyder and Michael M. Ting, "An Informational Rationale for Political Parties," *American Journal of Political Science* 46, no. 1 (2002): 90–110; James M. Snyder and Michael Ting, "Roll Calls, Party Labels, and Elections," *Political Analysis* 11 (2003): 419–444. But see also: Keith Krehbiel, "Where's the Party?" *British Journal of Political Science* 23, no. 2 (1993): 235–266.

a voters' understanding of a party brand.[26] Indeed, voters likely incorporate many other forms of information they receive from and about the party—including cues they receive from the president, presidential candidates, governors, and other political actors.

So, while party brands are fundamental to how political parties operate, providing voters with signals that might produce a brand that is both popular and consistent enough for it to help the party in elections requires coordination and consensus, not just in Congress but more broadly across the party. If the party succeeds at this, it can lower the bar to electoral participation since, at the most basic level, a clear and appealing party brand allows a voter to show up at a polling station, look at a ballot, have no familiarity with any of the specific candidates' qualifications or policy positions, but still be able to make the right choice for themselves on the basis of the candidate's partisanship. But no single actor or institution fully controls what their party's brand looks like. Additionally, many partisan actors are likely to *try* to move the brand in a direction that best suits their specific purposes. But while this may be in their personal interest, in doing so, these different actors within the party can undermine the broader effort of creating a brand that works best for the party as a whole, since the more the party presents itself as heterogeneous to voters, the more muddled the party brand becomes, and the lower the informational value of the heuristic will be. Party leaders therefore must look for a way to try to override conflicting signals and present voters with a clear, national, image.

National Committees and Party-Branding Activities

I argue the national committees are the institutions party leaders have long looked to for producing such a national brand. Both the DNC and RNC are well suited for this role because they developed an infrastructure specifically tailored toward providing publicity on behalf of their national party. Additionally, since the committees are the only national party organizations, the DNC and

[26] In fact, it is not entirely clear voters that are strongly affected by legislative achievements. Woon and Pope have found that voters do indeed rely on party brands in deciding their vote and that they update their assessment of those brands based on changes in congressional voting behavior; legislation (and governing success more broadly) is also not a guarantee for electoral rewards. But Galvin and Thurston find no real evidence that major policy success is rewarded by voters. See: Jonathan Woon and Jeremy C. Pope, "Made in Congress? Testing the Electoral Implications of Party Ideological Brand Names," *Journal of Politics* 70, no. 3 (2008): 823–836; Daniel J. Galvin and Chloe N. Thurston, "The Democrats' Misplaced Faith in Policy Feedback," *The Forum* 15, no. 2 (2017): 333–343.

RNC have at least some legitimacy to speak on behalf of their party. This party branding role is not new. In fact, the necessity of creating organizations capable of engaging in nationwide branding efforts is what drove national committee development in the second half of the 19th century. In the early decades of their existence, both the DNC and RNC organized national conventions but otherwise were inactive. Lacking permanent headquarters, the DNC and RNC functioned only as "committees of correspondence," charged with "keeping various elements of the party in touch between presidential elections."[27] A shift in this role occurred in the late 19th century as electoral reforms enacted during the Progressive Era, changes in the media landscape, and an increased focus on national issues by interest groups necessitated a change in how parties mobilized voters during election campaigns.

As Michael McGerr has argued, parties traditionally relied on "spectacle politics" to mobilize voters. But in the wake of Progressive Era reforms, parties instead had to start relying on "educational campaigns" to achieve the same goal.[28] Among the more crucial reforms in this regard was the introduction of the secret ballot (commonly known as the Australian ballot), which directly undermined the traditional party machine structure and created an electoral connection between elected officials and voters. Prior to the introduction of the secret ballot, local party organizations dominated elections by printing their own ballots and distributing them among voters.[29] Because "each party's ballot had a distinctive size and color," and because the act of casting the ballot was public, the party's workers who distributed them "could tell at a glance who was voting for which party."[30] As a result, parties could mobilize voters through vote buying: party workers could bribe voters with money, goods, or services and check that voters voted "correctly" in return for these favors.[31] But the parties' ability to buy votes decreased after party ballots were replaced by the secret ballot in the 1880s and 1890s. With the act of voting now (increasingly) private and secret, the existing system of mobilization became less effective.

While intended to undermine the party system, the secret ballot inadvertently strengthened parties. Under the new system, the cost of "bolting" the party increased since access to an official ballot was now constrained. Candidates

---

[27] Cotter and Bibby, "Institutional Development of Parties and the Thesis of Party Decline," 2–3.

[28] Michael McGerr, *The Decline of Popular Politics: The American North, 1865–1928* (Oxford: Oxford University Press, 1986).

[29] Richard Bensel, "The American Ballot Box: Law, Identity and the Polling Place in the Mid Nineteenth-Century," *Studies in American Political Development* 17 (2003): 1–27.

[30] Robert E. Mutch, *Buying the Vote. A History of Campaign Finance Reform* (New York: Oxford University Press, 2014), 16.

[31] Alan Ware, *The American Direct Primary: Party Institutionalization and Transformation in the North* (Cambridge: Cambridge University Press, 2002).

previously could more easily leave their party and distribute their own ballots but, in the Australian ballot system, faced a much higher hurdle in doing so. As the secret ballot became the norm across the country, party nominations increased in value because they became the key to accessing the ballot.[32] But as historian Michael Schudson notes, the new system also meant voters now "needed more information to cast a ballot than the loyal partisan of the nineteenth century."[33]

To help provide this information, candidates looked toward their national party organizations. As Daniel Klinghard has argued, the parties now no longer were able to rely on a "conception of party principles as subject to compromise and local interpretations, as local campaigners stretched party platforms to suit public opinion."[34] But parties could also not provide voters with a new clearer "conception" automatically: to inform voters, they needed to educate them. And doing so "required a national party apparatus possessing organizational capacities to reach voters directly, bypassing state and local organizations."[35]

---

[32] John F. Reynolds, *The Demise of the American Convention System, 1880–1911* (Cambridge: Cambridge University Press, 2006). Other reforms of the Progressive Era also contributed to the parties' shift toward educational campaigns. Around the same time, states began to pass laws that explicitly excluded (recent) immigrants from voting. These restrictions on the franchise, as well as Jim Crow legislation that banned Black voters from electoral participation across the South, deliberately excluded a set of voting groups that traditionally had been the easiest targets for local party machines. The 19th century also saw a noticeable increase in the number of interest groups pushing for national—rather than local—policies to deal with problems of the new industrial age, increasing attention to the importance of national politics and, therefore, national political parties. Another crucial element in this regard was the rise of nonpartisan newspapers. While the "yellow journalism" of the popular papers produced by publishers such as Joseph Pulitzer and William Randolph Hearst in the late 19th century were hardly high-quality journalistic products, they represented a crucial shift from partisan to nonpartisan media in American politics. See: Jonathan M. Ladd, *Why Americans Hate the Media and How It Matters* (Princeton, NJ: Princeton University Press, 2012); McGerr, *The Decline of Popular Politics*, 135; Michael Schudson, *The Good Citizen: A History of American Civic Life* (New York: The Free Press, 1998) 174–182; Daniel J. Tichenor and Richard A. Harris, "Organized Interests and American Political Development," *Political Science Quarterly 117*, no. 4 (2002) 587–612. For just two examples of the role of interest groups in pushing for national policies at the time, see: Elizabeth Sanders, *Roots of Reform: Farmers, Workers, and the American State, 1877–1917* (Chicago, IL: University of Chicago Press, 1999); Theda Skocpol, *Protecting Soldiers and Mothers: The Political Origins of Social Policy in the United States* (Cambridge, MA: Belknap Press of Harvard University Press, 1992).

[33] Schudson, *The Good Citizen*, 185.

[34] Daniel Klinghard, *The Nationalization of American Political Parties, 1880–1896* (New York: Cambridge University Press, 2010), 104. As Adam Silver shows, state party platforms in the late 19th century began to nationalize: while in the middle of the century there was considerable regional variation within the same parties, they began to produce more uniform policy agendas in the 1880s and 1890s. See: Adam M. Silver, *Partisanship and Polarization: American Party Platforms, 1840–1896* (Lanham, MD: Lexington Books, 2022).

[35] Klinghard, *Nationalization of American Political Parties*, 109.

As a result, national committees began to expand their roles within their parties. The DNC and RNC now no longer organized just the national conventions; they also prepared and distributed campaign materials during presidential elections. During the 1888 campaign, the RNC organized a series of Republican "clubs," which—as described by a party organizer—worked on "educating the people on the great questions which should absorb their interest" through "the circulation of newspapers, the distribution of public speeches, and the encouragement of public discussion."[36] Similarly, the DNC prepared campaign literature and materials even before the national convention had met to select the presidential nominee and vote on the party's platform.[37] During the campaign, the DNC expanded its campaign headquarters to prepare a national educational campaign:

> Party headquarters now occupied three floors of a Manhattan office building. The "department of oratory" assigned speakers to rallies; the "telegraphic bureau" sent out "proper Democratic news" to the press; [DNC secretary William S.] Andrew's Literary Bureau wrote articles and pamphlets; another bureau prepared documents for the printer; yet another mailed out Andrew's productions to newspapers and local party committees. A dazzled reporter claimed that "never before, even in 1876, under Mr. Tilden, were there such facilities for the spread of Democratic literature through the country."[38]

These developments produced a major reappraisal of the national committees as political institutions. Journalist Rollo Ogden, writing in *The Atlantic Monthly* in 1902, described the "quiet and almost unperceived usurpations of political power by the party National Committee, during the past fifteen or twenty years."[39] Similarly, political scientist Jesse Macy wrote in 1904 that "historically speaking, the committee has grown in consequence and power with the growth of the party" and "supplanted the irregular and self-appointed agencies of the early days and assumed prestige and authority."[40] While the DNC and RNC did

---

[36] Cited in McGerr, *The Decline of Popular Politics*, 82.

[37] Andrews also called on the DNC to collect addresses and personal data "for a million-and-a-half Democrats and independents," a move that would allow the national party to bypass the traditional local party machines and communicate with voters directly. The DNC did not execute Andrews's plan to collect these addresses due to financial constraints on the campaign. See McGerr, *The Decline of Popular Politics*, 85.

[38] Ibid., 86.

[39] Rollo Ogden, "New Powers of the National Committee," *The Atlantic Monthly*, January, 1902, 76.

[40] Jesse Macy, *Party Organization and Machinery* (New York: The Century Company, 1904) 65.

not immediately use their new publicity role outside of election years, over time party leaders began to realize that providing voters with "educational" information on behalf of the party did not need to be an activity limited solely to election campaigns: instead, committees could provide continuous publicity campaigns aimed at shaping voters' perception of the party's brand.

As a result, after the 1912 election both parties kept their national committees active outside of election years. In the decades that followed, both committees continued to invest in this publicity role—in part by continuously creating new types of publicity tools to reach out to voters with. This included advertisements in all types of media formats, magazines, radio shows, TV programs, websites, and online programs. In addition to this, the committees' chairs use their position to appear in the media and present their party's position on salient policy issues to a broader public. In doing so, the national committees try to help voters connect the party to specific policy positions, convince them that the party is particularly interested in representing their group or community, and attack the opposite party—including through what Frances Lee describes as "nonideological appeals accusing the other party of corruption, failure, or incompetence."[41] To help achieve this, committees began creating new (temporary) political party institutions and provided them with the power to set policy positions on behalf of the national party. While the committees do not have the power to force elected officials to embrace those policies, they could then promote those policies through their publicity tools as the party's official positions on issues. Notably, in executing this branding role, the committees are very much a product of the time periods in which they are active. This means both committees often engage in very similar activities around the same time, such as embracing new types of political communication or relying on similar political strategies. For example, after the DNC created the Democratic Advisory Council (DAC)—an intra-party organization that could set national policies for the party—in the second half of the 1950s, the RNC created its own version after the 1964 election. And both the DNC and RNC returned to the DAC format regularly in the decades that followed.

Of course, not all activities that the DNC and RNC engage in are branding focused. Both committees have continuously provided the kind of services scholars previously focused on, and these services are meaningful to party members. But the branding role is fundamental to the role national committees play within their parties: the necessity of producing a national party brand in the wake of the Progressive Era reforms is what drove the institutional expansion

---

[41] Frances E. Lee, *Insecure Majorities: Congress and the Perpetual Campaign* (Chicago, IL: University of Chicago Press, 2016), 2.

of both organizations in the first place, and, moving forward, party branding represented something of crucial importance to politicians. Since parties need a brand that voters find appealing, and individual politicians cannot easily create such a brand themselves, they look toward national committees to help achieve it for them.

Importantly, the national committees often have considerable agency to decide what *kind* of brand to promote. That is, national committee chairs can decide what policies the committee will promote, what voting groups it targets, and what topics it picks to differentiate their party from the opposition. In doing so, the committees can change their approaches in radical ways. For example, under DNC chair John Raskob (1928–1932), the DNC pushed the Democratic Party to embrace opposition to Prohibition. During World War II, the RNC worked to produce unity on moving past the party's previous isolationism. In the 1950s, under chair Paul Butler, the DNC moved from attempting to preserve the New Deal–era party coalition to embracing a clear liberal agenda—which included strong support for civil rights. More recently, the national committees engaged in similar choices. Under DNC chair Howard Dean (2005–2008), the committee relied on a "50-state strategy" aimed at expanding the Democratic Party's voting coalition to include White voters with conservative viewpoints. Part of this process included trying to downplay the Democrats' support for abortion rights and appealing to evangelical Christian voters. And, after the 2012 election, the RNC produced a report calling on the GOP to appeal to minority voting groups and embrace immigration reform efforts.

Each of these attempts—and many of the others discussed in this book—were controversial within the parties at the time. Some actors in the parties celebrated the committees' choices. Others opposed them for principal reasons—arguing that the national committees lacked authority to make such calls on behalf of the party, regardless of whether they agreed with them or not. But most of those who opposed specific national committee branding efforts did so because they feared that, if successful, these activities would adjust voters' understanding of the party's brand away from their preferred image. Crucially, the concern was not that the national committees' embrace of certain policy positions would bind individual elected officials to support them as well. All actors involved—both in- and outside the national committees—understood that the DNC and RNC have no such powers. Rather, these political actors feared that if the committees successfully rebranded their parties, it would affect those politicians opposing these brands as well. After all, if voters rely on their understanding of a party's brand in their voting decisions, *changing* the brand can bring in new voters but also alienate existing ones. For example, by appealing to one group (evangelical Christians) and the issues they find important, the party is at the same time providing other groups in society (LGBT voters) information about the kind of priorities it has in a way that may make those voters less likely to vote for that party in the future. Politicians within the party who rely on those voters' support therefore may be concerned if the national committees' branding choices contradict their own political strategies.

Because of this, the DNC and RNC are not institutions merely providing services to candidates requesting them: throughout the 20th century (and, to a lesser extent, beyond) both national committees have systematically engaged in party-branding activities, and those in charge of the national committees often have had considerable agency in determining what type of party brand to promote and have used this agency to take sides in major intra-party debates about specific policies, voting groups, or broader ideological directions the party should pursue.

Constraints on National Committee Branding Efforts

But national committee agency in determining *what* brand to promote or even *whether* to engage in branding is not constant. As the cases presented in this book will show, there are two broad types of constraints on national committees' ability to engage in branding: short-term limitations that may result in a committee decreasing its branding role for a period of time and then a return to investing in such efforts later, and a longer-term process of American political development that has made it increasingly difficult for national committees (or, indeed, any partisan institutions) to engage in the type of major branding efforts that they previously did.

The short-term limitations are sometimes based on specific historical events that limit a committees' ability to act. For example, national committees may face major difficulties in fundraising and paying off campaign debts, thereby limiting their ability to pay for new branding efforts. At other times, individual committee chairs lacked interest in running their organizations, resulting in a less active committee. But a more structural short-term limitation on national committee branding efforts concerns presidential control over the committee. While national committee chairs of parties out of the White House have considerable agency in determining what kind of brand to promote, this is not true for chairs of parties with incumbent presidents. Since presidents have the de facto power to select and replace the national committee's chair, the DNC or RNC acts as an agent of the president when their party holds the White House. As a result, what national committees do when their party is in the White House is the product of the president's preferences. Such preferences can be based on a variety of political contextual situations, and there are times when presidents can see major benefits to having a national committee engage in active branding on their behalf. Under these conditions, presidents use their national committees to promote their preferred brand—that is, the policies they support as well as their own political interests (such as their re-election efforts). These activities are generally centered on promoting a party image in line with what the president believes will serve the party and themselves best. That is, the committee will back major legislative efforts by the administration, celebrate the president's achievements in office, and more generally connect the image of the party to that of the president.

Such presidential use of national committee branding may be a mixed bag for the party. In some cases, focusing publicity on the president's image and policies may benefit both president *and* party. After all, presidents are the most visible and well-known political actors in the United States and, in situations where the president is popular with the public, the party understandably would want to connect itself as much as possible to them. But presidential self-promotion through national committees can also come at a cost to the party. On the most basic level, national committees may be prioritizing their resources in support of the president rather than other candidates on the ticket. Additionally, not all presidents or administration policies are popular, and party members may grow frustrated with a national committee supporting policies they themselves oppose. For example, during Bill Clinton's first term in office, the DNC promoted both his legislative agenda and his re-election efforts extensively. These activities included advertisement campaigns on behalf of Clinton's healthcare legislation, and a major series of campaign ad buys on behalf of his re-election campaign as early as the summer of 1995. Many Democrats at the time complained about Clinton's use of the DNC—protesting that the national committee focused exclusively on helping Clinton while ignoring the needs of other Democrats. Thus, an in-party national committee that is actively engaged in branding can be controversial within the party.

But not all presidents see value in having a national committee actively engaged in branding in the first place—even if they can control the committee's messaging. As Philip Klinkner has argued, out-parties, because they recently lost a presidential election, have a "powerful motivation for changing their personnel, organizational structure, internal party procedures, and platforms since past methods have failed to achieve victory."[42] Because of this, out-party committees almost always have an incentive to engage in major branding efforts. Presidents also have strong incentives to want their party to do well and may

[42] Klinkner, *The Losing Parties*, p. 1.

believe their national party organizations can help achieve this. Indeed, Daniel Galvin has shown that presidents like Dwight Eisenhower, Richard Nixon, Gerald Ford, and Ronald Reagan invested considerable time and energy into building up their national party organizations in different ways. Yet, Galvin also shows that presidents like Lyndon Johnson and Jimmy Carter let their national party organizations decline.[43] Why would presidents do this? Galvin argues presidential party building (that is, presidents actively working to strengthen their party's organization) occurs when presidents believe their party is electorally weak, most commonly in situations where their party is in the minority in Congress. In contrast, majority party presidents lack the incentive to invest in party building and will focus their attention on more urgent matters. But the relationship between president and party is also often deeply complicated. As Sidney Milkis has argued in his landmark book *The Presidents and the Parties*, many presidents feel constrained by other actors in their party and often prefer to act independently. With the expansion of the size and power of the federal government under the New Deal and beyond, presidents could achieve such independence by engaging in executive action and self-promotion without ever having to deal with their national party organization.[44]

Additionally, using national committees as branding organizations may not serve the president's interests. Presidents can be expected to want to legislate and govern. While national publicity programs might help increase public support or put pressure on co-partisans in Congress to back the president's agenda, they can also be disruptive if the committees are emphasizing issues on which there is no consensus within the party. Because of this, presidents may be concerned about "rocking the boat" within their party. Additionally, they may consider that a national committee aggressively promoting specific issues or bills may poison the well with the opposition party on crucial issues on the legislative agenda. Presidents often need to rely on support from the opposition in the House and (particularly) Senate to pass major pieces of legislation. Even if a topic or target of national committee branding is not controversial within their own party, a purely partisan promotion effort could antagonize the opposition by framing issues along party lines, and presidents might find it harder to work with contra-partisan legislators to pass legislation. As a result, presidents may prefer to see national committees decrease their branding role, resulting in organizational decline of the institution.[45]

---

[43] Galvin, *Presidential Party Building*

[44] Sidney M. Milkis, *The Presidents and the Parties: The Transformation of the American Party System since the New Deal* (New York: Oxford University Press, 1993).

[45] In previous work, I argued that this concern is particularly strong among majority party presidents (those in the White House while their party also has majorities in House and Senate) as they are trying to maintain their majorities. However, the same logic applies for minority presidents who

Separate from temporary decreases in publicity operations, the national committees' branding role has also become more complicated in recent years. This appears to be the product of two broad changes in American party politics. The first concerns the changing nature of presidential selection since the 1980s. After the McGovern–Fraser reforms of the 1970s, both parties moved toward relying on primaries and caucuses as the process of selecting their presidential nominees. Over time, presidential candidates in both parties also started their election campaigns earlier, and it has become common for presidential candidates to announce their candidacy early in the year *before* the presidential election. These long presidential primary campaigns constrain national committees' branding abilities in two ways. With presidential candidates in the party campaigning for close to two years, much of the media's attention may be focused on them rather than any branding signals the national committee may be sending out. Second, with candidates debating each other within the party, the national committees are in a more complicated position in taking positions on issues. After all, if the committees take sides in these conflicts during the (invisible) primaries, they run the risk of being accused of interfering in the presidential selection process. The long presidential primaries thus limit the space national committees have to introduce and execute major publicity efforts on behalf of the party.

The second change concerns the dramatically different media and political communication landscape of the late 1990s and early 21st century. The introduction of (mostly conservative) talk radio and ideological news networks such as Fox News (on the right) and MSNBC (on the left) has added an easily accessible and popular form of semi-partisan communication entirely out of the control of the national committees. Even more important in this regard has been the introduction of the Internet and social media as political communication tools. While both committees use these tools, they dramatically lowered the bar for sharing political communication with audiences of practically unlimited size at almost no cost. For much of the period covered in this book, national committees had some form of monopoly on political communication through their investments in technology such as radio and TV studios or their control over mailing lists of politically interested Americans. But in the age of Facebook, Twitter, and YouTube such a monopoly has disappeared. Indeed, high-profile partisan (and nonpartisan) political actors can now reach millions of voters directly, instantly, and basically for free.

need to work with the opposite party to pass legislation and achieve other goals when their party is in the minority in the House and/or Senate. See: Boris Heersink, "Party Brands and the Democratic and Republican National Committees, 1952–1976," *Studies in American Political Development* 32, no. 1 (2018): 79–102.

Combined, these two types of constraints on national committee branding suggest that we should see (1) a temporary decrease in branding when a national committee finds itself under the control of a president who does not believe such partisan branding is in their interest, and (2) a general decline in major branding operations by both committees starting in the 1980s with the rise of long presidential primary campaigns and accelerating in the 2000s with the introduction of more easily accessible political communication tools. The first type of short-term constraint should reveal itself in a decline of national committees as organizations under some (but not all) presidents, followed by reinvestments in the committees' publicity role after a presidential election loss. The second type of constraint suggests the committees' branding role may be finite. Indeed, as their ability to dominate national branding efforts on behalf of the party disappears, the committees in the early 21st century are facing a new political reality that requires a reinvention of their role in the party to remain politically relevant.

Summary of the Argument

This book presents a major reassessment of the role and influence the DNC and RNC play within their parties and in American politics more broadly. I argue that national committees have a clear but previously unacknowledged role within their parties—and one political actors believe to be incredibly important: helping shape their party's national brand. They do so by engaging in major publicity campaigns, as well as by trying to set party policies on behalf of the national party. When their party is out of the White House, national committees in particular have an incentive to engage in such branding activities, and when they do, they also have the agency to promote a brand they believe is best for their party. As a result, national committees often take sides in major intra-party conflicts on policy and ideology. In contrast, when a party is in the White House, presidents control the national committee. Some presidents see value in using their committees for branding purposes. But others believe such branding is not helpful. As a result, we should see some presidents neglect their national party organizations. Finally, developments in recent years—including changes in political communication and the introduction of the invisible primary—limit the national committees' ability to engage in such branding efforts, increasingly leaving parties without institutions that can try to coordinate the process of producing a coherent party image.

I test this branding theory by looking at changes in the quantity of branding activities by the national committees over time, and by assessing the choices national committees make in what party brand they promote, how they go about doing so, how the specific image of the party they promote changes over time, and how other actors in the party responded to the committees' choices in this regard. Methodologically, I do so in two ways. First, I rely on qualitative case studies that cover the full history of both the DNC and RNC between 1912 and 2016.[46] These case studies are based on primary and secondary sources—including meeting transcripts, internal documents, publicity materials, and contemporaneous news coverage. These sources show the kind of branding activities the national committees engaged in at different moments in time—that is, what kind of political communication tools the committees used and what image they chose to project—as well as the logic political actors at the time presented as to why they were engaging in these actions. I show that political actors in- and outside of the national committees clearly articulate the importance of having the DNC and RNC engage in party-branding activities, but that these activities were also often controversial within the parties.

But while these qualitative case studies are helpful in showing such specific details, they are not necessarily as effective in measuring the quantity of national committee branding efforts over time. Unfortunately, producing a quantitative data set that measures such activity consistently for both parties is complicated. Since both national committees are private institutions, they are not required to maintain and share their internal documents and data. While collections of archival materials are available, they are generally limited to specific actors—for example, individual national committee chairs. Because of this, collecting consistent data sources from *within* the national committees with the purpose of creating a quantitative data set covering activities by both the DNC and RNC across a substantial period of time has been practically impossible. In this book, I present a new data set measuring both national committees' activities across the 20th century and beyond by relying on a metric of these activities that is *external* to the institutions: media coverage of the kind of activities both national committees engaged in over time. Specifically, I collected every *New York Times* article published between 1913 and 2016 that mentioned either national committee or its chairs and coded those articles for the type of committee activities reported. I use this data to test quantitatively under what conditions the national committees increase or decrease their branding role.

The outline of this book is as follows. In Chapter 2, I present the new quantitative data set and analysis showing that national committees of parties in the White House significantly decrease their branding role, but not service activities. Chapter 3 focuses on the DNC and RNC's initial development into permanently active organizations between the 1912 and 1932 presidential elections. I show that the DNC—despite considerable growing pains—built up an impressive publicity division during the Hoover administration, and that John Raskob, the committee's chair, tried to use this publicity tool to push the Democratic Party to embrace opposition to Prohibition. In contrast, despite early branding efforts during the Wilson effort, the RNC's role remained more limited (with one notable and disruptive exception) as the party was in the White House. Chapter 4 looks at both national committees' activity during the Roosevelt and Truman administrations. I show that on the Democratic side, the DNC declined dramatically while the Democrats were in the White House—particularly under FDR—though the committee did see occasional jolts of branding activity when it benefited the incumbent presidents. In contrast, the RNC began to expand its branding role and tried to help the Republican Party to find a comprehensive response to the New Deal. In particular, the RNC tried to coordinate a consistent Republican response to World War II and the role the United States would play in a postwar international community.

In Chapter 5, I look at the national committees' attempts at pushing their respective parties in a clear ideological direction in the period 1953–1968. In these years, both parties increasingly found themselves navigating major intra-party disagreements on issues such as civil rights. While the national committees generally tried to maintain a "big-tent" approach, at times chairs with strong ideological preferences attempted to push their party in a clear liberal or conservative direction. Notably, while under Dwight Eisenhower the RNC continued to be active, I show that under John F. Kennedy and Lyndon Johnson the DNC declined dramatically. Chapter 6 looks at the period between 1969 and 1980, during which the Democratic Party faced years of limited fundraising, major debts, and continued intra-party disagreements. I show that DNC chairs in this period worked at maintaining intra-party unity by producing policies and promotional activities acceptable across the party. Meanwhile, the RNC engaged in supportive activities on behalf of the Nixon and Ford administrations, but after the 1976 Jimmy Carter victory the RNC attempted to alter the GOP's image by prioritizing its appeals to Black voters. At the same time, however, the DNC saw another period of decline due to Carter's lack of interest in the organization.

Chapter 7 assesses the period between the 1980 and 2000 elections. In this period, subsequent DNC chairs consistently aimed to alter the Democratic Party image by promoting centrist policy positions on issues such as military spending, crime, and government spending. Meanwhile, during the Reagan administration the RNC engaged extensively in promotional activities supporting Reagan's policies and his own re-election efforts—presenting the GOP consistently as "Reagan's party." After Bill Clinton's victory in 1992, the RNC invested in new publicity tools—including television programs and Internet activities. Unlike his Democratic predecessors, Clinton relied extensively on the DNC during his first term—using the committee to back his legislative agenda and support his re-election. However, in this period the ability of national committees to try to set out policy agendas for their parties became more limited as the presidential primaries started increasingly early. Chapter 8 looks at the DNC and RNC between the 2000 and 2016 elections. In this period, both presidents—George W. Bush and Barack Obama—came into the White House with well-developed campaign organizations and, as a result, showed little interest in their national committee. But even out-party committees in this period faced major hurdles in engaging in major branding operations—because of the ongoing issue of early invisible primaries but also due to the expansion of competing political communication sources in the form of talk radio, ideological news networks, and the Internet. Finally, in Chapter 9, I present a conclusion that discusses the main takeaway points of the preceding chapters, as well as an assessment of the future of national committees in a changing media and partisan environment.

2

Examining DNC and RNC Party Branding Quantitatively

Presidential Control and National Committee Branding Decline

As outlined in the previous chapter, there is reason to believe that while branding is a fundamental part of the national committees' role in American politics, there may be moments of systematic decline in these efforts, specifically in comparing in- and out-party national committee activities. To assess whether there is indeed change in the extent to which national committees increase or decrease their branding activities it would be helpful to measure these activities quantitatively. But doing so on the basis of data from within the committees is difficult. As private organizations, the Democratic National Committee (DNC) and Republican National Committee (RNC) have no obligation to save documents or make them available to researchers. Collections covering materials related to individual actors in the national committees are available but generally cover only one party for a limited time period. For example, RNC chair Ray Bliss's (1965–1968) archival collection—available at the Ohio Historical Society—is helpful when it comes to studying the RNC's activities under Bliss's leadership. But the exact types of documents included in this collection are not necessarily available for other periods and/or parties. As a result, producing a consistent data set measuring national committee activities on the basis of internal documents is practically impossible.

To help overcome this problem I rely on an alternative, indirect approach to measuring national committee activity by relying on media reports.[1] DNC and RNC activities are regularly reported in the news media, and since such reports

---

[1] Part of the data presented here—covering the period 1953–2012—was used for similar analysis in: Boris Heersink, "Examining Democratic and Republican National Committee Party Branding Activity, 1953–2012," *Perspectives on Politics* (forthcoming).

National Party Organizations and Party Brands in American Politics. Boris Heersink, Oxford University Press.
© Oxford University Press 2023. DOI: 10.1093/oso/9780197695104.003.0002

are published consistently and are publicly available, they can be used to produce a consistent metric for both parties and throughout a lengthy time period. In this chapter, I use this data to test whether national committees of parties "in" the White House do indeed, on average, reduce their branding activities. In the chapters that follow, I use the same data set to show shorter-term changes in national committee activities.

Data Collection

I collected *New York Times* reports of committee activities between January 1, 1913, and December 31, 2016. I use the *New York Times* because it is both the "paper of record" and consistently available online throughout this period. I collected each article that mentioned either the DNC or RNC or its chairs in that year through the ProQuest Historical Newspaper database.[2] In total, this produced a collection of 42,487 articles. As can be seen in Figure 2.1, which shows the yearly number of articles collected for both the DNC and RNC between 1913 and 2016, there is considerable variation across time and party in the amount of coverage both committees received.

However, these articles inevitably include some that mention the committees (or their chairs) but in a context that is not relevant to our purposes here. For example, the articles include obituaries of employees who previously worked at either national committee, wedding announcements that mention RNC or DNC staff, or ones that reference former DNC or RNC chairs or staff in a context unrelated to the national committees' then current activities. Additionally, there are specific news events that result in a dramatic increase in coverage. To be sure, some of these increases are likely the result of actual increases in committee activity. For example, some of the biggest spikes in Figure 2.1 occur during presidential election years in which the DNC and RNC plan and execute their party's national convention and presidential campaign. But some of the other spikes in Figure 2.1 are likely due to *New York Times* coverage of issues that were correlated with the national committees but did not reflect an increase in the organizations' activities. For example, in 1964 there were 638 articles that

---

[2] For example, to collect the articles for the DNC in 1963, the search query was "Democratic National Committee" OR "John Bailey," while for the RNC in 1963 the search query was "Republican National Committee" OR "William E. Miller," for the period between January 1, 1963, and December 31, 1963. For years when more than one person was DNC or RNC chair, the search query included all committee chairs that served at any point during the year. For example, for 1959—in which the RNC chairmanship shifted from Meade Alcorn to Thruston B. Morton—the search query was "Republican National Committee" OR "Meade Alcorn" OR "Thruston B. Morton."

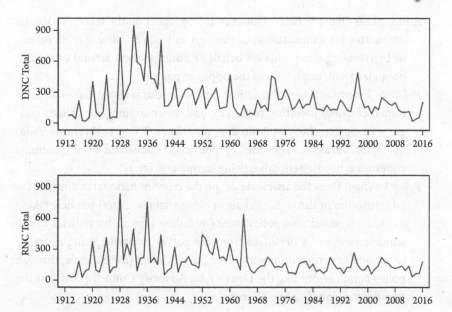

Figure 2.1. Total yearly *New York Times* articles mentioning the DNC or RNC and/or its chairs, 1913–2016.

mentioned either the RNC or its chairs in that year. These numbers are notably higher than in 1960 (352 articles) or 1968 (111 articles). The reason for this dramatic increase was likely the inclusion of former RNC chair Bill Miller as the vice-presidential candidate on the Republican ticket, as Miller's candidacy resulted in a major increase in references that did not indicate more actual activities by the committee. Similarly, in 1973 and 1974 the DNC (or its chair) was mentioned in 433 and 229 articles, respectively—considerably higher than in the comparable period 1969–1970 (147 and 173 articles) and 1977–1978 (249 and 130 articles). In this case, the increase largely concerned coverage of the Watergate scandal, and references to the break-in at the DNC during the 1972 presidential election.

To address this issue and to allow for analysis of the different types of activities the DNC and RNC are engaging in across time, I coded each article to assess whether they reported on DNC or RNC activity within the year the article appeared, and—if so—what type of activity (or activities) it reported on. If an article did not report on any activities in the list that follows, I dismissed the article as irrelevant. If it did, I coded for any of the activities as defined. Specifically, I looked for three broad categories of operations—branding, service, and other—and a subset of more specific types of activities that make up these broader categories. In terms of branding, I identified three specific types of activities:

Attack on the Opposite Party: Does the article report on the relevant national committee (as an institution or through its chair or other staff members, or by releasing statements on behalf of other political actors) criticizing politicians and/or policies of the opposite party?[3]

Publicity Programs: Does the article report on the relevant national committee creating, investing resources, and/or continuing a publicity program (including, but not limited to, magazines, TV or radio shows, radio or TV broadcasts of speeches by politicians sponsored by the national committee, newsletters, advertising campaigns, etc.)?[4]

Policy Position: Does the article report on the relevant national committee (as an institution or through its chair or other staff members) publicly taking a specific position on a policy issue (including support for policies by the administration of a president from the party) or participating in trying to set one in cooperation with other party leaders (for example, through policy commissions like the Democratic Advisory Council [DAC] or the Republican Coordinating Committee)?[5]

These activities cover different ways of shaping a party brand, by identifying policy positions for the party, attacking the opposite party[6] (which can further help differentiate the party from the opposition), and investing in, and using, the tools they rely on to present voters with those policy positions or attacks.

---

[3] Included in this coding is any situation where a national committee or its staff criticizes the opposite party, or any politician related to it, on its policies, its activities in government, or scandals, as well as any personal attacks against people within the opposite party. This coding does not include attacks or criticism against political actors who are not partisan. For example, an RNC statement criticizing the "liberal media" does not count as an attack on the opposite party. However, RNC statements criticizing Obamacare or attacking Obama as elitist would both count.

[4] Included in this coding are any articles that reference national committees creating their own publicity (for example, releasing new issues of magazines or TV advertisements, creating a radio or TV advertisement, paying for a series of advertisements to be aired in specific media markets) or paying for publicity on behalf of others (for example, paying for campaign advertisements on behalf of the party's candidates, or paying for the broadcasting of a TV or radio speech by a politician from its party).

[5] Included in this coding are any cases where a national committee takes a position in support of, or opposition to, specific legislation, Supreme Court cases or rulings, or broader political issues (i.e., supporting the civil rights movement, abortion rights, LGBT rights, etc.). The coding does not include any situation where specific issues are not mentioned by a national committee, i.e., a national committee refusing to comment on a policy; even if the refusal to comment might suggest a position, it does not count as a policy position in this coding.

[6] What Frances Lee describes as "nonideological appeals accusing the other party of corruption, failure, or incompetence." See: Frances E. Lee, *Insecure Majorities: Congress and the Perpetual Campaign* (Chicago, IL: University of Chicago Press, 2016), 2.

In terms of service activities, building on Daniel Galvin's description of party activities of committees under presidential control,[7] I identified the following four activities:

> *Campaign Service:* Does the article report on the relevant national committee providing campaign support for individual candidates—including presidential candidates, candidates for Congress, gubernatorial candidates, etc.—or the party as a whole, such as providing candidates' campaigns with money, opinion polls, training, strategic advice, organizing campaign appearances by the national committee chair or other party leaders, targeting voting groups, and mobilizing those groups through voter registration activities and Get Out the Vote drives?[8]
>
> *Human and/or Capital Development:* Does the article report on the relevant national committee engaging in candidate recruitment activities—that is, attempts by the national committee to convince potential candidates to run for office—training future candidates in campaign schools, hiring new staff members, or investing in its real estate or technology?[9]
>
> *Fundraising:* Does the article report on the relevant national committee engaging in fundraising activities—either on behalf of the committee itself or by having the national committee chair engage in fundraising activities on behalf of other party organizations or candidates?[10]

Finally, to fully cover the spectrum of national committee activity, I also coded for several other activities that do not fit in either the branding or service category, but that the national committees do engage in. While I do not present analysis of these articles, they are included in the data set. Specifically, I coded for the following activities:

---

[7] Daniel J. Galvin, *Presidential Party Building: Dwight D. Eisenhower to George W. Bush* (Princeton, NJ: Princeton University Press, 2009).

[8] Included in this coding are examples of the national committee directly participating in a campaign—for example, by sending campaign workers to a specific state or district during an election, or organizing Get Out the Vote drives in specific areas during a campaign—or examples where the committee provides financial support with the purpose of assisting campaigns—for example, if the committee donates money to a candidate.

[9] Included in this coding are any reports of national committee chairs or staff encouraging potential candidates to run for elected office, the committee organizing instruction courses for such potential candidates, and reports of the committee investing in its headquarters (i.e., renting or buying new office space, updating computer equipment) or its staff (hiring new staff members).

[10] Note: this excludes articles that only mention the DNC or RNC reporting a total amount they received over a time period, since based on the information available we do not know to what extent those funds come from active fundraising.

Patronage: Does the article report on the relevant national committee engaging in the division of patronage—that is, positions within the federal government—by managing job applicants and discussing job candidates with the administration?

Organization of National Conventions: Does the article report on the relevant national committee engaging in organization activities for an upcoming or ongoing national convention—including the selection of the convention city, setting rules for delegate selection and distribution, and the actual execution of the national convention?[11]

Generic: Does the article report on the relevant national committee engaging in any type of activity that does not fall in the categories outlined previously—including, but not limited to, the national committee chair holding meetings without additional agenda information, the committee chair resigning, a new committee chair being appointed, the announcement of staff retirements, the committee chair or the national committee as an institution expressing condolences, the committee chair expressing basic support for candidates of the party running in general elections, the committee chair presenting basic political positions in the media that do not fall in the category of policy positioning or attacking the opposite party, the committee chair providing predictions of election results, the committee chair discussing previous electoral strategies, etc.?

In coding each newspaper article, I relied on a dichotomous approach: if an article mentioned one or multiple activities that fell into the same category, I coded that article as "1" for that category, and "0" if it did not. In total, 19,655 of the articles collected reported at least one (and often, multiple) of the committee activities in the list. As can be seen in Figure 2.2, there is a notable difference in the total number of articles collected and those "relevant"—that is, those that mentioned one or more of the activities listed—which eliminates some of the more extreme variation across time and party. Still, there does remain considerable variation in coverage across party and time if we look at just these relevant articles. This variation makes it possible to test claims about whether national committees change their branding activity based on whether their party is in or out of the White House.[12]

---

[11] Included in this coding are any references to the actual organization of the convention (i.e., renting a hall, negotiating with cities, scheduling the event, etc.) but also to setting the rules of the convention and its related delegate selection process (including coverage of such reorganization activities as the McGovern–Fraser committee).

[12] While *New York Times* articles provide a consistent measure of national committee activity, it is important to note the limitations of the data as a metric of the *actual* activities both committees engage in. As a basic test of whether *Times* coverage of specific topics changes as national committee

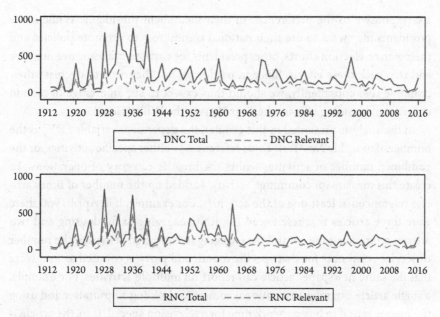

Figure 2.2. Yearly total and relevant *New York Times* articles mentioning the DNC or RNC and/or its chairs, 1913–2016.

Branding Decline under Presidential Leadership

I use this data set to test one component of the theory presented in the previous chapter. As outlined there, presidents are in de facto control of their national committees. In contrast to out-party committees—which practically always have an incentive to engage in major branding operations—in-party committees

activity on the topic changes, I compare descriptive data from the *New York Times* data I compiled with two key findings from Philip Klinkner's *The Losing Parties: Out-Party National Committees, 1956–1993* (New Haven, CT: Yale University Press, 1994): Klinkner argues that after the 1956 election, the DNC prioritized its policy role within the party, and that after the 1968 and 1972 losses, the DNC focused on procedural reforms. The *New York Times* data I collected shows changes in line with these findings: references to DNC policy positioning in *New York Times* articles were indeed notably higher in the period between the 1956 and 1960 elections; *New York Times* coverage of DNC policy position taking was highest in the period 1957–1960, when the average number of yearly references to policy activities by the DNC in the *Times* was 32.3. In comparison, for the period 1961–1992 the average number of yearly references was just 8.6. Meanwhile, in the period 1953–1968, the average yearly number of *New York Times* references to DNC convention organizing activities (the relevant measure of the type of organizational changes that the DNC focused on according to Klinkner's findings) was 13.2. In the period 1977–1992, the average number of yearly references was 17.8. But, in the 1969–1976 period, the average number of yearly *New York Times* references to DNC convention organizing activities was 29.9. These descriptive data suggest that *New York Times* coverage does adjust in response to changes in the actual activities by the DNC.

are responsive to the preferences of their incumbent presidents. While some presidents may want to use their national committees to promote policies and their own re-election efforts, other presidents see partisan branding as a negative and step back these efforts. Since in-parties are not theorized to decrease their branding role consistently, we should thus expect to see an average decline in coverage of branding efforts when a party is in the White House.

In the analysis presented in this chapter, the dependent variable (DV) is the number of monthly *New York Times* references to either specific activities, or the combined number of activities within the broader category of operations. To create this measure of committee activity, I added up the number of times articles referenced at least one of the activities. For example, if in April 1960 there were three articles that referenced the RNC engaging in fundraising and two articles referencing the committee engaging in campaign activities, the number of service references for that specific month and party is counted as five. Note that the same newspaper article can report on multiple activities. For example, a single article can refer to a national committee holding a fundraiser and using the money raised to buy network time for a television special. If so, the article is coded for reporting both fundraising and publicity activities. The resulting data set has an N of 2,496 (that is, 104 years times 12 months for both parties)— though in most models the DV is lagged, which means the N drops to 2,494.

The main independent variable in this analysis is whether a party held the White House or not. In some models, I include whether a president was a majority or minority president. In those cases, I rely on Goldman's definition of national majority parties as having

> majority status in at least four places simultaneously: (1) the electoral college, derived from pluralities in a sufficient number of states, that is, the party-in-the-electorate; (2) the presidency; (3) the Senate; and (4) the House of Representatives.[13]

Thus, a president with unified control of government will be considered a majority president, while a president whose party controls only one or zero houses of Congress is considered a minority president.

I include multiple control variables that could plausibly also cause difference in reported committee activity across time and party. Both national committees help organize and execute election campaigns, and we therefore expect increases in branding operations during presidential and midterm election

---

[13] Ralph M. Goldman, *The National Party Chairmen and Committees: Factionalism at the Top* (M.E. Sharpe, 1990), 569.

years. Therefore, I include a dummy variable for whether articles were published in presidential election or midterm election years. Note that because national committees do not wait until the end of a calendar year to begin incorporating the effects of elections, I apply the effects immediately to my coding. That is, if a party wins or loses the White House or majority status in the House and/or Senate, I use the day after the election that determined this as the tipping point, not the later point in time at which the elected officials are sworn in.[14] I also use this approach in coding for whether the activities described take place in an election year.[15]

Additionally, one party may structurally receive more coverage than the other. To control for this, I include a dummy variable identifying whether the article concerns coverage of the DNC. It is also possible that the amount of space in the *New York Times* fluctuated across time. To control for this, I include a continuous variable of the number of articles published on the first weekday of the year that include the word "and" as a metric of the amount of space available in the paper. The assumption here is that if more articles are found this way, it would indicate that there was more space available in the *Times* at that time. National committees can also find themselves facing major scandals concerning either their activities as an institution, or their chair. When these scandals occur, they might affect the committees' ability to function and/or the likelihood that the *New York Times* decides to publish stories about any DNC or RNC activities

[14] For example, the 1960 election took place on November 8. Prior to the election, Democrats had majorities in the House and Senate while Republicans held the White House. This meant the Democratic Party was the out-party in an election year on November 8. After the election, Kennedy became president-elect and Democrats maintained their congressional majorities. From the perspective of party leaders, this meant that after November 8, Kennedy was the de facto president and of a majority party, and the election year had ended. Thus, any newspaper articles published between January 1 and November 8, 1960, are coded to have appeared in a presidential election year in which Democrats were out of the White House. However, for any articles published between November 9 and December 31, 1960, Democrats are coded to hold the White House with unified control of government, and to not have been published in a presidential election year.

[15] Because the unit of analysis is the number of references to activities on a monthly basis, articles published in November before the election provide a problem, since this produces mixed results for the same month for whether the coverage took place in an election year. There is no obvious correct way to address this: for the data in this paper I dropped any newspaper articles that were published in November of an election year up through election day, thereby focusing the analysis exclusively on the majority of articles that correctly reflect the political context for the majority of the month. The only exception to the approach taken described here concerns the 2000 election when the Supreme Court's December 13 ruling ended the uncertainty over whether Republican candidate George W. Bush or Democratic candidate Al Gore was to be certified the winner of the election. For the year 2000, I keep all articles covering national committee activity in November as being published during a presidential election year but drop those that were published in December before the Supreme Court ruling. The results as presented here do not change regardless of which approach is used.

unrelated to the scandal. To control for this, I include a measure of the number of monthly articles mentioning scandals. The coding process followed the same setup as described earlier, and I defined scandal as follows:

> *Scandal:* Does the article report on the relevant national committee (or its chair or other staff members) being involved in a scandal (including, but not limited to, financial improprieties, criminal or congressional investigations into alleged crimes, sexual scandals, etc.)?

Finally, in some of the models I include year and month fixed effects to control for any additional unobserved variation—both in terms of consistent increases or decreases in newspaper coverage and/or committee activity at set moments across the year, or in specific years in which coverage and/or activity was notably higher or lower because of other factors. In the models that include fixed effects, I leave out control variables that are consistent across the year—that is, whether the year was a presidential or midterm election year, and the measure of *New York Times* size—since these would perfectly correlate with the specific-year fixed effect.

Results

To reiterate, the goal of this quantitative analysis is to assess whether national committees of parties in the White House are structurally less likely to engage in branding activities than those that are out of the White House. To do this, I rely on a data set that covers the number of monthly references to different types of activities the DNC and RNC engaged in as reported by the *New York Times* between January 1913 and December 2016. Since the dependent variable of this study concerns a (lagged) count of monthly references to branding and service operations in the *New York Times*, I rely on a negative binomial regression for most of the analyses presented here.[16]

Table 2.1 shows the results of a negative binomial model measuring the effect of a party being in the White House on the expected log count of the number of monthly *New York Times* reports on national committee branding operations— that is, the combined number of references to a national committee attacking the opposite party, using existing or new publicity programs, and/or presenting policy positions on issues. All models presented here include a one-month lag

---

[16] In the appendix to this chapter I present additional models—including the main analysis presented in Model 1, Table 3.1, with the control variables added one by one, a Poisson model, and a time-series negative binomial regression. All models result in the same basic findings.

Table 2.1. **Negative binomial regression of presidential and party status on monthly (lagged) *New York Times* coverage of national committee branding operations, 1913–2016.**

	(1)	(2)	(3)	(4)
White House	−0.456***	−0.446***	—	—
(Robust standard errors)	(0.066)	(0.044)	—	—
Majority president	—	—	−0.460***	−0.437***
	—	—	(0.087)	(0.062)
Minority president	—	—	−0.450***	−0.455***
	—	—	(0.076)	(0.061)
Pres. election year	0.606***	—	0.606***	—
	(0.072)	—	(0.071)	—
Midterm election year	0.018	—	0.019	—
	(0.072)	—	(0.071)	—
Democratic Party	−0.211**	−0.129**	−0.210**	−0.131**
	(0.064)	(0.044)	(0.065)	(0.045)
NYT size	0.002***	—	0.002***	—
	(0.000)	—	(0.000)	—
Scandal	0.017	−0.014	0.017	−0.014
	(0.023)	(0.018)	(0.023)	(0.018)
Fixed effects	—	Month & year	—	Month & year
Constant	0.630***	−2.438**	0.628***	−2.440**
	(0.092)	(0.707)	(0.094)	(0.707)
N	2,494	2,494	2,494	2,494
Pseudo R^2	0.022	0.113	0.022	0.113
Log pseudo likelihood	−5745.05	−5211.014	−5745.048	−5210.993
Alpha	1.493	0.724	1.492	0.724
Ln alpha	0.401	−0.324	0.401	−0.324

* $p < 0.05$, ** $p < 0.01$, *** $p < 0.001$.

on the dependent variable to allow for the possibility that national committees may need some short period of time to respond to a change in their party's majority or minority status. I present four versions of the main model testing the branding theory: in Models 1 and 2, the independent variable is whether a party is in the White House or not. Models 3 and 4 include the type of president—majority or minority—as separate variables. Models 1 and 3 include the control variables discussed in the previous section, while Models 2 and 4 exclude some of those controls in favor of year and month fixed effects.

In all models, the effect of a party being in the White House is, as predicted, negative and significant at the 0.001 level.[17] Meaning, regardless of whether a party has unified control of government or not, *New York Times* coverage of branding activity declines notably when a national committee's party holds the White House. This suggests that parties that hold the White House do indeed decrease their branding activities. But, aside from being statistically significant, does the coverage also decline in a *meaningful* way? While a negative binomial model is appropriate given the nature of the dependent variable, interpreting the substantial meaning of its coefficients is complicated. To provide some easier-to-interpret assessment of the practical implication of the size of the decline in *New York Times* coverage of branding operations, I present the results of an ordinary least squares (OLS) regression that uses the same variables as Model 1 in Table 2.1. The results, presented in Figure 2.3, suggest that monthly *New York Times* references to branding operations when a party controls the White House decline by 1.63. To put this number in context, the mean number of branding references by month for the period 1913–2016 was 3.58, so this effect represents a nearly 46% decrease in reported branding coverage—a considerable decline.

Combined, the results presented in Table 2.1 and Figure 2.3 are in line with the expectation of a negative effect for White House incumbency on national committee branding activity. However, it is possible that these results simply indicate that the committees of such parties are actually decreasing *all* of their activities—that is, both branding and regular service operations. While such a finding could still indicate a decline in national committee activity and influence, it would not be in line with the branding theory as outlined in the previous chapter. More problematically, it could also mean that the *Times* is decreasing coverage, not because committees are less active but because the *Times* is less interested in covering their ongoing activities once their party holds the White

[17] The results for the control variables included in Table 2.1 are in line with expectations as well: branding operation references increase in election years (when national committees are more actively appealing to voters), and the measure of *New York Times* size is positive and significant, indicating that as more articles were published in general, there were also more articles referencing branding operations.

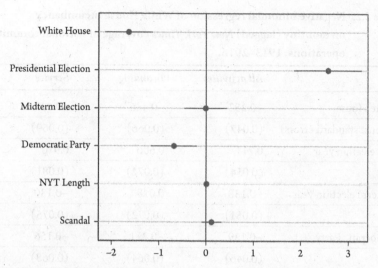

Figure 2.3. Linear regression of White House incumbency on monthly (lagged) *New York Times* coverage of national committee branding activity, 1913–2016.

House. To test whether this is the case or not, I present an assessment of different types of operations national committees can engage in. Table 2.2 includes the results from Model 1, Table 2.1, as well as similar models for all coded operations, and only the combined service operations. The results show that parties in the White House see a decline in all reported activity (significant at the 0.001 level). However, references to service operations (the combined references to campaign activities, candidate recruitment, human and capital development, and fundraising) are not significantly lower for parties in the White House. Thus, the decline in *New York Times* coverage for national committee activities when a party has a president in the White House is driven by a decline in coverage of branding activities, and not by an across-the-board decline in national committee activity. This suggests that in-party national committees specifically decrease their branding role.

To see whether any specific branding or service activities are more or less likely to be affected, I ran the same model as presented in Model 1, Table 2.1, for each individual activity in the data set. The results, presented in Figures 2.4 and 2.5, show that in terms of branding activities, parties in the White House are less likely to be reported to engage in attacks on the opposite party or to take policy positions (both significant at the 0.001 level). These are notable results since they represent relatively easy activities for a national committee to engage in: the financial cost of attacking the opposite party or taking a position on a policy issue is very low, and there is no organizational reason for why a party in the White House would have to decrease its activity in this regard. But these types

Table 2.2. **Negative binomial regression of White House incumbency on monthly (lagged)** *New York Times* **coverage of national committee operations, 1913–2016.**

	All activities	*Branding*	*Service*
White House	−0.252***	−0.456***	−0.037
(Robust standard errors)	(0.047)	(0.066)	(0.069)
Pres. election year	0.711***	0.606***	0.970***
	(0.054)	(0.072)	(0.081)
Midterm election year	−0.138**	0.018	−0.130†
	(0.051)	(0.072)	(0.075)
Democratic Party	−0.139**	−0.211**	−0.156*
	(0.046)	(0.064)	(0.068)
NYT size	0.002***	0.002***	0.003***
	(0.000)	(0.000)	(0.000)
Scandal	0.044*	0.017	0.060*
	(0.018)	(0.023)	(0.029)
Constant	1.599***	0.630***	−0.009
	(0.069)	(0.092)	(0.104)
N	2,494	2,494	2,494
Pseudo R^2	0.030	0.022	0.035
Log pseudo likelihood	−8231.915	−5745.05	−5162.291
Alpha	0.848	1.493	1.739
Ln alpha	−0.165	0.401	0.553

† $p < 0.10$, * $p < 0.05$, ** $p < 0.01$, *** $p < 0.001$.

of branding activities are also those that might be the most disruptive, and presidents may prefer to have their committees avoid them. The effect on references to publicity is also negative, though significant only at the 0.1 level. This may be because publicity investments are not as controversial. However, it is also possible that this might reflect an inherent limitation in the reliance on newspaper articles as a measure of ongoing committee activity. That is, the DNC or RNC might engage in ongoing publicity programs, but the *New York Times* might not consistently report on them every time a new issue or episode is released. In contrast, if a national committee attacks the opposite party or takes a position on a policy issue, this may be newsworthy each individual time it occurs.

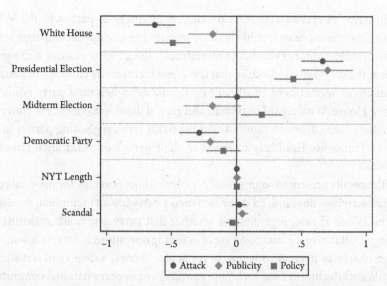

Figure 2.4. Negative binomial regressions of White House incumbency on monthly (lagged) *New York Times* coverage of national committee branding—attacks, publicity, and policy positioning—activities, 1913–2016.

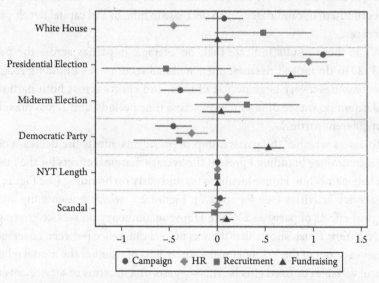

Figure 2.5. Negative binomial regressions of White House incumbency on monthly (lagged) *New York Times* coverage of national committee service—campaign, human and/or capital development, candidate recruitment, and fundraising—activities, 1913–2016.

In terms of service activities, national committees of parties in the White House are not more or less likely to be reported to engage in campaign activities or fundraising. For candidate recruitment, the effect is positive and significant at the 0.1 level—indicating that the *Times* increases its coverage of national committees' recruitment efforts of new candidates when their party holds the White House. With regard to human and capital development efforts, however, the effect is negative and significant at the 0.001 level, suggesting parties in the White House are less likely to invest in their party's organizational structure and staff.

The results presented suggest that *New York Times* coverage for national committee activities does indeed decrease when a party has an incumbent president in the White House, regardless of whether that party also holds majorities in Congress. But, while *Times* coverage of branding operations is notably lower, coverage of service operations is not. In particular, there is a clear (and statistically significant) decline in *New York Times* coverage of in-party national committees attempting to create a party brand by attacking the opposite party, and stating policy positions when their party has unified control of government. There is no notable difference in coverage between in-party and out-party committees engaging in campaign service and fundraising, but there is an increase in coverage on recruitment of candidates, and a decrease in human and capital development references.

While these results indicate that, on average, in-parties across the period 1913–2016 do indeed decrease their national committee's branding role, this data combines a very large period of time, and effects across both parties. To what extent do we see differentiation across time periods, and across presidents from different parties?

To assess whether the partisanship of presidents affects the decrease of national committee branding I present the average marginal effects for the interaction between White House incumbency and party on branding (see Figure 2.6) and service activities (see Figure 2.7). Figure 2.7, which presents the average marginal effects of party and White House incumbency on service coverage in the *New York Times*, shows that there is no real difference between coverage for parties in or out of the White House—regardless of whether the model relies on control variables or fixed effects. This suggests that in terms of service coverage, national committees of both Democratic and Republican presidents largely act similarly. In contrast, Figure 2.6—which presents the average marginal effects of party and White House incumbency on lagged branding coverage in the *New York Times*—shows clear differences between the two types of models. For the model that relies on control variables there is a decline in coverage for both parties when they are in the White House. However, the model that (predominantly) relies on fixed effects shows a different finding: here, the results for the

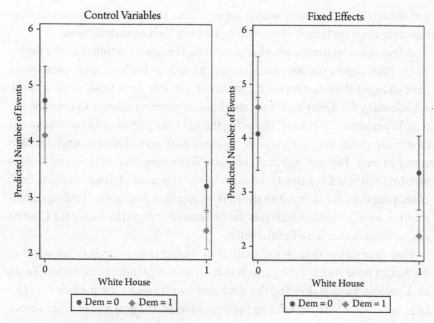

Figure 2.6. Average marginal effects of White House incumbency on monthly (lagged) *New York Times* coverage of national committee branding activities, 1913–2016—by party.

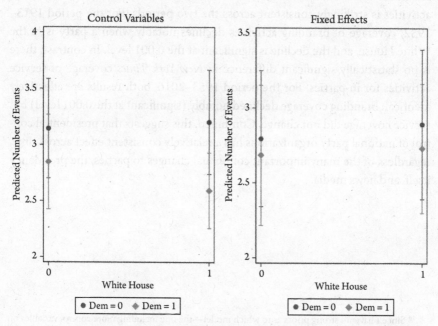

Figure 2.7. Average marginal effects of White House incumbency on monthly (lagged) *New York Times* coverage of national committee service activities, 1913–2016—by party.

Republican Party are largely similar between out- and in-party, but the decline in branding coverage largely appears to come from the Democratic side.[18]

A final consideration is whether comparing the effects within the time period 1913–2016 covers too broad a historical period, as both national committees have changed their institutional capacity in notable ways from 1912 onward. Additionally, the *Times* itself may also have changed its interest in covering national committees over time. Including the full time period in all models means inherently comparing coverage of (potentially) very different organizations acting in very different political contexts. To be sure, the inclusion of control variables and year fixed effects should help alleviate most of these concerns. Still, comparing the kind of activities the RNC engaged in during the Harding administration with the kind of activities the committee engaged in during the Clinton administration may have limited value.

One approach is to limit the analysis to shorter time periods to see whether the results hold within time periods that are arguably more comparable. To do so, I present models dividing the data into two smaller time periods—1913–1952 and 1953–2016. By limiting the time covered, the goal is to provide a more consistent comparison category and context for the type of activities that either or both national committees engaged in, and the kind of news coverage the *New York Times* provided. However, as can be seen in Tables 2.3 and 2.4, the results for White House incumbency on coverage of both branding and service activities is strikingly consistent across the two periods. For the period 1913–1952, coverage of branding activities declines notably when a party is in the White House, and the decline is significant at the 0.001 level. In contrast, there is no statistically significant difference in *New York Times* coverage of service activities for in-parties. For the period 1953–2016, both results are effectively identical: branding coverage declined notably (significant at the 0.001 level) but service coverage did not change. Combined, this suggests that presidential control of national party organizations has a relatively consistent effect across time, regardless of the many important contextual changes to parties, the presidency itself, and news media.

---

[18] Since I have no strong priors as to which model—the one including more control variables or the one relying more on fixed effects—is preferred, these results indicate that there is particular value in assessing the exact type of branding operations (or the lack thereof) Democratic and Republican presidents engaged in, as I do in in the remainder of this book.

Table 2.3. **Negative binomial regression of White House incumbency on monthly (lagged) *New York Times* coverage of national committee branding and service operations, 1913–1952.**

	Branding	*Branding*	*Service*	*Service*
White House	−0.536***	−0.439***	−0.019	0.104
(Robust standard errors)	(0.139)	(0.077)	(0.165)	(0.093)
Pres. election year	0.690***	—	1.441***	—
	(0.128)	—	(0.149)	—
Midterm election year	−0.148	—	−0.279†	—
	(0.132)	—	(0.151)	—
Democratic Party	−0.172	−0.039	−0.243	−0.146
	(0.135)	(0.076)	(0.171)	(0.092)
NYT size	0.002**	—	0.002*	—
	(0.001)	—	(0.001)	—
Scandal	0.057	0.010	0.028	−0.034
	(0.043)	(0.035)	(0.039)	(0.031)
Fixed effects	—	Month & year	—	Month & year
Constant	0.907**	−2.591***	0.321	−1.330*
	(0.278)	(0.709)	(0.283)	(0.615)
N	958	958	958	958
Pseudo R^2	0.018	0.144	0.038	0.135
Log pseudo likelihood	−2370.190	−2065.762	−2054.077	−1846.418
Alpha	2.017	0.744	2.640	1.200
Ln alpha	0.702	−0.296	0.971	0.182

† $p < 0.10$, * $p < 0.05$, ** $p < 0.01$, *** $p < 0.001$.

Data Use in Future Chapters

The results presented in this chapter rely on combining coverage of both the DNC and RNC across longer time periods and analyzing whether there is a consistent difference in *New York Times* coverage based on whether a party is in the White House or not, controlling for other relevant variables. However, because of the extensive size of the data set and the long time period covered, the data can also be leveraged to assess differences across committees in shorter

Table 2.4. **Negative binomial regression of White House incumbency on monthly (lagged)** *New York Times* **coverage of national committee branding and service operations, 1953–2016.**

	Branding	Branding	Service	Service
White House	−0.407***	−0.476***	0.024	0.008
(Robust standard errors)	(0.073)	(0.057)	(0.070)	(0.056)
Pres. election year	0.516***	—	0.614***	—
	(0.081)	—	(0.083)	—
Midterm election year	0.111	—	−0.073	—
	(0.0078)	—	(0.079)	—
Democratic Party	−0.180*	−0.185*	−0.034	−0.014
	(0.070)	(0.056)	(0.070)	(0.055)
NYT size	0.002***	—	0.003***	—
	(0.000)	—	(0.000)	—
Scandal	−0.011	−0.021	0.058†	0.023
	(0.023)	(0.017)	(0.033)	(0.016)
Fixed effects	—	Month & year	—	Month & year
Constant	0.675***	0.464	−0.146	−0.487
	(0.108)	(0.252)	(0.124)	(0.238)
N	1,536	1,536	1,536	1,536
Pseudo R^2	0.017	0.080	0.022	0.103
Log pseudo likelihood	−3337.835	−3123.709	−3026.700	−2776.064
Alpha	1.119	0.664	1.105	0.566
Ln alpha	0.112	−0.409	0.100	−0.570

† $p < 0.10$, * $p < 0.05$, ** $p < 0.01$, *** $p < 0.001$.

periods of time. For example, if we want to know whether under the leadership of President Jimmy Carter the DNC decreased its branding role, we could run a model similar to the one presented in this chapter but instead use Carter's incumbency as the independent variable. The results of such a model shows the effect of Carter's leadership on DNC branding or service activity coverage in the *New York Times*. But doing so reintroduces the issue about the proper comparison categories used in such an analysis: that is, is it appropriate to compare coverage of the Carter-era DNC to that of both national committees at any other moment in time across more than a century of history? While potentially interesting, we might be more interested to know whether the committee decreased its branding role in comparison with the type of activities it engaged in during the years directly preceding Carter's presidential election victory in 1976.

By limiting the data to a shorter period and coverage of just one party, such a comparison becomes possible. To illustrate this approach, I present the results of negative binomial regressions in Figure 2.8 In these models Carter's incumbency is the independent variable, and the lagged monthly *Times* coverage of only DNC branding activity is the dependent variable. I also limit the data to a more reasonable time period: specifically, I restrict the period covered to just articles published between January 1973 and November 1980. In doing so, the results show the effect of Carter's presidency on DNC activities in comparison with the previous presidential term when the party found itself out of the White House. As a result, these models provide a clearer assessment of the effect Carter's presidency had on coverage of DNC activities. The results in the left frame of Figure 2.8 show that under Carter coverage of the DNC's

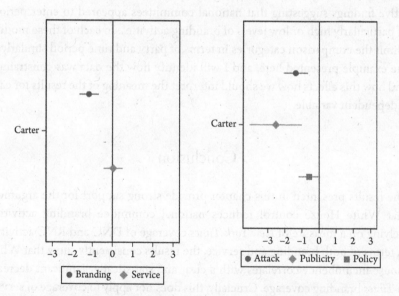

Figure 2.8. Negative binomial regression of Jimmy Carter's presidency on monthly (lagged) *New York Times* coverage of DNC branding and service activities, 1973–1980.
Note: This model includes variables controlling for presidential and midterm election years, a measure of *New York Times* length, and DNC scandals. The data coverage is limited to articles published between January 1973 and December 1980 covering only the DNC.

branding role declined (an effect significant at the 0.001 level). However, *Times* coverage of the DNC's service role did not change. And, as can be seen in the right frame of Figure 2.8, under Carter, coverage of all *types* of branding activities declined: attacks on the opposite party (significant at the 0.001 level), publicity activities (significant at the 0.001 level), and policy position taking (marginally significant at the 0.10 level). Crucially, because the data is limited to just coverage of the DNC and only for the period 1973–1980 these results indicate that under Carter there was a notable decline in branding coverage in comparison with the type of coverage the DNC received in between the 1972 and 1976 presidential elections—suggesting a notable decrease in the committee's branding role under Carter in comparison with the immediate period preceding his presidency (something that the case study of the Carter-era DNC later in this book confirms to be correct).

In the chapters that follow I use similar approaches to test the specific effects individual presidents or national committee chairs had on their parties' branding (and service) activities in comparison with coverage of their party in a relatively comparable time period preceding their time in office. I use these models to complement the qualitative case studies that will form the bulk of this book moving forward. In doing so, I present additional tests of any qualitative findings suggesting that national committees appeared to enter periods of particularly high or low levels of branding activities. In each of these models, I limit the comparison categories in terms of party and time period similarly to the example presented here, and I will identify how the data was constrained, and how this affects how we should interpret the meaning of the results for each independent variable.

Conclusion

The results presented in this chapter provide strong support for the argument that White House control reduces national committee branding activities. Relying on a measure of *New York Times* coverage of DNC and RNC activities in terms of both branding and service, the results consistently show that White House incumbency correlates with a clear and statistically significant decrease in *Times* branding coverage. Crucially, this does not apply to coverage of service activities—suggesting that the DNC and RNC do not scale back *all* their activities when their party holds the White House but that the decline is specific to their branding role. These results are not limited to just one time period— indeed, they are remarkably similar for the periods 1913–1952 and 1953–2016. Thus, despite the many changes in national committee capacity and news coverage over time, there does appear to be a consistent finding in terms of how presidential control affects national committee branding behavior: with a president in the White House, on average, there is a clear decline in national committee party branding.

To be sure, this analysis—while in line with the expectations outlined in Chapter 1—come with some clear limitations. First and foremost, the data reflects an external measure of national committee activity. While the *Times* does appear to adjust its coverage when there are clear shifts in committee behavior, perhaps not all activities are likely to get the same level of news coverage. Additionally, the coding process used to create this data set is dichotomous. That is, a *New York Times* article either mentioned a specific type of activity or it did not. The coding process does not distinguish between the importance of different activities. For example, an article mentions that the DNC starting a new magazine counts as a single reference to a publicity activity. But an article that mentions the RNC publishing a single advertisement in a newspaper also counts as a single reference to a publicity activity.

Combined, this means the analysis presented here suggests that national committees do adjust their branding role over time, and that they appear to do so based on whether their party holds the White House or not. But while we see a clear decline in branding activity for in-party national committees, branding never ceases entirely. And what committees are actually promoting as their party's brand is, of course, as (if not *more*) important as how much branding it engages in. Thus, the case studies in the chapters that follow will dig into the specific branding activities and policy positions the committees have taken, and what caused them to make decisions in this regard.

Appendix

Main Model Deconstructed

The model presented in Model 1, Table 2.1, includes different control variables. While these variables are each potentially relevant predictors of changes in *New York Times* coverage independent of White House incumbency, it is possible that the inclusion of such control variables is necessary to produce the outcome we see for the core independent variable, which may raise questions about whether their specific inclusion or coding is responsible for the outcomes. To ensure this is not the case, I present Table A.2.1, which shows the model used in Model 1, Table 2.1, but with each control variable added separately. This approach produces no difference in the results: White House incumbency is consistently a negative predictor of *New York Times* branding coverage, and in every model significant at the 0.001 level.

Table A.2.1. Negative binomial regression of presidential status on monthly (lagged) *New York Times* coverage of national committee branding operations, 1913–2016.

	(1)	(2)	(3)	(4)	(5)	(6)
White House	-0.412***	-0.430***	-0.430***	-0.428***	-0.448***	-0.456***
(Robust standard errors)	(0.071)	(0.071)	(0.071)	(0.071)	(0.065)	(0.066)
Pres. election year	—	0.640***	0.617***	0.618***	0.615***	0.606***
	—	(0.075)	(0.081)	(0.081)	(0.073)	(0.072)
Midterm election year	—	—	-0.012	-0.018	0.018	0.018
	—	—	(0.077)	(0.076)	(0.070)	(0.072)
Democratic Party	—	—	—	-0.122†	-0.213**	-0.211**
	—	—	—	(0.071)	(0.064)	(0.064)
NYT size	—	—	—	—	0.002***	0.002***
	—	—	—	—	(0.000)	(0.000)
Scandal	—	—	—	—	—	0.017
	—	—	—	—	—	(0.023)
Constant	1.463***	1.303***	1.306***	1.365***	0.631***	0.630***
	(0.049)	(0.053)	(0.064)	(0.072)	(0.092)	(0.092)
N	2,494	2,494	2,494	2,494	2,494	2,494
Pseudo R²	0.005	0.013	0.013	0.013	0.022	0.022
Log pseudo likelihood	-5850.485	-5803.393	-5803.378	-5800.965	-5745.470	-5745.05
Alpha	1.689	1.600	1.600	1.597	1.494	1.493
Ln alpha	0.524	0.470	0.470	0.468	0.401	0.401

† $p < 0.10$, * $p < 0.05$, ** $p < 0.01$, *** $p < 0.001$.

Poisson and Time-Series Models

The analysis presented in this chapter includes both negative binomial and linear regression models. Given the count data, the most appropriate model is the negative binomial regression. However—as is often the case—alternative models could also be applied to this data set. In Table A.2.2, I present the models

Table A.2.2. **Poisson regression of presidential and party status on monthly (lagged)** *New York Times* **coverage of national committee branding operations, 1913–2016.**

	(1)	*(2)*	*(3)*	*(4)*
White House	−0.461***	−0.401***	—	—
(Robust standard errors)	(0.069)	(0.048)	—	—
Majority president	—	—	−0.463***	−0.410***
	—	—	(0.092)	(0.070)
Minority president	—	—	−0.458***	−0.388***
	—	—	(0.075)	(0.063)
Pres. election year	0.619***	—	0.618***	—
	(0.078)	—	(0.078)	—
Midterm election year	0.007	—	0.007	—
	(0.074)	—	(0.075)	—
Democratic Party	−0.203**	−0.110*	−0.203**	−0.108*
	(0.068)	(0.049)	(0.071)	(0.050)
NYT size	0.003***	—	0.003***	—
	(0.000)	—	(0.000)	—
Scandal	0.027	0.001	0.027	0.001
	(0.021)	(0.019)	(0.021)	(0.019)
Fixed effects	—	Month & year	—	Month & year
Constant	0.583***	−2.468**	0.582***	−2.466**
	(0.095)	(0.715)	(0.099)	(0.716)
N	2,494	2,494	2,494	2,494
Pseudo R^2	0.092	0.381	0.092	0.381
Log pseudo likelihood	−9578.049	−6524.992	−9578.040	−6524.854

$^{*}p < 0.05, ^{**}p < 0.01, ^{***}p < 0.001.$

Table A.2.3. **Time-series negative binomial regression of presidential and party status on monthly *New York Times* coverage of national committee branding operations, 1913–2016.**

	(1)	*(2)*	*(3)*	*(4)*
White House	−0.468***	−0.450***	—	—
(Robust standard errors)	(0.055)	(0.044)	—	—
Majority president	—	—	−0.484***	−0.429***
	—	—	(0.069)	(0.063)
Minority president	—	—	−0.448***	−0.475***
	—	—	(0.070)	(0.063)
Pres. election year	1.117***	—	1.116***	—
	(0.067)	—	(0.067)	—
Midterm election year	0.432***	—	0.434***	—
	(0.065)	—	(0.065)	—
Democratic Party	−0.206***	−0.126**	−0.204***	−0.132**
	(0.054)	(0.044)	(0.054)	(0.046)
NYT size	0.002***	—	0.002***	—
	(0.000)	—	(0.000)	—
Scandal	0.025	0.010	0.025	0.010
	(0.018)	(0.016)	(0.018)	(0.016)
Fixed effects	—	Month & year	—	Month & year
Constant	0.409***	−2.132**	0.400***	−2.163***
	(0.082)	(0.703)	(0.085)	(0.703)
N	2,496	2,496	2,496	2,496
Pseudo R^2	0.043	0.107	0.043	0.107
Log pseudo likelihood	−5627.794	−5250.239	−5627.694	−5250.117
Alpha	1.281	0.767	1.281	0.767
Ln alpha	0.248	−0.265	0.247	−0.265

$^*p < 0.05$, $^{**}p < 0.01$, $^{***}p < 0.001$.

included in Table 2.1 but instead rely on a Poisson model—the results are not different in terms of direction or level of statistical significance for the core independent variables.

The models presented in the chapter rely on the assumption that *New York Times* coverage of national committee activity in each subsequent time period is not dependent on that in the previous period. That is, national committee activity and *New York Times* coverage of those activities in month *t* change independently of what the activity/coverage was at time *t−1*. This assumption does not need to be correct; indeed, an extensive literature on national committee activity has noted the institutional development of the DNC and RNC over time. Additionally, it is likely that there is seasonal variation—both in terms of election years (in which both national committees are more active) and possibly in terms of specific times of the year when national committees and/or the *New York Times* could be more or less active. For example, it is possible that the *Times* decreases its coverage of political events during summer months or during the winter holiday season. The inclusion of the election year control variables, and year-and-month fixed effects, should address most of these concerns. Nonetheless, the question of the effect of long-term institutional differences remains. To address this potential concern, I present the models from Table 2.1, but for the data when it is designated as a time-series data set (see Table A.2.3). The results are, again, unchanged in terms of direction and statistical significance.

Quarterly, Yearly, and Congressional Term Models

In the analyses presented, I rely on a monthly count of reported committee activities. The benefit of adding up the number of articles across a consistent time period is that it presents an easier-to-interpret result and cancels out specific

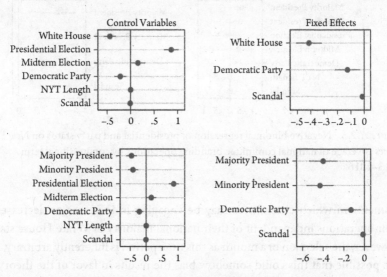

Figure A.2.1. Negative binomial regression of presidential and party status on quarterly *New York Times* coverage of national committee branding operations, 1913–2016.

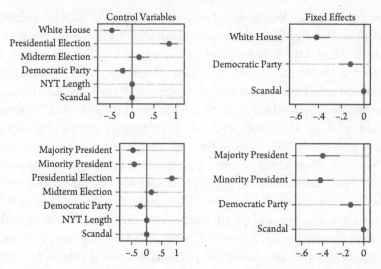

Figure A.2.2. Negative binomial regression of presidential and party status on annual *New York Times* coverage of national committee branding operations, 1913–2016.

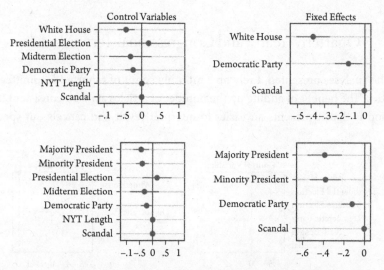

Figure A.2.3. Negative binomial regression of presidential and party status on *New York Times* coverage of national committee branding operations by congressional term, 1913–2016.

moments in which committees may be engaging in increases or decreases in their operations independent of their national majority or White House status. However, the selection of a month as this time period is inherently arbitrary, and it is possible that this could somehow bias the results in favor of the theory. In Figures A.2.1, A.2.2, and A.2.3 I present the models presented in Table 2.1 on data collected by quarter, year, and congressional term, rather than by month. Note that in this approach the issue of differentiating between articles published in the fourth quarter of election years becomes more problematic since it includes more articles that were published before and after an election that can change a party's national majority status. For this reason, I drop all articles published in November and December of presidential and midterm election years for the models discussed in this subsection. As indicated, the quarterly models include fixed effects for quarter and year, the yearly models include fixed effects for year, and the congressional term models include fixed effects for congressional terms. All results for either White House or majority/minority presidents are negative and statistically significant at the 0.01 level or below.

3

Building Permanently Active National Committees, 1912–1932

Both national committees in the late 19th century embraced a branding role during presidential campaigns but mostly remained inactive outside of election years. For both the Democratic and Republic National Committees (DNC and RNC) this changed after the 1912 election, when the parties determined to keep their committees "active" throughout the Wilson administration. On the side of the Republican Party, this decision may have been understandable given the major losses the GOP experienced in 1912 and the deep intra-party divisions the party faced between old guard conservatives and Progressives. In need of a coordinated rebranding effort, Republican leaders looked to the RNC to help unite the party. But while Democrats won the White House and congressional majorities, they too remained concerned about the nature of the victory. In particular, Democratic leaders—including Woodrow Wilson, the new president—understood that their success in 1912 was in no small part the product of the GOP's internal struggles. Therefore, the DNC also maintained headquarters and staff after Wilson's inauguration.

While the DNC and RNC now were "full-time" political organizations, their activities in this period were still modest, and both organizations faced growing pains in determining what role they should play within their parties, when to play it, and how to pay for it. Still, the cases presented in this chapter show both committees in the period 1912–1932 invested in branding activities, and engaged in attempts at defining a coherent, national policy agenda. For example, the RNC in the run-up to the 1920 election attempted to produce a coherent policy agenda in advance of platform discussions at the national convention. And during the Hoover administration, the DNC developed one of the most advanced publicity departments in American politics at the time and used it to attack the Republican Party's management of the Great Depression but also to push the Democratic Party to embrace opposition to Prohibition. In doing so,

National Party Organizations and Party Brands in American Politics. Boris Heersink, Oxford University Press.
© Oxford University Press 2023. DOI: 10.1093/oso/9780197695104.003.0003

the committees were focused on providing voters with a clear image of their party with the goal of improving its future electoral performances but in doing so also produced considerable backlash among opponents of those positions within their party.

Defending a Fragile Majority: The DNC during the Wilson Years, 1912–1920

The Democratic Party in 1912 won victories in the presidential race—which saw Woodrow Wilson win 435 electoral votes, to 88 for Progressive Party candidate Theodore Roosevelt, and a mere 8 for Republican candidate and incumbent president William Howard Taft—and in Congress. In the House, Democrats increased their existing majority considerably: with a gain of 61 seats, Democrats now held 291 seats to 134 for the Republicans, while in the Senate, Democrats managed to gain a small majority (see Figure 3.1). Combined, Democrats had won unified control of the federal government for the first time since 1892. However, Democratic politicians—most notably Wilson himself—were cautious in their interpretation of these election results. Indeed, they had good reasons to be suspicious of whether the 1912 successes would translate to future elections. Democrats had faced clear electoral disadvantages in both the

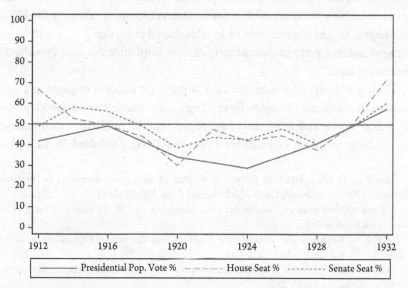

Figure 3.1. Democratic electoral performance in presidential, House, and Senate elections, 1912–1932. *Source: Congressional Quarterly's Guide to U.S. Elections*, 7th ed. (Washington, DC: Congressional Quarterly, 2016).

electoral college and congressional elections in the "System of 1896,"[1] and their victory in 1912 was in no small part caused by the internal rifts in the GOP— with Roosevelt and Taft splitting Republican support but, together, winning a majority of the popular vote.

This meant Democrats did not interpret 1912 as a major realignment in favor of their party. Rather, the 1912 victory represented a fragile advantage for their party, and one that could prove to be quite temporary. Because of this, Wilson determined that the party would instead keep the DNC active throughout his presidency in order to conduct "a continual campaign for the education of the people in Democratic doctrines."[2] Its core goal in this regard was publicity on behalf of the administration with the goal of securing Democratic victories in future elections. DNC chairman William F. McCombs—who had been a student of Wilson's at Princeton and had helped organize Wilson's presidential campaign[3]—argued for the necessity of a permanent communication effort, stating he did "not believe that, after an election, whether it results in victory or defeat, a committee should be dormant until a few months before another election" for "in order to assure a continuation of what we have accomplished, we must continue an organized army."[4] McCombs stressed the necessity of the national committee as the body that would create such an effort and asked DNC members to provide "suggestions and advice" so that "[two] years from now when we meet strong opposition, we can maintain ourselves in Congress and can organize ourselves for the great battle four years from now."[5] In response, members of the DNC voted to maintain the Wilson campaign's former headquarters in New York, establish a permanent Washington office for the DNC, and engage in "the organization of an educational campaign [...] with a continuous militant party organization from now until after the next Presidential election at least."[6]

During Wilson's first term, the DNC's publicity division engaged in a continuous promotional campaign by sending policy newsletters on a weekly basis to 10,000 weekly and 2,000 daily newspapers that did not have correspondents in Washington.[7] And in February 1914, the DNC published "A Record of

[1] See Scott C. James, *Presidents, Parties, and the State: A Party System Perspective on Democratic Regulatory Choice* (Cambridge: Cambridge University Press, 2000) 132–141.

[2] "Plans 4-Year Campaign," *Washington Post*, November 08, 1912; "Home of Party Here," *Washington Post*, December 24, 1912.

[3] Ralph M. Goldman, *The National Party Chairmen and Committees: Factionalism at the Top* (Armonk, NY: M.E. Sharpe, 1990) 220–221.

[4] William F. McCombs and Louis J. Lang, *Making Woodrow Wilson President* (New York: Fairview Publishing Company, 1921), 228.

[5] "McCombs Remains in Chair," *New York Times*, March 6, 1913.

[6] "Democrats Plan Fight," *New York Times*, May 17, 1913.

[7] "Palmer Is Chairman," *Washington Post*, May 17, 1913.

Achievement: The First Ten Months of Woodrow Wilson's Administration the Most Remarkable for Deeds in the Entire History of the Nation"—one of three political pamphlets celebrating the Wilson administration's (legislative) achievements with regard to taxation, tariffs, and currency revision, among others. These pamphlets were "intended to furnish the keynote for Democratic campaign speakers and editors in the Congressional and State campaign to be waged this year."[8] The DNC also released other campaign materials connecting congressional candidates to the achievements of the Wilson administration and in cooperation with the Democratic Congressional Campaign Committee (DCCC) released a "Democratic text book"—a 352-page publication celebrating the Democratic Party's achievements in the first two years of the Wilson administration, and outlining the party's plans for the future.[9] Additionally, the DNC helped organize Wilson's personal campaign activities in the 1914 midterm elections.[10] Notably, the DNC was not acting in a vacuum in making these decisions: the RNC also retained an active HQ and, after the RNC and the Republican Congressional Campaign Committee (RCCC) announced they had formed a joint campaign organization for the 1914 midterms, the DNC and DCCC followed suit.[11]

In the run-up to 1916, the DNC continued to engage in its "national educational and publicity campaign."[12] A. Mitchell Palmer, the chairman of the DNC's executive committee, proposed that the party should raise $100,000 (approximately $2.5 million by 2021 standards) for the specific purposes of "making a nation-wide educational campaign." Palmer called for this amount to be spent on "printer's ink during the immediate year,"[13] with the goal of promoting the Democratic Party and the Wilson administration to the public—since, "[we] are not afraid of the result if the work of the Democratic Party is put squarely before the people, and the misrepresentations by those adversely affected are exposed. These will be accomplished by an educational campaign."[14] The DNC also created a "foreign bureau" to create publicity for "citizens of foreign birth and descent who depend mostly on the language of the mother country for information and instruction regarding political affairs in the land of freedom."[15]

[8] "10 Months of Achievement," *New York Times*, February 7, 1914. See also: "Wilson in 1916, His Party's Slogan," *New York Times*, February 16, 1914.

[9] "Texts for Campaign," *Washington Post*, September 27, 1914; "Democratic Textbook Out," *New York Times*, September 22, 1914.

[10] "Wilson to Go on Stump," *New York Times*, July 28, 1914.

[11] "Palmer Is Chairman." See also: "Gardner Quits Fight," *New York Times*, August 9, 1913.

[12] "$100,000 Democratic Fund," *New York Times*, April 12, 1915.

[13] Ibid.

[14] Ibid.

[15] "Seeking Foreign Vote," *Washington Post*, August 22, 1916.

Prior to the 1916 presidential campaign, Wilson replaced McCombs with Vance McCormick, a former newspaper publisher and mayor of Harrisburg, and a Wilson administration veteran.[16] Running against former Supreme Court justice Charles Evan Hughes, Wilson managed a close victory in the electoral college, and a slightly bigger victory in the popular vote. In the House, Republicans won more seats, but Democrats were able to maintain their official majority through arrangements with third-party members. In the wake of the razor-thin election, McCormick, like his predecessor, stressed the ongoing need for a permanently active DNC.[17] However, due to the considerable deficit the party built up during the campaign, the DNC was left with a debt of $600,000—a remarkable amount at the time. The committee's investment in publicity programs during Wilson's second term proved limited.[18] Still, DNC figureheads remained focused on the committee's responsibility for maintaining permanent publicity campaigns. DNC Assistant Treasurer W. D. Jameson in February 1917 stressed that, despite the committee's financial woes, "[we] are going to start our campaigns now, and we are going to keep the country Democratic. The party will have its salesmen everywhere to sell its goods."[19] However, the DNC's attempt to turn the 1918 midterms into a referendum on Wilson's leadership during World War I did not pay off: Republicans won an actual majority in the House and won back the Senate.[20] After the 1918 midterm defeat, McCormick resigned as DNC chairman to serve as the chair of the American delegation at the postwar negotiations in Versailles but advised the party to ensure that the "organization work of the committee" should be "vigorously prosecuted"[21] during the remaining years of the Wilson administration and the run-up to the 1920 election.

Wilson selected Homer S. Cummings, a long-term committee member from Connecticut, as McCormick's successor.[22] Under Cummings, the DNC remained active in terms of publicity by creating a set of subcommittees to prepare campaigns among women—who, after the passage of the Nineteenth Amendment were to be voters across the country for the first time in 1920—and foreign-born voters.[23] Additionally, the DNC actively supported one of the

[16] Goldman, *The National Party Chairmen*, 221. McCombs officially resigned but did so in response to signals from Wilson that he would not be kept on to manage the president's 1916 reelection campaign. See: "M'Combs Will Quit as Committee Head," *New York Times*, April 25, 1916; "M'Cormick to Run Wilson's Campaign," *New York Times*, June 16, 1916.

[17] "M'Cormick to Fight for 1918 Congress," *New York Times*, November 22, 1916.

[18] "Democrats Raise $450,000 of Deficit," *New York Times*, February 28, 1917.

[19] Ibid.

[20] "Line Up for Congress," *Washington Post*, October 21, 1918; "M'Adoo and Hays in Party Conflict," *Washington Post*, October 28, 1918.

[21] "Democratic Chairman to Be Chosen Feb. 26," *New York Times*, January 16, 1919.

[22] Goldman, *The National Party Chairmen*, 225.

[23] "Democrats Meet to Get $5,000,000 Fund," *New York Times*, September 27, 1919.

Wilson administration's core legislative agenda goals by supporting the League of Nations.[24] The DNC also announced a major drive to get at least one million small donors to contribute to a campaign fund intended to help the party's publicity machine in the run up to the 1920 election, with the goal of carrying "the message of the Democratic Party to the humblest home in the land."[25]

But the party was deeply divided in 1920: without Wilson as its unifying figure, the first ballots of the 1920 convention produced a contest between two leading candidates, William Gibbs McAdoo, Secretary of the Treasury and Wilson's son-in-law, and A. Mitchell Palmer, Attorney General and former chair of the DNC executive committee. With neither man capable of winning the necessary two-thirds majority to clinch the nomination, after the seventh ballot, James M. Cox—the governor of Ohio—emerged as the new frontrunner. Still, it would take 44 ballots before Cox was finally nominated as the party's compromise candidate.[26] In the general election campaign, the committee's campaign efforts were dampened by lackluster fundraising, and committee workers were even locked out of the main campaign headquarters in New York at one point because the DNC had failed to pay rent.[27] Given the circumstances, the 1920 election results were, unsurprisingly, dramatic: Republicans expanded their majorities in Congress and regained the White House in a landslide victory for their candidate, Warren G. Harding.

Rebuilding a Broken Party: The RNC in 1912–1920

With Democrats winning unified control of government in 1912, the GOP faced a dramatic reversal of fortunes after four consecutive and comfortable presidential election victories. Adding insult to injury, the Republican losses were mostly the result of internal divisions. In the spring of 1912, incumbent president William Howard Taft had faced off against former Republican president Theodore Roosevelt for the party's presidential nomination. Taft triumphed on the first ballot at the Republican National Convention after Roosevelt bolted from the party when it became clear he did not have the votes necessary to win.

[24] "Cummings Urges Backing for Wilson," *New York Times*, March 13, 1919; "Cummings Makes League of Nations the Issue for 1920," *New York Times*, March 15, 1919; "Sees Third Run for Wilson if League Fails," *New York Times*, May 29, 1919; "Nation for League, Cummings Finds," *New York Times*, July 30, 1919.

[25] "Democrats Seeking $5,000,000 for 1920," *New York Times*, August 24, 1919.

[26] *CQ Guide to U.S. Elections*, 6th ed. (Washington, DC: CQ Press, 2010) 711.

[27] "Democrats Barred from Own Headquarters," *New York Times*, November 3, 1920.

But Taft's success at the convention came at a high price, as Roosevelt decided to run in the general election as a third-party Progressive candidate. With both Roosevelt and Taft on the ballot, the Republican vote was split, and Taft ended up a distant third in both the popular and electoral vote. Meanwhile, in Congress, Democrats increased their majorities in the House and gained control of the Senate. While RNC chairman Charles D. Hilles argued that the responsibility for Taft's defeat rested "squarely and solely upon Mr. Roosevelt,"[28] in the aftermath of the election Republican leaders understood the necessity of healing the internal divisions between the progressive and conservative Republican wings. Indeed, Taft, after the election, called on the party to convince progressive Republicans who had abandoned the party in 1912, to rejoin: "without compromising our principles we must convince and win back former Republicans and we must reinforce our ranks with constitution loving Democrats."[29]

Republican leaders pointed to the RNC as the organization that could help the party in its process of unification. Newspaper reports noted RNC members "have offered various suggestions for the reopening of party activity" and favored "a general publicity and educational campaign to strengthen public support of Republican principles and to take advantage of any 'mistakes' the Democratic administration may make."[30] In late November 1912, at a meeting at the White House with Taft and Hilles, RNC members urged them to "take part in the movement to establish active, 'militant' headquarters for the party, to be opened at once, and to lead a general party reorganization movement during the next four years."[31] With support of the outgoing president and incumbent RNC chair, the RNC thus maintained active headquarters throughout the Wilson administration.

In the years that followed, the RNC would play an active role in two important ways. First, the committee tried to use its role as the organizer of the party's national conventions to provide an olive branch to the Progressive wing of the party. Second, the committee used its publicity role to attack the Wilson administration and to help shape the party's policies—particularly in the run-up to the

---

[28] Meanwhile, RNC operative Frances B. Gessner, who worked in organizing the Republican campaigns in Ohio and West Virginia, argued that Taft's loss was in part due to Republican voters switching to Wilson out of fear for a Roosevelt victory: "There was no sentiment in [Ohio and West Virginia] for Wilson. It was just a Roosevelt hoodoo that was working. I heard lots of Republicans announce publicly that they were going to vote for the Democratic candidate just because they wanted to be sure of knocking Roosevelt out, and predict this will be found to be the case everywhere when the vote is analyzed." See: "T.R. Solely to Blame," *Washington Post*, November 6, 1912; "Determined to Beat Moose, so Republicans Voted for Wilson," *New York Times*, November 8, 1912.

[29] "Taft, Owning Defeat, Calls to Deserters," *New York Times*, November 11, 1912.

[30] "Taft Halts Booms," *Washington Post*, November 27, 1912.

[31] Ibid.

1920 Republican National Convention. In terms of party unification, the focus of both progressives and conservative Republicans initially was on settling long-standing debates about intra-party rules. In May 1913, in anticipation of the first RNC meeting of the year, progressive Republicans who had not bolted from the party in 1912 met in Chicago to discuss their demands.[32] The participants of this meeting argued that major concessions by the RNC would be necessary to unite the party. Senator Lawrence Yates Sherman (IL) noted that much of the conversation between these progressives had focused on "whether the National Committee should be as inflexible in character as it has been" and that "the [national] committee would" have to "be amenable to public opinion and keep pace with what was going on"[33] within the party.

While one of the biggest items on the progressive wish list—an off-year national convention to help reorganize the entire Republican Party—would end up being denied, the progressives were successful in achieving another core demand: a decrease in the size of Southern representation at Republican National Conventions.[34] Since the first Republican convention, all states were given a number of delegates in line with the size of their congressional representation, and Southern states consistently made up about a quarter of Republican convention delegations. After the end of Reconstruction, as Democrats began to create a de facto single-party system through violence and threats against (Black) Republican voters and candidates and (later) through Jim Crow–era legislation aimed at blocking Black electoral participation almost entirely, the region's influence on crucial party decisions such as presidential and vice-presidential selection became controversial.[35] While Southern states held a quarter of Republican convention votes, they increasingly contributed next to no electoral votes, Senate seats, or House seats. By 1912—as the *Washington Post* noted—it became

> quite generally admitted among Republican leaders that it is a grotesque folly for a group of Southern States which never choose a Republican presidential elector and seldom elect a Republican member of Congress or senator to control between one-fourth and one-third of the members of the Republican national convention.[36]

[32] "Hilles Issues a Call," *New York Times*, May 8, 1913.

[33] "Republicans Meet; Plan Party Reform," *New York Times*, May 12, 1913.

[34] "Outlook for Conciliation," *New York Times*, May 24, 1913; "Republicans Plan Reform Convention, *New York Times*, May 13, 1913; "Old Guard Decides against Convention," *New York Times*, May 20, 1913; "Republicans Veto Party Convention," *New York Times*, December 16, 1913; "Republicans Vote Delegate Reforms," *New York Times*, December 17, 1913.

[35] Boris Heersink and Jeffery A. Jenkins, *Republican Party Politics and the American South, 1865–1968* (New York: Cambridge University Press, 2020).

[36] "Aim to Unite Party," *Washington Post*, December 7, 1912.

But decreasing the size of Southern representation at the national convention proved complicated. The decline of Republican electoral success in the South also opened up possibilities for national party leaders—including presidential hopefuls like William McKinley in 1896—to use the "rotten borough" Southern state party organizations to their benefit. These political actors realized Southern convention support could be bought by paying bribes to state party leaders or promising them control over patronage. As a result, proposals to decrease the role of the South at Republican conventions were blocked or settled through negotiations behind the scenes. This approach was widespread: as president, Theodore Roosevelt had built his own relations with Southern party leaders and, in 1908, had handed control of these Southern machines to Taft. Yet, during the 1912 nomination, Roosevelt and other progressive Republicans attacked the role of the South, arguing that the region had stolen the Republican nomination.[37]

In 1913, progressive Republicans used their leverage to force major changes to the delegate division process. During an RNC meeting in May 1913, members of the committee voted to establish a special committee to investigate the delegate rules that progressives claimed had undermined Roosevelt's performance at the 1912 convention.[38] The committee radically altered the delegation division process: rather than provide states with delegates based on their population size, the new proposal based delegation size in part on the party's electoral performance. Specifically, each state would receive two at-large delegates at the 1916 convention, but congressional districts would receive a delegate only if the GOP vote in 1914 was 7,500 or greater. The proposal was ratified by both the RNC and two-thirds of party organizations of states that had voted Republican in 1908.[39] With Black voters in the South banned from voting due to Jim Crow legislation, and many Republican state party organizations unable or unwilling to run candidates in all congressional districts, the new plan resulted in a considerable decline in Southern representation at national conventions. While in 1912, the South made up 23.4% of delegates, in 1916 this declined to 17.6%. To be sure, the size of Southern delegations would remain an issue in future conventions, and national party leaders continued "buying" Southern support in the years that followed. However, the 1913 decision did produce a permanent

---

[37] Heersink and Jenkins, *Republican Party Politics and the American South*; Boris Heersink and Jeffery A. Jenkins, "Southern Delegates and Republican National Convention Politics, 1880–1928," *Studies in American Political Development* 29, no. 1 (2015) 68–88.

[38] "Harmony the Note of Republican Talk," *New York Times*, May 25, 1913.

[39] "Republicans Vote Delegate Reforms," *New York Times*, December 17, 1913; "Plan Cut in South in G.O.P. Delegates," *New York Times*, April 8, 1914.

decrease of Southern influence at Republican National Conventions until the party's electoral resurgence in the region.[40]

In addition to dealing with convention representation, Hilles also engaged in the type of branding activities Republicans had urged the RNC to engage in after the 1912 election. A major part of this concerned attacks on the Wilson administration. In an August 1913 article in the *New York Times*, Hilles criticized its foreign and economic policies and described the election of a "complete Democratic administration" as a "calamity to the nation."[41] The RNC invested in its publicity division by creating a new press bureau that had the goal of "[forwarding] the propaganda of Republicanism"[42] across the country. Additionally, in the run-up to the 1914 midterm campaign, the RNC worked with the RCCC in trying to produce a comprehensive campaign effort—though, as Ralph Goldman notes, in doing so the more conservative leadership of the RNC had to work with Progressive Republican Rep. Frank P. Woods (IA), resulting in "much apprehension on both sides."[43]

Despite these efforts, some Republicans still complained that the RNC was not doing enough. In the run-up to the 1916 election, several committee members called for further expansion and professionalization of the organizational structure of the RNC. Nebraska member R. B. Howell noted that members of the national committee had "very little to do" because "work was almost entirely confined to a sub-committee that was selected on the last day or the day following the last day of the Convention four years ago."[44] Instead, Howell argued, the RNC needed to become a "powerful body for the advancement of the Republican Party, a body very similar to the body that manages the affairs of the two great Political Parties of Great Britain."[45] Regardless of such

[40] Heersink and Jenkins, *Republican Party Politics and the American South*; "Republicans Vote Delegate Reforms"; "Plan Cut in South in G.O.P. Delegates"; "Republicans Cut Down Delegates," *New York Times*, October 26, 1914.

[41] "The Republican Party and the Future," *New York Times*, August 31, 1913. See also: "Hilles Calls Committee," *New York Times*, October 30, 1915. Along similar lines, but outside of the RNC, the RCCC itself also moved in the direction of activities focused on the national party, rather than individual candidates, when RCCC Chairman Woods announced that "the committee's work from now on would not be in the line of direct aid to individual candidates but would consist of furnishing information to voters. ("Campaign Plan Ready," *Washington Post*, August 30, 1913.) For a full overview of the historical development of the DCCC and RCCC see Robin Kolodny, *Pursuing Majorities. Congressional Campaign Committees in American Politics* (Norman: University of Oklahoma Press, 1998).

[42] "Old Guard Decides against Convention."

[43] Goldman, *The National Chairmen*, 278.

[44] Paul Kesaris, Blair Hydrick, and Douglas D. Newman, *Papers of the Republican Party* (Frederick, MD: University Publications of America, 1987), Reel 1, Frames 25–27.

[45] Ibid.—as will be noted later in this chapter, the British party organization system would prove to be an inspiration to the RNC during the New Deal era as well.

criticism, by the 1916 national convention the party found itself in a better position than four years earlier. To be sure, this was partly due to the failure of the Progressive Party to capitalize on Roosevelt's performance in the previous election. During the 1914 midterms, Progressives lost three of their nine seats in the House and won only one in the Senate. Indeed, the party's role largely was one of a spoiler for Progressive candidates who ran in the Democratic or Republican party in races against conservatives.[46] Roosevelt declined the 1916 Progressive Party presidential nomination over his support for American involvement in World War I and endorsed Republican nominee Charles Evan Hughes instead.

In the 1916 election Republicans performed better than they had four years earlier but still came up short in the presidential race, though a flip in California—which Wilson won by just 3,773 votes—would have put Hughes in the White House. Democrats also retained their majority in the Senate and control of the House through support of Progressive and Socialist members. In the aftermath of the election, some Republicans again argued that the RNC had not been aggressive enough during the first Wilson term. Republican Senator John W. Weeks (MA), in December 1916, attacked the RNC's role in the party, arguing that "if any private business attempted to conduct itself as did the National Committee it would go into bankruptcy in a short time."[47] Instead, Weeks called for a "permanent, continuously active National Committee which would be in the field the year around instead of being moribund except for a brief period before and after election days."[48]

The man responsible for further expanding the committee along these lines—William Russell Wilcox—proved a poor choice for this role. Hughes had selected Wilcox as RNC chair after the 1916 convention. Wilcox, a lawyer in New York and active in New York Republican politics, was an appealing candidate because he had long-standing connections to both Hughes and Roosevelt. In 1907, Hughes—then governor of New York—had appointed Wilcox chairman of the metropolitan branch of the state's Public Service Committee, which essentially provided Wilcox with control over state patronage. While progressive Republicans were supportive of the Wilcox selection, others were critical. Nicholas Murray Butler, the president of Columbia University and a delegate to Republican National conventions throughout the early 20th century, complained that Wilcox "has no acquaintance, no political sagacity, and nothing but good intentions and amiability to help him."[49] Wilcox's standing with conservatives did not improve after the 1916 election, as they blamed him

---

[46] Goldman, *The National Chairmen*, 278.

[47] "Overhaul Party Is Republican Demand," *New York Times*, December 2, 1916.

[48] Ibid.

[49] Both cited in Goldman, *The National Chairmen*, 282.

for Hughes's defeat.[50] And Wilcox himself had no interest in running the RNC as an active organization: although the RNC voted to maintain its headquarters and hold annual meetings of the full committee, Wilcox opposed having the RNC engage in additional activities.[51] After members of the RNC requested an early start to the 1918 midterm campaign, Wilcox informed them that "his other duties interfere with his being active" as RNC chair, and that any attempt to "rehabilitate the committee long before a national campaign"[52] would mean his resignation.

Wilcox's ineffective leadership of the RNC ended in early 1918 when he took a position in the wartime U.S. Railroad Wage Commission. Despite his own limited interest in the institution, Wilcox nonetheless used his farewell address to call for the RNC to "become a very active organization"[53] which should help shape a national party by connecting local state party organizations to the national Republican leadership in Congress. In the open race to succeed Wilcox, reporters and political insiders considered RNC vice-chairman John T. Adams (a conservative) to be his most likely successor. However, in the run-up to the RNC meeting that would elect the next chair, Adams was accused of holding pro-German sympathies.[54] After a bitter clash behind closed doors, conservatives and progressives in the RNC selected a compromise candidate instead: Will Hays, a lawyer from Indiana who had supported Taft in 1912 and had been state chairman of the Indiana GOP since 1914.[55]

Hays lifted the committee out of the slumber it had been in under Wilcox' leadership. Under Hays, the RNC not only maintained headquarters in Washington, DC, but also opened field offices in New York, Chicago, and San Francisco.[56] As part of the war effort, Hays coordinated Republican Party activists to volunteer for Liberty Loan drives. While these activities were partly based on patriotism— Hays argued that "all political issues at home must be subordinated to the one

[50] Ibid., 285.

[51] Ibid., 286.

[52] "Republicans Plan an Early Campaign," *New York Times*, December 21, 1917.

[53] Indeed, Willcox argued that he had no doubt that "had this complete organization which I refer to—this complete harmony—[...] existed between the States, [...] and had the instructions of the National Committee been followed in all of the States, Hughes and Fairbanks would have been elected." Kesaris et al., *Papers of the Republican Party*, Reel 1, Frame 123.

[54] See: "Assert Adams Is Pro-German," *New York Times*, February 12, 1918; "Pro-German Letter Written by Adams," *New York Times*, February 13, 1918; "Halt Election of Party Head," *New York Times*, February 13, 1918; "Adams Drops Out, Hays Elected," *New York Times*, February 14, 1918.

[55] Goldman, *The National Chairmen*, 283, 286–287.

[56] "Republicans Make Ready," *New York Times*, April 13, 1918; "Headquarters at Capital," *New York Times*, June 30, 1918; "G.O.P. Chiefs Coming Here," *Washington Post*, July 1, 1918; Goldman, *The National Party Chairmen*, 288.

uppermost cause of winning the war"[57]—they also provided local party workers with a chance to build contacts with new voters. And Hays continued uniting progressives and conservatives in the GOP, declaring that "[all] the old factions of the party [...] were now together, and the meaning of the terms Bull Moose, Old Guard, and Reactionaries were now forgotten."[58] Hays increased collaboration between the RNC and the RCCC, resulting in a fully co-organized midterm campaign in 1918. The central message of this campaign—designed by the RNC—was an attack on the Wilson administration's War Department for its handling of World War I.[59] Hays even managed to reunite Roosevelt and Taft, convincing the two former presidents to meet and compose a joint statement in which they criticized Wilson's approach to the war effort and called for the election of Republican candidates to Congress.[60]

The RNC's publicity division also expanded its role, producing weekly news sheets that were sent to 5,145 newspapers each week. Additionally, the RNC created a Speaker's Bureau, allowing it to coordinate requests for appearances of national party leaders at events across the country.[61] Hays also used his position as RNC chair to help set party policy for the GOP, kicking off the 1920 campaign with a speech in March 1919 in which he attacked the League of Nations and pledged that Republicans "will accept no indefinite internationalization as a substitute for fervent American nationalism."[62] Hays further increased the influence of the RNC by establishing an Advisory Committee on Politics and Platform. This committee was the first attempt by a national committee to take control of the process of drafting the party's platform prior to the national convention. Hays noted that "heretofore platforms had been written on short notice without prior preparation or study" but that the Republican Party would benefit from a platform based on a "careful study of national conditions."[63] In doing so, the RNC—in the assessment of the Washington Post—placed "issues above candidates"[64] by producing a draft platform before a presidential nominee was

[57] "Must Win Peace, Says Hays," New York Times, May 25, 1918. After the announcement of the fourth liberty loan drive in September 1918, Hays stated that "the entire Republican organization in every voting precinct in this country shall be a fighting force in this Liberty Loan drive, all else is chores"; "Will Drop Politics to Get behind Loan," New York Times, September 26, 1918; "The Republican Declaration," Chicago Daily Tribune, September 28, 1918.

[58] "Republicans Rally to Support Hays," New York Times, March 2, 1918.

[59] "Baker as a Campaign Issue for the Republicans," New York Times, February 3, 1918. See also: "The Republican Party's Attitude," New York Times, June 30, 1918; "'I Say Fight,' Is Hays's Reply to Wilson Appeal," New York Times, October 28, 1918.

[60] "Taft and Roosevelt in Appeal to Voters," New York Times, November 1, 1918.

[61] Kesaris et al., Papers of the Republican Party, Reel 1, Frame 345.

[62] "G.O.P. Campaign on Nationalism." New York Times, March 8, 1919.

[63] "Hays Gives Bases of Party Planks," New York Times, February 5, 1920.

[64] "G.O.P. Convention at Chicago, June 8," Washington Post, December 11, 1919.

selected or convention delegates had even been selected. The RNC's Advisory Committee selected 21 topics—including railroads, agriculture, national economy, military affairs, tariffs, taxation, conservation, social problems, immigration, postal reform, and the high cost of living—and sent questionnaires to "prominent Republicans" to gauge their views on what positions the GOP should take in the 1920 platform.[65] With surprise presidential nominee Warren Harding on the ballot in the 1920 presidential election, Republicans found themselves back in the White House and with majority control in Congress after the 1920 election.

The DNC as Out-Party, 1921–1932

These 1920 election results radically changed the political environment both national committees functioned in. In the wake of the election, William G. McAdoo, widely seen as a potential presidential candidate for the 1924 election, blamed the results on a lack of political communication, and lamented the party's "failure to get the Democratic side before the people through proper publicity."[66] To improve conditions, McAdoo suggested that the DNC should not only maintain permanent headquarters but also appoint a full-time chairman—that is, a chair who could devote all their time to working on behalf of the national party and not combine it with other positions. Combined, McAdoo argued, this should result in "the establishment and maintenance of permanent national headquarters with sufficient force to carry on [the DNC's] legitimate operations"[67] during the Harding administration.

During the four years that followed the DNC did just that and dramatically increased its branding role. Under George White—a former member of Congress from Ohio who had been selected as DNC chair by Cox– the committee created a new executive committee with the goal of providing "counsel [on] an efficient organization of the National Committee"[68] and to take "every possible advantage of the political mistakes that may be made in the Republican Party during the Harding administration."[69] White moved the DNC's campaign headquarters

[65] "Republicans Seek Data for Platform," *New York Times*, March 28, 1920; "G.O.P. Questionnaire," *New York Times*, April 4, 1920; "Currency Questionnaire," *New York Times*, April 13, 1920; "Republicans Seek Ship Plank Data," *New York Times*, April 18, 1920.

[66] "McAdoo on Party's Needs," *New York Times*, January 9, 1921; "Envy the Elephant," *Los Angeles Times*, January 9, 1921.

[67] "McAdoo on Party's Needs," *New York Times*.

[68] "White Names 16 Democrats to 'Counsel' on Reorganizing the National Committee," *New York Times*, February 3, 1921.

[69] "White Now Faces Democratic Split," *New York Times*, February 5, 1921.

back to Washington from New York and appointed a full-time executive secretary in charge of managing HQ.[70] White also appointed Richard Linthicum—a former writer for the editorial page of the *New York World*—as a full-time publicity chairman whose task was to shape the Democratic response to the Harding administration.[71] Despite these efforts, White's tenure as chairman of the DNC proved to be short-lived. After the disastrous 1920 election, White faced considerable criticism from allies of McAdoo in- and outside of the DNC. To stay in office, White attempted to preempt any challenges to his leadership by refusing to call a meeting of the full DNC, which would have the power to hold a vote to replace him with a new chairman.[72] This strategy proved successful initially, as the committee did not meet in the spring or summer of 1921.[73] However, when the DNC finally did meet in November 1921, White lacked majority support among the committee membership and resigned.[74]

DNC members elected Cordell Hull, a former congressman from Tennessee who had lost his re-election campaign in 1920, as White's replacement.[75] As DNC chair, Hull further expanded the committee's activities, and in particular its publicity role. Speaking to the press the day after his election as chair, Hull pledged he would develop the committee into "the most militant and efficient organization"[76] in American politics and promised to "proceed at once with establishment of a systematic and thorough organization in the various States and counties" and "to maintain an efficient publicity bureau to get unbiased and accurate facts relating to the shortcomings of the Republican administration before the average citizens."[77]

Hull had a keen understanding of the potential of the DNC as a political organization, particularly at times when the party did not control the White House. Writing in his autobiography, Hull explained that with "the Party out of power and in the minority in both Houses of Congress, whoever occupied the office of chairman of the National Committee was in the highest position of Democratic

[70] "Burt New Aid to White," *Washington Post*, February 21, 1921.

[71] Thomas J. Queenan, *The Public Career of George White, 1905–1941* (PhD diss., Kent State University, 1976), 149; "Job for Newspaperman," *New York Times*, April 14, 1921.

[72] See: "Democrats Move to Oust White," *New York Times*, February 7, 1921; "Clark and Flood Line Up for White," *New York Times*, February 8, 1921; "Plan to Oust White Charged to M'Adoo," *New York Times*, February 9, 1921.

[73] "Committee Backs Chairman White," *New York Times*, February 18, 1921.

[74] "Democrats to Meet in St. Louis on Nov. 1," *New York Times*, October 11, 1921; "White Will Drop Out if Democrats Agree," *New York Times*, October 31, 1921.

[75] "Democrats Elect Hull as Chairman," *New York Times*, November 2, 1921.

[76] "New Chairman Aims to Unite Democrats," *New York Times*, November 3, 1921.

[77] Ibid.

Party leadership in the nation."[78] In contemporaneous private correspondence, Hull expanded on his understanding of his role as chairman of a national committee. Between 1921 and 1924, Hull frequently corresponded with former president Wilson, and they discussed their concerns about their party's electoral woes and the role the DNC could play in alleviating them. Hull showed particular attention to the necessity of a coherent national party brand for Democrats to be able to retake control of the House and Senate. In May 1922, Hull wrote to Wilson that he had "exercised all possible efforts to stump out and minimize all factionalism wherever the same existed" and that "no Democrat had a right to put forward his personal ambition during this year [. . .] where to do so might to any substantial extent jeopardize the success of the party in the November election."[79] In another letter to Wilson in August 1922, Hull complained that he had been "preaching constantly to Democratic leaders the great and urgent necessity for general organization and educational work among the rank and file of Democrats," concluding that "we are in serious need of more cohesion and better party spirit."[80]

In the run-up to the 1922 midterms, Hull focused most of his attentions on fundraising—a necessity given the debts the DNC still had to pay off from the 1920 campaign. Thanks in large part to Democratic Victory Clubs—a set of local party organizations created by Hull to ensure that the DNC would receive a constant stream of income through donation subscriptions by regular citizens—Hull managed to erase the DNC's debts and worked with the DCCC to organize the party's national 1922 midterm campaign.[81] But Hull also frequently attacked the Harding administration, and the DNC organized a training school for speakers and campaign workers.[82] In the election, Democrats failed to

[78] Cordell Hull and Andrew Henry Thomas Berding, *The Memoirs of Cordell Hull* (New York: Macmillan Company, 1948), 113.

[79] Cordell Hull to Woodrow Wilson, May 27, 1922, Reel 1, Cordell Hull Papers, Library of Congress (hereafter cited as Cordell Hull Papers).

[80] Cordell Hull to Woodrow Wilson, August 23, 1922, Reel 1, Cordell Hull Papers.

[81] Hull claims the Victory Clubs brought in around $70,000 in the first 10 months of 1923 (Cordell Hull to Woodrow Wilson, October 27, 1923, Reel 2, Cordell Hull Papers), a far cry from the $1 million the Victory Clubs were intended to raise before the 1924 election ("Democrats to Seek $1,000,000 For 1924," *New York Times*, March 24, 1923) but nonetheless a significant amount for the perpetually cash-strapped DNC. The DNC would remain in financial difficulties throughout Hull's term: in January 1923, Hull wrote to FDR that "[our] financial troubles are enough to run one crazy every twenty four hours here at the office." See: "Cordell Hull to Franklin Delano Roosevelt, January 18, 1923," Box 2, Folder 12, Personal Papers 1920–1928, Franklin Delano Roosevelt Presidential Library (hereafter cited as FDR Personal Papers 1920–1928).

[82] "Cordell Hull Asks World Trade Union," *New York Times*, January 6, 1922; "Hull Assails Rule of the Republican," *New York Times*, March 6, 1922; "No One to Defend Congress, Says Hull," *New York Times*, March 31, 1922; "Cox for the League as Campaign Issue," *New York Times*, April 3, 1922; "To Train Women Speakers," *New York Times*, April 9, 1922; "Newberry Assailed by Hull in Michigan,"

regain majorities in Congress but still performed well, winning six seats in the Senate, and 77 in the House—one of which was Hull's, who regained his House seat. In the wake of the election, Democratic politicians and the press celebrated Hull as one of the principal architects of a Democratic revival.[83]

After the 1922 midterms, Hull expanded the DNC's activities further. In a letter to Wilson in February 1923, Hull noted that the committee now sent "weekly literature and up-to-date facts" to "about five thousand country weeklies and one thousand local dailies."[84] The DNC's research department had also begun collecting "considerable data" to assist Democrats in Congress, and the committee organized weekly meetings with "a great many leading Democrats" at the DNC's offices "for purposes of conference and exchanges of information"[85] and to provide Democrats an opportunity to coordinate on the party's response to salient policy issues.[86] Additionally, the DNC created the National School of Democracy "to instruct Democratic women in public speaking and party administration."[87] Hull himself continued to be a major spokesperson for the party in the media, criticizing the Harding (and, later, Coolidge) administration for its "misrule and extravagance."[88]

New York Times, April 20, 1922; "Calls for Overturn of 'Worst Congress,'" *New York Times*, June 23, 1922; "Lays World Plight to Republican Rule," *New York Times*, August 3, 1922.

[83]   Goldman, *The National Party Chairmen*, 311.

[84]   Cordell Hull to Woodrow Wilson, February 28, 1923, Reel 1, Cordell Hull Papers.

[85]   Ibid.

[86]   In 1924, the National Democratic Club, a New York–based organization independent from the DNC, began publishing the *National Democratic Magazine*, a new publication aimed at reporting the "Democratic viewpoint." While the DNC was not responsible for this publication, both Hull and Linthicum were contributors to the first issue. See: "Democrats Start National Magazine," *New York Times*, March 2, 1924.

[87]   Goldman, *The National Party Chairmen*, 314; "Course on Politics," *New York Times*, January 22, 1923. While Hull's achievements in this regard were impressive, initial plans for the expansion of the DNC were even more extensive. One early plan, proposed by Linthicum, concerned the creation of a Democratic National Association that would unite Democratic voters in a membership organization that would provide the DNC with an annual fee of $10 per member ("Suggested Plan for Democratic National Association," December 3, 1921, Reel 1, Cordell Hull Papers). Even more extensive was Hull's suggestion (in an effort to "stump out and minimize factionalism wherever the same existed") "to develop a plan under which some of our Democratic leaders in the House and myself [. . .] will announce a policy [. . .] of giving to each section of the country their reasonable representation with respect to committee chairmanships in the House" (Cordell Hull to Woodrow Wilson, May 27, 1922, Reel 1, Cordell Hull Papers).

[88]   "Democrats Elated at Dever Landslide," April 5, 1923. See also: "Calls Congress Failure," *New York Times*, March 5, 1923; "Start Joint Inquiry on Sugar Gambling; Hoover Is Assailed," *New York Times*, March 24, 1923; "Says Republicans Ignore the Women," *New York Times*, May 21, 1923; "Adams Is Accused of Party Sabotage," *New York Times*, May 31, 1923; "Disputes Harding on Economy Claim," *New York Times*, June 22, 1923; "Attacks J.T. Adams as World Court's Foe," *New York*

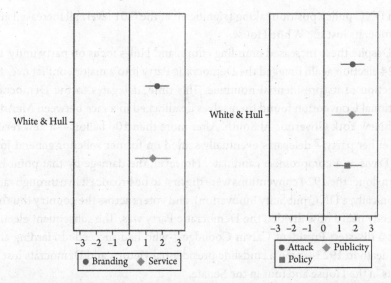

Figure 3.2. Negative binomial regressions of George White and Cordell Hull's DNC chairmanship on monthly (lagged) *New York Times* coverage of DNC branding and service activities, 1917–1924. *Note:* These models include variables controlling for presidential and midterm election years, a measure of *New York Times* length, and DNC scandals. The data coverage is limited to articles published between January 1917 and June 1924 covering only the DNC.
Source: Data collected by author.

The difference between the DNC's activities in the period 1921–1924 and before is also reflected in *New York Times* coverage of DNC publicity activity under its White and Hull. Figure 3.2 shows the results of negative binomial regressions in which White and Hull's incumbency as DNC chairs is the independent variable and the lagged monthly *Times* coverage of DNC branding and service activities are the dependent variables. In this model, the data is limited to those articles covering the DNC published between January 1917 and June 1924 (the month before Hull's term as chair ended)—thereby comparing coverage of the DNC under White and Hull to that in Wilson's second term. The results show that coverage of combined branding activities increased during the White and Hull era (significant at the 0.001 level) as did combined service coverage (significant at the 0.05 level). Notably, coverage of all three types of branding activities increased: *Times* references to DNC attacks on the Republican Party (significant at the 0.001 level), DNC publicity efforts (significant at the 0.01 level),

Times, September 17, 1923; "Blames Republicans for Farmers' Ills," *New York Times*, September 24, 1923; "Hull Says Scandals Are Campaign Issue," *New York Times*, January 27, 1924.

and DNC policy position taking (significant at the 0.01 level) all increased after Democrats lost the White House.

Despite these increased branding efforts and Hull's focus on party unity, the 1924 election again dragged the Democratic Party into a major conflict over the selection of its presidential nominee. This time, delegates to the Democratic National Convention found themselves deadlocked in a race between McAdoo and New York Governor Al Smith. After more than 100 ballots—a new record for either party—delegates eventually settled on former solicitor general John W. Davis as a compromise candidate. However, the damage by that point had been done: the 1924 conventions were the first to be broadcast live through radio (ironically, a DNC publicity innovation), and voters across the country thus had directly heard how divided the Democratic Party was. The subsequent election was a disaster: President Calvin Coolidge—who had succeeded Harding after his death in 1923—won a landslide presidential victory, and Democrats lost 24 seats in the House and four in the Senate.

After such a defeat, the DNC would have been expected to invest further in publicity programs after the election. Instead, many political actors within the party complained that the DNC failed to live up to these expectations.[89] To the extent that this is true, this may have been due to financial constraints: with few donations coming in after the 1924 convention, the party ran up a $300,000 deficit by the end of the campaign.[90] DNC chair Clem Shaver—the former state chairman of the Democratic Party in West Virginia, who had been appointed by Davis[91]—was forced to spend most of his time in office raising money, though with little success. While Shaver announced in the spring of 1925 that the deficit from the 1924 campaign had largely been cleared up and the committee would "start an offensive by expanding the skeleton organization now in Washington into a bureau which will give active help to the party,"[92] in practice the debt remained. During testimony before a Senate committee on party finances in July 1926, Shaver confirmed that the DNC had collected only $2,000 for that year's midterm campaign and that it did not have a budget planned for the year. Democratic Senator James A. Reed (MO) concluded that Shaver's testimony indicated the DNC was in effect "nearly bankrupt."[93] As the Washington Post reported, these financial limitations most directly affected the DNC's publicity

---

[89] To be sure, the New York Times data collected for this book shows no decline in branding activities in the 1925–1928 period in comparison with 1921–1924.

[90] "Deficit of Democrats Put at about $300,000," New York Times, December 4, 1924.

[91] Goldman, The National Party Chairmen, 317.

[92] "Democrats to Drop Policy of Silence," New York Times, May 8, 1925; "Democrats Wipe Out 1924 Campaign Debt," New York Times, June 7, 1925.

[93] "Party Chiefs on Stand," New York Times, July 3, 1926.

role: "Shaver discontinued the publicity activities of the National committee" because they were "too costly and were not profitable."[94]

While such a decline was perhaps unavoidable given the committee's financial state, other party leaders criticized Shaver for it. After the 1924 election, both the National League of Young Democrats and the New York Democratic Club called on Shaver to organize more frequent DNC meetings, and to create national off-year conventions to help the party set clear policy positions in midterm elections. Additionally, the groups called for permanent DNC offices to be created in major American cities to ensure consistent outreach to voters there.[95] And Representative William Allan Oldfield of Arkansas, the chair of the DCCC, complained that the "lack of adequate publicity" from the DNC "has been the greatest handicap of the Democratic Party in State and national politics."[96]

One of the more comprehensive critiques of Shaver's leadership came from Franklin Delano Roosevelt (FDR), who had been the vice-presidential candidate on the 1920 Democratic ticket. In December 1924, FDR sent a letter to Democratic leaders across the country outlining certain "fundamental truths" he believed should guide the party moving forward:

1. That the National Committee, or its executive machinery should function every day in every year and not merely in Presidential election years. 2. That the National Committee should be brought into far closer touch with the State organizations. 3. That the executive machinery for year in and out work should be put on a continuing and business like financial basis. 4. That publicity for fundamental party policy and for the dissemination of current information should be greatly extended. 5. That party leaders from all sections should meet more frequently in order to exchange views and plan for united party action.[97]

[94] "Shaver Is Reported Ready to Resign as National Chairman," *Washington Post*, May 27, 1925. To fill the void left by the DNC in this period, the DCCC published the *National Democrat*, a magazine intended to promote Democratic policies. Richard Linthicum—who had been publicity director of the DNC during the Hull era—was involved in the magazine, though the DNC does not appear to have been. See: "Another National Weekly," *New York Times*, May 18, 1925; "F.W. Steckman to Edit National Democrat," *New York Times*, May 20, 1925.

[95] Goldman, *The National Party Chairmen*, 320–321.

[96] "Another National Weekly," *New York Times*.

[97] Franklin D. Roosevelt to Randolph, December 5, 1924, Reel 2, Cordell Hull Papers. FDR's call for more frequent national conventions was not new: in November 1921 he suggested to DNC chairman Cordell Hull that the DNC should organize a "yearly get-together conference" to "secure better team work and cooperation" and to "get a certain amount of enthusiasm into the state unitsswhich [sic] is bound to follow a general meeting of this kind." See: "Franklin Delano Roosevelt to Cordell Hull, November 4, 1921," Box 2, Folder 12, FDR Personal Papers 1920–1928.

FDR's concern—as expressed in a letter to Shaver in March 1925—was that "the Democratic party has been becoming more and more a party of un-unified units, each fighting in their own particular territory with courage and [...] with conspicuous success, but without any general direction and without the tremendous advantage of effective help from other parts of the country."[98] As FDR's biographer James Macgregor Burns has argued, FDR wanted the party to "unite more closely, get rid of its "factionalism" and "localism," to do a better publicity job, to get on a firmer financial basis"[99]—all of which required a stronger national committee.

But despite largely positive feedback from other Democrats, there was little to no follow through on FDR's letter from the side of the DNC.[100] In a personal letter, Roosevelt accused Shaver of having "more the Washington viewpoint, which is always in favor of doing nothing rather than the real feeling of the Democrats throughout the country generally."[101] And, in a letter written in the spring of 1927 to a political supporter, FDR complained that

> the present Chairman of the National Committee has very frankly declined to assume any responsibility whatever. The National Committee itself has been perfectly willing to remain even more dormant than this and as a result the body which should guide us and keep us enthusiastic in between elections is, for all practical purposes, non-existent.[102]

While financial limitations may have been the main driving force in limiting DNC activities in the period 1925–1928, there were other considerations at play as well. One constraint was opposition by Southern Democrats to national publicity activities by the DNC. As part of a de facto one-party system in the South, these Democrats faced little to no threat to their re-election in general elections. As a result, Southern Democrats were generally not concerned with

[98] "Franklin Delano Roosevelt to Clem Shaver, March 4, 1925," Box 4, Folder 8, FDR Personal Papers 1920–1928.

[99] James MacGregor Burns, *Roosevelt: The Lion and the Fox* (New York: Harcourt, Brace and Company, 1956) 95.

[100] Roosevelt received several hundred replies to his original letter—with most state party leaders expressing agreement with all five of his "fundamental truths." See: Boxes 5 and 6, FDR Personal Papers 1920–1928.

[101] "Franklin Delano Roosevelt to Clem Shaver, April 7, 1925," Box 4, Folder 8, FDR Personal Papers 1920–1928.

[102] Cited in Laurence Robert Jurdem, *Return to the Arena: The Reemergence of Franklin Delano Roosevelt, 1921–1928* (PhD diss., University of Louisville, Proquest, UMI Dissertations Publishing, 1997), 137.

the need to build a national party brand or an organization capable of helping create one. Crucially, Southern Democrats were also not particularly open to the *kind* of national brand the DNC might promote. Burns argues that conservative Democrats feared a "concerted national effort by the party" would undermine their strategy of "deserting the party platform and taking a position congenial to local interests."[103] FDR himself concluded that the combination of the national committee's financial troubles, and the South's unwillingness to support committee investments, meant that "we have practically no leaders in a National sense at all."[104]

The 1928 election—another victory for the GOP—did nothing to solve the divide within the party. However, it did produce a surprising solution to the committee's financial woes and set in motion a dramatic expansion of DNC branding efforts. Hoping to avoid another catastrophic convention, delegates in 1928 were relatively unified in their support for Smith as the party's presidential nominee. This did not help the party much in the election, which Republican nominee Herbert Hoover won in a landslide—in no small part due to Southern hostility toward Smith as the first Catholic presidential candidate on a major party ticket.[105] However, Smith did get to select the party's new national committee chair. As the replacement of the inept Shaver, Smith chose businessman John J. Raskob. This was, by all accounts, a surprising pick. Raskob worked his way up from being the personal secretary of Pierre DuPont to becoming vice president of General Motors but generally identified as a political independent. Even in early 1928, Raskob, in declining an offer to be state chairman of the GOP in Delaware, argued that he was "such a strong believer in voting for good men regardless of party that it would be unfair for me to be aligned too closely

---

[103] Burns, *Roosevelt*, 96.

[104] Ibid. Shaver's survival in office for four years may have been assisted by the fact that the party was heavily divided between supporters of Smith and McAdoo for the 1928 nomination. While neither group was pleased with Shaver's performance, they also preferred "no action taken that will make it more difficult to restore harmony in the party"—that is, unseating Shaver would have introduced a battle over his succession and whether a McAdoo or Smith supporter would take his place. See: "Ritchie Boom Rises for the Presidency," *New York Times*, January 18, 1926.

[105] Hoover performed considerably better in the South than Republican presidential candidates had traditionally done since the end of Reconstruction. Hoover himself interpreted this success as evidence that his personal appeal could break the one-party system, in part due to his role managing relief efforts in the wake of the 1927 Mississippi flood. However, Heersink, Peterson, and Jenkins have shown that Hoover actually performed *worse* in those counties affected by the flood. Instead, Hoover's strong performance in the South mostly appears to have been based on backlash against Smith's Catholic faith. See: Boris Heersink, Brenton D. Peterson, and Jeffery A. Jenkins, "Disasters and Elections: Estimating the Net Effect of Damage and Relief in Historical Perspective," *Political Analysis* 25 (2017): 260–268.

with any party."[106] Raskob was thus by no means a devout Democrat but accepted the position for two reasons. First, Raskob had become a close personal friend to Smith. While the two had only met in 1926, they had bonded over a shared "rags-to-riches" personal history and their Catholic faith. Smith incorporated Raskob in his "Golfing Cabinet"—a set of wealthy New York donors to his campaigns who competed for his attention with his more progressive political advisers in Albany.[107] Second, Raskob was a strong opponent of Prohibition, based both on his own personal unwillingness to abide by the law and his conviction that the amendment was the product of anti-Catholic and anti-immigrant politics. Additionally, Raskob was concerned that a ban on alcoholic beverages could function as a slippery slope and inspire similar bans on other products— including those he had personal financial interests in.[108] As chairman of the DNC, Raskob believed he might be able to use his new political influence to steer one of the two major parties away from Prohibition.

Raskob remained chair after Smith's defeat. While controversial during his time in office, Raskob managed to maintain his position largely because he also functioned as the committee's most reliable lender. For example, in one month during his chairmanship Raskob contributed $10,000 to the DNC—covering nearly all of the committee's operating costs that month.[109] Raskob's willingness to function as the committee's personal credit provider was important because the DNC had a deficit of $1.6 million at the end of the campaign.[110] Additionally, Raskob's business connections meant Democrats were now also competitive among other donors. As Robert E. Mutch notes, Raskob "brought in three times as many $5,000-plus donors as had contributed in any of the four previous presidential campaigns. Some of these donors [. . .] were reliable Democratic backers, but most were giving to the party for the first time."[111]

Raskob used this influx of money to expand the DNC's publicity division radically. But in doing so, Raskob went much further than his predecessors in either party in claiming that the DNC not only should promote policies but also *determine* positions the party as a national institution supports.[112] The result was

[106] Cited in David Farber, *Everybody Ought to Be Rich: The Life and Times of John J. Raskob, Capitalist* (Oxford: Oxford University Press, 2013), 220.

[107] Ibid., 224.

[108] Ibid., 227.

[109] Douglas B.S. Craig, *Rehearsal for Revolt: The Ideological Turmoil of the Democratic Party, 1920–1932* (PhD diss., University of Virginia, 1989), 431.

[110] "Democrats Facing Deficit of $1,500,000," *Chicago Daily Tribune*, November 17, 1928; "Huge Sum Owed by Democrats," *Los Angeles Times*, November 17, 1928.

[111] Robert E. Mutch, *Buying the Vote: A History of Campaign Finance Reform* (New York: Oxford University Press, 2014), 90.

[112] Early in his tenure, Raskob and congressional party leaders agreed that "[future] policies of the Democratic party, at least for the next three years, probably will be determined by its spokesmen in

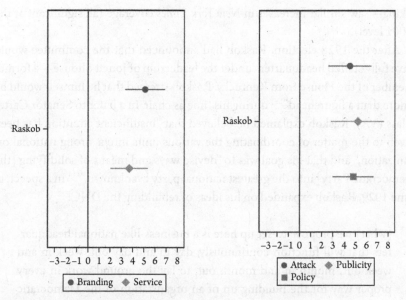

Figure 3.3. Negative binomial regressions of John Raskob's DNC chairmanship on monthly (lagged) *New York Times* coverage of DNC branding and service activities, 1925–1932. *Note:* These models include variables controlling for presidential and midterm election years, a measure of *New York Times* length, and DNC scandals. The data coverage is limited to articles published between January 1921 and June 1932 covering only the DNC.
Source: Data collected by author.

a dramatic expansion of DNC branding activities in comparison with the Shaver era. The effects of this are clear in the *New York Times* coverage of the Raskob era. Figure 3.3 shows the results of negative binomial regressions in which Raskob's incumbency as chair is the independent variable and the lagged monthly *Times* coverage of DNC branding and service activities are the dependent variables. In this model, the data is limited to those articles covering the DNC published between January 1925 and June 1932 (the month before Raskob's term as chair ended)—thereby comparing coverage of the Raskob-era DNC with that of the Shaver-era DNC. The growth in DNC activity across the board is self-evident: the combined coverage of branding and service increased dramatically (both statistically significant at the 0.001 level), and each individual branding activity—DNC attacks on the GOP, publicity activities, and policy position

the United States Senate." However, in practice, Raskob quickly attempted to steer the party toward embracing policies he preferred. See: "Senators to Guide Democratic Party," *New York Times*, April 21, 1929.

taking—saw similar increases in *New York Times* coverage (all significant at the 0.001 level).

After the 1928 election, Raskob had announced that the committee would have fully staffed headquarters under the leadership of Jouett Shouse—a former member of the House from Kentucky. Raskob stressed that he himself would be "more than a figurehead"[113] during his time as chair. In a letter to Senator Carter Glass (VA), Raskob explained he believed that "insufficient attention has been given to the matter of coordinating the various units into a strong national organization," and that his goal was to "devise ways and means of solidifying [the Democratic Party] into the greatest national party ever known."[114] In a speech in June 1929, Raskob expanded on his ideas of rebuilding the DNC:

> [what] we propose to set up here is a business-like national headquarters that will function continuously, day in and day out, week in and week out, month in and month out, to lay the ground work in every proper way for the building up of an organization of the Democratic party, for the education of the people as to what is taking place in the conduct of their government by the party now in power, and for an earnest effort to win them to the support of our party, first in the election of the next Congress and later in the election of the next President of the United States. With this in view, three major activities will be undertaken—organization, publicity and research.[115]

To achieve this, the DNC created a new publicity bureau. Shouse, writing in an article in the *Atlantic Monthly* in 1931, explained that the division had "the dual purpose of educating the electorate and affording some proper understanding of the Democratic point of view."[116] The division produced daily press releases and sent them to major and minor newspapers across the country. In 1931, the committee began a weekly "radio educational campaign on issues and policies" broadcast on CBS.[117] Through these publicity efforts the DNC attacked the Hoover administration's handling of the unfolding economic collapse and issues such as the Smoot–Hawley tariff. In a particularly notable stunt, the DNC took advantage of conflict within the GOP on the issue of farm relief: Republican

[113] "Raskob to Summon Democratic Chiefs to Build Up Party," *New York Times*, December 5, 1928.

[114] Cited in Roy H. Lopata, *John J. Raskob: A Conservative Businessman in the Age of Roosevelt* (thesis, University of Delaware, 1975), 114.

[115] "Democrats Cheer Raskob and Shouse as Party Builders," *New York Times*, June 11, 1929.

[116] Jouett Shouse, "Watchman, What of the Night?," *The Atlantic Monthly* 147 (February 1931), 251.

[117] "Democrats to Radio," *New York Times*, October 5, 1931.

Senator William Borah (ID) had given a speech criticizing Hoover for his failure to help farmers. The DNC paid to print millions of copies of the speech and cooperated with Borah to use his congressional franking privileges to send copies to farmers across the country.[118] Notably, the "Democratic perspective" the DNC promoted included considerable space for Raskob's friend Smith. The DNC paid for a national radio broadcast of a Smith speech in January 1929 and published a book of Smith's 1928 campaign speeches.[119] Combined, in Raskob's own assessment, the DNC's publicity division was "able successfully to acquaint the people of the United States with the weaknesses, false claims and failures of the Republican party when in power."[120] And, in the estimation of reporter Frank R. Kent, the Raskob-Shouse-led publicity division was the "most elaborate, expensive, efficient, and effective political propaganda machine ever operated in the country."[121]

But Raskob did not merely invest in new publicity programs; he also tried to use these programs to adjust the Democratic Party's position on Prohibition. Raskob's conviction that the DNC had a central task in providing new ideas and policies in the years between national conventions represents an important reassessment of the role national committees should play in intra-party politics. Raskob's goal was to use the DNC to make the repeal of the Eighteenth Amendment party policy before the start of the 1932 convention—essentially presenting support for repeal as a fait accompli once delegates gathered. Though unsuccessful in this regard, Raskob made several attempts to achieve this. The most notable effort came in early 1931 when Raskob announced he would put the issue of Prohibition to a vote in a DNC meeting scheduled for March. Supporters of Prohibition, particularly Southern conservatives, were outraged: Senator Cameron A. Morrison (NC) warned Raskob that if he carried "out the will of these nullifiers of the Constitution of the United States and [sought] to determine the policy of the Democratic Party" he would "meet defeat before the committee" or "if they carry the committee, the committee will receive the worst drubbing that any set of men ever received in American politics in the next Democratic Convention."[122]

FDR's role in this chapter of the DNC's attempts at updating the party's brand was notable. When FDR advocated for a stronger national committee during the

---

[118] "Hoover-Borah Split on Farm Relief Is Seen," *The Miami News*, April 28, 1929; "Democrats Using Speech by Borah," *New York Times*, September 1, 1929.

[119] See: "Smith to Talk to Nation on Radio Wednesday," *New York Times*, January 11, 1929; "30,000 Smith Books Bring in $125,000," *New York Times*, February 18, 1929.

[120] "Raskob Upholds Attacks on Hoover," *New York Times*, September 3, 1930.

[121] Cited in Craig, *Rehearsal for Revolt*, 425.

[122] "Southern Senators Warn Party Wets," *New York Times*, February 17, 1931.

Shaver era he had run into opposition from the South. Now, a considerably more active DNC was again running into opposition from conservative Democrats. But the 1928 election had changed FDR's own political strategy: his election as governor of New York meant he was now in a strong position to run for president in 1932. But to win the nomination, he would need Southern support at the convention. As a result, FDR's supporters on the DNC—chiefly among them James Farley, the chair of the Democratic Party in New York—opposed all attempts to bring Prohibition to a vote. Privately, FDR wrote to Harry F. Byrd, the former governor of Virginia who had expressed his concern about Raskob's attempts at using the DNC to oppose Prohibition,[123] that "[you] are absolutely right that the Democratic National Committee has no authority, in any shape, manner or form, to pass on or recommend national issues or policies."[124] Publicly, Farley issued a statement criticizing Raskob for confusing "the powers of the national committee by seeking to create an issue or issues on which the national committee cannot by any strength of the imagination bind the party."[125] To be sure, FDR had good reasons to oppose an expansion of DNC power under Raskob's control. Both Raskob and Shouse, while officially not picking sides, wanted Smith to be the nominee again in 1932. Indeed, when it appeared that Smith might not run again, Raskob and Shouse began to encourage other candidates to join the race to keep Roosevelt from winning the nomination.[126]

But the negative response to Raskob's attempts at setting party policy was not limited exclusively to those Democrats who were on FDR's side in the looming 1932 nomination contest and activated a broader debate about the proper role of a national committee. Bernard Baruch—a financier, former political adviser to Woodrow Wilson, and a personal friend of Raskob—wrote Raskob to strongly warn him against using the DNC to

> put forth what it may think is the Democratic position on the great questions. This is not its business, certainly not as much as it is the leaders in Congress. The convention that nominates the presidential

---

[123] Byrd noted that "[the] Democratic Committee has no right to make a platform for the party. It has never done so before. [. . .] It is not a courageous action because it is taking a short cut, as it is traditional that the Democratic party makes its policies by the action of the individual Democrats speaking through precinct meetings, thence to the State conventions, and thence to the national convention"; "Harry F. Byrd to Franklin Delano Roosevelt, February 28, 1932," Box 20, Folder 14, Governor of New York Papers, Franklin Delano Roosevelt Presidential Library (hereafter cited as FDR Governor of New York Papers).

[124] "Franklin Delano Roosevelt to Harry F. Byrd, March 2, 1931," Box 20, Folder 14, FDR Governor of New York Papers.

[125] Goldman, The National Party Chairmen, 334.

[126] See Lopata, John J. Raskob, 185–191.

candidate is the body which makes the platform and declares its position on all questions and the nominee is the one to expound its principles. I can think of nothing that would be so destructive of the magnificent chances the Democratic Party has before it as to attempt to have the National Committee declare for its policies or views upon great questions of the day.[127]

The opposition prevented Raskob from bringing Prohibition to a vote, though he did use the DNC meeting to call on the 1932 Democratic National Convention to support a new constitutional amendment allowing individual states to opt out of the Eighteenth Amendment.[128] And despite their failure to get the national committee to confirm the party's opposition to Prohibition, Raskob and Shouse continued to push an anti-Prohibition agenda. In April 1931, Raskob sent a letter to every member of the DNC asking them to provide him with personal recommendations for the planks that should be included in the 1932 platform, and particularly with any suggestions regarding how the party should deal with Prohibition. The intent behind this survey was to show a groundswell of support among party leaders across the country for a "wet" plank.[129] Around the same time, Shouse published an article in *The Democratic Bulletin*—the newsletter of the Women's National Democratic Club of Washington—calling for the party to embrace a so-called beer-plank, which would outlaw hard liquor but allow the manufacturing of wine and beer.[130] In November 1931, Raskob again tried to show Democratic opposition to Prohibition by sending a survey to 90,000 DNC donors requesting their views on the issue.[131]

Raskob and Shouse both failed in their attempt to settle the Prohibition issue before the 1932 convention and in keeping FDR from winning the Democratic presidential nomination. Instead, sizable majorities of delegates at the convention passed both a wet plank *and* nominated FDR.[132] But Raskob's role was

---

[127] Cited in ibid., 159.

[128] Ibid., 162. This position did not please Southern Democrats either: Senator Joseph T. Robinson (D) warned Raskob and the DNC that they could not "inscribe on the banner of the Democratic Party the skull and crossbones of an illegal trade." See: ibid., 163.

[129] "Raskob Insists Party Decide It's Wet or Dry," *Chicago Daily Tribune*, April 6, 1931; "Wet, Dry Issue Raskob Appeal Stirs His Party," *Chicago Daily Tribune*, April 7, 1931; "Raskob Canvasses Party's '32 Policies, Stressing Dry Law," *New York Times*, April 6, 1931.

[130] "Shouse for Beer as a Party Plank," *New York Times*, September 21, 1931.

[131] "Raskob Asks 90,000 if Party Platform Is to Be Wet or Dry," *New York Times*, November 23, 1931; "Raskob's 'Wet' Poll Viewed as Strategy to Block Roosevelt," *New York Times*, November 24, 1931.

[132] Raskob—realizing that Smith lacked the necessary delegates to be nominated—made a last-minute attempt to push Owen Young (the chairman of General Electric) as the Democratic presidential candidate at the beginning of the 1932 convention. See Faber, *Everybody Ought to Be Rich*, 283.

important, and even FDR admitted that under Raskob and Shouse "for the first time since 1920 we are getting real publicity from the National capitol."[133] Indeed, the assessment of reporter Frank Kent that the DNC's publicity division helped shape "the public mind in regard to Mr. Hoover"[134] came to be broadly shared, and Raskob's DNC would be presented as an example of an effective out-party national committee response to an incumbent president in the decades that followed. Additionally, Raskob's attempts at using the DNC for program-matic purposes more forcefully than ever before also introduced the concept that national committees ought to have the power and responsibility of setting party policies—an argument that the RNC had made earlier in the 1910s, and that both parties' committees would double down on in the future.

The RNC under Harding, Coolidge, and Hoover

After the 1920 election restored the GOP to unified control of government, the RNC's role initially proved complicated. Republican presidential candidate Warren G. Harding—a surprise dark horse nominee at the party's 1920 convention—won a landslide victory while in the House and Senate, Republicans now held considerable majorities in both chambers (see Figure 3.4). But the return of Republican control of the White House introduced the question of what the RNC's role—invigorated as an independent organization under the leadership of Will Hays—would be moving forward. While Hays managed Harding's campaign, he resigned in the spring of 1921.[135] As his replacement, Harding selected John T. Adams—the committee's vice-chair whose attempt to become chairman in 1918 had failed due to accusations of his sympathy for Germany in the war. Adams was a businessman from Iowa who had long been active in state politics there and had joined the RNC as the state's representative in 1912. Crucially, Adams was also a strong supporter of the old guard conservative wing of the GOP and a major critic of American foreign intervention.[136]

---

[133] "Franklin Delano Roosevelt to Fred W. Johnson, November 6, 1929," Box 74, Folder 3, FDR Governor of New York Papers.

[134] Cited in Faber, *Everybody Ought to Be Rich*, 254.

[135] Hays did implement a resolution passed by the national convention calling for another reassessment of the size of Southern representation at future conventions. Initially, this resulted in a plan that would have cut the South's delegation. However, after Harding's death, Calvin Coolidge—who was not certain he could win his own nomination at the 1924 national convention but could rely on Southern support due to federal patronage—canceled these plans. See: Heersink and Jenkins, *Republican Party Politics and the American South*.

[136] Goldman, *The National Chairmen*, 286.

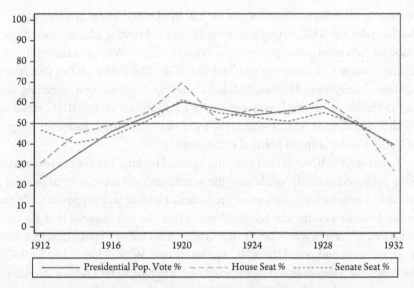

Figure 3.4. Republican electoral performance in presidential, House, and Senate elections, 1912–1932. *Source: Congressional Quarterly's Guide to U.S. Elections, 7th ed.* (Washington, DC: Congressional Quarterly, 2016).

During the first half of the Harding administration the RNC faced major debts. In October 1922, the *New York Times* concluded that the GOP's midterm campaign managers were "confronted with a depleted treasury and refusal of contributions from sources heretofore depended upon"[137] and that the RNC's role in the midterm elections appears to have been notably limited. But the 1922 midterms set in motion a different role for Adams. Republicans lost seats in both the House and Senate, which increased the power of Western Republican progressives who regularly worked with liberal Democrats on legislation.[138] In response, Adams began using his position as RNC chair to attack not just Democrats but also those progressives within the GOP that cooperated with them. This alone would have been uncommon for a national committee, but Adams extended this approach to criticizing actions by the Harding administration as well. Adams caused major controversy in the spring of 1923 after he attacked European allies as "crooks" for failing to pay the United States for the presence of American troops in Europe. An RNC statement accused Great Britain and other allies of trying to "bilk the United States by hook or crook" for military expenses, which it deemed "typical of the attitude of England and European Powers toward this

[137] "Republicans Uneasy over the Election," *New York Times,* October 15, 1922.
[138] See Jeffery A. Jenkins and Charles Stewart III, *Fighting for the Speakership. The House and the Rise of Party Government* (Princeton, NJ: Princeton University Press, 2013), 284–291.

country in all matters. They are out to 'job' the United States at every turn."[139] Additionally, the RNC strongly disagreed with the Harding administration's position on American participation in the World Court.[140] While the committee officially withdrew its statement attacking U.S. allies after pushback from Secretary of State Charles Evan Hughes,[141] Adams continued defending it—arguing that any criticism of his statement represented opposition to the RNC standing "with the 16,000,000 voters who, in the 1920 elections, voted against the League of Nations and European political entanglement."[142]

To be sure, the RNC did not fully turn against Harding. The committee consistently published materials celebrating the administration's successes and paid for a scheduled nationwide broadcast of the address Harding was supposed to deliver in San Francisco during the fateful "Western tour" he was engaged in at the time of his death.[143] But it was Adams's attacks against his fellow Republicans that drew most attention and pitted the RNC against its own White House. In May 1923, the New York Times assessed that it would be "impossible for [Adams] to remain much longer in his official position. In the course of nature he would be removed from it next year, but the party leaders ought to help nature along by getting rid of him as soon as possible."[144] However, party leaders—and, specifically, Harding—for unclear reasons were unwilling to "help nature along": despite plenty of calls for Adams to be removed, no action was taken to force him to call an RNC meeting at which the committee could vote to remove him as chair. And Harding did not use his authority to force Adams to resign either.

After Harding's death in August 1923, Adams continued his attacks on Republican progressives. In September, 1923, the RNC released a statement again opposing any U.S. membership of an international court.[145] In February, 1924, Adams called for the resignation of Attorney General Harry M. Daugherty in relation to the corruption scandals that had plagued the

---

[139] "Sages at Washington," New York Times, May 25, 1923.

[140] Congressional Republicans also opposed U.S. participation in a World Court. See: "Republicans Charge Allies Are 'Crooked,'" New York Times, May 24, 1923; "'Allied Crooks' Circular Gives Harding Shock," Chicago Daily Tribune, May 25, 1923; "Harding Harassed by Party Managers," New York Times, May 26, 1923.

[141] "Republicans Annul Attacks on Allies at Hughes's Order," New York Times, May 25, 1923; "Incredible Stupidity," New York Times, May 26, 1923.

[142] "Adams Raps Critics of Committee Slur on Allied Nations," New York Times, May 30, 1923.

[143] Harding's health deteriorated during the tour, and the San Francisco speech had to be canceled. Harding died days later. See: "A Forehanded Committee," New York Times, March 1, 1923; "5,000,000 Will Listen to Harding by Radio as He Speaks Tuesday in San Francisco," New York Times, July 28, 1923.

[144] "An Impossible Chairman," New York Times, May 31, 1923.

[145] "Republican Fight on Court Renewed," New York Times, September 13, 1923.

Harding administration.[146] Adams finally overplayed his hand when, in spring 1924, he authored a series of articles published in the *National Republican*, a magazine which previously had been published by the RNC but which had split off as an independent publication.[147] The split was based on the *National Republican*'s editorial staff's desire to be able to uphold "only those members of the Republican Party who are faithful to the principles of the regular organization" and to oppose "men classed as Republicans who have not kept step with party principles and policies"[148]—that is, progressives. But while the magazine was now separate from the national party organization, Adams was one of the magazine's major stockholders and a regular contributor, making it hard to distinguish between the publication's positions and the RNC's. As a result, both the media and progressive Republicans interpreted attacks against the progressive wing of the GOP in the magazine as coming from the RNC chair himself. In May 1924, Coolidge forced Adams to resign.[149]

In the wake of Coolidge's victory in 1924, the RNC's activities receded. Coolidge had named his friend William Butler as the new chair. However, after the death of Senator Henry Cabot Lodge (R-MA) in November 1924, Butler also was appointed senator. Between these two jobs, Butler's focus was clearly on the Senate. While he expressed his belief in "the necessity of strong efforts to win in the congressional elections of 1926,"[150] the RNC engaged in few activities of note and the committee met only irregularly. When it did, the committee focused on organizing the 1928 convention.[151] While the RNC still maintained headquarters in Washington, DC, it did so with only limited staff. Additionally, the RNC engaged in few publicity activities. Butler himself was also largely invisible: with the exception of a spring 1927 fact-finding tour to prepare for the 1928 campaign, the chairman remained out of the spotlight.[152]

The decline in the RNC's activities during Coolidge's post-1924 term is evident in the coverage the RNC received in the *New York Times*. Figure 3.5

---

[146] "Adams Hits Lodge Group," *New York Times*, February 23, 1924.

[147] The status of the *National Republican* prior to 1924 was complicated, but the *New York Times* described it as "generally considered the organ of the Republican National Committee" in a June 1923 article. See: "Hirshfield Applauded in Organ of Adams," *New York Times*, June 17, 1923.

[148] "Republican Organ Adopts New Policy," *New York Times*, April 24, 1924.

[149] "Coolidge Chooses Butler to Succeed Adams as Chairman," *New York Times*, May 2, 1924.

[150] "Must Fight in 1926, Declares Butler," *New York Times*, May 21, 1925.

[151] Kesaris et al., *Papers of the Republican Party*, Reel 2, Frame 443.

[152] A *New York Times* columnist, in discussing a speech Butler gave in Philadelphia in May of 1925, mocked the aloof RNC chair as not having been heard of for some time: "there was a general impression that he had taken refuge in the Citadel of Protection there to brood over the wonders that his abracadabra has wrought for the textile industries of his State and on his singular personal triumph in reviving the tariff issue—till President Coolidge said No." See "Senator Butler Is Found," *New York Times*, May 22, 1925.

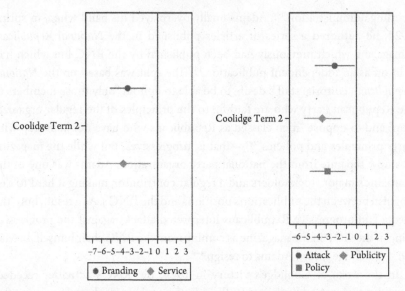

Figure 3.5. Negative binomial regression of Calvin Coolidge's incumbency as president during his second term on monthly (lagged) *New York Times* coverage of RNC branding and service activities, 1921–1928. *Note:* This model includes variables controlling for presidential and midterm election years, a measure of *New York Times* length, and RNC scandals. The data coverage is limited to articles published between January 1921 and December 1928 covering only the RNC.
Source: Data collected by author.

shows the results of negative binomial regressions in which Coolidge's incumbency as president after the 1924 election is the independent variable and the lagged monthly *Times* coverage of RNC branding and service activities are the dependent variables. In this model, the data is limited to just those articles covering the RNC that were published between January 1921 and October 1928—thereby comparing *Times* coverage of the RNC during Coolidge's post-1924 term with that during the period in which the RNC was mostly led by Adams. The results show a decline in *Times* coverage of combined branding and service activities (significant at, respectively, the 0.01 and 0.05 levels). *Times* coverage decreased for RNC attacks on the Democratic Party (significant at the 0.05 level), publicity activities (0.001), and RNC policy position taking (0.01). Combined, these results thus show that RNC's activities declined dramatically during Coolidge's post-1924 term.

This inactivity largely continued under Herbert Hoover. After winning the presidential nomination at the 1928 convention, Hoover selected Hubert Work as Butler's successor. Work was a doctor in Colorado before he became active in the state's Republican Party and had been a member of the RNC since 1913. During the Harding and Coolidge administrations, Work was Secretary of the

Interior and the first of the cabinet to support Hoover's candidacy.[153] Despite this, Work and Hoover fell out after the convention, and the RNC was largely excluded from planning the campaign itself.[154] After Hoover's victory, Work remained RNC chair and proposed a decentralization of organizational activities within the party: while he stressed the necessity of central headquarters, Work also called on state party organizations to raise their own funds and create their own campaign materials rather than rely on the national party organization.[155] The rift between Work and Hoover remained, and as a result Work stayed an outsider to the Hoover administration and resigned in June 1929.

In contrast to Work, Hoover initially showed some interest in expanding the RNC but in practice achieved little. In this regard, he was not helped by a series of scandals and issues regarding the national committee's chairs during his presidency. Hoover had selected Claudius Huston, the former assistant secretary of commerce, as the next RNC chair. During his first speech as chair, Huston proclaimed that "the work of a national party organization is no longer a mere spasmodic campaign effort"[156] and that his "program as Chairman will be that of seeking to build up [...] an organization which will ensure full expression of that public confidence which stands with and by the Republican Party."[157] However, Huston resigned a year later due to a scandal surrounding his personal finances.[158]

Huston's resignation took effect just weeks before the 1930 midterms, and Hoover replaced him with Senator Simeon D. Fess (OH). As a sitting senator, Fess had little interest in actively running the RNC and largely relied on the committee's executive director, Robert Lucas, a former commissioner of internal revenue, for its day-to-day management. Fess intended to resign after the 1930 midterms, with Lucas as his likely successor.[159] However, during the midterms Lucas actively campaigned against the re-election of Republican senator George W. Norris of Nebraska and was later found out to have "secretly

[153] Goldman, *The National Party Chairmen*, 302.

[154] Ibid., 381.

[155] Kesaris et al., *Papers of the Republican Party*, Reel 3, Frame 316.

[156] Ibid., Frames 367–368.

[157] Ibid., Frame 369.

[158] Huston was accused of having used funds for the Tennessee River Improvement Association to support his personal stock margins. Despite this controversy, Huston remained in office for another few months before announcing his resignation in July 1930. See: "Huston Expected to Quit as Republican Chairman," *The New York Times*, March 21, 1930; "Lobby Fund for Stock Margin to Unseat Huston," *Chicago Daily Tribune*, March 22, 1930; "New Post Planned when Huston Quits," *New York Times*, July 12, 1930.

[159] "Old Guard Victory in Choice of Fess," *New York Times*, August 10, 1930. See also: Glen Jeansonne, *The Life of Herbert Hoover: Fighting Quaker, 1928–1933* (New York: Palgrave Macmillan, 2012), 184–185.

ordered and paid for literature to be distributed in Nebraska [. . .] on behalf of former Senator Gilbert M. Hitchcock, the Democratic senatorial nominee."[160] Once Lucas's activities were exposed he became an unacceptable replacement, and Fess remained in office—despite his clear lack of interest in the job—until the summer of 1932.[161] Thus, despite the GOP's poor performance in 1930 and its upcoming landslide defeat in 1932, the RNC's role remained nearly nonexistent during the Hoover administration.

Conclusion

In the wake of the 1912 election both the DNC and RNC remained "active" throughout the Wilson administration and beyond. Much of the committees' subsequent activities were inspired by party leaders identifying a problem—providing voters with a clearly articulated, *national*, party brand—and identifying the DNC and RNC as the solution to that problem. Indeed, national committee chairs such as Will Hays, George White, Cordell Hull, and John Raskob focused on building up their committee's publicity role and using it to promote what they believed to be the most effective party brand to win electoral support in future elections.

During the Wilson administration, with the Republican Party deeply divided between conservatives and progressives, the RNC's role largely focused on bridging gaps between the two wings. But while modest in comparison with the type of branding activities national committees would engage in later, the RNC—particularly toward the end of the second Wilson term—did innovate in crucial ways. Most notably, in the run-up to the 1920 convention, the RNC began drafting a national platform well before delegates were selected. On the Democratic side, Hull in particular was one of the earliest committee chairs to have a clear vision of the role the DNC could play in coordinating a national Democratic message. And under Raskob, the DNC created one of the most advanced political publicity tools in existence at the time and used it to try to push the Democratic Party to embrace opposition to Prohibition. While Raskob was unsuccessful in forcing his party to take such a position prior to the 1932 convention officially, both the publicity division he built and the broader concept of a national committee trying to set party policies would heavily influence both national committees in the future.

---

[160] "G.O.P. Leader Is Held Hidden Foe of Norris," *Washington Post*, December 20, 1930.
[161] Goldman, *The National Party Chairmen*, 386–388.

But this period also saw two clear exceptions to the branding theory's predictions. One was the DNC's lackluster performance during the chairmanship of Clem Shaver (1924–1928), when the committee maintained only a skeleton staff at its headquarters, likely due to the committee's dismal financial status. Still, when the DNC did fall short in this period, Democratic leaders like FDR criticized Shaver for this lack of activities. The other was the tenure of RNC chair John T. Adams during the Harding administration. While the RNC declined under Coolidge and Hoover, under Harding the RNC not only remained active in promoting party policies but frequently went against the president's preferences. Indeed, under Adams, the RNC openly criticized the Harding administration on its foreign policy positions. While not predicted, Adams' activities do illustrate why incumbent presidents might prefer a less branding-active national committee. As an outspoken member of the party's conservative wing, Adams criticized fellow Republicans and even the administration, but, in so doing, Adams mostly produced an example of why future incumbent presidents might want to control and—sometimes, silence—their national committees.

4

National Committees and the New Deal, 1933–1952

During the Hoover administration, the Democratic and Republican National Committees (DNC and RNC) were on divergent paths. On the one hand, the RNC had played no major role within the GOP during the Coolidge and Hoover years. With the GOP comfortably winning presidential elections and majorities in Congress, there was seemingly no need for an active RNC—with even the committee's chairs often showing little interest in running the organization. In contrast, while the DNC had faced major financial problems during the Coolidge administration, it had developed into an impressive communication tool for the Democratic Party during the Hoover years. Notably, under the leadership of committee chair John Raskob, the DNC used organizational investments not just to attack Hoover but to also try to set national policy positions on behalf of the party, in particular by embracing opposition to Prohibition.

The 1932 election would push both committees into opposite directions. With the GOP now facing the worst electoral performances in its history, the RNC began developing a national response to the New Deal. This proved to be a difficult process, with considerable disagreements in the party on how it should position itself on the expansion of the federal government under FDR. And, given the party's poor performance in the 1934 and 1936 elections and Democratic presidential victories in 1940, 1944, and 1948, the RNC's attempts at reframing the party's image were clearly not successful in terms of regaining electoral support. Yet, RNC chairs in this period were instrumental in producing the party's electoral strategy. This included promoting specific policy positions (such as rejecting the GOP's previous isolationism during World War II) and identifying new voting groups the party should target to improve its electoral performance (such as a new focus on appealing to Southern Whites after the 1948 election).

National Party Organizations and Party Brands in American Politics. Boris Heersink, Oxford University Press.
© Oxford University Press 2023. DOI: 10.1093/oso/9780197695104.003.0004

In contrast, the DNC declined during the New and Fair Deal years. This decline was not instantaneous: under FDR's first term, the DNC remained active in trying to shape the public's perception of the party and assist its president. But after FDR's landslide victory in 1936, the DNC ceased to be a helpful tool to him, and the organization would not play much of a role in the remainder of his time as party leader. Under Truman, the DNC also remained mostly on the sidelines. The one exception occurred when the committee temporarily regained its usefulness to Truman's personal political goals: after the dramatic Democratic losses in 1946, and with his 1948 re-election now in clear jeopardy, Truman revitalized the DNC and its publicity role. But, after Truman's surprise victory, the DNC again largely was relegated to the sidelines.

A National Committee in Decline: The DNC under FDR, 1933–1945

In the first years after Roosevelt's victory the DNC continued using the publicity machine Raskob had created, though now with the goal of supporting the new Democratic president and administration. James Farley—who had been promoted by FDR to DNC chair at the 1932 Democratic National Convention—used his position to support the administration's legislative agenda and to try to coordinate its messaging. For example, in 1933, Farley called on Democrats in Congress to support the repeal of Prohibition.[1] In that same year, Farley announced all radio speeches given by members of the Roosevelt administration would have to be pre-approved by DNC executive secretary Richard F. Roper, in the hopes of providing voters with "a balanced diet of words which might prove useful in the forthcoming Congressional campaigns."[2] Additionally, DNC publicity chairman Charles Michelson maintained a weekly column titled "Dispelling the Fog," which was published (inconsistently) in a number of local newspapers until 1941—often next to a similar column by a representative of the RNC. So, while not as active and visible as it had been during the Hoover years, the DNC still continued to play some branding role on behalf of the new administration.

Notably, the DNC engaged in these activities while facing new problems in its financial well-being. While Raskob had been successful in increasing the number of donors to the party, much of the money needed to create his expansive (and

---

[1] See: "Farley's Plea for Big Repeal Vote," *New York Times*, May 23, 1933; "Farley to Urge Repeal Fight by All Campaign Workers," *New York Times*, May 24, 1933.

[2] "Farley Moves to Regulate Talks to Provide Balanced Radio Diet," *New York Times*, September 24, 1933.

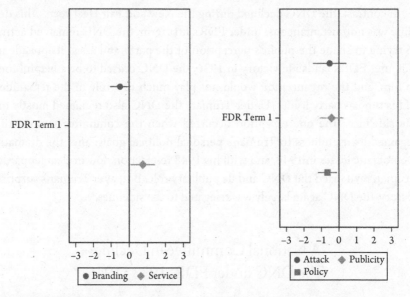

Figure 4.1. Negative binomial regressions of FDR's incumbency as president during his first term on monthly (lagged) *New York Times* coverage of DNC branding and service activities, 1929–1936. *Note:* These models include variables controlling for presidential and midterm election years, a measure of *New York Times* length, and DNC scandals. The data coverage is limited to articles published between January 1929 and October 1936 covering only the DNC.
Source: Data collected by author.

expense) publicity division had come in the form of loans he himself had provided. While he still controlled the DNC, this was not an issue. And, had Al Smith or another candidate who Raskob approved of won the 1932 nomination and the presidency, Raskob perhaps might have chosen a path that would have allowed the DNC to pay off these loans at a slower rate. However, with his political opponent in the White House, Raskob now expected to be repaid. After the 1932 presidential election, the DNC had a combined debt of nearly $750,000. While the committee managed to pay off some of this, the DNC still had a deficit of $477,000 after the 1934 midterms.[3]

Combined, the Democrats' return to the White House correlated with a still minor decline in branding activities, which is reflected in the *New York Times* coverage the committee received during FDR's first term in the White House. Figure 4.1 shows the result of negative binomial regressions in which FDR's incumbency during his first term in office is the independent variable and the

[3] "Farley Maps Drive to Pay Party Debt," *New York Times*, February 15, 1933; "Democratic Fund $21,294 on Oct. 25," *New York Times*, November 2, 1934.

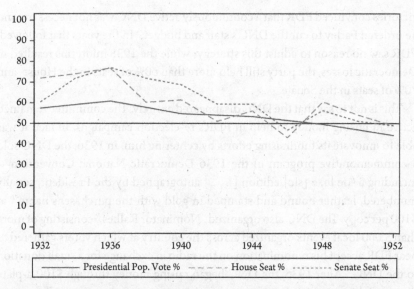

Figure 4.2. Democratic electoral performance in presidential, House, and Senate elections, 1932–1952. *Source: Congressional Quarterly's Guide to U.S. Elections, 7th ed.* (Washington, DC: Congressional Quarterly, 2016).

lagged monthly *Times* coverage of DNC branding and service activities are the dependent variables. In this model, the data is limited to those articles covering the DNC published between January 1929 and October 1936—thereby comparing coverage of the DNC under FDR's first term to that of the Raskob era. While the combined coverage of branding shows a negative coefficient, it is only marginally statistically significant (at the 0.10 level). In contrast, coverage of DNC service activities increased during FDR's first term (significant at the 0.05 level). With regard to specific branding activities, each of the coefficients is negative, but only one—DNC policy position taking—is statistically significant (at the 0.05 level).

But the DNC's decline accelerated after FDR was re-elected in 1936. As historian Sean J. Savage argues, this second victory changed FDR's perspective on the national committee: while he had previously called for the DNC to play a leading role in structuring internal debate within the party, FDR now "no longer found it necessary for the DNC to become a major vehicle for liberalizing Party ideology."[4] This updated view of the DNC was in no small part affected by the Democratic Party's new comfortable electoral position: the party managed to expand on its 1932 majorities in both 1934 and 1936 (see Figure 4.2). These

---

[4] Sean J. Savage, *Roosevelt: The Party Leader, 1932–1945* (Lexington: The University Press of Kentucky, 1991), 81.

victories convinced FDR that a continuously active DNC was not necessary, and he ordered Farley to cut the DNC's staff and budget.[5] In the years that followed, FDR saw no reason to adjust this strategy: while the 1938 midterms resulted in Democratic losses, the party still held more than 60% of seats in the House, and 70% of seats in the Senate.

This is not to say that the DNC disappeared entirely. The committee remained active in raising money to help in FDR's re-election campaigns. In fact, it was able to innovate its fundraising efforts by centering him. In 1936, the DNC sold a commemorative program of the 1936 Democratic National Convention— including a "de luxe [sic] edition [. . .] autographed by the President, serially numbered, leather bound and stamped in gold with the purchaser's name"[6] at $100 per copy. The DNC also organized "Nominator Rallies," consisting of more than 5,000 local events organized across the country at which voters gathered to hear FDR accept his renomination on the radio in exchange for a small donation to the DNC.[7] After 1936, the DNC began raising money through $100-a-plate dinner nights, at which Democrats at gatherings across the country listened to local speakers and national political figures whose addresses were broadcast simultaneously to the events by radio. These dinner nights proved to be highly successful and allowed the DNC to raise major sums of money.[8]

But the DNC's grassroots campaign activity still declined: much of the logistics underlying the 1936 campaign was no longer organized by the DNC and instead was taken over by organized labor.[9] As Sidney Milkis has argued, this was in part an electoral strategy on the side of FDR, as "the principal problem FDR faced in [the 1936] campaign was to appeal to activists in the labor movement

[5] FDR demanded that the DNC's monthly budget would not exceed $6,000 a month. See: James A. Farley, *Jim Farley's Story: The Roosevelt Years* (New York: Whittlesey House, 1948), 49.

[6] "Letter from the DNC Treasurer to Mr. Louis Abrons, October 24, 1936," Box 34, Folder 1, FDR Papers as President Official File 300. The cost for each deluxe book is identified in: "Safeway Stores Inc. to Mr. W. Forbes Morgan, December 8, 1936," Box 46, Folder 3, Papers as President Official File 300, Franklin Delano Roosevelt Presidential Library (hereafter cited as FDR Papers as President Official File 300).

[7] "Democrats Pushing Sale of Their Book," *New York Times*, June 1, 1936; "Farley Opens New Drive for Campaign Cash," *Chicago Daily Tribune*, June 4, 1936; "Democrats Gain $500,000," July 1, 1936; "Memo for Hon. Forbes Morgan, August 3, 1936," Box 603, Folder 1932–1939, Papers as President—President's Personal File, Franklin Delano Roosevelt Presidential Library (hereafter cited as FDR Papers as President, President's Personal File).

[8] See: "Dinners to Raise Democratic Fund," *New York Times*, February 23, 1937; "Hail 'Happy Days' at Victory Dinner," *New York Times*, March 5, 1937; "Campaign Funds Reported for 1937," *New York Times*, January 4, 1938; "Jackson Day Dinners Brought In $221,545," *New York Times*, March 12, 1939; "45 States' Democrats Dine Loyally Tonight," January 8, 1940; "Democrats to Issue Book to Aid Funds," *New York Times*, August 8, 1940; "$100 Dinners as Usual," January 5, 1941.

[9] Savage, *Roosevelt*, 82.

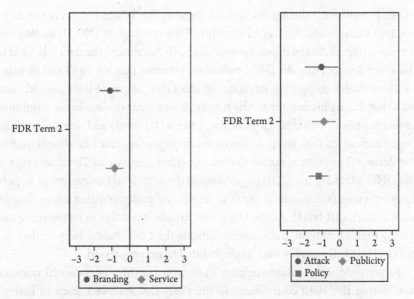

Figure 4.3. Negative binomial regressions of FDR's incumbency as president during his second term on monthly (lagged) *New York Times* coverage of DNC branding and service activities, 1933–1940. *Note:* These models include variables controlling for presidential and midterm election years, a measure of *New York Times* length, and DNC scandals. The data coverage is limited to articles published between January 1933 and October 1940 covering only the DNC.
Source: Data collected by author.

and other independent progressives who might work for him but refused to do so through the Democratic party."[10] By separating FDR's 1936 re-election campaign from his party, and by relying on auxiliary organizations and committees, the FDR re-election effort could recruit volunteers in a way that the DNC may not have been able to. After 1936, the DNC's role was weakened further due to the deterioration of FDR's relationship with Farley. While FDR remained silent on whether he intended to seek a third term in office, Farley—who also served as postmaster general—harbored his own presidential ambitions. With Farley openly discussing a presidential campaign, FDR began to exclude him from his inner circle but retained him as DNC chair.[11] As a result, FDR barely relied on the DNC during his second term in office.

The continued decline of the DNC is illustrated in *New York Times* coverage as well. Figure 4.3 shows the results of negative binomial regressions in which

[10] Sidney M. Milkis, *The President and the Parties: The Transformation of the American Party System since the New Deal* (New York: Oxford University Press, 1993), 76.

[11] Farley, *Jim Farley's Story*, 68–76.

FDR's incumbency during his second term in the White House is the independent variable and the lagged monthly *Times* coverage of DNC branding and service activities are the dependent variables. In this model, the data is limited to those articles covering the DNC published between January 1933 and October 1940—thereby comparing coverage of the DNC during FDR's second term with that during his first term. The results show a clear decline in the combined coverage of both branding (significant at the 0.001 level) and service activities (significant at the 0.01 level). In terms of coverage of specific branding activities, the decline is consistent across the board, with a decrease in *Times* coverage of the DNC attacking the GOP (significant at the 0.05 level), engagement in publicity activities (significant at the 0.05 level), and policy position taking (significant at the 0.001 level). As the DNC was already less active in its branding role during FDR's first term, these results indicate the DNC fading away further as a political institution as his time in the White House progressed.

Farley resigned as chairman after FDR won his third presidential nomination during the 1940 convention. In the years that followed, each of Farley's successors focused mostly "on maintaining the intra-party cohesion necessary for raising funds"[12] and none initiated major publicity programs. Bronx party leader Ed Flynn succeeded Farley at the 1940 convention. While Flynn intended to be chairman only until after the election, he remained in office until 1943 with little enthusiasm for the job.[13] By then, this perhaps was a common sentiment within the DNC: Michelson, its long-serving publicity chair, complained in a 1942 newspaper interview that "it's been true for two years" that he "wanted to quit and take it easy"[14] but remained in office until January 1945.[15] By this time, the committee was left "in a state of dormancy, with only a skeleton staff"[16] of around a dozen workers.[17] Flynn resigned after he was nominated to become ambassador to Australia,[18] and FDR replaced him with Postmaster General Frank C. Walker, who took "the chairmanship with great reluctance"[19] and remained

[12] Savage, *Roosevelt*, 82.

[13] In his autobiography, Flynn noted that he "had taken the position as National Chairman with the understanding that I would resign immediately after the election"; however, "[it] was not easy to find a successor," and, as a result, "[things] drifted for a while." See: Edward J. Flynn, *You're the Boss*, (New York: The Viking Press, 1947), 170.

[14] "Won't Resign Now, Michelson Says," *New York Times*, October 23, 1943.

[15] "Hannegan to Give Politics Full Time," *New York Times*, January 23, 1945.

[16] Ralph M. Goldman, *The National Party Chairmen and Committees: Factionalism at the Top* (Armonk, NY: M.E. Sharpe, 1990), 355. See also: Savage, *Roosevelt*, 100–101.

[17] Hugh A. Bone, *Party Committees and National Politics* (Seattle: University of Washington Press, 1958), 38.

[18] "E.J. Flynn Quits Party Committee," *New York Times*, January 27, 1943. Flynn was never confirmed and asked FDR to withdraw his nomination. See: Goldman, *The National Party Chairmen*, 356.

[19] "Walker Persuaded to Succeed Flynn," *New York Times*, January 15, 1943.

in office for just one year.[20] Walker's replacement became Robert E. Hannegan, a Democratic politician from Missouri, and the DNC all but endorsed a fourth term for FDR, passing a resolution in January 1944 "earnestly [soliciting FDR] to continue as the great world leader."[21] In the 1944 campaign, the Congress of Industrial Organizations (CIO), a federation of industrial unions supportive of the New Deal, organized most campaign activities: while in the 1936 campaign the DNC had employed 700 full-time staff at its HQ, during the 1944 campaign the committee had just 250 paid employees.[22]

During FDR's presidency, the DNC thus lost all the progress made during the Raskob era. While in 1932, the DNC's publicity division in particular was widely celebrated as one of the most innovative in American politics, the *New York Times* summarized the state of the party in the tail end of the FDR era as being "in the condition of an aging athlete who has grown soft and fat through laziness and overconfidence" based on FDR's conviction "that he could be reelected each time he faced the polls."[23] Of course, it is debatable whether FDR's beliefs in this regard represented *overconfidence*. After all, Democrats won every presidential election with him on the ballot comfortably and remained in the majority in Congress. And FDR achieved this without having to rely on the DNC. Indeed, during his first term in office, he realized he could rely on unions rather than the Democratic Party's own national organization to do campaign work on his behalf. As a result, for most of his presidency "there was little cooperation between the White House and the Democratic National Committee."[24]

Seeking a Response to the New Deal: The RNC, 1933–1945

While the 1932 election elevated the Democratic Party to a period of comfortable majorities in presidential and congressional elections, it left the GOP in disarray. In the wake of the 1929 economic crash, Republicans had already lost a considerable number of seats in Congress but still managed to hold on to their majorities. But 1932 proved to be a complete rejection of the party: in addition

---

[20] Savage, *Roosevelt*, 101. Walker's autobiography—based on an unfinished manuscript written before his death—does not contain any references to his service as DNC chairman. See: Robert H. Ferrell, ed., *FDR's Quiet Confidant: The Autobiography of Frank C. Walker* (Niwot: University Press of Colorado, 1997).

[21] "Party Chiefs Ask Roosevelt to Stay as World Leader," *New York Times*, January 23, 1944.

[22] "Washington Calling: Rebuilding the Democratic Party," *The Washington Post*, November 13, 1944.

[23] "Democrats Tackle Job of Reviving Party Zeal," *New York Times*, October 5, 1947.

[24] Ibid.

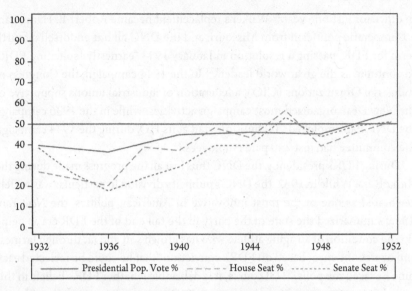

Figure 4.4. Republican electoral performance in presidential, House, and Senate elections, 1932–1952. *Source: Congressional Quarterly's Guide to U.S. Elections,* 7th ed. (Washington, DC: Congressional Quarterly, 2016).

to Hoover's landslide defeat, Republicans lost 101 seats in the House and 12 in the Senate—leaving it with, respectively, only 23.2% and 37% of seats. And, while Republican leaders did not yet know this, things would only get worse in 1934 and 1936 (see Figure 4.4). The RNC—which had faced years of neglect under Coolidge and Hoover—initially produced a somewhat anemic response to this new electoral reality. The committee's chair, Everett Sanders, was selected by Hoover to replace Simeon Fess at the 1932 Republican National Convention. Sanders was born and raised in Indiana and had served in the House of Representatives for four terms before becoming President Calvin Coolidge's personal secretary.[25] Hoover selected Sanders in the hope that he could help the party in the Midwest, though this proved an impossible mission. Sanders remained in office after the election but faced considerable health issues throughout his chairmanship, which limited his activities.[26] Sanders remained in office until June 1934, while Republican party leaders tried to find a replacement who could help organize a coherent response to the New Deal.

While Sanders did not steer the RNC toward a more active role, he did believe the committee should be a crucial part of the GOP's rebuilding efforts. In a speech in 1933, Sanders argued that "the very existence of a vigilant, well

[25] Goldman, *The National Party Chairmen,* 370.
[26] Ibid., 392.

organized minority party" was "the best preventive against economic and political excesses upon the part of the party in power."[27] Others in the party agreed: Hoover, in a letter to Sanders from May 1934, called for a more active RNC, as "government based on the proper functioning of two political parties" required "vigorous activity on the part of the party; and indeed, it is only through such organized discussion of public questions that our people may arrive at the truth."[28] But Sanders and congressional party leaders failed to agree on a fund-raising scheme to help pay for midterm campaign activities, and congressional Republicans announced they would go it alone. In doing so, they announced they would create a new press bureau and research unit focused on economic policies. Several weeks later, Sanders (by then, hospitalized) announced his intention to resign.[29]

Hoover suggested Sanders's replacement should be "from outside the leadership of his administration, preferably someone from the Midwest with practical organizational experience and a capacity for fund-raising."[30] During the chairmanship election, the contest focused on two candidates: Iowa state chairman John D. M. Hamilton and former undersecretary of state Henry P. Fletcher. While Hamilton was a better match with Hoover's outline, it was Fletcher who won a comfortable majority, and Hamilton was given the post of general counsel.[31] Under Fletcher, the RNC took on a much more active role in the party than it had since the Harding administration. Crucially, the committee began to identify a national argument the GOP could present against the New Deal. Fletcher proposed readjusting the GOP's ideological positions and that the Republican Party would have to be rebuilt "along more liberal lines, but opposed to New Deal theories."[32] Fletcher argued that such a reassessment was necessary because the GOP's performance in the 1934 midterms—in which the party lost another 14 seats in the House and 10 seats in the Senate—meant it risked going "the way of the Whig organization if it did not present appealing issues and a united front in the next Congress."[33]

To help achieve this, Fletcher began to expand the committee's staff. The goal was for the RNC to mimic the kind of activities the DNC had engaged in during

[27] "Address to the Young Republican Rally," June 29, 1933, Container 4, Folder 1, Everett Sanders Papers, Manuscript Division, Library of Congress, Washington, DC (hereafter cited as Everett Sanders Papers).

[28] Herbert Hoover to Everett Sanders, May 30, 1934, Container 1, Folder 3, Everett Sanders Papers.

[29] Goldman, *The National Party Chairmen*, 393.

[30] Ibid., 394.

[31] Ibid., 394–395.

[32] "Fletcher to Speed Party Rebuilding," *New York Times*, November 8, 1934.

[33] Ibid.

the Hoover era. Fletcher reinstated the RNC's Speakers Bureau to coordinate visits by national party leaders to local campaign events and fundraisers. The RNC also opened up offices in Chicago and added a full-time executive assistant to the chairman to the HQ staff.[34] To help the party appeal to younger voters, the RNC added a youth division that published *The Trumpeter*—a monthly news-letter.[35] Finally, Hamilton organized a grassroots conference in 1935, bringing together 6,000 Republicans from 10 states in the Midwest.[36] A few months later, the RNC voted to invest in Grass Roots Clubs aimed at increasing Republican voter involvement in the party, as well as by supporting youth and women's organizations.[37]

The reinvigoration of the RNC under Fletcher in comparison with Sanders's period as chair is evident in *New York Times* coverage of the committee in this period. Figure 4.5 shows the results of negative binomial regressions in which Fletcher's incumbency as RNC chair is the independent variable and the lagged monthly *New York Times* coverage of RNC branding and service activities are the dependent variables. In this model the data is limited to just those articles covering the RNC that were published between January 1933 and May 1936 (the last full month of Fletcher's chairmanship)—thereby comparing *Times* cov-erage of the Sanders and Fletcher era. The results show that coverage increased for both the combined branding (significant at the 0.05 level) and service (at the 0.001 level) activities. Regarding the specific branding activities, *New York Times* coverage increased across all categories—with more coverage of RNC attacks on the Democratic Party (significant at the 0.05 level), publicity efforts (at the 0.05 level), and policy position taking (at the 0.01 level) than during the Sanders era.

Fletcher's term as RNC chair ended at the 1936 national convention. The party's new presidential nominee, Kansas governor Alfred Landon, had a long-standing relationship with Hamilton and selected him to lead the RNC and manage his campaign. Landon lost to FDR in the GOP's second consecutive landslide defeat while Democrats expanded their majorities in Congress even further. After the election, Hamilton offered his resignation, though this was largely a gamble on his part: as Hamilton explained to a supporter in a private letter sent in December 1936, he

---

[34] "Republican Groups to Seek Formula," *New York Times*, April 28, 1935.

[35] Goldman, *The National Party Chairmen*, 396–397.

[36] "The Grassroots Republican Conference, Springfield, Illinois, June 10–11 1935," Container 1, Folder 1, John D. Hamilton Papers, Manuscript Division, Library of Congress, Washington, DC (hereafter cited as John D. Hamilton Papers). See also: Elliot A. Rosen, *The Republican Party in the Age of Roosevelt. Sources of Anti-Government Conservatism in the United States* (Charlottesville: University of Virginia Press, 2014), 21–22.

[37] Goldman, *The National Party Chairmen*, 396.

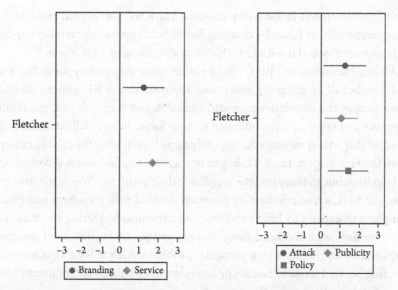

Figure 4.5. Negative binomial regression of Henry P. Fletcher's RNC chairmanship on monthly (lagged) *New York Times* coverage of RNC branding and service activities, 1933–1936. *Note:* This model includes variables controlling for presidential and midterm election years, a measure of *New York Times* length, and RNC scandals. The data coverage is limited to articles published between January 1933 and May 1936 covering only the RNC.
Source: Data collected by author.

thought this course wise for several reasons. First, if the resignation is refused I shall be the Chairman in my own right. Second, refusal will result in an approval of the conduct of the [1936 presidential] campaign and there can be no future backbiting. Finally, I will be in a position to insist on reorganization in the states which need it which I certainly would not be able to do if I myself had not offered my resignation.[38]

Hamilton's gamble paid off: the RNC voted to refuse his resignation and he remained chair through the 1940 national convention.

During FDR's second term, the RNC expanded its permanent staff to 51 employees and increased the budget of its research division. To fund this expansion, and to pay off the deficit the party was left with after the Landon campaign, the RNC inaugurated several new fundraising programs. This included the unification of national and state appeals to avoid duplicate solicitations, and the introduction of Lincoln Loyalty Dinners—fundraisers in the mold of the

[38] John D. M. Hamilton to A. L. "Dutch" Schultz, December 4, 1936, Container 1, Folder 4, John D. Hamilton Papers.

DNC's Jefferson and Jackson Day Dinners. The RNC also copied Hull's idea of Democratic Victory Clubs by charging Republican supporters membership fees. This approach netted the RNC $700,000 in donations in 1938 alone.[39]

Under Hamilton, the RNC also became more engaged in providing publicity on behalf of the party and trying to coordinate a Republican message. For example, the committee provided candidates with speech kits: pre-written speeches and talking points intended to help Republican candidates across the country shape their message during campaigns.[40] Following the DNC's example from the Harding era, the RNC began to organize regular weekend conferences to help Republican Party leaders coordinate their positions. To assist in this process, the RNC's research division prepared detailed policy analyses and invited nonpartisan experts to brief candidates and lawmakers. During the meetings, "for two days each weekend these various groups sat together and discussed ways and means of improving particular problems, such as legislative measures pending before House or Senate, or amendment of bills, or amendment of statutes already on the books."[41]

The RNC also played an important role in countering FDR's court packing plan. In the wake of Roosevelt's massive 1936 victory and a series of Supreme Court decisions rejecting the constitutionality of New Deal laws, FDR proposed adding one justice to the court for every justice aged 70 or older. Such a scheme would give him considerable sway in reshaping the court as a liberal institution and produced massive opposition among both Republicans and conservative Democrats. The RNC prepared data and speeches in opposition to FDR's attempt at expanding the size of the Supreme Court that were used by both Republican *and* Democratic opponents of the plan. In May 1937, the RNC paid for and created a number of national radio addresses challenging the plan. Hamilton helped coordinate payments from Republican donors to other groups opposing court packing to ensure broad public opposition.[42]

In November 1937, Hamilton announced a new RNC committee, existing of no less than 100 members selected by the RNC's executive committee, which would prepare the platform for the 1940 presidential election campaign. During

---

[39] See: Paul Kesaris, Blair Hydrick, and Douglas D. Newman, *Papers of the Republican Party* (Frederick, MD: University Publications of America, 1987), Reel 5, Frames 298, 277–278, and 392–394.

[40] Daniel J. Galvin, "The Transformation of Political Institutions: Investments in Institutional Resources and Gradual Change in the National Party Committees," *Studies in American Political Development* 26, no. 1 (2012): 60–61. As will be discussed, the DNC also used such speech kits after the 1952 elections.

[41] Kesaris et al., *Papers of the Republican Party*, Reel 5, Frames 947–948.

[42] Goldman, *The National Party Chairmen*, 405.

an RNC meeting, Hamilton explained that a comprehensive and clear party platform was necessary since the GOP lacked a consistent message:

> Surely we cannot be worse off than we are now. We have no common bond—except the name—that unites Republicans anywhere. Men are elected to Congress from different sections of the country, calling themselves Republicans […] yet holding diametrically opposed views on public questions.[43]

To Hamilton, the heterogenous nature of the GOP meant that "there's no wonder, when you talk to the average man about the Republican Party, he asks you what the Party stands for."[44] With Landon's massive loss in 1936 and Republicans now holding fewer than 18% of seats in the Senate and 21% of seats in the House, Hamilton argued that it was time the national party organization took control of shaping the party's image: "if there has ever been a time when we must be audacious, it is now."[45]

Hamilton's assessment of the RNC's role in this regard was inspired by a visit he made to the United Kingdom in 1937 during which he interviewed a number of politicians, volunteers, and staff members of the Conservative Party. Hamilton concluded that "it is a primary principle of the Conservative system […] that 'politics' is not a seasonal or spasmodic interest"[46] and that the Conservative approach suggested that in a modern media landscape, parties could not survive solely on the basis of volunteer activity. Instead, "the backbone of the system is made up of the various paid agents of the Party,"[47] and the RNC would need to professionalize further to provide the constant messaging necessary to inform voters of the party's policies.

To achieve this, Republican leaders from across the country—appointed by Hamilton and the RNC's executive committee—began meeting in March 1938. In the two years that followed, the committee interviewed experts on different policy issues in public hearings across the country. Once those testimonies resulted in policy proposals, they were sent to the RNC, where a team under the direction of Glenn Frank, the former president of the University of Wisconsin, compiled them into a coherent national program of action. To

[43] Kesaris et al., *Papers of the Republican Party*, Reel 5, Frame 435.

[44] Ibid.

[45] John D. M. Hamilton to Frances Bolton, October 25, 1937, Container 2, Folder 4, John D. Hamilton Papers.

[46] "Memorandum on Conservative Party Organization," June 1937, Page 2, Container 2, Folder 2, John D. Hamilton Papers.

[47] Ibid.

be sure, Republicans in Congress were skeptical about the RNC's attempts at setting party policy and believed they had the sole right to make these types of decisions. Even Frank himself concurred on that point, stating that "the custodians of party policy in the interims between National Conventions are the Republican members in the Senate and the House when, as now, the party is not in power."[48] Still, the two-year process produced a document outlining a GOP response to the New Deal. In February 1940, the RNC released *A Program for a Dynamic America*—a 33,000-word document that criticized the centralization and spending of the administration and backed free enterprise as the best solution to the ongoing unemployment crisis.[49]

At the 1940 Republican National Convention, Wendell Willkie—a businessman who had gained national fame through his fight against public ownership of utilities—won the party's presidential nomination. A political outsider and former Democrat, Willkie selected Joseph W. Martin as the next RNC chair. Martin had been elected to the House of Representatives in 1924 and was now the party's minority leader. But neither the Willkie gamble nor FDR's controversial decision to run for a third term did much to help the GOP's electoral fortunes: Democrats maintained their congressional majorities, and while Willkie did better than Landon, FDR was easily re-elected again.

As former chair, Hamilton expressed concerns about the state of the RNC after the end of his term. For example, in 1944, Hamilton wrote that "we never seem to learn in the Republican Party that activities are a year round proposition and not something to be indulged in spasmodically every four years."[50] This seems to have been a bit of an overstatement, as the RNC remained active in publicity and policy-setting attempts throughout the remainder of FDR's presidency. After the 1940 election, Martin remained RNC chair until after the 1942 midterms. As chair, Martin created subcommittees to deal with a variety of issues facing the party, including its internal organization and publicity programs; attempts at reaching out to Black voters, farmers, voters in the South, and women; and issues related to large-city problems.[51] The RNC also adopted a plan to nationalize the party's midterm campaign by assigning Republican workers specific responsibilities assigned by the party's HQ.

But both parties agreed to suspend political activities temporarily after the Pearl Harbor attacks and the United States' entry into World War II.[52] However,

---

[48] Quoted in Goldman, *The National Party Chairmen*, 408.

[49] Ibid., 407–408.

[50] John D. M. Hamilton to Roy Garvin, May 5, 1944, Container 5, Folder 1, John D. Hamilton Papers.

[51] "Republicans Name Seven Study Units," *New York Times*, June 9, 1941.

[52] "Republican Meeting Off," *New York Times*, December 22, 1941.

this truce did not last long: in February 1942, RNC publicity director Clarence Budington Kelland noted that a wartime political "recess" would mean "the destruction of the two-party system, the erection of the tyranny of the one-party system and the disappearance of the republic."[53] Thus, the RNC quickly returned to its midterm campaign efforts. And, while Martin claimed, "no administration in time of war ever had greater cooperation than we have given the present Administration,"[54] he and other RNC leaders soon began criticizing the administration's handling of the war.

In doing so, RNC officials criticized FDR while trying to remain supportive of the broader war effort. Kelland suggested that the GOP would "compel efficiency in our program of materials for victory," guarantee "the appointment of proper efficient men to see that the job of production is done," and ensure that the administration would spend money for victory and "not fritter it away for press agents, fan dancers, coordinators of ping-pong and political boondoggling."[55] The focus on "efficiency" became a core RNC talking point in the run-up to the midterm elections. In April, Martin noted "inefficient transportation facilities which constitute a bottleneck preventing planes, tanks, guns and munitions from reaching our fighting forces in sufficient quantities in time."[56] In September, RNC assistant chair Frank E. Gannett accused FDR of "bungling" the war effort and threatening "to usurp" law-making powers with the goal of "muzzling" the press and noted that the American people were "losing patience with the conduct of the war."[57] And, in October, Kelland suggested that the "war can be shortened and the day of victory brought nearer by the election of a Republican Congress."[58]

The 1942 midterm results saw Republicans gain 47 seats in the House and 9 in the Senate. The RNC celebrated the results as a major comeback for the party: Gannett claimed they marked "a definite change in the trend of public opinion" and gave the GOP "encouragement that when the next election comes around we shall complete the job."[59] After the election, Harrison E. Spangler—an RNC member from Iowa—was elected as the next national committee chair. Spangler, who was a compromise candidate acceptable to both conservative members of the RNC and those who supported Willkie,[60] announced he would

---

[53] "Kelland Opposes Political Recess," *New York Times*, February 13, 1942.

[54] "Hails Republicans for Action in War," *New York Times*, April 19, 1942.

[55] "Offers War Program for Republicans," *New York Times*, March 29, 1942.

[56] "Kennedy Is Urged by Martin as Ship 'Czar' to 'Smash Bottleneck' by Speeding Output," *New York Times*, April 26, 1942.

[57] "Gannett Assails War Leadership," *New York Times*, September 30, 1942.

[58] "Says Republicans Can Shorten War," *New York Times*, October 11, 1942.

[59] "Gannett Sees 'Wholesome Effect,'" *New York Times*, November 5, 1942.

[60] Goldman, *The National Party Chairmen*, 395, 480–481.

"devote his full-time effort to rebuilding and perfecting the party organization"[61] in the run-up to the 1944 presidential election campaign.

One of the issues Spangler faced was the ongoing difference of opinion within the GOP about the role the United States would play in the postwar world. The GOP traditionally had been dominated by isolationists and had retained that position even as the threat of Nazi Germany expanded. After the 1940 election, but before the United States entered the war, Willkie had come out in support of Roosevelt's Lend-Lease plan to help provide military support to Great Britain. Yet, despite his support, a majority of Republicans in Congress opposed the plan.[62] Under Spangler, the RNC began embracing an internationalist approach to a post–WW II future. In April 1942, the RNC approved a resolution that called for both the "relentless prosecution of the war" and "cooperative efforts for peace after the war."[63] Spangler argued that "you no longer can say that the Atlantic and Pacific oceans are moats around America."[64] He expanded on this in a January 1943 article in the *American Magazine*, in which he argued that America's role in foreign affairs could not be constrained to its own hemisphere after the war:

> [We] have partners in this war, partners who have fought, bled, and sacrificed. It would seem to be both improper and ungrateful were the United States to announce a plan or fabricate a mechanism for post-war procedure without consultation and agreement with our three great partners, China, Russia, Great Britain. [. . .] we shall need the collaboration of our partners in peace exactly as we need it now in war. We must be willing and wise to collaborate, but that collaboration must be without impairment of our national independent nation, without surrendering our individuality as an independent State.[65]

To produce a clear and broadly shared Republican position on this topic, Spangler created the Republican Post-War Advisory Council.[66] This council consisted of 49 members elected by the RNC and Republican leaders in Congress,[67] though it notably excluded Willkie, Hoover, and Landon.[68] The

[61] "Spangler Projects Unity Conferences," *New York Times*, December 9, 1942.

[62] "Republicans Assay Position," *New York Times*, March 30, 1941.

[63] "Republican Stand Stirs House Debate," *New York Times*, April 22, 1942.

[64] "Spangler Projects Unity Conferences," *New York Times*, December 9, 1942.

[65] "Spangler Outlines Republicans' Aims," *New York Times*, January 7, 1943.

[66] "Republican Post-War Policy," *New York Times*, June 2, 1943.

[67] James A. Gazell, "Arthur H. Vandenberg, Internationalism, and the United Nations," *Political Science Quarterly* 88, no. 3 (September 1973): 375–394.

[68] Hank Meijer, "Hunting for the Middle Ground: Arthur Vandenberg and the Mackinac Charter, 1943," *Michigan Historical Review* 19, no. 2 (Fall 1993): 1–21. See also: Simon David Topping, *The*

council represented a complicated balancing act: in the assessment of the *New York Times*, the RNC had to "walk a tightwire between the old pre-Pearl Harbor isolationists […] and the highly militant Willkie-led internationalists."[69] Indeed, Michigan senator Arthur Vandenberg, a member of the Senate Foreign Relations Committee and leading voice in the council, wrote in his diary in August 1943 that he found himself "hunting for the middle ground between those extremists at one end of the line who would cheerfully give America away and those extremists at the other end of the line who would attempt a total isolation which has come to be an impossibility."[70]

The council met in September 1943 on Mackinac Island in Michigan. The conference represented an opportunity for isolationists (such as Ohio senator Robert A. Taft), supporters of international cooperation (such as New York governor Thomas Dewey), and those in between (Vandenberg) to debate foreign policy suggestions submitted by Republicans from across the country. But it was clear that the isolationists were not in a position of strength. While this wing had been successful in undermining the League of Nations, most in the party had come to realize World War II required a different approach. Hiram Johnson, the isolationist senator from California, noted in his diary that after World War I "a few of us" were able to convince the people of "the utter futility and weaknesses of this League, […] designed solely to exercise our own country's sovereignty in behalf of all the world." Now, Johnson believed, "all of the press, and certain of the politicians, would go even further than the League sought to go" while nearly everybody who had been successful in opposing the League "passed away, and it makes me feel very sad to be the only one left, and to find myself neither physically nor mentally fitted for the new task."[71]

The council statement—largely written by Vanderbilt and adjusted through negotiations with Dewey—called for disarmament across the world and some form of international organization. In the assessment of *Time* magazine, this was "far more specific" than internationalists had hoped for and committed the GOP to "responsible participation by the United States in postwar cooperative organization among sovereign nations to prevent military aggression and to attain permanent peace with organized justice in a free world."[72] Indeed, the statement was

Republican Party and Civil Rights, 1928–1948 (PhD diss., University of Hull, March 2002), 270; "Republicans Call Platform Parley," *New York Times*, July 24, 1943; "G.O.P. Leaders Meet to Draft 1944 Platform," *Chicago Daily Tribune*, September 5, 1943; "GOP at Mackinac Left Doors Open," *New York Times*, September 12, 1943.

   [69] "Republicans Approach Touchy Post-War Issue," *New York Times*, June 6, 1943.
   [70] Quoted in Gazell, "Arthur H. Vandenberg," 380–381.
   [71] Quoted in Lawrence W. Levine, "The 'Diary' of Hiram Johnson," *American Heritage* 20, no. 5, 1969, accessed online at https://www.americanheritage.com/diary-hiram-johnson.
   [72] Quoted in Meijer, "Hunting for the Middle Ground," 17.

well received by internationalist Republicans: Vermont senator Warren Austin praised the statement as "marvelous, absolutely marvelous. We have broken through the old shell of isolationism. We have gone farther than we could possibly have gone had we continued the fight."[73] With Mackinac receiving considerable media coverage (for every Republican delegate at the conference there were two reporters[74]), the agreement represented an important signal to voters of the GOP's postwar intentions. Thus, through the RNC's coordinating role, the GOP embraced a clear internationalist outlook on foreign affairs, including American participation in what would become the United Nations.

At the 1944 national convention, Dewey easily won the presidential nomination on the first ballot and appointed Herbert Brownell as the new RNC chairman. Brownell had grown up in Nebraska but practiced law in New York and had become friendly with Dewey. Brownell successfully ran for state assembly in 1932 and served as Dewey's campaign manager for his 1942 gubernatorial run.[75] As chair and campaign manager, Brownell was the public face of the 1944 campaign. While Dewey became the fourth consecutive Republican presidential nominee to lose to FDR, as Goldman notes, many Republican leaders viewed the loss as "honorable"[76] given the closer margin than in the previous elections (Dewey received nearly 46% of the popular vote and won 12 states). Nonetheless, in the wake of the defeat, Brownell admitted that "some intensive work has to be done"[77] on formulating national Republican policies. Thus, Brownell promised during the upcoming presidential term a "vigorous, progressive, all-year program of party activity"[78] with particular focus on devising "ways and means to bring the record of the Republican party to the attention of the American people."[79]

Truman as Party Leader: The DNC, 1945–1952

During FDR's long occupancy in the White House, the DNC had declined, as the organization had little value to the president. After FDR's death in April 1945, his successor Harry Truman initially had a similar outlook. Truman had been added to the ticket in 1944 to replace Vice President Henry Wallace because

[73] "Republican Stand Pleases Both Sides," New York Times, September 9, 1943.

[74] "Reporters to Outnumber Delegates," New York Times, September 3, 1943.

[75] Goldman, The National Party Chairmen, 483.

[76] Quoted in ibid., 486.

[77] "Republican Unity Seen by Brownell," New York Times, December 20, 1944.

[78] Quoted in Goldman, The National Party Chairmen, 487.

[79] "Vandenberg Stand Sought for Party," New York Times, January 22, 1945.

Democratic leaders feared the prospect of a Wallace presidency should FDR not survive his fourth term. Hannegan had strongly supported the selection of Truman, who was a longtime ally of his and a fellow Missouri Democrat.[80] But while Hannegan remained DNC chair, in the run-up to the 1946 midterms his attention was mostly focused on his position as postmaster general.[81] The DNC did engage in some limited publicity activities in 1946—including producing radio broadcasts of several Truman speeches.[82] But the committee largely relied on a stale message, attempting once again to use FDR to inspire voter turnout.[83] The DNC even produced a series of radio commercials featuring the late president's voice—a strategy the RNC dismissed as "grisly."[84] The DNC also organized a number of "harmony" meetings between Southern Democrats (frustrated with Truman's pro-union policies) and the administration to improve communications.[85] At the same time, Truman was attacked by liberals in the party. In particular, Wallace—now secretary of commerce—and Florida senator Claude Pepper criticized Truman for his foreign policy toward the Soviet Union, resulting in Wallace's firing from the cabinet weeks before the midterm elections.[86]

Although Democrats had faced midterm losses since 1938, the 1946 election saw Republicans regain their majorities in Congress for the first time since the New Deal realignment. With Truman's re-election in 1948 now in serious jeopardy, the DNC sprung back to life after years of lethargy. In early 1947, Hannegan made two important new hires: Gael Sullivan as executive director and Jack Redding as publicity director.[87] Sullivan and Redding worked closely with Hannegan and (after his resignation in the fall of 1947) with his successor,

[80] Sean J. Savage, *Truman and the Democratic Party* (Lexington: The University Press of Kentucky, 1997), 17–19.

[81] Additionally, Hannegan's influence with Truman appears to be limited, and in 1946 he was blocked from attending White House staff meetings. See: Robert H. Ferrell, ed., *Truman in the White House: The Diary of Eben A. Ayers* (Columbia: University of Missouri Press, 1991), 121–122, 145.

[82] "Truman to Speak for Party Tonight," *New York Times*, March 23, 1946; "Maps Democrat Speeches," *New York Times*, September 10, 1946.

[83] "Hannegan Upholds Roosevelt Policy," *New York Times*, August 17, 1946.

[84] "Roosevelt 'Voice' to Flood Airways," *New York Times*, October 29, 1946; "Roosevelt Disk Use Old," *New York Times*, October 30, 1946.

[85] "Harmony Table Set by Hannegan," *New York Times*, March 17, 1946; "Democratic Row Kept Up by Phone," *New York Times*, April 4, 1946; "House Democrats Enraged Again as Party Letters on Foe Hit Them," *New York Times*, April 13, 1946.

[86] "Party Campaign Ban Shaped for Both Wallace, Pepper," *New York Times*, September 21, 1946; "Democratic Leaders Get Pepper to Speak," *New York Times*, September 28, 1946; "Michigan, Indiana Will Hear Wallace," *New York Times*, October 10, 1946.

[87] "Democratic Post Is Given Sullivan," *New York Times*, February 13, 1947; "Democrats Name Redding," *New York Times*, March 27, 1947.

Rhode Island senator Howard J. McGrath.[88] As Redding recalled, "for many years the National Committee publicity staff had consisted of only a director and a secretary in political off years and was beefed up only for the actual campaign."[89] Now, the DNC was once again turned "into a beehive of activity."[90] These activities had a clear goal: electing Truman in 1948.[91] Hannegan explicitly instructed Redding in the spring of 1947 that he should not "do anything unless it advances the cause of President Truman's election. We do not want publicity for the sake of publicity."[92]

The DNC relied on two main approaches: first, because Sullivan and Redding believed newspapers were supportive of Republicans, it invested in more radio broadcasts. Second, it amped up its communication toward party volunteers to have the Democrats' talking points promulgated by word of mouth. The DNC created a new newsletter, Capital Comment—a four-page publication the committee used to set the tone for the upcoming 1948 campaign. In the first issue, the DNC focused on the issue of cost of living—a topic Sullivan believed would be the main focus in the upcoming presidential election[93]—and criticized manufacturers and Republicans in Congress for an increase in the cost of consumer products.[94] Capital Comment received considerable media attention, and Redding concluded that the newsletter "gave us the means to reach our party workers" while also producing "newspaper publicity. For these two reasons the publication was of tremendous value, particularly as we found Democratic political workers throughout the country responding to the material in it."[95]

In September 1947 and January 1948 the DNC organized major "radio rallies," which saw Democrats across the country gather at meetings to listen to addresses by national leaders from different states.[96] For the first radio rally—broadcast by ABC—Democrats met in 2,981 counties across the country. Promoted as

[88] "Hannegan Resigns, M'Grath Succeeds as Party Chairman," New York Times, September 28, 1947; Jack Redding, Inside the Democratic Party (Indianapolis, IN: The Bobbs-Merrill Company, Inc., 1958), 91.

[89] Redding, Inside the Democratic Party, 42.

[90] Goldman, The National Chairmen, 423.

[91] Hannegan publicly called on Truman to be nominated as early as February 1947. See: "Hannegan Appeals for Truman in '48," New York Times, February 7, 1947.

[92] Redding, Inside the Democratic Party, 44.

[93] "Sullivan Hits Record," New York Times, August 10, 1947.

[94] "Sullivan Blames Industry for Prices," New York Times, May 2, 1947; Redding, Inside the Democratic Party, 56–58.

[95] Ibid., 61.

[96] "Democrats Plan Broadcast to Challenge GOP Claims on Record in Congress," New York Times, August 12, 1947; "Air Rally for Democrats," New York Times, August 22, 1947; "News of Radio," New York Times, December 19, 1947; Savage, Truman, 63.

"the first nationwide political meeting of the air,"[97] the "show" saw a number of Democratic leaders—including Mayors William O'Dwyer (New York City) and Hubert Humphrey (Minneapolis), and Senators John Sparkman (Alabama), Francis J. Myers (Pennsylvania), and Brien McMahon (Connecticut)—follow each other giving speeches in their home states.[98] In the estimation of the DNC, 63 million Americans were exposed to the program, either by listening to the live broadcast (or its rebroadcasts in the days or weeks after), or through news coverage of the event.[99]

The DNC's publicity division focused its resources on defending Truman and his administration, and attacking Republican leaders—most notably, Senator Robert A. Taft. The division produced radio commercials that attacked Republicans as being pro-business and insensitive to the average American, a theme Truman would run on in 1948.[100] The DNC also increased its coordination with local party leaders: state party leaders were invited to visit Washington, DC, and have a short meeting with Truman. After this brief face-to-face time with the president, the local party leaders were shuttled to DNC headquarters to meet with Sullivan and Redding, where they were briefed on the national strategy with regard to organization and publicity.[101] The DNC supported Truman despite the fact that his nomination was not secured. A number of Democratic leaders actively tried to convince General Dwight Eisenhower to run for the Democratic presidential nomination. But Hannegan instructed Redding that "your loyalty is to the President."[102]

At the 1948 convention, any real challenges to Truman's nomination failed to materialize, but the convention did produce a major schism in the party. After 1946, Truman had begun slowly to embrace civil rights—in part to ensure Black voters would support him in 1948. This had already enraged Southern Democratic governors, who, in a meeting with McGrath, had complained about the administration's changing stand on civil rights. In response, McGrath sided with Truman, dismissing any possibility of compromise: "As Chairman,

[97] Redding, *Inside the Democratic Party*, 83.

[98] "'Democrats on Air' Open Fight on GOP," *New York Times*, September 3, 1947.

[99] Redding, *Inside the Democratic Party*, 82–84.

[100] Savage, *Truman*, 78.

[101] "Democrats Slate Series of Parleys," *New York Times*, April 2, 1947; Redding, *Inside the Democratic Party*, 87.

[102] This exchange occurred after Hannegan announced his retirement but before McGrath was officially installed as the new DNC chair. Redding planned to offer his resignation to McGrath but was dissuaded by Hannegan, who told him, "Take this back. No one is going to do anything with it. You can't quit. I appreciate the offer as a genuine compliment to me and to Gael; but your loyalty is to the President, not to me. It isn't necessary for you to make the gesture. Just sit tight" (Redding, *Inside the Democratic Party*, 91–92).

I'm not going to push this thing one spot further than the President's message. But neither will I withdraw one inch from the confines of that message."[103] At the convention, the party went further than before, with delegates voting to include a progressive civil rights plank in the platform. In response, delegates from the South walked out of the convention and, later that summer, announced they would run their own presidential candidate (South Carolina governor Strom Thurmond) as the "Democratic" candidate in a number of Deep South states. Meanwhile, Wallace decided to challenge Truman from the left with his own presidential campaign. As a result, Truman faced not just Republican nominee Thomas Dewey but also two competitors from within the Democratic Party.

Despite some assessments that the DNC was irrelevant in Truman's surprise 1948 victory,[104] the committee's publicity division remained highly active during the general election campaign. As historian Sean J. Savage has argued, the DNC was "impressively innovative in devising ingenious methods for promoting Truman's candidacy"[105] and linking Republican presidential candidate Thomas Dewey to the conservative wing in the Republican Party. DNC radio commercials in the 1948 general election campaign mocked GOP opposition to Truman's economic policies and quoted Taft's response to a question of how Americans should respond to rising food prices ("Eat less.").[106] During Truman's 1948 whistle-stop tour, the national committee assisted the president by providing details on the locations he gave speeches at. Redding took credit for having Truman engage in this tactic: in the spring of 1947 a strategic memo from the DNC suggested "the greatest assets Mr. Truman had were his own forthright manner and his smile, I suggested putting the President on the rear end of a train and exposing him to as many people as time and spirit would allow."[107] And the strategy appears to have worked: research measuring the effect of Truman visits on vote share has found that the Truman whistle stops added on average 3 percentage points to Truman's vote in visited counties.[108] On election night, voters returned Truman to the White House (despite Thurmond winning 39 electoral

---

[103] Ibid., 137.

[104] In the snarky book *The Truman Merry-Go-Round* by veteran reporter Robert S. Allen and William V. Shannon, the authors dismiss McGrath's role in the general election campaign as issuing "a few press releases, an occasional weary exhortation, and [looking] most of the time as if he wished he knew what was going on" (Robert S. Allen and William V. Shannon, *The Truman Merry-Go-Round* [New York: The Vanguard Press, Inc., 1950], 104).

[105] Savage, *Truman*, 78.

[106] Ibid., 78–79.

[107] Redding, *Inside the Democratic Party*, 52.

[108] See: Boris Heersink and Brenton D. Peterson, "Truman Defeats Dewey: The Effect of Campaign Visits on Election Outcomes," *Electoral Studies* 49 (2017), 49–64.

votes in the Deep South) and restored Democratic majorities in both the House and Senate.

But Truman's victory also saw the end of the team that had reinvigorated the DNC. Sullivan had already resigned in the spring of 1948, and Redding left the committee to work in the administration as Assistant Postmaster General. Finally, McGrath announced his retirement as chairman in August 1949 after Truman nominated him to be attorney general.[109] Truman replaced McGrath with William M. Boyle Jr., a product of the Pendergast Democratic machine in Kansas City. Boyle hired new staff to run the publicity and research divisions of the national committee, and, for the first time in its history, the DNC invested in buying (rather than leasing) a building to house its permanent headquarters.[110] Under Boyle, the DNC engaged in some branding efforts—including organizing regional conferences and publishing materials supporting Truman's legislative proposals.[111] But in comparison with the period 1947–1948, the DNC was clearly a less active organization with Boyle focused more on representing the administration in negotiations with Democrats in Congress, while the DNC publicity division faced limited funding.[112]

The 1950 midterms saw Democrats lose seats in House and Senate but hang on to a small majority in both. While Boyle declared the election a victory for the party, Democratic elected officials blamed the DNC for the party's losses.[113] In particular, Representative Wayne Hays of Ohio argued that while the RNC had provided damaging publicity against Democrats, the DNC had been too quiet.[114] Boyle resigned in the fall of 1951 after accusations of financial impropriety, and Truman replaced him with Frank E. McKinney—a banker and owner

---

[109] "Sullivan Resigns Democratic Post," *New York Times*, April 29, 1948; "M'Grath Sets Date to Pick Successor," *New York Times*, August 14, 1949; Redding, *Inside the Democratic Party*, 296.

[110] "Dryer to Get Democratic Post," *New York Times*, July 9, 1950; "Democrats Offer Job to Writer for The New York Post, *New York Times*, August 7, 1950; "Democratic Party Acquires Building," *New York Times*, August 8, 1950; "Post Reporter to Head Democratic Publicity," *New York Times*, August 9, 1950.

[111] "Democrats to Push Regional Parleys," *New York Times*, June 15, 1949; "2D Democratic Talk Set," *New York Times*, September 5, 1949; "Democrats Gather on Coast Sept. 18," *New York Times*, September 11, 1949; "Truman Aims Guide Party, Boyle Says," *New York Times*, September 19, 1949; "Harmony Meeting Set by Democrats," *New York Times*, January 8, 1950; "Democrat Parley Bars Rights Issue," *New York Times*, January 28, 1950; "Boyle Predicts Big Fete," *New York Times*, February 25, 1950; "Democrats to Set New England Talk," *New York Times*, April 3, 1950; "Democrats Plan Parley," *New York Times*, March 29, 1950; "Party Booklet Backs Truman Health Plan," *New York Times*, May 1, 1950; "Democrats Print M'Arthur 'Facts,'" *New York Times*, April 28, 1951.

[112] Goldman, *The National Chairmen*, 430; Allen and Shannon, *The Truman Merry-Go-Round*, 74; Savage, *Truman*, 79.

[113] "Boyle Finds Election Democratic Victory," *New York Times*, November 18, 1950.

[114] Savage, *Truman*, 71.

of major league baseball teams—who remained in office for just a few months.[115] In the run-up to the 1952 convention, the DNC mostly became preoccupied with responding to charges of corruption and accusations of communist interference within the Truman administration.[116] And, after Truman announced he would not accept a nomination for a third term in the White House, the DNC all but ceased its publicity role until the convention selected a new presidential candidate and party leader—thus postponing any major investments in its branding role until after the 1952 election.

The RNC during the Truman Years, 1945–1952

While Brownell did not intend to be a full-time RNC chair after the 1944 election and remained in office for a short period of time, under his leadership the "all-year" program he had promised in the wake of Dewey's defeat did result in concrete investments in the committee. Brownell expanded the size of HQ staff to focus on "research, investigation, and publicity."[117] Brownell hoped the RNC could help Republicans "show more clearly the fallacies of New Deal doctrines" and "ferret out the waste, extravagance and bungling" of the administration. Additionally, the committee would have "a publicity staff to drive home in every possible way the Republican message."[118] This included the creation of the Republican Rural News Service, which regularly provided 4,000 small newspapers in agricultural areas with press releases, the *Republican News*—a party publication sent to around 200,000 people every month—and a biweekly *Chairman's Letter*.[119] Brownell was careful to note that he believed Republicans in Congress would set policies while his own role was presenting "our Republican viewpoint to the people. We are not going to rely on the blunders and errors of the New Deal opposition as a means of attaining success in the next election. We are going to have an aggressive program of our own."[120] But Brownell also argued that the GOP needed "a positive, constructive blue-print of party policy for the

[115] "Boyle Quits Post as Party Leader; Defends Conduct," *New York Times*, October 14, 1951; "McKinney, New Chairman, Warns Democrats on Gifts," *New York Times*, November 1, 1951.

[116] "Truman, M'Kinney Attack Grafters in the Government," *New York Times*, November 27, 1951; "M'Kinney Lashes 'Negative' Critics," *New York Times*, December 14, 1951.

[117] Goldman, *The National Party Chairmen*, 487.

[118] "The GOP Looks Ahead," *New York Times*, January 28, 1945.

[119] F. Suzanne Bowers, *Republican, First, Last, and Always: A Biography of B. Carroll Reece* (Newcastle upon Tyne, UK: Cambridge Scholars Publishing), 68; Michael Bowen, *The Roots of Modern Conservatism: Dewey, Taft, and the Battle for the Soul of the Republican Party* (Chapel Hill: The University of North Carolina Press, 2011), 29.

[120] "Republicans Plan 'Aggressive' Drive," *New York Times*, January 21, 1945.

guidance of Party members in the national legislature"[121] and that it needed to come to "fundamental agreement on the principles or purposes" under which it intended to govern: "We must first decide whether we wish to go to Chicago or to Pittsburgh before we can debate the particular route which we think will best get us there."[122]

To find such direction, congressional Republicans under the leadership of Taft produced a "statement of aims and purposes," which the RNC endorsed. Brownell subsequently appointed a Special Committee on Development of National Policy tasked with producing a coherent Republican message for the 1946 midterm campaign.[123] In doing so, Brownell attempted to rephrase the Taft statement using more "moderate rhetoric"—including rephrasing sections on union rights.[124] The RNC also created a foreign affairs section—led by Hugh R. Wilson, the former ambassador to Germany—to provide Republicans in Congress with policy briefs.[125] Wilson attended the San Francisco Conference (which produced the UN Charter) as an observer and urged Republicans to adopt a policy of "intimate collaboration with Russia in every possible way"[126] to preserve peace in the aftermath of the war.

In February 1946, with the reorganization of RNC HQ complete, Brownell announced his retirement.[127] In the contest to replace him, two candidates received the most attention: former Connecticut senator John A. Danaher and Representative Brazilla Carrol Reece from Tennessee.[128] With Danaher receiving support from the Dewey wing of the party, Reece became the favored candidate of the conservative Taft wing, while a third candidate—New York banker John W. Hanes—received support from the small remnants of the Willkie supporters within the national committee.[129] After two ballots in which no candidate received a majority, the supporters of Hanes—hoping to limit the influence of Dewey in the party—switched to Reece, handing him the chairmanship.[130]

[121] Quoted in Bowen, *The Roots of Modern Conservatism*, 31.

[122] "Report of Herbert Brownell Jr. to Republican National Committee at Indianapolis, Indiana, January 22, 1945," Kesaris et al., *Papers of the Republican Party*, Series A, Reel 7, Frame 756.

[123] David W. Reinhard, *The Republican Right since 1945* (Lexington: The University Press of Kentucky, 1983), 10; "Republicans Back Party Policy Draft," *New York Times*, December 9, 1945; "Brownell Names Policy Committee," *New York Times*, December 15, 1945.

[124] Bowen, *The Roots of Modern Conservatism*, 33.

[125] "Hugh R. Wilson Joins Republican Advisers," *New York Times*, April 12, 1945; "Truman Asks World Chiefs to End the Political Impasse," *New York Times*, October 19, 1945.

[126] "H.R. Wilson Urges Amity with Russia," *New York Times*, May 29, 1945.

[127] Goldman, *The National Party Chairmen*, 487–488.

[128] "Reece or Danaher Likely to Be Made Chairman of GOP," *New York Times*, April 1, 1946.

[129] Reinhard, *The Republican Right*, 11.

[130] Goldman, *The National Party Chairmen*, 490; "Republicans Elect Reece as Chairman," *New York Times*, April 2, 1946.

As *Time* magazine described him, Reece was "something of a rarity in politics: a popular and successful Republican below the Mason Dixon line."[131] Indeed, Reece was one of only two Republican members of Congress from a former Confederate state in the 79th Congress and had been in the House nearly continuously since 1921. During this time, he had built up a "staunchly conservative record."[132] As RNC chair, the first major task facing Reece was winning the 1946 midterms—the first since FDR's death. Reece focused the campaign on socialism and the power of unions within the Democratic Party. In an editorial in the *Republican News*, Reece described the "party which bears the name of Democrat" as having

> ceased to exist as such. It consists today of three important elements—the Solid South, held in bondage by the chains of racial discrimination; the big machines—Kelly, Hague, Flynn, Pendergast; and the radical group devoted to Sovietizing the United States. Of these three the last-named group is the most important and the most powerful.[133]

Thus, during the 1946 campaign, Reece doubled down on the message that "the choice which confronts America this year is between Communism and Republicanism"[134] by attacking both the Democratic Party (as having "fallen into the hands of the Red reactionary group"[135]) and labor unions. And the approach seemed to pay off: running under the slogan "Had Enough?," Republicans won control of Congress for the first time since 1932.[136]

But with majorities came the responsibility of legislating. In an editorial in *The Republican News* Reece called on Congress to "clean up the mess inherited from fourteen years of Democrat confusion and misrule and to set the nation on the high road to prosperity."[137] In early February 1947, in a letter sent to 7,500 Republican office holders, Reece identified a series of campaign promises the GOP would have to deliver on.[138] And plenty of such promises were made: Reece himself had claimed the GOP would eliminate 90% of the federal bureaucracy,[139]

---

[131] Quoted in Bowers, *Republican, First, Last, and Always*, 65.

[132] Reece lost his renomination battle in the 1930 election but won the nomination again in 1932; Reinhard, *The Republican Right*, 11.

[133] "G.O.P. Sure It Can Win the House," *New York Times*, June 16, 1946.

[134] Lewis L. Gould, *Grand Old Party: A History of the Republicans* (New York: Random House, 2003), 310.

[135] "GOP Chairmen Back Reece," *New York Times*, June 10, 1946.

[136] Reinhard, *The Republican Right*, 17.

[137] "Parties' Chiefs Hit at Other's Efforts," *New York Times*, January 9, 1947.

[138] "Campaign Promise to Cut Income Tax Repeated by Reece," *New York Times*, February 2, 1947.

[139] Reinhard, *The Republican Right*, 17.

while other Republicans had promised both tax cuts and major cuts in the federal budget.[140] The new Republican majorities were successful in some areas: the GOP was able to pass the Taft–Hartley Act and overrode President Harry Truman's veto with bipartisan support. It also supported Truman's Marshall plan for aid to Europe—a major investment in postwar rebuilding efforts aimed at limiting communist influence in Western Europe. But most of the campaign promises—including attempts at passing a tax cut –failed to pass.[141]

The result was a good amount of intra-party sniping. Republican Senator Raymond Baldwin (CT) concluded that the failure to legislate would lead "everyone but die-hard Republicans" to admit that "we started off very badly."[142] In response, Reece called on Republican elected officials to be unified in Congress as "every Republican in Congress today represents both his party and his individual constituency":

> it was the party which elected him. He is a member of a team, one which he joined of his own free will and with full realization of the responsibilities he was assuming. He has a vote, like every other member, in the selection of the captains of the team and, to carry the figure one step further, in the selection of the quarterbacks. A successful team is one which executes the signals called by the duly chosen quarterback. Differences of opinion as to the choice of a particular play are ironed out in the huddles before the plays are called, not afterward. Team play is the first essential of success.[143]

But Reece's call for unity had little effect: Senator Wayne Morse (OR) dismissed him as a "chore boy" for the old guard who had merely produced a "brazen demand for reactionary control of the Republican Party."[144] Combined, in the assessment of the *Nation* the GOP's return to power was off to a rocky start: "Not even in the latter stages of the New Deal were the Democrats battling each other as Republicans are today."[145]

Despite these setbacks, Reece was confident that "the people, the Republicans and sound Democrats, have come to the conclusion that the only agency through

[140] Ibid., 20–21; "Martin Pledges Reductions in U.S. Spending and Taxes," *New York Times*, January 4, 1947.

[141] Reinhard, *The Republican Right*, 20–21; "Truman Supported by 71 Democrats," *New York Times*, June 21, 1947; "House Overrides," *New York Times*, July 19, 1947.

[142] Reinhard, *The Republican Right*, 23.

[143] "Reece Urges GOP in Congress to End Discord, Use Team-Work," *New York Times*, March 3, 1947.

[144] "Morse Raps Reece on GOP Team-Play," *New York Times*, March 4, 1947.

[145] Reinhard, *The Republican Right*, 24.

which the type of government in which they believe can be achieved is the Republican party"[146] and that the GOP would finally regain the White House. At the 1948 convention Dewey once again controlled a majority of delegates and won the nomination. In an attempt at building party unity, Dewey allowed Speaker of the House Martin to select Pennsylvania Representative Hugh Scott as the next RNC chair. Given Truman's low approval ratings and major splits in the Democratic Party, the general consensus throughout the fall campaign was that Dewey was almost guaranteed a victory. His subsequent defeat and the GOP's loss of its congressional majorities was thus a major and unpleasant surprise. In the wake of the election, much blame was placed on those involved in running the Dewey campaign—including Dewey himself.[147]

Scott was not exempted from this criticism but nonetheless decided he would try to remain RNC chair. During the first RNC meeting after the election an attempt at removing him from office failed—though his majority was small (54 to 50 votes).[148] Scott's survival in part was achieved by him reminding committee members that they had been supportive of his strategy during the campaign. These reminders had particular effect since Scott also revealed he had secretly recorded their conversations at the time. Participants at the RNC meeting found messages slipped under their doors informing them of the tapes, and Scott confirmed he had brought transcripts of the tapes with him "to keep the record straight."[149]

Scott left the meeting with big plans and shortly after appointed a midterm strategy committee and an agricultural division to help the party appeal to voters in farm states. Scott also stressed the importance of an effective publicity approach, arguing that "to get majority acceptance of the Republican product [...] it must be well and attractively packaged to enlist public interest and public support."[150] Yet, his survival at the RNC meeting proved to be a Pyrrhic victory. Republicans in Congress mostly ignored the RNC and began organizing their own activities, including creating a "committee on public information" aimed at replacing the RNC's publicity role.[151] In February 1949, Clarence Budington

---

[146] "GOP Leaders See Easy '48 Victory," New York Times, October 24, 1947.

[147] Dewey's style of campaigning was criticized as being underwhelming to voters and lacking specific policy proposals. Heersink and Peterson in their analysis of the Truman and Dewey campaign visit effects find that the Dewey visits had no positive effect on his vote share. See: Heersink and Peterson, "Truman Defeats Dewey."

[148] Goldman, The National Party Chairmen, 496.

[149] Reinhard, The Republican Right, 57.

[150] Kesaris et al., Papers of the Republican Party, Series A, Reel 9, Frame 87.

[151] Goldman, The National Party Chairmen, 495–497; Bone, Party Committees and National Politics, 164; "Republicans Put Farm Vote First," New York Times, April 26, 1949; "Young GOP to Seek Farm-Labor Help," New York Times, June 25, 1949; "Gabrielson Named New GOP Chairman," New York Times, August 5, 1949.

Kelland—the former RNC publicity director, and a committee member from Arizona—criticized the 1948 campaign effort as too centered on appeasing "groups and blocs. We have fished for racial voters or sectional votes with evasions. We have not realized our duty to our party, to our country, and to posterity." If the GOP were to survive, Kelland argued, it would need to "erect itself as a restraining dam to contain and hurl back this flood"[152] of Democratic policies. In July, Kelland initiated a drive to make Guy Gabrielson, an RNC member from New York, the new chairman. To achieve this, Kelland, Gabrielson, and 23 other RNC members met in Pittsburgh to strategize.[153] Several days later, Dewey and Taft met to discuss the GOP's upcoming midterm campaign—in which both men were facing re-elections—and the RNC chairmanship controversy. Shortly after the Dewey–Taft meeting, Scott announced his resignation. In the leadership election, Gabrielson was elected the next RNC chairman by a small majority of committee members.[154]

While Gabrielson, a former state legislator in New York, announced he intended to be "an impartial presiding officer,"[155] he was largely seen as a supporter of Taft. After his election as chair, Gabrielson announced yet another reorganization of the committee and appointed a special adviser on labor affairs in an attempt to appeal to rank-and-file union members.[156] In terms of policy, Gabrielson undermined the strategy committee founded by Scott by denying it funding.[157] Instead, Gabrielson created his own policy committee with "a strong 'Old Guard' element"[158] which set out to create a new statement of purposes for the 1950 midterms.[159] The outcome was *Restatement of Principles and Objectives*, an update of the Taft-produced 1945 statement. The document was presented during a major gathering of 11,000 Republicans in the Uline Arena in Washington, DC, and advocated for balanced budgets, support for Taft–Hartley, and free world trade with protections for American industry against "underpaid foreign labor," and it included criticism of Truman-era policies.[160] Meanwhile,

[152] Gould, *Grand Old Party*, 321.

[153] Reinhard, *The Republican Right*, 57.

[154] Goldman, *The National Party Chairmen*, 498–499.

[155] "Gabrielson Named New GOP Chairman," *New York Times*, August 5, 1949.

[156] Goldman, *The National Party Chairmen*, 499; "Gabrielson Plans Business-Like GOP," *New York Times*, August 17, 1949.

[157] Goldman, *The National Party Chairmen*, 499.

[158] "Which Way for the G.O.P.," *New York Times*, December 27, 1949.

[159] "Search for a Policy," *New York Times*, December 1, 1949; "G.O.P. Chief Names Anti-New Dealers to Help Set Policy," *New York Times*, December 26, 1949; "Republicans Frame Policy for Election," *New York Times*, February 2, 1950.

[160] Reinhard, *The Republican Right*, 60; Bone, *Party Committees and National Politics*, 60; "G.O.P. Poses Issue For '50 as Liberty versus Socialism," *New York Times*, February 7, 1950.

after the United States entered the Korean war in the summer of 1950, the RNC relied on the same message it used in World War II, with Gabrielson warning that the GOP would not hesitate to criticize the Truman administration's "fumbling, stumbling ineptness"[161] in executing the war.[162]

But Gabrielson's tenure as RNC chair hit a speed bump in the fall of 1951 when it was revealed that his company Carthage Hydrocol had received a loan from the Reconstruction Finance Corporation (RFC) and had been allowed to defer repayments. A similar issue had come up surrounding DNC chair Boyle and became part of a series of scandals plaguing the administration. Gabrielson's position was less suspect as chair of the out-party (making it unlikely for him to have received preferential treatment from the Truman administration), but Republican opposition to the RFC was difficult to balance with the party chairman's corporation benefiting from it.[163] A number of Republicans, including California senator Richard Nixon, called on Gabrielson to resign, but he retained support from a majority of the RNC executive committee and remained in office until the 1952 national convention.[164]

As a result of these scandals, Gabrielson's public role decreased in the second half of his chairmanship and, with it, the RNC's broader publicity role. This decline is evident in the coverage the New York Times produced of the RNC under Gabrielson. Figure 4.6 shows the results of negative binomial regressions in which Gabrielson's incumbency as RNC chair is the independent variable and the lagged monthly coverage of RNC publicity and service activities are the dependent variables. In this model, the data is limited to just those articles covering the RNC published between January 1945 and June 1953 (the last full month in which Gabrielson was chair)—thereby comparing Times coverage of the RNC under Gabrielson's leadership with that during the previous RNC chairs in 1945–1949. Times coverage of the combined RNC branding activities declined under Gabrielson (significant at the 0.001 level), while no change in coverage occurred for combined service activities. The results for each individual branding activity show a clear decrease in coverage across all categories: Times

[161] "G.O.P. to Support Our Korean Policy," New York Times, August 1, 1950.

[162] "G.O.P. Gears Drive to Foreign Policy," New York Times, August 29, 1950; "Parties Open Fire over Foreign Policy," New York Times, September 9, 1950.

[163] "R.F.C. Hearing Weighed for Political Effects," New York Times, March 11, 1951; "Byrd and House Republicans Call for Abolition of R.F.C.," New York Times, March 14, 1951; "White House Aid, Lithofold Linked," New York Times, September 20, 1951; "Gabrielson Admits Dealing with R.F.C.; Denies 'Influence,'" New York Times, September 23, 1951; "Gabrielson Gives Defense of Loan," New York Times, October 1, 1951.

[164] Simon Topping, Lincoln's Lost Legacy: The Republican Party and the African American Vote, 1928–1952 (Gainesville: University Press of Florida, 2008), 161–162; "G.O.P. Votes Faith in Party Chairman," New York Times, October 2, 1951.

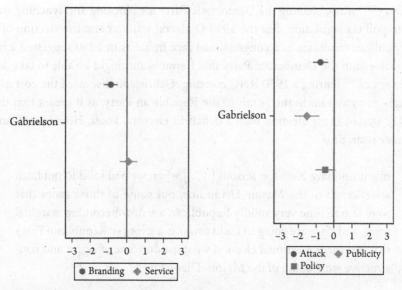

Figure 4.6. Negative binomial regression of Guy Gabrielson's RNC chairmanship on monthly (lagged) *New York Times* coverage of RNC branding and service activities, 1945–1952. *Note:* This model includes variables controlling for presidential and midterm election years, a measure of *New York Times* length, and RNC scandals. The data coverage is limited to articles published between January 1945 and June 1952 covering only the RNC.
Source: Data collected by author.

coverage declined for RNC attacks on the Democrats (significant at the 0.001 level), publicity efforts (significant at the 0.001 level), and RNC policy position taking (significant at the 0.10 level).

While the RNC's branding activities may have declined under Gabrielson, his leadership did introduce a renewed focus on the American South as a potential area for Republican growth. Throughout the existence of the "Solid" Democratic South, Republican leaders—including presidents such as Harding and Hoover—regularly attempted to reinvigorate local state party organizations in the former Confederacy, but with little success.[165] Under Reece (himself from the South), appealing to Black voters was still a core component of the GOP's electoral strategy. Indeed, Reece's nomination was seconded by Perry Howard, a Black man who was a long-standing RNC member and state party leader in Mississippi.[166] Reece praised the GOP as the party founded to "wipe out human

[165] Boris Heersink and Jeffery A. Jenkins, *Republican Party Politics and the American South, 1865–1968* (New York: Cambridge University Press, 2020).
[166] "Republicans Elect Reece as Chairman," *New York Times*, April 2, 1946.

slavery"[167] while blaming the Democratic Party for blocking anti-lynching and anti–poll tax legislation. But the 1948 Dixiecrat walkout and the election of a Republican candidate in a congressional race in Texas in 1950 suggested a regional split in the Democratic Party that Republicans might be able to take advantage of.[168] During a 1950 RNC meeting, Gabrielson discussed the cost of a single-party system in the South to the Republican Party, as it meant that the GOP started every election with a deficit in electoral votes, House seats, and Senate seats. This

> might not have been too serious [. . .] when we had solid Republican states north of the Mason–Dixon line, but some of those states that were at one time very solidly Republican are now becoming marginal areas, and if we are going to build towards a stronger Republican Party that can carry a national election we must do some effective and constructive work south of the Mason–Dixon line.[169]

Gabrielson therefore created a new committee to investigate ways in which the GOP could improve its performance in the South.[170]

Gabrielson made appearances in the South, speaking to both Republicans and Dixiecrats.[171] During a trip to Atlanta, Gabrielson noted that the GOP's appeal to voters would be based on "states running their own affairs and the cutting down of federal bureaucracy" and that the GOP would not abandon its support for civil rights for Black Americans, stating that "we must do away with second-class citizenship in this country and make everybody, regardless of race, color, or creed, equal."[172] But during a speech in Alabama in February 1952, Gabrielson explicitly tried to connect the Republican Party to the (segregationist) Dixiecrat movement:

> Our friends call themselves States' Righters and we call ourselves Republicans. But they oppose corruption in government and so do we. We want the Dixiecrats to vote for our candidate. The Dixiecrat

---

[167] "Democrats Held Failing on Rights," New York Times, February 16, 1948.

[168] "Victory in Texas Elates the G.O.P.," New York Times, May 8, 1950.

[169] Quoted in Heersink and Jenkins, Republican Party Politics and the American South, 171.

[170] "G.O.P. Spurs Drive to Bar Third Term," New York Times, January 27, 1951.

[171] As Simon Topping notes, Gabrielson may also have had presidential politics in mind: Southern delegates at the Republican National Convention could become pivotal in selecting the 1952 presidential nominee and were considered likely supporters of Taft, whose candidacy Gabrielson was considered to be supportive of as well. See: Topping, Lincoln's Lost Legacy, p. 162.

[172] Ibid.

movement is an anti-Truman movement. The Dixiecrat party believes in states' rights. That's what the Republican Party believes in.[173]

While an early attempt, Gabrielson's outreach to White Southerners was a clear step in the direction that would come to define much of the party's Southern strategy in the decades that followed: appealing to White Southerners as a way to break the Democratic domination of the South and, as a result, dramatically altering the makeup of the GOP.

Conclusion

During the New Deal years both national committees adjusted their activities and roles within their parties in response to the new electoral reality they now faced. While the DNC had expanded during the Hoover administration by taking on an aggressive role in providing national publicity for the party and even attempting to set party policies, under President Franklin Delano Roosevelt the committee declined. This decline was not instantaneous: during FDR's first term in the White House, the DNC still retained a role in publicizing the administration's achievements. But the Democratic Party's continued successes convinced him that the DNC was unnecessary to his political survival, and that relying on outside (union) support was a more effective strategic approach. Thus, the DNC became not only largely invisible outside of election years, but even less important during presidential campaigns. The one exception in this period concerned the 1948 election. With Democrats losing control of both House and Senate in 1946 and with the party deeply divided, Truman realized the value of revitalizing the DNC. But this effort was clearly aimed at helping him win re-election: the DNC staff in 1947–1948 prioritized Truman above all other factions in the party, and after the surprise 1948 victory, the DNC again became largely dormant.

In contrast, the RNC after years of easy victories in the 1920s now faced a massive voter deficit in comparison with the New Deal coalition. While under RNC chair Everett Sanders the committee's response was initially limited, from Henry P. Fletcher onward every Republican committee chair in this period tried to use the RNC to provide national publicity on behalf of the party and regain the electoral support the party had lost. Many of these chairs also tried to shape the specific image they were promoting. To be sure, these attempts did

---

[173] Quoted in Joseph E. Lowndes, *From the New Deal to the New Right: Race and the Southern Origins of Modern Conservatism* (New Haven, CT: Yale University Press, 2008) 36.

not necessarily produce a clear-cut alternative to the New Deal—instead they generally focused on supporting the free market and criticizing governmental overreach and waste. But at times, the RNC's involvement was consequential, including helping navigate the Republican Party into shedding its isolationism and helping embrace active U.S. involvement in the post–World War II international order, and embracing a "Southern strategy" aimed at appealing to White voters in the region under Guy G. Gabrielson.

Combined, the cases presented in this chapter follow the expectations of the branding theory. On the side of the out-party, RNC chairs consistently tried—though, admittedly, with limited success—to try to forge an alternative image of the Republican Party that could convince voters to return to the GOP. They did so by contrasting the two parties through the GOP's criticism of the New Deal and FDR, but also by spotlighting the party's own positions. In contrast, the in-party committee's role changed in line with the whims of the incumbent president. Under FDR, the DNC became less helpful to him and, thus, declined. Under Truman, the DNC re-emerged but only to the extent that it helped the incumbent president. Thus, by the time the 1952 election saw Democrats finally lose their grip on the White House, their national committee was in a weak state. Meanwhile, the new Republican president—Dwight Eisenhower—would need to decide how to use (or not use) the RNC.

"We Either Have a National Party or We Do Not Have," 1953–1968

Dwight Eisenhower's victory in the 1952 election ended the Democrats' two decades hold on the White House. But Eisenhower's presidential election victory placed neither party in a position of electoral strength. While Republicans now held the White House, they only maintained a majority in Congress for two years. Meanwhile, Democratic leaders had to grapple with the collapse of the New Deal coalition. In the years that followed, both parties faced the same basic assignment: (re)building a reliable electoral coalition that would provide both presidential victories and majorities in Congress. In executing that assignment, both the Democratic and Republican National Committees (DNC and RNC) had to grapple with a broader question: Would they be more successful if their parties continued to reflect a broad ideological spectrum or if, instead, the parties became two clearly opposite ideologically homogeneous forces in American politics? In the decades that followed, DNC and RNC chairs generally fell into the former category. That is, party chairs from 1952 onward often chose a path centered on "unity" and tailored to keep a broad array of ideological actors inside their party. But the DNC and RNC were not consistent in this regard. Specifically, in the period 1953–1968 both committees at times promoted a clear and strong ideological image, with the goal of radically altering voters' perception of the national party brand.

Much of the debate in this period centered on the question of how each party would balance appealing to two central voting groups: Black voters and White Southerners. After the Dixiecrat walkout in 1948 and Dwight Eisenhower's strong performance in the South in 1952, Democratic leaders initially prioritized securing Southern support in future elections. This meant that the DNC—now for the first time since 1933 the out-party—stepped up its publicity role but promoted an image of the Democratic Party designed to be inclusive toward all wings within the party by avoiding issues that were controversial to Southern

White politicians and voters—most notably, civil rights. But this approach did not last: after a major decline in Black support in the 1956 election, the DNC switched its strategy and now began promoting the Democratic Party as a clearly liberal national institution. This included the committee embracing civil rights, support for unions, and the further expansion of the federal government. Yet, despite this major surge of DNC activity in the 1950s, Democratic presidents JFK and LBJ oversaw another major decline of the organization—in no small part because the committee did not serve their political needs.

In contrast, Republican president Dwight Eisenhower invested heavily in the RNC with the goal of using the organization to shape and promote the GOP in his image—that is, as a right-of-center party focused on managing rather than destroying the post–New Deal federal government. But after Richard Nixon's defeat in the 1960 election, presidential control of the RNC ended as well. In the subsequent leadership vacuum, conservatives took control of the RNC and began using the organization to appeal explicitly to Southern White voters. While not a new strategy, the messaging began to embrace opposition to civil rights. But this conservative takeover proved temporary: after Goldwater's dramatic defeat in 1964, moderates regained control of the RNC and returned to the type of branding it had engaged in under Eisenhower.

The DNC during the Eisenhower Years: "Unity" versus Liberalism

The 1952 election left the Democratic Party in a complex electoral situation. For the first time since 1928, a Republican had won the White House—and had done so with overwhelming success: Eisenhower had even won Texas, Florida, Virginia, and Tennessee—a major achievement for a Republican candidate in a region that until 1948 had been the "solid" Democratic South.[1] And, Republican success was not limited to the presidency: in the House, Republicans gained 22 seats leaving Democrats in the minority (see Figure 5.1). In the Senate, Republicans gained a single seat, resulting in a split 48-48 division of seats. However, with Vice President Richard Nixon presiding, Republicans controlled the Senate as well. Democrats now had to reassess their electoral strategy, and the role of the South in the party would be a fundamental issue. The New Deal coalition had relied on the party's long-term dominance in the South in combination with its ascendency in other parts of the country. But this put pressure on

---

[1] Additionally, Eisenhower came within roughly 5,000 votes of winning South Carolina and received more than 45% of the vote in Louisiana and North Carolina.

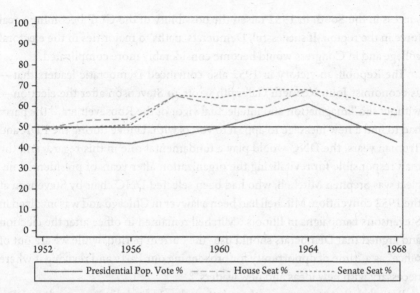

Figure 5.1. Democratic electoral performance in presidential, House, and Senate elections, 1952–1968. *Source: Congressional Quarterly's Guide to U.S. Elections, 7th ed.* (Washington, DC: Congressional Quarterly, 2016).

the position of Southern conservatives within the party. Prior to 1932, Southern Democrats were effectively the majority of a minority party. With the massive victories of the FDR era, the influence of the Southern wing decreased, and Southerners found themselves in the minority.

Initially, this did not cause major issues. Indeed, as Eric Schickler has shown, Southern members of Congress were loyal supporters of most early New Deal legislation. But as the Democratic Party began to cater to the Black voters that had begun to support the party in the 1930s, Southern legislators became more hostile.[2] FDR's attempts to shift the power balance within the party through a "purge" of conservative congressional candidates in the 1938 primaries failed, and for the remainder of the New Deal the Democratic Party was divided between a liberal Northern and conservative Southern wing. This relationship became even more complicated after FDR's death. In 1948, Southern delegates walked out of the Democratic convention in protest of the party's stance on civil rights and ran a States Rights Democratic Party ticket in the presidential election.[3] While the Dixiecrat revolt failed to prevent Truman's re-election, Eisenhower's

[2] Eric Schickler, *Racial Realignment: The Transformation of American Liberalism, 1932–1965* (Princeton, NJ: Princeton University Press, 2016).

[3] Southern members of Congress also began organizing within the Democratic caucus around this time as well. See: Ruth Bloch Rubin, *Building the Bloc: Intraparty Organization in the U.S. Congress* (New York: Cambridge University Press, 2017).

success in the South in 1952 raised the possibility of the GOP becoming a real force in the region. If successful, Democrats' paths to majorities in the electoral college and in Congress would become considerably more complicated.

The Republican victory in 1952 also convinced Democratic leaders that—as economist John Kenneth Galbraith wrote to Stevenson after the election—without the "imagination and intellectual vigor of the Roosevelt era,"[4] the party had to find a new message to appeal to voters with. Unlike during the FDR and Truman years, the DNC would play a fundamental role in this regard, and the man responsible for revitalizing the organization after years of presidential neglect was Stephen Mitchell, who had been selected DNC chair by Stevenson at the 1952 convention. Mitchell had been a lawyer in Chicago and was involved in Stevenson's campaigns in Illinois.[5] Mitchell remained in office after the election and argued that Democrats should use "the current period, while we are out of office" as a "time of opportunity for broadening our Party and reviving it where necessary with new ideas and new leaders."[6]

But what that reviving and broadening should look like was unclear. With Black and union voters increasingly important outside of the South, the party could not ignore the policy demands of these crucial groups. But without the South, Democrats had no easy path to regaining the White House. Equally important, Democratic majorities in the House and Senate relied on the South: of the 48 Senate seats Democrats held in the Eighty-Third Congress, nearly 46% were from states that had been part of the Confederacy. Combined, Democratic leaders faced a conundrum: how can a broad ideologically and geographically divided party be electorally successful without alienating crucial, but opposing, groups within its coalition?

During the Eisenhower years, the DNC came up with two different answers to this question. After 1956, liberals—frustrated with another presidential loss and a decline in support from Black voters and union members in the Northeast—used the DNC to try to create a liberal and pro–civil rights national party brand. But prior to 1956, the strategy was different: with neither conservatives nor liberals willing to abandon the party or able to move away from each other, Democratic leaders saw few options but to continue the party's marriage of ideological convenience. In doing so, the DNC worked harmoniously with congressional Democratic leaders—many of them Southerners. In December 1952,

[4] Cited in Arlene Lazarowitz, *Years in Exile: The Liberal Democrats, 1950–1959* (New York: Garland Publishing, 1988), 78.

[5] Ralph M. Goldman, *The National Party Chairmen: Factionalism at the Top* (Armonk, NY: M.E. Sharpe, Inc., 1990), 441.

[6] Stephen Mitchell to Lawrence M.C. Smith, January 7, 1954, Container 24, Folder 4, Stephen Mitchell Papers, Harry S. Truman Presidential Library (hereafter cited as Stephen Mitchell Papers).

Mitchell reported that he intended for the DNC to seek "an effective liaison with the Democratic members of Congress,"[7] that the committee would function as "sort of a Department of Supply," and that he would "endeavor to do what we can to support the articulate voices of the Party which, of course, are in the Senate of the United States, and in the Congress."[8] In this design, the DNC would promote the party's national policy positions, but those policies would be set by the party's leadership in Congress.

That the DNC would need to up its publicity game after the 1952 election was broadly agreed upon. Indeed, multiple leading Democrats insisted that an aggressive DNC publicity program would be necessary, referring to the branding role the DNC had played under John Raskob's leadership during the Hoover administration.[9] Stephen Spingarn, a former aide to President Harry Truman, suggested to Stevenson that the party would need to engage in "a continuous hard-hitting and coordinated effort to keep steadily before the country each and every gap between Republican campaign promises and actual performance."[10] To achieve this, Spingarn argued, the party needed a "strong, resourceful and imaginative leadership at the Democratic National Committee," and, in particular, "a strong Research Division" and "an equally strong publicity division."[11]

In January 1953, Mitchell announced that the DNC intended to operate its "public affairs activities—publicity, research, speaker's bureau—at campaign tempo"[12] during the Eisenhower years. To help facilitate this, Mitchell reorganized the DNC by creating a new Public Affairs division. This division was headed by DNC staffer Clayton Fritchey and included an expanded "research-publicity-strategy group" that was "staffed with impressive new talent from among the refugee New and Fair Dealers."[13] The research subdivision predominantly provided members of Congress with "guidance and leadership"[14] by coordinating attacks against Republicans. The division was highly active

---

[7] "Revitalized Party Seen by Mitchell," *New York Times*, December 3, 1952.

[8] Transcript Democratic National Committee Eastern Regional Conference Meeting, February 14, 1953, Container 113, Folder 13, Democratic National Committee Meeting Transcripts, Democratic National Committee Records, John F. Kennedy Presidential Library (hereafter cited as DNC Meeting Transcripts).

[9] "President Calls Stevenson Head of Nation's Democrats," *New York Times*, November 8, 1952.

[10] Stephen J. Spingarn to Adlai E. Stevenson, November 6, 1952, Container 413, Folder 1, DNC Chairman's Files 1956–1960, Records of the Democratic National Committee, John F. Kennedy Presidential Library (hereafter cited as DNC Chairman's Files 1956–1960).

[11] Ibid.

[12] "Report to Members of the Democratic National Committee and State Chairmen," January 20, 1953, Container 219, Folder 2, Records of the Democratic National Committee, Harry S. Truman Presidential Library (hereafter cited as Records of the DNC).

[13] "Democrats in Congress Find New Role Not Bad," *New York Times*, February 15, 1953.

[14] Ibid.

during the Democrats' time as a minority party in the 1950s. In 1953 alone it produced reports on agriculture, civil service, social security, defense cuts by the Eisenhower administration, monetary policies, and Democratic policies against Communism. It also produced a speech kit consisting of pre-written speeches identifying the Democratic positions on salient policy issues that candidates were encouraged to incorporate verbatim in their stump speeches. In his introduction of the speech kit, Philip M. Stern of the DNC's research division wrote that it was his "hope that, when you are called on to fill speaking engagements, you will be able to select those 'Speech Sections' which will be of interest to your audience and put them together to make a complete speech."[15] The issues for which the DNC provided Democrats with ready-made speeches included high prices, the GOP's public power "sell-out," farmers, veterans, education, labor, big business administration, housing and rents, sales tax, small businesses, social security, "corruption GOP style," civil service, and tight money.[16]

The DNC's publicity division also invested heavily in a major innovation in direct communication to voters through the creation of the *Democratic Digest*—the DNC's own monthly magazine. A publication with the same name had previously existed as the DNC's Women's Division's newsletter, and national committees had relied on such newsletters in the past to promulgate their positions to the party faithful. But the *Digest* introduced in May 1953 was a fundamentally different communication tool. Unlike the previous newsletters, the *Digest* was available to consumers through subscription services and for sale at newsstands across the country. Each issue was printed at a run of 100,000 copies. The DNC presented the *Digest* as "the voice of the Democratic party,"[17] which would identify "the campaign issues for the party and [project] them in terms easy for the public to understand."[18]

Initially, the *Digest* largely consisted of repurposed political materials, such as transcribed speeches by Democratic politicians and reprinted articles and cartoons from newspapers. However, over time the Public Affairs division began to produce original. In the assessment of political scientist Roger H. Marz, writing in 1957, the *Digest* represented "an essentially new form of activity in the American party arena."[19] To be sure, the magazine was no money-making venture: while the *Digest* had 20,000 subscribers before the first issue was published

---

[15] "Speech Sections," August 29, 1953, Container 22, Folder 2, Stephen Mitchell Papers.

[16] Ibid.

[17] "Pocket Sized Digest Planned by Democrats," *Chicago Daily Tribune*, May 31, 1953. See also: "Democrats to Issue 'Digest' Monthly 25-Cent Magazine," *New York Times*, May 31, 1953.

[18] "In the Nation," *New York Times*, July 19, 1955.

[19] Roger H. Marz, "The Democratic Digest: A Content Analysis," *American Political Science Review* 51, no. 3 (1957): 696.

and 40,000 by September 1953,[20] it never became financially self-sustaining. Rather, the DNC paid the *Digest's* deficits because it believed the magazine provided it with a direct form of communication to promote the party. In 1954, Fritchey, during a DNC meeting, noted that after "the defeat of 1952, we found more than ever that the problem of communications […] for our party was still paramount, even more so after losing the voice in the House committees" and that the Democrats needed "a special instrument for effectively projecting its views into general circulation."[21] Fritchey noted that for every copy sold, there were estimated to be seven or eight people reading that copy, producing direct readership of around 700,000 to 800,000 people, or "about six persons to every precinct in the United States."[22]

The DNC also used the *Digest* to target the media: throughout its existence, news media regularly reported on items published in the *Digest*. Fritchey compared the DNC's strategy with "the old Republican theory in the economics phase, of the trickle-down theory, which does not trickle down at all."[23] By having "thought leaders" read the *Digest*, this put "into circulation the thoughts and impressions which finally motivate a nation, particularly on that fateful day when they go to the polls."[24] And in Fritchey's assessment the *Digest*

> is now closely followed by editors and publishers, by columnists and commentators, by political writers, educators, clergymen, civic leaders, lecturers, by the producers of radio and TV forums which have audiences in the millions. […] In the world of thought, opinion does trickle down. It is certainly a fact that the thinkers in any country influence the nonthinkers. That is why I attach so much importance to the circulation and prestige of the *Democratic Digest*.[25]

Fritchey also regularly encouraged news organizations to report on items in the *Digest*:

> when one of the news services failed to carry a story on the issue of the *Democratic Digest* a few days ago, when it came out, we got in touch with

[20] Report to Members of the Democratic National Committee and State Chairmen, September 4, 1953, Container 114, Folder 4, DNC Meeting Transcripts.

[21] Ibid.

[22] Ibid.

[23] Ibid.

[24] Ibid.

[25] Ibid.

friendly publishers. They brought pressure to bear and we had the story out to 2,000 more papers than it would have gone out to otherwise.[26]

But the party brand the DNC was promoting had to be acceptable to both conservatives and liberals. With civil rights objectionable to Southern conservatives and Eisenhower maintaining his popularity in the South, the DNC avoided attacking the president or discussing issues that would disturb the fragile ideological alliances within the party.[27] The DNC research division produced no documents related to race or civil rights in this period.[28] Between 1953 and 1956, the Digest also ignored civil rights, with the sole exception being two articles that referred to racial integration of the military, which, by then, was a fait accompli.[29] Instead, the DNC highlighted issues Democrats could agree on, such as blaming congressional Republicans for the national economic down-turn, more federal assistance for farmers, and attacking Vice President Richard M. Nixon.[30] One particularly notable DNC foe was Senator Joe McCarthy (R-WI). During one of McCarthy's speaking tours in 1954, the DNC sent "truth kits" countering McCarthy's attacks to editors of newspapers, radio and television station commentators, and Democratic officials in the cities that McCarthy appeared in.[31]

This approach to branding—attacking Republicans but avoiding clear policy positions that could disrupt the balance between conservatives and liberals—is also reflected in the New York Times coverage the DNC received under Mitchell. Figure 5.2 shows the results of negative binomial regressions in which Mitchell's incumbency as DNC chair is the independent variable, and the lagged monthly Times coverage of DNC branding and service activities are the dependent variables. In this model, the data is limited to those articles

---

[26] Transcript Meeting of the DNC Executive Committee, April 1, 1953, Container 114, Folder 1, DNC Meeting Transcripts.

[27] Gallup polls between February 1953 and June 1955 show that Eisenhower's approval ratings consistently remained above 60% in the South. In some months, approval for Eisenhower in the South was even higher than his national approval rating. See: George Gallup, The Gallup Poll, 1949–1958 (New York: Random House, 1972).

[28] "Numerical Index of 1953 Research Division Documents," Container 22, Folder 1, Stephen Mitchell Papers.

[29] The two exceptions were: "Communists Failed to Convert Negro POWs," Democratic Digest 4 (November 1953); "All Americans Can Fight," Democratic Digest 12 (July 1954).

[30] "Democrats Set Farm Panel," New York Times, April 30, 1954; "Mitchell Scores Farm Policy," New York Times, August 22, 1954; "Democrat Rally Set," New York Times, August 27, 1954; "Democrats Aim '54 Drive at Downswing," Washington Post, February 23, 1954; "Democrats Meet on Fall Strategy," New York Times, March 5, 1954.

[31] "'Truth Kits' Sent to Fight McCarthy," New York Times, February 6, 1954; "Mitchell Assails 'Hate' Campaign," New York Times, March 18, 1954.

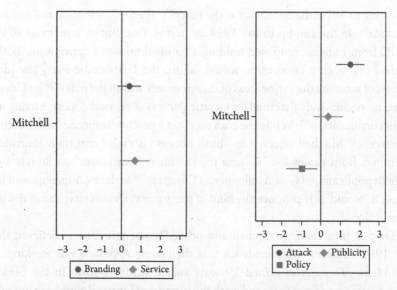

Figure 5.2. Negative binomial regressions of Stephen Mitchell's DNC chairmanship on monthly (lagged) *New York Times* coverage of DNC branding and service activities, 1949–1954. *Note:* This model includes variables controlling for presidential and midterm election years, a measure of *New York Times* length, and DNC scandals. The data coverage is limited to articles published between January 1949 and November 1954 covering only the DNC.
Source: Data collected by author.

covering the DNC published between January 1949 and November 1954 (the last full month in which Mitchell was DNC chair)—thereby comparing coverage of the DNC under Mitchell with that during Truman's presidency after the 1948 election. The results show interesting variation: the general change of *Times* coverage of all branding activities under Mitchell is positive but not significant. However, this null finding is the result of two opposite effects in the *types* of DNC branding the *Times* reported on. On the one hand, there was an increase in coverage of the DNC attacking the Republican Party (significant at the 0.001 level). But coverage of the DNC taking policy positions *decreased* under Mitchell (significant at the 0.05 level). These results underline the strategic choices the DNC made during the first Eisenhower term: positive policy positions could alienate *some* voters in the party, and thus the DNC instead focused on attacking the GOP.

While the DNC's unity approach mostly managed to avoid conflict, tensions remained. In February 1953, Senator Richard B. Russell (GA) gave a radio speech in North Carolina that the DNC intended to rebroadcast nationwide. However, Russell used this speech to warn "self-styled liberals" that they were carrying the party to "the most disastrous defeat in American political history" by trying to "drive the South out of the party."[32] The DNC canceled the national broadcast. In the run-up to the 1954 midterms, Paul Butler, a member of the DNC from Indiana, proposed holding a national midterm convention. Butler argued that such a convention would "afford the Democratic Party the ideal means of scouting the major areas of disagreement within the party"[33] and "demonstrate persuasively that the Democratic Party is alive, awake, alert, a living national organization."[34] While the plan received a positive response from political observers,[35] Mitchell rejected it—both because it could constrain individual members from professing "a liking for President Eisenhower" while rejecting "the Republican Old Guard influence in Congress"[36] in their campaigns, and because it "would only produce the kind of party rows [Democrats] had at the last convention."[37]

Despite these issues, Mitchell and other Democratic leaders believed that the 1954 midterms were evidence that their unity approach was working. In the House, Democrats gained 19 seats and majority control. In the Senate, Democrats gained two seats and, with the support of former Republican but now Independent Senator Wayne Morse (OR), who caucused with the Democrats, managed to win a tight majority. Mitchell announced his resignation as chair after the election so he could help Stevenson win the 1956 nomination.[38] As the *New York Times* noted, Mitchell during his chairmanship had relied on "a fixed, intelligent plan" to reorganize "the party machinery and binding up the wounds inflicted by factionalism."[39] Indeed, in his last report to the committee after the 1954 election, Mitchell stressed that "one of our primary goals has been to build a greater degree of unity among Democrats of all regions—particularly to eliminate or reduce the old frictions between Northern and Southern Democrats":

> [D]uring our years of success, we had drifted apart. As soon as we suffered our 1952 defeat, we all saw that we could no longer afford the

[32] "Democrats Face New Defeats if South Is Lost, Russell Says," *Washington Post*, March 1, 1953.

[33] "Democrats Get Plan for a '54 Convention," *New York Times*, April 2, 1953.

[34] "Democrats Ponder 1954 Rally," *Washington Post*, April 2, 1953.

[35] The *Washington Post* in an op-ed concluded that "midterm conventions of both parties would also serve the national interest by sharpening campaign issues and promoting party cohesiveness" ("Midterm Conventions," *Washington Post*, April 3, 1953).

[36] "Democrats Cooling on Off-Year Convention: Leaders Fear Platform-Writing Wrangles," *Washington Post*, August 11, 1953.

[37] "Democrats Borrow Eisenhower Tactic: A Study Committee," *Wall Street Journal*, September 15, 1953. See also: "Convention Plan Decried," *New York Times*, April 5, 1953; "Democrats Cooling on Off-Year Convention."

[38] See: Goldman, *The National Party Chairmen and Committees*, 447.

[39] "In the Nation," *New York Times*, December 7, 1954.

luxury of feuding among ourselves. And once we became disposed to cooperate, we discovered that the differences among us had been magnified—that the matters on which we agreed were vastly more important than the matters on which we disagreed.[40]

After Mitchell announced his resignation, Harry Truman and Adlai Stevenson initially tried to persuade Thomas Finletter, the former secretary of the air force, to run for the position of DNC chair. However, Finletter declined, leaving Truman and Stevenson without an obvious alternative candidate to back. Meanwhile, Butler had announced his candidacy and, as the only DNC member running, had received considerable support from other committee members and Mitchell. At the DNC meeting that elected Mitchell's successor, Butler easily won a majority of committee votes.[41] While Butler's votes came from DNC members from all parts of the country, he was particularly popular among Southern DNC members: Southerners made nominating speeches on Butler's behalf, and Butler received 95% of Southern committee votes, in comparison with 67% of the total committee.[42] In his acceptance speech, Butler expressed his pride in having had support "from all sections of the country" and stated that he was

> against any sectionalization of our Party by any issue, activity or any proceeding in the Democratic Party, and [would] attempt to serve the Party and all members of the Party, all sections of our Country, with the same degree of understanding and appreciation of their problems in their local areas as they certainly are entitled to at all times.[43]

While still supportive of the South, Butler's leadership did produce an immediate change in tone. Unlike Mitchell, Butler had no qualms about going after Eisenhower directly.[44] In January 1955, the DNC privately circulated analyses of the State of the Union that were more critical than those put forward

[40] "Report to the Democratic National Committee," December 4, 1954, Container 23, Folder 7, Stephen Mitchell Papers.

[41] "Democrats Elect Butler as Chairman," *Chicago Daily Tribune*, December 5, 1954.

[42] "Transcript of DNC Meeting," December 4, 1954, Container 223, Folder 7, Records of the DNC.

[43] Ibid.

[44] "Political Nuances," *New York Times*, December 7, 1954. In response, Eisenhower described Butler as the kind of politician "who, looking in the glass, sees only reflections of doubt and fear and the kind of confusion he often tries to create." See: "Knockout of Bystander," *New York Times*, December 9, 1954.

by Democratic congressional leaders such as Senate Majority Leader Lyndon Johnson (TX). The documents consisted of "a heavy unsparing and detailed assault upon the very Presidential document that the Johnsonians in Congress had on the whole little criticized."[45] DNC critiques on the ratification of a mutual defense treaty with the Republic of China, Eisenhower's 1955 budget, and a proposed school construction bill followed.[46] In each of these instances, Butler stretched the boundaries of the DNC's role as outlined by Mitchell after the 1952 defeat: the committee not only provided members of Congress with information on policy issues; it now also took specific stances on them, which sometimes were counter to those taken by Speaker of the House Sam Rayburn (TX) and LBJ.

But Butler stayed clear from civil rights, despite pressure to take a position. In a letter to Butler, Senator Hubert Humphrey (MN) warned that Democrats would "suffer at the ballot boxes,"[47] as Black voters in the Northeast were increasingly disappointed in the party. Still, civil rights was absent from a DNC list of top 10 policy issues for 1956.[48] And while Butler criticized the Eisenhower administration's claims that it had produced significant progress on civil rights as "a fraud upon the American people,"[49] the DNC made no attempts to push for a more expansive civil rights plank in the 1956 platform, as Butler explained that "the time is not right" for civil rights.[50] Even the brutal murder of Emmett Till—the 14-year-old boy from Chicago lynched by White men after he had been accused of offending a local White woman in Mississippi—would not move Butler. Despite pleas by the NAACP, Representative James Roosevelt (CA), and California DNC member Paul Ziffren to merely call for a fair trial of Till's murderers,[51] Butler refused, writing in response that he could not interfere

[45] "Democrats Wary on China Treaty," New York Times, January 12, 1955. See also: "Democratic Party Attacks Program Set by Eisenhower," New York Times, January 8, 1955; "Democratic Analysis of President's Speech," New York Times, January 8, 1955.

[46] "Democrats Wary on China Treaty," New York Times, January 12, 1955; "'Confidential' Memo Attacks Ike's Budget," Chicago Daily Tribune, January 19, 1955; "Democrats' Memo Raps President's School Bill," Los Angeles Times, February 21, 1955.

[47] Hubert H. Humphrey to Paul Butler, February 7, 1956, Container 441, Folder 21, Chairman's Files, 1956–1960.

[48] "10 Top Issues for '56 Listed by Democrats," Chicago Daily Tribune, December 18, 1955

[49] "Butler Charges 'Fraud' on Rights," New York Times, March 6, 1956.

[50] "Rip Butler over 'Time Not Right' Stand," Chicago Defender, February 11, 1956.

[51] See: A.E. Johnson to Paul Butler, September 19, 1955, Container 457, Folder, 10, Chairman's Files, 1956–1960; Manny Rohatiner to Paul Butler, October 12, 1955, Container 457, Folder 10, Chairman's Files, 1956–1960; James Roosevelt to Paul Butler, October 17, 1955, Container 457, Folder 10, Chairman's Files, 1956–1960; Paul Ziffren to Paul Butler, January 12, 1956, Container 457, Folder 10, Chairman's Files, 1956–1960.

publicly because he was "Chairman of all Democrats, white and Negro, North and South."[52]

Butler's support for the unity approach ended after the 1956 election. At first glance, the election results may not seem particularly surprising: while Stevenson lost to Eisenhower again, Democrats managed to maintain their majorities in Congress. Given Eisenhower's popularity, Stevenson's loss could hardly have been surprising. Indeed, both LBJ and Rayburn believed that the results vindicated their strategy of cooperating with Eisenhower.[53] But, liberals found the 1956 election results deeply concerning. One issue was that the goal of the unity approach—regaining Southern votes—had failed: in fact, Eisenhower improved slightly on his 1952 performance in the region. The second theme Democratic liberals noted in the results of the 1956 election was "large-scale defections of Negroes and laborers from the Democratic fold."[54] Indeed, Eisenhower received close to 40% of the Black vote.[55] As political analyst Samuel Lubell concluded, the results raised the peculiar paradox of "the Negro and the white Southerner [casting] a protest vote against one another by voting for the same man, Dwight D. Eisenhower."[56]

Liberals believed the "the compromising attitude [. . .] toward the South" put forward by Rayburn, LBJ, and the DNC "hurt the party far more than it helped."[57] Butler's own analysis of the election results stressed Eisenhower's success among Black voters, as well as with Catholics and union members.[58] Butler also concluded that, despite he himself talking "softly" on civil rights, "he got the label anyhow of being too liberal" and that with "a surprisingly noticeable shift of Negro votes to the Republican side"[59] the party would need to change its approach.

But such a change was unlikely to come from Congress, where Southern Democrats had dominant roles on committees due to the seniority system.

---

[52] Paul Butler to Paul Ziffren, February 16, 1956, Container 457, Folder 10, Chairman's Files, 1956–1960.

[53] Philip A. Klinkner, *The Losing Parties: Out-Party National Committees, 1956–1993* (New Haven, CT: Yale University Press, 1994), 15.

[54] "Democratic Row: Northern "Liberals" Prepare to Do Battle with the South for Control of the Party," *Wall Street Journal*, December 14, 1956.

[55] Everett Carll Ladd Jr. and Charles D. Hadley, *Transformations of the American Party System: Political Coalitions from the New Deal to the 1970s* (New York, NY: W.W. Norton & Company, 1975); David A. Bositis, *Blacks & the 2012 Democratic Convention* (Washington, DC: Joint Center for Political and Economic Studies, 2012).

[56] Cited in Sean J. Savage, *JFK, LBJ, and the Democratic Party* (Albany: State University of New York Press 2004), 36.

[57] "Democratic Row: Northern 'Liberals' Prepare to Do Battle".

[58] Ibid.

[59] "Top Man on Democratic Totem Pole," *Chicago Defender*, April 26, 1958.

Since Southern Democrats rarely faced competitive general elections, they had a much easier time staying in office and building up seniority than Democrats from other parts of the country. The result was that Southern Democrats in Congress held controlling positions in many committees, giving them a major source of power to prevent liberal Democrats from producing legislation they disagreed with. Butler explained the mechanics of the "regionalized" congressional Democratic leadership in a 1959 television interview, in which he argued that the problem was caused by

> the procedures and rules governing the Congress, where seniority applies and where members of the Democratic Party from Southern states, both members of the Senate and House, have longer service, [...] and the seniority system lends itself to the build up of power and influence, control of committees; by Southern Democrats, when the Democrats are in control of Congress. And this point of view generally expressed by these Southern leaders does not represent the national point of view.[60]

This left the DNC as the remaining channel for liberals to try to change the Democratic Party's brand. In November 1956, the DNC's executive committee gathered in a private meeting to discuss the election results. In a lengthy and tense discussion, members from the South and other regions discussed their assessments of how the party should move forward. Liberals on the executive committee expressed their dismay that Republicans had bypassed Democrats on civil rights. Ziffren expressed his fear that "the Republican Party is going to pose, or at least try to pose as a great liberal party, a champion of civil rights."[61] David Lawrence, mayor of Pittsburgh and a DNC member from Pennsylvania, argued that "Eisenhower is liable to do the thing that we accused him of not doing" on civil rights: "accepting the real leadership and the hard work of striving for the things that he is supposed to believe in."[62] The liberals also discussed the problems they ran into in countering the congressional Democratic party's policies with regard to civil rights and labor rights. Lawrence explicitly argued that the dominance of conservative Southerners in Congress made it impossible to appeal effectively to Black voters:

[60] Celebrity Parade, WMAL-TV, July 5, 1959, Container 460, Folder 21, Chairman's Files, 1956–1960.

[61] Transcript DNC Executive Committee Meeting, November 26–27, 1956, Container 119, Folder 4, DNC Meeting Transcripts.

[62] Ibid.

There isn't any question that in a great many areas in the north we lost a substantial colored vote and labor vote; and the arguments about [Senator James] Eastland [MS] on the one hand, and [Chairman of the House Committee on Education and Labor Graham A.] Barden [NC] on the other hand were just unanserable [sic], you couldn't answer them. […] We could go into all the details of what Roosevelt did for the colored people, and what Truman did, and what we have done in cities and in states for them. But that was too long-drawn-out. They just say, "Eastland"; they say "Barden"; and that answered all kinds of arguments.[63]

To solve this problem, the DNC would have to try to override the image produced by Democrats in Congress. As Jacob Arvey, a DNC member from Illinois, argued, Southern Democrats were also "elected on the Democratic Platform," and they should not have the right to ignore it once elected, since "we either have a National Party or we do not have."[64] If Congressional Democrats did not act to implement the party's platform, then the DNC had the right to step in and promote the party's "true" policies. To achieve this, the executive committee voted to install a "new 17 man top level advisory committee to formulate party policy and shape a "liberal" legislative program."[65] Southern members on the executive committee abstained in protest.[66] In the press release announcing the creation of the new organization—the Democratic Advisory Council (DAC)—Butler stressed that its goal was to produce a national Democratic image: "the Council will be a vehicle for rallying national support behind constructive programs and organizing and giving voice to opposition to unwise programs which ill-serve the national interest."[67] Additionally, the DAC would serve as a voice for "millions of Democrats not represented in Congress" and would engage "in an unprecedented effort to make a national political party more responsive and more responsible to its members and to the public."[68]

Notably, the DAC was inspired by recent political science research. Political scientists writing the 1950 American Political Science Association (APSA) report *Towards a More Responsible Party System* called for a party system with higher internal cohesion to provide voters with two ideologically homogenous and

---

[63] Ibid.

[64] Ibid.

[65] "Democrats Name Group to Shape Party's Policies," *Chicago Daily Tribune*, November 28, 1956.

[66] Ibid.

[67] Publicity Division Press Release B-1491, April 9, 1957, Container 449, Folder 1, Chairman's Files, 1956–1960.

[68] "Democratic Chiefs Split over Policies," *Chicago Daily Tribune*, January 4, 1957.

distinct parties. The report criticized parties' reliance on national conventions to set policies because they were "unwieldy, unrepresentative and less than responsible in mandate and action."[69] The authors suggested that parties instead should create a "party council" to "consider and settle the larger problems of party management" by proposing a draft of the platform and interpreting it in between national conventions.[70] The APSA report had a major influence on the DNC in this era, as several political scientists—including James Sundquist and Bernard C. Hennessy—worked at the DNC in the 1950s.[71] Paul Willis, a political scientist from Indiana University, worked closely with Butler at the DNC and had provided him with a copy of the APSA report in 1953.[72]

Butler announced the preliminary DAC member list in December 1956. The list included party elders—including Truman, Stevenson, and Eleanor Roosevelt—congressional Democrats such as Rayburn, LBJ, House Majority Whip Carl Albert, and Senators Hubert Humphrey, Mike Mansfield (MT), and JFK (MA), and Democratic governors such as Averell Harriman (NY), G. Mennen Williams (MI), and Ernest W. McFarland (AZ). But the suggested list Butler produced was something of a political ploy, as Butler (correctly) assumed Rayburn, LBJ, and Albert would refuse to serve.[73] Butler ensured that the members of the DAC he believed *would* accept had a strong liberal slant: even the Southern members were seen as moderates.[74] Additionally, the DAC's steering commission—consisting of five members—included only one Southerner while the other members (Stevenson, Harriman, Williams, and Ziffren) were all liberals.[75] Combined, there was little doubt, as the *Wall Street Journal* concluded, that "Northern party leaders planned to use this advisory

[69] *Toward a More Responsible Two-Party System* (New York: Rinehart, 1950), 37.

[70] Ibid., 5.

[71] Stephen Mitchell to Basil L. Walters, Container 14, Folder 13, Stephen Mitchell Papers; Cornelius P. Cotter and Bernard C. Hennessy, *Politics without Power: The National Party Committees* (New York: Atheron Press, 1964).

[72] George C. Roberts, *Paul M. Butler: Hoosier Politician and National Political Leader* (Lanham, MD: University Press of America, 1987), 36, 60; Paul Butler to Dr. Walter H.C. Leves, January 31, 1955, Container 446, Folder 34, Democratic Chairman's Files, 1956–1960.

[73] "Democrats Name 20 to Chart a Program," *New York Times*, December 6, 1956; "Rayburn Balks Party Plan to Sit as Adviser," *Chicago Daily Tribune*, December 9, 1956.

[74] "Democrats Name 20 to Chart a Program."

[75] Gravel, the DNC committee member from Louisiana, member of the DNC's executive committee, and the only Southerner on the DAC's executive committee, was ousted as DNC member by Louisiana's Democratic Party for being too liberal on segregation. Remarkably, the DNC allowed Gravel to remain on the committee regardless. "Democrats Press Civil Rights Bills," *New York Times*, February 18, 1957; "Party Ousts Louisianan," *Washington Post*, October 9, 1958; "Butler Rejects Removal of Aide," *New York Times*, October 10, 1958.

group as a weapon to prod Senator Johnson and House Speaker Rayburn of Texas into more "liberal" legislation."[76]

When the DAC gathered for the first time in 1957 its members quickly determined that, as former New York senator Herbert H. Lehman argued, the council had "to have the right, even if it means a fight with the congressional leadership, to force the point of view"[77] of what it considered to be the Democratic Party's positions. Lehman warned that parties could not rely on presidential candidates to introduce new policy positions to voters during a campaign. Rather, the national party as an institution would need to expose voters to these policies through a process of continuous branding activities:

> Adlai Stevenson, or anybody else, who may be our nominee, may go around the country and talk his head of [sic] and heart out, but that isn't going to do the thing unless the issues have been made in Congress and unless the leadership is going to be influenced by what this Advisory Committee proposes and suggests and urges.[78]

Thus, the DAC immediately began presenting a rejection of the unity approach. In its first statement the DAC proclaimed that "we can win in 1960 only if we begin now to hammer out a forceful, coherent policy and to keep communicating it to the public."[79] Immediately, the organization embraced civil rights, calling on members of Congress to "redeem party pledges by supporting civil rights legislations" and requested "legislation to end discrimination of all kinds."[80] The council criticized Eisenhower and Democratic governor of Arkansas Orval Faubus, for their handling of the Little Rock school controversy.[81] The DAC also passed a resolution criticizing anti-labor right-to-work legislation—issuing a clear rebuttal of Democratic Senator John L. McClellan's (AR) attempt to add such a bill as a poison pill amendment to the 1957 Senate civil rights bill.[82]

[76] "Northern "Liberals" Prepare to Do Battle with the South for Control of the Party," *Wall Street Journal*, December 14, 1956.

[77] Proceedings of Advisory Council of the Democratic National Committee Meeting, February 15–16, 1957, Container 120, Folder 3, DNC Meeting Transcripts.

[78] Ibid.

[79] Cited in Klinkner, *The Losing Parties*, 25.

[80] "Democrats Agree on Rights Policy," *New York Times*, February 17, 1957.

[81] DNC Publicity Division Press Release B-1560, September 15, 1957, Container 449, Folder 1, Chairman's Files, 1956–1960.

[82] Transcript of Meeting of the Advisory Council of the Democratic National Committee, May 5, 1957, Container 121, Folder 7, DNC Meeting Transcripts. See also: "M'Clellan Scored on Right-to-Work," *New York Times*, May 9, 1957.

Butler also became vocal in his support for civil rights. In September 1958, Butler called out Democratic Governors Faubus, J. Lindsay Almond (VA), and Marvin Griffin (GA) for their failure to implement civil rights reforms and stated that they did "not represent the position of the Democratic Party."[83] Butler went even further in a TV interview before the 1958 midterms, telling Southern Democrats that "if they did not like the party's official stand in favor of integration they could find asylum either with the Republicans or in a third political party."[84] The DAC thus gave Butler and the DNC the cover they needed to oppose segregation and support civil rights. Criticizing the RNC's attempts at reaching out to Southern Whites by stressing states' rights, Butler in a 1959 TV interview explained that "our National Party and spokesmen for our National Party, whether they speak in the North or the South, or the East or West are holding to the position that the Democratic Party must take a strong moral position on this issue."[85]

But the DAC did not limit itself to civil rights. The council called for increased federal government spending, expressed opposition to Eisenhower's "tight-money" policy, and blamed the (perceived) drop in American military power and economic performance on budget cuts.[86] The DAC also created specialized advisory subcommittees on a broad range of issues. Former Secretary of State Dean Acheson became the chair of the DAC's Advisory Committee on Foreign Policy.[87] In September 1957, a committee dealing with economic issues was announced, chaired by John Kenneth Galbraith. In the months that followed, the DAC created specialized committees on party finances, political technology and development, labor, and other issues.[88] The subcommittees had considerable autonomy, but Butler supervised the organization through a three-member Administrative Committee that "directed advisory committees as to what topics to pursue, approved pamphlets coming from advisory committees for distribution to the DAC, considered political ramifications of DAC appointments,

[83] "Butler Assails Southern Governors," Daily Defender, September 9, 1958.

[84] "Smathers Chides Butler on Rights," New York Times, October 22, 1958.

[85] Transcript Celebrity Parade, WMAL-TV, July 5, 1959, Container 460, Folder 21, Chairman's Files, 1956–1960.

[86] See: Democratic Advisory Council Press Release, February 16, 1958, Container 449, Folder 1, Chairman's Files, 1956–1960; "Economic Policy in 1958—a Statement by the Democratic Advisory Council," February 2, 1958, Container 449, Folder 1, Chairman's Files, 1956–1960; "America's Present Danger and What We Must Do about It—a Statement by The Democratic Advisory Council," February 1, 1958, Container 449, Folder 1, Chairman's Files, 1956–1960. Also see: Klinkner, The Losing Parties, 33.

[87] DNC Publicity Division Press Release B-1562, September 24, 1957, Container 449, Folder 1, Chairman's Files, 1956–1960.

[88] Roberts, Paul M. Butler, 111.

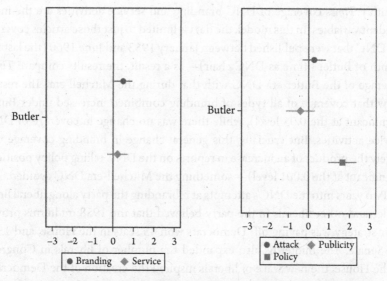

Figure 5.3. Negative binomial regression of Paul Butler's DNC chairmanship on monthly (lagged) *New York Times* coverage of DNC branding and service activities, 1953–1960. *Note:* This model includes variables controlling for presidential and midterm election years, and a measure of *New York Times* length. The DNC scandals variable is omitted in these models due to collinearity. The data coverage is limited to articles published between January 1953 and June 1960 covering only the DNC.
Source: Data collected by author.

and implemented plans for congressional liaison."[89] With the exception of Southern members' opposition to civil rights policy papers, dissent within the DAC was rare. Largely, this was the product of liberal domination of the council. For example, the Advisory Committee on Labor Policy produced policy proposals strongly supportive of unions—unsurprisingly so, as its members included George M. Harrison (the president of the Brotherhood of Railway Clerks), Joseph D. Keenan (the international secretary of the International Brotherhood of Electrical Workers), and Arthur J. Goldberg (special counsel of the AFL-CIO).[90]

The shift in DNC strategy is reflected in *New York Times* coverage in this period. Figure 5.3 shows the results of negative binomial regressions in which Butler's incumbency as DNC chair is the independent variable, and the lagged

[89] Ibid., 113.

[90] Democratic Advisory Council Press Release, June 12, 1958, Container 449, Folder 1, Chairman's Files, 1956–1960; Chairman Report to the Members of the Democratic National Committee, February 27, 1959, Container 122, Folder 8, DNC Meeting Transcripts.

monthly *Times* coverage of DNC branding and service activities are the independent variables. In this model, the data is limited to just those articles covering the DNC that were published between January 1953 and June 1960 (the last full month of Butler's time as DNC chair)—as a result, the results compare *Times* coverage of the Butler-era DNC with that during the Mitchell era. The results show that coverage of all types of branding combined increased under Butler (significant at the 0.05 level), while there was no change in coverage of DNC service activities. But crucially, this general change in branding coverage was largely the product of an increase in reports on the DNC taking policy positions (significant at the 0.001 level)—something the Mitchell-era DNC avoided.

Two years into the DNC's attempts at rebranding the party along liberal lines, Butler and other liberals in the party believed that the 1958 midterms proved their strategy was paying off: Democrats won 45 seats in the House, and 15 in the Senate. The midterms also expanded the number of liberals in Congress. In the House, the new wave of liberals inspired the creation of the Democratic Study Group, which pushed for increased power for party leaders at the expense of the seniority system.[91] In the Senate, the class of 1958 included future liberal stalwarts like Edmund Muskie (ME), Philip Hart (MI), and Eugene McCarthy (MN). As Barbara Sinclair has noted, these "new Democratic senators differed from their senior party colleagues in region of origin, ideological proclivities, and electoral security" and were a "markedly liberal group."[92] Meanwhile, the DNC's activities hit a nerve with Southern Democrats. Hugh N. Clayton, a DNC member from Mississippi, expressed opposition to the DAC early on.[93] Rayburn, in February 1959, warned Butler that he had "no patience with people who claim to be Democrats who say they want to run other people who claim to be Democrats out of the party."[94] Senator Robert C. Byrd (WV) in a lengthy personal letter to Butler cautioned that "if we hope to be victorious next year, we should and we must adopt unity as our watchword [underline in original]" and that "our Party is big enough for the liberals, the conservatives, and the middle-of-the-roaders [...] if it is a Party that seeks to cast out all of the liberals, or, conversely, all of the conservatives, then it will cease to be the Democratic Party."[95] And Senator Spessard Holland (FL) told Butler that "the great bulk of

[91] David W. Rohde, *Parties and Leaders in the Postreform House* (Chicago, IL: University of Chicago Press, 1991), 7.

[92] Barbara Sinclair, *The Transformation of the U.S. Senate* (Baltimore, MD: The Johns Hopkins University Press), 31.

[93] Hugh N. Clayton to Paul Butler, December 18, 1956, Container 434, Folder 21, Chairman's Files, 1956–1960.

[94] "Follow Steps of F.D.R., Party Urged," *Los Angeles Times*, March 1, 1959.

[95] Robert C. Byrd to Paul M. Butler, July 10, 1959, Container 449, Folder 7, Chairman's Files, 1956–1960.

our members are distinctly out of sympathy with the pronouncements of the Advisory Council which seems to be running directly counter to the efforts of the leadership and the majority of the Democrats in both Senate and House."[96] Other Southern Democrats threatened to bolt from the 1960 convention and run a Dixiecrat ticket.[97]

But this did not deter the DNC and DAC. In the run-up to the 1960 convention, the DNC tried to expand its new influence to the process of drafting the party's new platform. The committee organized a series of public hearings across the country "so that citizens can appear and suggest planks for the platform."[98] Butler argued that this showcased "the increasing importance which we, as a Party, attach to our national platform, not merely as a campaign document, but as a living expression of our party's deepest conviction, principle and promise, to be acted upon affirmatively once elected."[99] Around the same time, the DAC introduced a new civil rights subcommittee chaired by Eleanor Roosevelt, which drafted the platform's civil rights plank and called on Congress to go "squarely on record as opposed to racial segregation in public schools" and "to enact additional laws to protect [. . .] rights of American citizens to register and vote free of discrimination based on race, color, religion or national origin."[100] Despite protests from Southern members of the DAC, the 1960 platform included the civil rights proposal.

Regardless of the DNC's activities, the assessment of its performance under Butler overwhelmingly has been negative. Political reporters writing about the DNC and DAC mostly focused on the fact that the committee failed to produce legislative successes. The *Chicago Daily Tribune* concluded that the DAC's program was "dying on the vine"[101] because Southern Democrats ignored its policy papers. Similarly, the *New York Times* concluded that Butler achieved few, if any, victories in his fights with Democratic congressional leaders.[102] Retrospective

---

[96] Spessard L. Holland to Paul Butler, July 11, 1959, Container 449, Folder 7, Chairman's Files, 1956–1960.

[97] "Dixiecrats Set Up Worry for Party," *New York Times*, March 29, 1959.

[98] "Democrats 'Share Work' on Platform," *Washington Post*, March 8, 1960.

[99] DNC Publicity Division Press Release B-2025, March 7, 1960, Container 17, Folder B-2025, Publicity Division.

[100] "Democratic Split on Rights Widens," *New York Times*, March 16, 1960.

[101] "Butler Group Sees Program Dying on Vine," *Chicago Daily Tribune*, July 13, 1959.

[102] "Butler Needs Allies in Democratic Battle," *New York Times*, July 19, 1959. Butler also became controversial due to a series of gaffes—such as his suggestion in March 1960 that Eisenhower had "something to answer for" after the death of 19 members of the Navy in an air disaster during the president's visit to Brazil. Butler added, "What right has he to take the Navy Band on a tour around the world? Was this a political sow or something?" After criticism from both Democratic and Republican leaders, Butler apologized. See: "Butler's Series of Blunders Seen Damaging Value as Party Chairman," *Los Angeles Times*, March 8, 1960.

assessments have not been kinder, as political scientists writing in the 1960s and '70s concluded that Butler's attempt at implementing the APSA report's recommendations had failed.[103] There is no denying that Democrats in Congress did not follow the DAC's policy prescriptions. But the DNC was not trying to force compliance from Democrats in Congress: they were trying to provide voters with a new image of the Democratic Party. In this regard, the DNC's influence may have been more important. As James Sundquist has argued, the "uncompromisingly liberal stand" the DAC took on civil rights sent a strong message to voters that the "moderation" of LBJ and Rayburn and the "outright defiance" of Southern Democrats "was not the Democratic party's position."[104] And the DAC's liberal economic policies, and its positions on the environment and Medicare helped shape a policy platform the party would go on to enact during the Kennedy and Johnson administrations.[105]

Combined, the DNC was revitalized during the eight years the Democratic Party was out of the White House. While at the end of the Truman administration the committee was largely in hibernation, under Mitchell and Butler the committee's staff and budget were expanded, and major investments were made in its publicity role. But how the committee presented the Democratic Party to voters changed dramatically. After the 1952 election, Mitchell (and, later, Butler) made the strategic assessment that appeasing the South was the easiest path toward Democratic success in 1954 and 1956. To achieve this, the DNC effectively ignored civil rights—despite the fact that the issue was clearly becoming increasingly salient. Not until the "unity" approached showed its biggest cost—that is, Black and other liberal voting groups in the Northeast abandoning the party for Eisenhower in 1956—did the DNC change its strategy. Regardless of the extent to which the DNC's activities during the second Eisenhower term

---

[103] Daniel M. Ogden, "Party Theory and Political Reality inside the Democratic Party," paper delivered at the 1960 meeting of the American Political Science Association, New York (Ann Arbor, MI: University Microfilm, Inc.); Daniel M. Ogden, "Paul Butler, Party Theory, and the Democratic Party," in *Comparative Political Problems: Britain, United States and Canada*, ed. John E. Kersell and Marshall W. Conley (Scarborough: Prentice-Hall of Canada, Ltd., 1968), 117–125; Evron M. Kirkpatrick, "'Toward a More Responsible Two-Party System': Political Science, Policy Science or Pseudo-Science?," *The American Political Science Review* 65, no. 4 (December 1971): 965–990.

[104] James L. Sundquist, *Politics and Policy. The Eisenhower, Kennedy and Johnson Years* (Washington, DC: The Brookings Institution, 1968), 409–410.

[105] On Medicare the DAC was ahead of the curve, and its support may have played a role in placing the issue on the 1960 platform. While a bill creating Medicare had been introduced in Congress in 1957, it had failed to move forward in either the House or Senate in part because of opposition from conservative Democrats. The DAC endorsed Medicare in 1958, and despite the fact that Democratic congressional leaders failed to bring Medicare to a vote, the Democratic platform of 1960 endorsed the program. See: ibid., 410–414.

helped shape the party, this meant that by the time JFK won the 1960 presidential election the new president-elect inherited control of a controversial national party organization.

Eisenhower as Party Leader:
The RNC, 1953–1960

With Dwight Eisenhower's victory in the 1952 presidential election, the RNC now found itself back in an unfamiliar situation: under the control of an incumbent president. Traditionally, scholars who studied Eisenhower largely dismissed his role as party leader—portraying him as a president who was essentially above party politics.[106] In recent years, this image has been altered through the research of Daniel Galvin, who has shown that Eisenhower was in fact a very active leader of the GOP, who invested considerable time and energy in party matters. Crucially, Eisenhower also believed the Republican Party could only be successful as a moderate, right of center party. In taking this perspective, Eisenhower placed himself in the middle of what would become a multi-decade intra-party struggle between conservatives and moderates over what type of party the GOP should be. As Geoffrey Kabaservice summarized this conflict, conservatives considered the New Deal "to be wholly alien to the American tradition" and wanted the GOP "to eradicate it."[107] In contrast, moderates—while critical of the expanded federal government—hoped to "to rationalize and reform the New Deal rather than repeal it."[108] Eisenhower clearly placed himself in the moderate camp, arguing that "the Republican Party must be known as a progressive organization or it is sunk."[109] It is undeniable that Eisenhower

---

[106] As Galvin notes, Ralph Ketcham argued that Eisenhower was an exception to the modern presidents who engaged in partisan politics, but Bibby and Huckshorn concluded that Eisenhower was "generally oblivious to party affairs," and Sundquist argued that there was "no evidence" Eisenhower supported party-building activities. See: Ralph Ketcham, *Presidents above Party* (Chapel Hill: University of North Carolina Press, 1987), 231, 234; John F. Bibby and Robert J. Huckshorn, "The Republican Party in American Politics," in *Parties and Elections in an Anti-Party Age: American Politics and the Crisis of Confidence*, ed. Jeff Fishel (Bloomington: Indiana University Press, 1978), 55; James Sundquist, *Dynamics of the Party-System* (Washington, DC: Brookings Institution, 1983), 287; Daniel J. Galvin, *Presidential Party Building: Dwight D. Eisenhower to George W. Bush* (Princeton, NJ: Princeton University Press, 2010), 41–42.

[107] Geoffrey Kabaservice, *Rule and Ruin. The Downfall of Moderation and the Destruction of the Republican Party. From Eisenhower to the Tea Party* (New York: Oxford University Press, 2012), 25.

[108] Ibid., 15.

[109] Cited in Galvin, *Presidential Party Building*, 51.

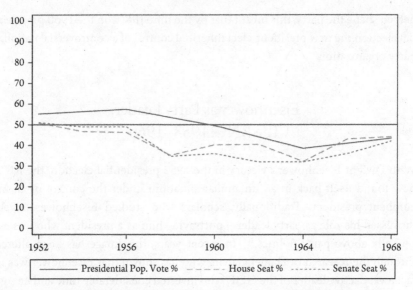

Figure 5.4. Republican electoral performance in presidential, House, and Senate elections, 1952–1968. *Source: Congressional Quarterly's Guide to U.S. Elections, 7th ed.* (Washington, DC: Congressional Quarterly, 2016).

failed to end this debate in his side's favor: the battle between moderates and conservatives would continue through the 1960s and '70s, until the election and presidency of Ronald Reagan effectively validated the GOP as a (majority) conservative party. But Eisenhower certainly *tried*, and the RNC was crucial in this effort. Indeed, Eisenhower's investments in the RNC as an organization were inherently linked to his desire to use this organization to reshape the GOP in his image.

To be sure, Eisenhower's interest in the RNC as an organization was limited early in his presidency. With Republican majorities in Congress (see Figure 5.4), and the development of a surprisingly effective working relationship with Robert Taft—who had been Eisenhower's opponent in the testy nomination battle—the new president may not have had much reason to focus on the RNC. But after Taft's sudden death in July 1953, Eisenhower became frustrated with the inconsistent support he received from Republicans in Congress and having to work with Democrats to form legislative majorities. As Galvin notes, this experience led Eisenhower to the determination that "the Republican Party should be revitalized, brought into the service of building support for his administration, and made more attractive to the median voter."[110]

---

[110] Ibid., 45.

Eisenhower's first selection for RNC chair after the 1952 election had been Wesley Roberts, a Kansas businessman.[111] However, Roberts had to resign only a few months later after being accused of defrauding the Kansas state government.[112] As his replacement, Eisenhower selected Leonard W. Hall, a member of the House from New York and chair of the Republican Congressional Campaign Committee (RCCC) during the 1952 campaign.[113] Eisenhower gave Hall a clear assignment as to what he expected of the RNC moving forward: the committee should be developed into "the 'selling organization' for the Administration and the entire Party."[114] To help achieve this, Eisenhower instructed Hall to get rid of RNC members who failed to support the administration's policies, and to create a team of Republican leaders to help improve relations between committee and administration.[115]

Unlike under FDR and Truman on the Democratic side, the RNC under Eisenhower thus had a clear assignment to continue its branding activities with the goal of supporting the administration. In response, the RNC invested new programs aimed at party-building and promotional activities. Television, then still a new medium, was a particularly important part of the committee's publicity strategy. During the 1952 campaign, the committee had paid for several broadcasts—including of a speech given by Eisenhower in Boston on the last night of the campaign. This broadcast—which appeared on both radio and television—cost the committee nearly $300,000. Combined, the RNC spent more than four times what it spent in 1948 on radio and TV in the '52 campaign. The rise of TV required the RNC to invest in new technology: in the previous decades it had relied on a "radio platter service," allowing Republicans in Congress to record audio messages and ship them to radio stations in their states or districts. The cost of such a service was as low as $6 for a 14-minute broadcast. But to produce a similar television version would cost $86. Since the committee was "going to have to make maximum use of television and radio"[116] in the run-up to the 1954 midterms, the committee would need to raise more money.[117]

---

[111] Previously Eisenhower had selected Arthur Summerfield to be RNC chair after winning the Republican presidential nomination. Summerfield resigned to become postmaster general in the Eisenhower administration.

[112] "Roberts Elected Chairman of GOP," *Los Angeles Times*, January 18, 1953; "GOP's Roberts Involved in Kansas Investigation," *Washington Post*, March 10, 1953; "Roberts Resigns as GOP Chairman," *Los Angeles Times*, March 28, 1953.

[113] "Hall to Be Chosen G.O.P. Head Friday," *New York Times*, April 8, 1953.

[114] Cited in Galvin, *Presidential Party Building*, 45.

[115] Ibid.

[116] Paul Kesaris, Blair Hydrick, and Douglas D. Newman, *Papers of the Republican Party* (Frederick, MD: University Publications of America, 1987), Series A, Reel 13, Frame 824.

[117] Ibid., Frames 822–824.

In 1953, the RNC paid for several television (and radio) broadcasts promoting the Eisenhower administration. For example, in August 1953, the RNC produced a television program for ABC in which Speaker of the House Joseph W. Martin praised Eisenhower's "refreshing toughness" in foreign policy, and in reversing the "fixed policy of huge spending" by the federal government.[118] The committee also supported the Eisenhower administration through more traditional approaches. *Straight from the Shoulder*, a new party publication used by the RNC to communicate directly with party workers, was published consistently throughout Eisenhower's first term and used to attack Democrats when they criticized Eisenhower.[119] Hall also functioned as a cheerleader on behalf of the administration, praising Eisenhower for producing a ceasefire in Korea and supporting his cuts in the military budget.[120] During the 1954 midterm campaign, the RNC filmed an Eisenhower speech in Los Angeles and made both the film and five million copies of its text available for distribution by Republican state parties.[121]

The RNC's continued branding role during Eisenhower's first term is reflected in the coverage it received in the *New York Times* in this period. Figure 5.5 shows the results of negative binomial regressions in which Eisenhower's incumbency during his first term is the independent variable and monthly lagged *Times* coverage of RNC branding and service activities are the dependent variables. In this model the data is limited to just those articles covering the RNC published between January 1949 and October 1956—thereby comparing *New York Times* coverage of the RNC during Eisenhower's first term in the White House with that of the committee during the preceding four years. The results show no statistically significant difference in *Times* coverage of combined branding and service activities. And, with regard to the specific branding activities, *Times* coverage did not change between the Truman years and the first Eisenhower term either: none of the coefficients are statistically significant. These null findings suggest that, in

---

[118] "News Summary & Index," *New York Times*, August 11, 1953; "Martin to Review Session on TV," *New York Times*, August 9, 1953.

[119] Kesaris et al., *Papers of the Republican Party*, Series A, Reel 14, Frame 177; "Harriman Called Yalta 'Architect,'" *New York Times*, April 29, 1955; "G.O.P. Sees 'Smear' in Investigations," *New York Times*, November 6, 1955; "Hall Challenges 'Road-Block' Foes," *New York Times*, November 8, 1955; "Knowland Says He'll Wait until Feb. 15 on Candidacy," *New York Times*, January 16, 1956; "G.O.P. Maps Drive to Tag Congress as 'Do-Nothing,'" *New York Times*, April 2, 1956; "G.O.P. Paper Derides 'General' Stevenson," *New York Times*, May 3, 1956; "Congress Scored for 'Reluctance,'" *New York Times*, August 5, 1956.

[120] "Hall Hails President for Korean Attitude," *New York Times*, June 7, 1953; "President's Truce Role Hailed," *New York Times*, June 9, 1953; "Hall Rallies G.O.P.," *New York Times*, June 10, 1953; "Hall Defends Air Budget," *New York Times*, June 28, 1953.

[121] "Eisenhower Film in Campaign," *New York Times*, September 28, 1954.

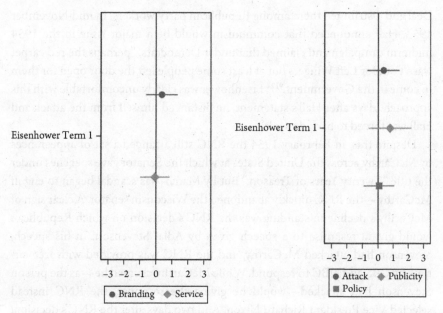

Figure 5.5. Negative binomial regression of Dwight Eisenhower's incumbency as president during his first term on monthly (lagged) *New York Times* coverage of RNC branding and service activities, 1949–1956. *Note:* This model includes variables controlling for presidential and midterm election years, a measure of *New York Times* length, and RNC scandals. The data coverage is limited to articles published between January 1949 and December 1956 covering only the RNC.
Source: Data collected by author.

comparison with the last four years at out-party, the RNC did not decrease its branding activities after Eisenhower became president: the RNC remained active at roughly the same level as it had been during the Truman years.[122]

But while the RNC did not change the quantity of its branding, the type of message it was trying to promote was noticeably different. An example of this was the RNC's changing perspective on how to deal with Joe McCarthy. During the Truman administration, the RNC had backed McCarthy's efforts to—in the words of RNC chair Gabrielson—bring "out to the American people the tremendous infiltration of pinks and fellow-travelers into our Government."[123] After Eisenhower entered the White House, the RNC initially continued to support McCarthy. In the fall of 1953, the RNC ordered 50,000 copies of a Senate report on communist subversion in the federal government during the New

---

[122] Though it is worth noting that under RNC chair Guy Gabrielson the RNC's branding role had declined in comparison with the previous out-party chairs (see Chapter 4).

[123] "Gabrielson Backs M'Carthy on Reds," *New York Times*, February 3, 1952.

Deal and distributed them among Republican party workers. In mid-November 1953, Hall announced that communism would be a major issue in the 1954 midterm campaign and claimed that under Democrats, "perhaps the red carpet wasn't out for Left Wingers but at least some people left the door open for them to come in the Government."[124] Eisenhower was clearly uncomfortable with this approach: days after Hall's statement, he distanced himself from the attack and Hall was forced to back down.[125]

Despite this, in February 1954 the RNC still arranged a set of appearances by McCarthy across the United States at which the Senator gave speeches under the title "Twenty Years of Treason." But by March—as scandal began to engulf McCarthy—the RNC quickly abandoned the Wisconsin senator. A clear sign of McCarthy's decline in standing was the RNC's decision on which Republican would give a response to a speech given by Adlai Stevenson. In his speech, Stevenson had attacked McCarthy, and the RNC was provided with free air-time by CBS and NBC to respond. While McCarthy claimed he—as the person Stevenson had attacked—would be giving the response, the RNC instead selected Vice President Richard Nixon. And two days after the RNC's decision, McCarthy faced a major public attack by reporter Edward R. Murrow—a crucial moment in his eventual demise as a leading political figure.[126]

But while 1954 proved to be the undoing of McCarthy—with the Army–McCarthy hearings in April–June and the Senate's condemnation of McCarthy in December—Eisenhower remained concerned with the broader conservative movement within the GOP and concluded, "the Republican Party must be completely reformed and revitalized."[127] To achieve this, Eisenhower expanded the RNC—hoping that he would be able to increase the number of moderates active within the party. The RNC created a GOP campaign school in 1955 to train Republican local party workers and potential candidates in get-out-the-vote activities and use of different publicity tools, including direct mail, radio, and TV.[128] Eisenhower incorporated the independent Citizens for Eisenhower groups into the RNC, helping increase the number of moderate Republicans

[124] "Hall Asserts G.O.P. Views Communism as Big 1954 Issue," New York Times, November 16, 1953

[125] "Hall Backs Eisenhower on End of Red Issue in '54," New York Times, November 19, 1953.

[126] "'Appeasement' Scored," New York Times, April 14, 1954. See also: "Red Inquiry Report Distributed by G.O.P.," New York Times, November 3, 1953; "Senate Report Financed," New York Times, November 4, 1953; "M'Carthy Itinerary Set," New York Times, February 4, 1954; "M'Carthy a Big Gun in the Republican Arsenal," New York Times, February 7, 1954; "Who Speaks for the G.O.P.," New York Times, March 10, 1954; "Television in Review: Rebuttal," New York Times, March 10, 1954; "TV and McCarthy," New York Times, March 14, 1954.

[127] Cited in Galvin, Presidential Party Building, 51.

[128] Ibid., 46.

active within the party's official organizations.[129] And Eisenhower engaged in extensive fundraising activities, including a series of "Salute to Eisenhower" dinners transmitted by television to $100-a-plate dinners across the country.[130]

Throughout 1955 and 1956, with the next presidential election approaching, the RNC continued promoting Eisenhower and his administration's policies. In October 1955, the RNC announced it would sign contracts with radio and TV networks for two million dollars' worth of broadcast time during the 1956 presidential election.[131] By the end of the year, the RNC was running its HQ on a campaign basis and planning Eisenhower's campaign visits for fall 1956.[132] Hall continued to see television as "the backbone of the campaign,"[133] as "on television you can get practically the same impact as from a personal appearance."[134] And the RNC helped the administration with its much maligned farm policies by expanding the committee's farm division and hiring a PR firm to appeal to farmers facing decreasing prices and income.[135]

With Eisenhower safely re-elected in 1956, Hall resigned as chair, and Eisenhower selected Connecticut RNC member Meade Alcorn as his replacement.[136] Under the first two years of Alcorn's leadership, the RNC remained engaged in some activities, though it did not initiate any major new publicity or policy efforts on behalf of president or party. But Eisenhower's massive victory—winning more than 57% of the popular vote and 41 states—did little to smooth over the ideological fights within the GOP. In part, this was because Eisenhower provided few to no coattails for Republicans in Congress: after losing their majorities in the 1954 midterms, the GOP remained in the minority in Congress after 1956. Rather than cement Eisenhower's control of the party, the election emboldened his conservative critics. In April 1957, during a regional RNC conference, Arizona senator Barry Goldwater criticized the Eisenhower administration for failing to repudiate the New Deal and proposing a $71.8 billion budget. Goldwater argued that Eisenhower had betrayed "the people's trust"

---

[129] Galvin, *Presidential Party Building*, 48–55.

[130] "The Busy Republicans." *New York Times*, September 15, 1955; "Election Budget of G.O.P. $7,000,000," *New York Times*, June 26, 1956.

[131] "G.O.P. '56 Air Time Set at $2 Million," *New York Times*, October 30, 1955; Reel 14, Frame 912.

[132] Kesaris et al., *Papers of the Republican Party*, Series A, Reel 14, Frame 912.

[133] "Campaign Special: TV or Train," *New York Times*, April 29, 1956.

[134] "Election Budget of G.O.P. $7,000,000," *New York Times*, June 26, 1956.

[135] "Benson Rejects Pig Killing Plan," *New York Times*, December 10, 1955; "G.O.P. Promoting Its Farm Policy," *New York Times*, December 13, 1955; "Eisenhower Seeks Farm Bill Speed," *New York Times*, January 1, 1956; "New Book Published," *New York Times*, October 12, 1956.

[136] "Hall Quits as G.O.P. Chairman," *New York Times*, January 12, 1957; "Alcorn Selected Chairman by GOP," *Los Angeles Times*, January 23, 1957; "Alcorn Takes Over as GOP Chairman," *Washington Post*, February 2, 1957.

and that he would represent "the rather brief tenure of his splinterized concept of Republican philosophy."[137]

This division concerned Alcorn, who noted that

> the thing we need to worry about is that the discussion of what a modern Republican is as compared to what some other kind of Republican is is the threat that the discussion of it may lead to actual division, and I think that would be a catastrophe for the Republican Party [...].[138]

After further losses in the 1958 midterms, Eisenhower determined that the party needed a "broadly based committee to analyze Republican difficulties and failures and to work out the finest possible plan we could develop for their correction."[139] During a press conference, Eisenhower stated that "a political party has a certain façade, sort of a certain face, that becomes recognized. And I think that some of the features of this face have been distorted in popular conviction and imagination unfairly."[140] To achieve this, the RNC appointed a committee to produce a "concise, understandable statement of our party's long-range objectives in all the areas of political responsibility in the light of the social, technological and economic developments [...] during the years immediately ahead."[141]

The committee—led by Charles H. Percy—produced the report *Decisions for a Better America*, published in September 1959 and available for purchase in book form.[142] The program reflected a perspective in line with Eisenhower's views with some lip service toward the conservative side. For example, the section on Human Rights and Needs stated that "the federal government has a role to play only when individuals, communities or states cannot by themselves do the things that must be done"[143] yet also called for a major federal role in education.[144] Additionally, the program endorsed federal action against school segregation, government support for housing construction and the creation of more nursing homes, and spending as much as $36 billion by 1976 to support scientific research.[145] While Kentucky Senator Thruston B. Morton, a "true-blue

---

[137] Cited in Galvin, *Presidential Party Building*, 59.

[138] Kesaris et al., *Papers of the Republican Party*, Series A, Reel 15, Frame 691.

[139] Cited in Galvin, *Presidential Party Building*, 60.

[140] "Republicans Pick 44-Member Group to Draft a Credo," *New York Times*, February 26, 1959.

[141] "G.O.P. to Stress Long-Term Policy," *New York Times*, March 14, 1959. See also: "Republicans Pick 44-Member Group to Draft a Credo," *New York Times*, February 26, 1959.

[142] Republican Committee on Program and Progress, *Decisions for a Better America* (Garden City, NY: Doubleday & Company, Inc., 1960).

[143] Ibid., 30.

[144] Ibid., 33.

[145] "G.O.P. Study Urges More Science Aid," *New York Times*, October 5, 1959.

Eisenhower man"[146] who had succeeded Alcorn as RNC chair after his resignation in April 1959, supported the report, conservatives in the GOP rejected it and wrote their own alternative program, *Meeting the Challenges of the Sixties.*[147]

A final component of Eisenhower's attempt at reshaping the GOP in his image was a major RNC program aimed at appealing to Southern voters. Somewhat ironically, both before and after Eisenhower's presidency appealing to (White) Southern voters had been a conservative strategy. But Eisenhower's strong performance in the South—which had so dramatically affected Democratic strategy in the 1950s—also produced opportunities for the GOP. Breaking up the one-party South had been a long-term goal of the Republican Party ever since the end of Reconstruction, and Republican presidents—including Warren G. Harding and Herbert Hoover—had attempted to rebuild Southern party organizations, though with little electoral success.[148] Eisenhower—a military hero born in Texas—proved to be capable of outperforming the previous GOP presidential candidates in the South. Even before his inauguration in 1953, Eisenhower ordered the RNC to create a Committee on the South to produce a "long range program for expanding the Republican party in the South."[149] RNC chair Summerfield, in early 1953, noted that "we have a glorious opportunity in the South and we must avail ourselves of it to the utmost."[150] But while the RNC planned some activities and identified a number of competitive House races, the committee appears to have achieved little.[151]

After the 1956 election the RNC again voted to appoint a committee to investigate "the ways and means of further developing the Republican Party in the South."[152] The core issue facing the party was how to convince voters to vote not just for Republican presidential candidates, but also for GOP down-ballot candidates. As Louisiana RNC member John Minor Wisdom noted, "it is a far cry from carrying a state for a presidential election and electing a Congressman and Senator in the local houses."[153] The RNC created a new division within its HQ focused on appealing to Southern voters. Known as Operation Dixie, the

[146] "New Chairman Held True-Blue Ike Man," *Washington Post*, April 12, 1959. See also: "Alcorn to Quit, Paper Reports," *Washington Post*, April 1, 1959; "President, Nixon, Spur G.O.P. for '60," *New York Times*, April 11, 1959; "Morton Wins Eisenhower OK as Party Chief," *Los Angeles Times*, April 11, 1959; "Chicago Selected as '60 G.O.P. Site," *New York Times*, April 12, 1959.

[147] Ibid., 62.

[148] Boris Heersink and Jeffery A. Jenkins, *Republican Party Politics and the American South, 1865–1968* (New York: Cambridge University Press, 2020).

[149] Galvin, *Presidential Party Building*, 63.

[150] Kesaris et al., *Papers of the Republican Party*, Series A, Reel 13, Frame 824 (p. 827).

[151] "G.O.P. Denounces 'Locking in' of Jobs," *New York Times*, March 1, 1953.

[152] Kesaris et al., *Papers of the Republican Party*, Series A, Reel 15, Frame 555.

[153] Ibid., Frame 556.

project was led by I. Lee Potter, who had been the Virginia GOP's state chair.[154] Potter went on speaking tours in the South promoting the Republican Party and worked on recruiting candidates and activists in the region.

But "selling" the GOP in the South proved complicated due to the increased salience of civil rights. During his first term, Eisenhower's record in this regard was mixed. While he pushed for the end of segregation in Washington, DC, and moved to end discriminatory employment practices by government contractors, on *Brown v. Board of Education*—the unanimous 1954 Supreme Court decision establishing that racial segregation in public schools was unconstitutional—Eisenhower moved deliberately slowly. And, in the run-up to the 1956 convention, Eisenhower reportedly scrapped a draft civil rights platform plank that stated support for the Court's ruling.[155] But civil rights were an issue the administration could not ignore forever. After Eisenhower ordered the National Guard to intervene in the Little Rock integration crisis in September 1957, his popularity in the South declined. Although Potter publicly dismissed this—noting some "dampening of enthusiasm" but arguing that the "southern conservative Democrat certainly has nothing to look forward to in his own national party's stand"[156]—privately he wrote that "I have been into every one of the Southern States and I can tell you that there has been severe damage done [...] [Southern Democrats] feel that this is an invasion of the rights of the States."[157]

Operation Dixie thus spotlighted the basic Southern problem both parties wrestled with in the 1950s: if the cost for electoral success in the South was condoning segregation, was a party willing to (continue to) pay that price? Under Eisenhower, the RNC would not answer that question entirely affirmatively. But with the end of Eisenhower's second term, and Nixon's loss in the 1960 presidential election, the RNC would see a drastic change in leadership and a different assessment of the Southern question.

DNC Decline during the Kennedy and Johnson Years, 1961–1968

With JFK's victory in 1960, Democrats were now back in unified control of government. JFK as the incoming president also took control of the DNC and

---

[154] Ibid., Frame 708.

[155] Jim Newton, *Eisenhower: The White House Years* (New York: Anchor Books, 2011), 217.

[156] "Potter Admits Troop Use Hurts GOP," *Washington Post*, October 3, 1957.

[157] Quoted in: Galvin, *Presidential Party Building*, 65.

appointed John M. Bailey as the new national committee chair.[158] Prior to his election as DNC chair, Bailey had been the chair of the Connecticut Democratic Party and a consistent supporter of JFK's political ambitions.[159] Bailey would become one of the longest-serving committee chairs, remaining in office until the 1968 national convention. But even before the inauguration, the DNC began a process of "retrenchment,"[160] which saw the committee fire staff members and cut programs. In mid-November 1960, the DNC terminated the *Democratic Digest*.[161] The DNC also ended the DAC: newspapers reported that JFK planned "a quiet death" for the institution that had "served to emphasize the deep liberal-conservative split within the party."[162] The decision to end the DAC was a clear consequence of the party being back in the White House: Bailey acknowledged that the DAC had "served a function" but moving forward "policy should be made at the White House and by the leadership of Congress."[163]

The DNC did not immediately abandon all branding activities. As under FDR's first term in office, the committee initially promoted JFK's policies through a program called "Operation Support." Active mostly between 1961 and 1963, the program promoted JFK's legislative agenda to local party leaders and voters. The DNC sent information on bills the administration supported to party organizations in districts of members of Congress who opposed the plans.[164] As part of this project, the DNC sent telegrams "to the Democratic chairman in the member's state or district advising him of the vote and suggesting that he get the 'facts' of the situation as widely publicized as possible." Additionally, the DNC's women's division created "kits" containing "pocket-sized pamphlets devoted to aspects of the Kennedy program, setting out basic facts, arguments in their behalf, and what the individual could do to enhance prospects of enactment."[165] The DNC also organized conferences at which Kennedy administration officials explained their policy positions to local Democrats. For example, the DNC used Operation Support to support JFK's proposed tax cuts plan. In doing so

[158] At the 1960 Democratic National Convention Kennedy had selected Senator Henry "Scoop" Jackson (WA) as Butler's replacement. Jackson made it clear at the time that he would only serve during the 1960 general election campaign.

[159] Goldman, *The National Party Chairmen*, 470; "Bailey Will Hold Two Party Posts," *New York Times*, December 25, 1960.

[160] "Democrats Cut National Headquarters Staff," *Washington Post*, November 17, 1960.

[161] Despite some attempts at having the magazine survive as an independent project, the last issue was a celebration of the Kennedy inauguration published in January 1961. "Digest Suspends," *New York Times*, November 18, 1960; "Party Digest Shifts," *New York Times*, November 22, 1960.

[162] "Advice without Consent," *Wall Street Journal*, December 19, 1960.

[163] "Democrats End Advisory Council," *New York Times*, March 12, 1961.

[164] "Democrats Open Drive for Tax Cut," *New York Times*, August 31, 1963; "Democrats Mail Tax Cut Publicity," *New York Times*, October 15, 1961.

[165] "Party Will Press Kennedy Program," *New York Times*, April 5, 1961.

the DNC mostly targeted Republican districts. However, the DNC was forced to apologize after it was revealed that it had also sent materials to Tennessee to influence Senator Albert Gore.[166]

Operation Support appears to have come about in response to a similar frustration Eisenhower experienced in his first term. JFK found himself with an unreliable Democratic congressional majority and hoped the DNC would help tie individual members of Congress to his administration's policies. As Galvin has noted, the DNC "aimed to activate the natural Democratic majority to bring pressure to bear on Congress in *this* session, on behalf of certain policies that were being considered *now* [emphasis in original]," though in doing so "it looked no further than the current legislative calendar."[167] But the impact of Operation Support appears to have been limited and the effort was short-lived: after JFK's death in 1963, Operation Support activities ended as well.

The DNC's changing role during the Kennedy years is also represented in the coverage the committee received in the *New York Times* in this period. Figure 5.6 shows the results of negative binomial regressions in which JFK's incumbency is the independent variable and monthly lagged *Times* coverage of DNC branding and service activities are the dependent variables. In this model the data is limited to just those articles covering the DNC published between January 1957 and October 1963 (the last full month of JFK's life and presidency)—thereby comparing *Times* coverage of the DNC under JFK with that during the Butler era after the 1956 election. The results show no statistically significant difference in *Times* coverage of combined branding and service activities. But the results for specific branding activities do show a clear decline in *Times* coverage of DNC policy position taking (significant at the 0.01 level)—reflecting the change between the DNC's focus on policy setting under Butler and its support for the Kennedy administration after the 1960 election.

Early attempts by Bailey to reorganize the DNC as an organization also quickly fizzled out. While the DNC provided advice to Black and Latino action groups, it did not actively organize voter registration drives. And Bailey was "careful not to antagonize southern Democratic politicians and state committees"[168] since the position of Southern Democrats in the party had improved somewhat after 1960. As the *New York Times'* Arthur Krock wrote after the election, the results meant that JFK "and the 'liberal' non-Southern party majority that nominated him on a platform repugnant to the South, are deeply in debt to the Southern

[166] "Democrats Mail Tax Cut Publicity," *New York Times*, October 15, 1963; "Democrat Takes Blame for Tax-Cut Slap at Gore," *Los Angeles Times*, October 22, 1963.

[167] Galvin, *Presidential Party Building*, 166.

[168] Savage, *JFK, LBJ, and the Democratic Party*, 153. See also: Galvin, *Presidential Party Building*, 175–177.

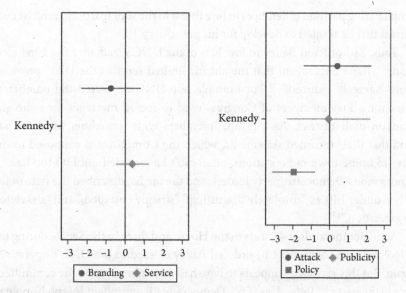

Figure 5.6. Negative binomial regression of JFK's presidencies on monthly (lagged) *New York Times* coverage of DNC branding and service activities, 1957–1963. *Note:* This model includes variables controlling for presidential and midterm election years, a measure of *New York Times* length, and DNC scandals. The data coverage is limited to articles published between January 1957 and October 1963 covering only the DNC.
Source: Data collected by author.

leaders"[169] since without the electoral votes from Alabama, Arkansas, Georgia, Louisiana, North Carolina, South Carolina, and Texas, JFK would have lost the election. Thus, Bailey and the DNC staff "tried their best to avoid favoring one faction or candidate over another in intraparty disputes within the states"[170] rather than engage in intra-party debates as under Butler.

The DNC's decline as an organization became particularly clear after JFK's assassination in November 1963 and LBJ's landslide victory against Republican presidential nominee Barry Goldwater a year later. After his massive election victory, LBJ saw no further use for the organization. Indeed, LBJ was successful in pushing through major pieces of legislation that had stalled under JFK—including the 1964 Civil Rights Act—by relying on a broad coalition of Democrats and Republicans. At the same time, LBJ also attempted to placate (conservative) Democrats on other policy issues. A publicity-centered DNC would not serve either purpose, since, as Sean Savage has argued, "LBJ perceived a strong, national party organization with regular publicity [. . .] activities

---

[169] "The Parties' Futures," *New York Times*, November 13, 1960.
[170] Savage, *JFK, LBJ, and the Democratic Party*, 154.

emphasizing partisan differences to be a threat to the suprapartisan, centrist consensus that he wanted to develop for his presidency."[171]

Thus, LBJ ordered Bailey to fire 30% of the DNC's staff after the 1964 election.[172] These cuts meant that the already limited services the DNC provided were "savagely reduced."[173] For example, the DNC decreased the number of telephone lines members of Congress used to record messages for radio stations in their district. As a result, "members with something timely to say find that their recorded statements, which the Committee is supposed to deliver to home-town radio stations, often can't be recorded until it's too late."[174] Anonymous Democratic party leaders, and the media, described the state of the DNC under LBJ as "absolutely disgusting," "sharply curtailed," and "a skeleton organization."[175]

After Democrats lost 47 seats in the House and three in the Senate during the 1966 midterm elections, LBJ ordered Bailey to expand the DNC's operations again. But this expansion appears to have had no major effect on the committee's role in the party.[176] Indeed, in 1967, Democratic PR consultant Joseph Napolitan wrote Postmaster General Lawrence O'Brien to complain about lack of support from the DNC:

> In 1966 I tried to get from the Democratic National Committee some research material demonstrating the differences between the Democratic Party and the Republican Party. After weeks of fruitless discussion, I had my own office do the research and prepare the material. [...] In July [1967], I tried to get the National Committee to arrange some background briefings on foreign affairs for LeRoy Collins who is

[171] Ibid., 160.

[172] See: "The Democratic Deficit," Washington Post, September 23, 1965; "Democrats Reduce Jobs in National Committee," Los Angeles Times, December 22, 1965; "Demo Committee Cuts Staff," Chicago Defender, December 25, 1965; "Republicans Intensifying Efforts in Big Cities as Democrats Cut Back Their Urban Staff," New York Times, December 29, 1965.

[173] "Campaign Breakaway," Washington Post, March 25, 1966.

[174] Ibid.

[175] See: "Campaign Breakaway"; "Democrats in Distress," Wall Street Journal, March 30, 1966; "President Failed to Satisfy Governors on National Committee Shortcomings," Washington Post, January 1, 1967; "Democrats Grope for Fresh Ideals, for Fresh Ideas," New York Times, January 2, 1967.

[176] A November 1967 mailer in which the DNC attacked Democratic critics of the Vietnam War was described by Washington Post columnists Evans and Novak as "the sophomoric tone of 'Campaign '68" and described as "a jumbled, poorly-written eight-page compilation of anecdotes and pronouncements" that revealed "once again the low level of competence at the Democratic National Committee." See: "Democratic Campaign Letter Gibes at Many Anti-LBJ Party Leaders," Washington Post, November 24, 1967.

running for the Senate seat George Smathers will vacate. I couldn't even get an answer to my letter or phone calls, and I also drew a blank at The White House. [...] It is in the area of mass media that the National Committee really is inefficient. The literature produced for Johnson in 1964 was atrocious—not just bad, but awful. [...] I also get the impression that the Democratic Party has got fat in power, that it has lost rapport with the people, and relies too much on outmoded methods and organizations for delivering a vote they no longer control.[177]

Not until 1968—when the combination of Vietnam, race riots, and challenges from, first, Eugene McCarthy and, later, Senator Robert F. Kennedy (NY) in the 1968 presidential primaries scuttled the LBJ presidency—did the DNC take on a role of publicizing issues again. At a set of regional meetings in early 1968, Johnson administration officials and other Democratic leaders (such as former DNC chair James Farley) deflected criticism on the Vietnam War and other issues. The DNC also produced a set of pamphlets defending the administration and distributed them among party activists.[178] However, this too proved to be short-lived, and after LBJ announced his intention not to run for re-election, the DNC ended all major fundraising efforts and public conferences until the national convention.[179] After eight years in the White House, the DNC had once again seen the investments of the previous out-period being undone through presidential disinterest.

Conservative Takeover and Moderate Backlash: The RNC during the JFK–LBJ Era

After the disappointment of the 1960 election, moderates and conservatives within the GOP agreed that the RNC would have to be responsible for creating a new national image for the party: Barry Goldwater argued that the RNC should "re-establish itself to its rightful position as the governing body of the Party,"[180] while Governor Nelson Rockefeller (NY) argued that the RNC should be "the actual agency heading the Party in the next four years."[181] But there was no

[177] Memo from Joseph Napolitan to Lawrence F. O'Brien, September 1, 1967, Box 221, Folder 7, Democratic National Party Files, 1961–1975, John F. Kennedy Library (hereafter cited as Democratic National Party Files, 1961–1975).

[178] Savage, *JFK, LBJ, and the Democratic Party*, 165.

[179] "Major Fund-Raising Halted by Democrats," *Washington Post*, April 5, 1968.

[180] Kesaris et al., *Papers of the Republican Party*, Series B, Reel 1, Frame 280.

[181] "Nixon, Rockefeller Discuss Role of Party in Leadership Dilemma," *Washington Post*, December 3, 1960.

consensus on what the RNC should actually do. Crucially, the fact that the 1960 election was so close—JFK received a comfortable majority of the electoral vote (303 to 219), but the difference in the popular vote was a mere 112,827 votes, less than half a percentage point—made it so that both conservatives and moderates had a compelling argument for why their strategy would be the best path forward for the party.

Moderates argued that the party's weak point was its performance in major cities, especially among Black voters. RNC chair Morton noted that "when you lose in the cities by 1.8 [million votes] and you lose an election by 112,000 clearly we have a job in certain metropolitan areas."[182] Even a small improvement among Black voters could have made a meaningful difference. JFK won Illinois by 8,858 and New Jersey by 22,091 votes. Had both states flipped to Nixon, JFK would have dropped under 270 electoral votes. Additional gains in Missouri (which JFK won by 9,980 votes) or Minnesota (22,018 votes) would have provided Nixon a majority of the electoral vote. Nixon lost many of these states by underperforming in the major cities: in Cook County, IL (which includes Chicago), JFK ran ahead of Nixon by more than 318,000 votes. Even in Pennsylvania, where JFK beat Nixon by a comfortable 116,000 votes, he was ahead by more than 331,000 votes in Philadelphia. A path toward an electoral college majority in future presidential elections—moderates argued—thus required only slightly improving the party's performance in big cities.

Conservatives contended that the lack of a clear conservative party brand was to blame for Nixon's defeat. Goldwater claimed the 1960 election showed the "necessity for a return to a vigorous, forward-looking, dynamic conservative philosophy which will clearly identify the Republican Party and Republican candidates as supporters of a concept of government totally different from that which Mr. Kennedy and his people offer the nation."[183] In particular, conservatives suggested that the party should focus even more on the South. While JFK won Alabama, Arkansas, Louisiana, North Carolina, South Carolina, and Texas,[184] his margin of victory in these states was often small—less than 5 percentage points in North Carolina, South Carolina, and Texas. Flipping these states alone would have gotten Nixon close to an electoral college majority. Additionally, the South also offered the GOP the chance to win more seats in Congress and end Democratic majorities there. But that path would not be feasible if the party focused on marginally improving its performance with Black voters in big cities.

---

[182] Kesaris et al., *Papers of the Republican Party*, Series B, Reel 1, Frame 88.

[183] "The Republican Party's Choices Are Conservatism or Liberalism," *Los Angeles Times*, November 20, 1960.

[184] Mississippi narrowly voted for a slate of delegates pledged to Virginia Senator Harry F. Byrd.

With Morton remaining as chair, the RNC initially followed the moderates' prescription. Morton ordered the creation of a 14-member committee tasked with improving Republican performance in big cities. The committee was chaired by Ray C. Bliss, the chair of the Ohio Republican Party, broadly seen as a skilled party machine operator.[185] But moderate control of the RNC after 1960 proved short-lived. Morton announced his resignation in the spring of 1961 to focus on his own Senate re-election campaign in 1962. The RNC voted to replace him with conservative congressman William E. Miller from New York.[186]

As chair, Miller focused his attention on making major investments in the RNC's PR division. Speaking at an RNC meeting in January 1962, Miller argued that

> In the area of publicity and promotions, I know you will agree with me that there is room for improvement, today, in the public image of the Republican Party. I propose that we go about creating more interest by effectively presenting these Republican leaders and Republican issues to the voters of the 50 states. The short-range public relations objective will be to use promotional techniques to aid us in the 1962 elections, but also to keep them consistent with the long-range public image that we must create in the general.[187]

Others agreed: in a presentation to the RNC in January 1962, advertising executive Duke Burgess advised the committee that "now is the time to create a public image of the word 'Republican' [. . .]. Now is the time to sell the resurgent Republican Party. It will cost far less now; it is easier to sell now."[188] The RNC dedicated a considerable part of its budget to publicity: in 1962, the divisions that made up the RNC's publicity arm comprised a third of its monthly operating budget.[189] The RNC used these funds to continue producing a biweekly newsletter (*Battle Line*—sent to 100,000 subscribers), speech kits for Republican

---

[185] "G.O.P. Names Panel to Scan Urban Vote," *New York Times*, January 29, 1961.

[186] "G.O.P. Is Expected to Name Miller," *New York Times*, May 27, 1961. Ray Bliss—the moderate chairman of the GOP in Ohio—was the only other candidate but withdrew his candidacy before the vote. Despite concerns by some Republicans that Miller's "views were too conservative and that the party needed a full-time chairman" (ibid.), this left Miller as the only acceptable candidate, and the RNC voted unanimously to elect Miller as its new chair in its June meeting.

[187] Kesaris et al., *Papers of the Republican Party*, Series B, Reel 1, Frame 623.

[188] Ibid., Reel 1, Frame 770.

[189] This consisted of the Public Relations, Research, and Speaker's Bureau divisions. Combined, these three publicity divisions counted for $339,400 of the RNC's total $1.3 million 1962 budget—the largest subset within the budget. Within publicity, Public Relations represented more than 61% of expenses. See: ibid., Reel 2, Frame 484.

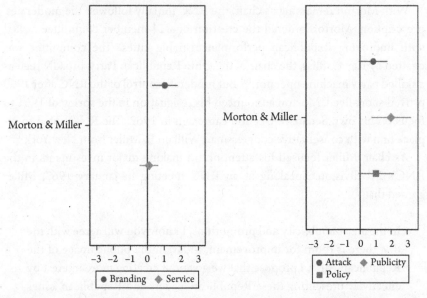

Figure 5.7. Negative binomial regression of Thruston Morton and William Miller's RNC chairmanships on monthly (lagged) *New York Times* coverage of RNC branding and service activities, 1957–1964. *Note:* This model includes variables controlling for presidential and midterm election years, a measure of *New York Times* length, and RNC scandals. The data coverage is limited to articles published between January 1957 and June 1964 covering only the RNC.

Source: Data collected by author.

candidates, and *Ratio*—a weekly radio program sent to independent and small affiliate radio stations that lacked correspondents in Washington, DC.[190]

The RNC's increase in publicity is reflected in *New York Times* coverage in this period. Figure 5.7 shows the results of negative binomial regressions in which the RNC chairmanship of Morton and Miller is the independent variable, and the lagged monthly *Times* coverage of RNC branding and service activities are the dependent variables. In this model the data is limited to just those articles covering the RNC that were published between January 1957 and June 1964 (the last full month of Miller's term as chair)—thereby comparing the coverage of the RNC during most of the Kennedy–Johnson term with that during Eisenhower's second term in office. *New York Times* coverage of combined branding activities increased during the Morton–Miller out-party era (significant at the 0.01 level), but there was no change in coverage of service activities. Specifically, the *Times* increased its coverage of RNC publicity activities (significant at the 0.01 level), as well as attacks on the Democratic Party and RNC

[190] Ibid., Reel 1, Frames 636–638.

policy position taking (both marginally significant at the 0.10 level) in comparison with the second Eisenhower term.

But Miller's most important project was improving the GOP's performance
in the South. As Phillip Klinkner argues, Miller "knew that the Republicans'
only chance to capture the House was to win seats in the South and that a big
city strategy offered no such hope."[191] Miller and the conservatives' strategic argument was strengthened by the surprise victory of Texas senatorial candidate
John Tower in the race to win LBJ's old seat in 1961. The committee's publicity
division began targeting Southern White voters and in doing so pushed a conservative party brand to convince them to switch their partisan allegiance. The
Eisenhower-era Operation Dixie was a crucial element in the RNC's strategy
during the 1962 midterm campaign, as the RNC spent 10 times as much on
Operation Dixie what it spent on the Big City Panel.[192] In April 1962, the RNC
began producing *The Republican Southern Challenge*, a newsletter aimed at
(White) Southern voters. By 1964, the newsletter had become a monthly publication with a distribution list of 39,000 people that "emphasized 'conservatism,'
and [...] pushed hard for a two-party system in the South."[193] Additionally, the
RNC ran ads in Southern newspapers and magazines criticizing the Democratic
Party for neglecting Southern needs.[194] In the 1962 midterms, Republicans
gained four House seats in the former Confederacy.[195] The RNC's research division concluded that "the most impressive aspect of the 1962 election was the
sharp increase in Republican strength in the South,"[196] noting a popular vote
increase of 243.8% there in comparison with the 1958 midterms. Miller boasted
that "we worked to find good candidates, and we provided the money—more
than a quarter of a million dollars—to help them get started, as well as supporting
them with tailor-made campaign materials. You have seen the results."[197] The
RNC ramped up its Southern strategy and approved a "massive 1964 GOP assault on Democratic strongholds in the segregationist South."[198]

---

[191] Klinkner, *The Losing Parties*, 54; Joseph E. Lowndes, *From the New Deal to the New Right: Race
and the Southern Origins of Modern Conservatism* (New Haven, CT: Yale University Press, 2008), 45–
68; Galvin, *Presidential Party Building*, 63–67.

[192] Klinkner, *The Losing Parties*, 59.

[193] Cited in ibid., 55.

[194] Ibid.

[195] Republicans gained one seat each in Florida, North Carolina, Tennessee, and Texas. See: "GOP
Snaps 1-Party Grip in the South," *Washington Post*, November 8, 1962.

[196] *Congressional Quarterly Almanac, 88th Congress, 1st Session, 1963 Vol. XIX* (Congressional
Quarterly Service, Washington DC, 1963), 1168.

[197] Kesaris, *Papers of the Republican Party*, Series B, Reel 2, Frame 577.

[198] "GOP Leaders Approve All-Out Drive in South," *Los Angeles Times*, December 8, 1962.

But this new version of Operation Dixie was controversial among moderates in the party. *Advance*, a magazine published by the Young Republican organization, criticized the RNC for supporting segregationist candidates in the South, while Senator Kenneth Keating (NY) warned that Republicans would be "forever a minority party"[199] if they supported segregationist policies in their efforts to win in the South. In contrast, conservatives celebrated Operation Dixie, believing that—as the *Washington Post* summarized the logic—"Republicans are impractical fools to worry about the Northern Negro voters, because nothing will tempt the Negroes from their solid Democratic allegiance."[200] Miller defended the Dixie approach, arguing that "our successes in the South need no apology. They are the product of hard and intelligent efforts on the part of people dedicated to the Republican principle of freedom and sound government."[201]

The 1964 presidential nomination of Barry Goldwater complemented the RNC's Southern strategy. In June, days after narrowly defeating New York governor Nelson Rockefeller in the California primary, Goldwater became one of just six Republican senators to vote against the 1964 Civil Rights Act. As Kabaservice has argued, while Republican support for the act had been pivotal for its passage in Congress, Goldwater's opposition meant that "the credit—even the glory—that the Republican Party should have enjoyed" for supporting it "was effectively negated."[202] Goldwater's control over a majority of convention delegates also meant conservatives could set the Republican platform and control the general election campaign. Goldwater successfully demanded that the party drop a proposed plank confirming that the Civil Rights Act was constitutional and during his acceptance speech stated that no person "should violate the rights of some in order to further the rights of others."[203]

During the campaign when Strom Thurmond, the segregationist Democratic senator from South Carolina who ran as a Dixiecrat candidate against Truman in 1948, switched to the Republican Party in September 1964, Burch welcomed Thurmond to the party—describing him as "a man of rare honesty, courage, and integrity."[204] While the National Negro Republican Assembly protested this welcome, Goldwater embraced Thurmond and appeared with him across the South. Walter Lippmann, writing in the *Los Angeles Times*, noted that Goldwater's

---

[199] "G.O.P. Is Attacked for Its Aid to Segregationists in the South," *New York Times*, November 26, 1962; "Keating Urges G.O.P. to Shun Segregation in Bid for the South," *New York Times*, December 1, 1962.

[200] "The Southern Strategy," *Washington Post*, December 7, 1962.

[201] "GOP Leaders Approve All-Out Drive in South."

[202] Kabaservice, *Rule and Ruin*, 101.

[203] "South's GOP Chiefs Reassured on Rights," *Washington Post*, July 11, 1964.

[204] "Thurmond Given Praise and Scorn," *New York Times*, September 17, 1964.

campaign strategy "was not so much to win this election but to inaugurate the so-called southern strategy in order to lay the foundations for a radically new Republican Party." Lippmann also noted that while Goldwater did not discuss civil rights during his campaign appearances, "there was no need to mention civil rights or to take notice of the existence of a large Negro population when he could consort publicly with Sen. Strom Thurmond."[205]

The conservative experiment of 1964 resulted in one of the largest defeats in Republican Party history, with LBJ receiving slightly more than 61% of the popular vote and 486 electoral votes. The one silver lining was Goldwater's success in the South: of the six states Goldwater won, five (Alabama, Georgia, Louisiana, Mississippi, and South Carolina) were in the South. Goldwater also came close to winning Florida (where he received 49% of the vote) and Virginia (46%) and won 49% of votes cast in the former Confederacy. To be sure, this Southern success did not impress moderates. Oregon governor Mark Hatfield called on the GOP to re-establish "a broad middle-ground philosophy and [to] outline positive positions on civil rights, medicare, taxation, conservation, education, and foreign aid."[206] New York senator Jacob Javits warned that "the Republican party faces not only a major reconstruction job throughout the nation; it also faces the difficult task of exorcising the image which the 'Southern strategy' created—that of an impending transformation to a 'lily white' party."[207] And Senate Minority Leader Everett Dirksen blamed the 1964 loss directly on the RNC and its failure to produce a winning party image, arguing that "we failed to present a clear-cut image and sell it to the voters. [...] It was the fault of those whose business it was to project the true Republican image. It was the national committee's business and it flubbed the job."[208] While Goldwater attempted to maintain Burch as chair after the election, moderates used the defeat to force a challenge to his leadership. As Burch and Goldwater came to the realization that they would not have a majority within the RNC, Burch resigned as chair.[209] Burch's successor was Ray Bliss, chair of the GOP in Ohio and former chair of the RNC's Big City committee.

Under Bliss, the RNC continued its publicity efforts. Indeed, Bliss announced that the RNC would run "a 12-month a year, 24-hour a day" permanent election campaign.[210] The committee expanded its budget and the amount it devoted to

[205] "Goldwater Lays Foundation for a Radically New Republican Party," *Los Angeles Times,* September 23, 1964.

[206] "Aide Expects Barry to Make Unity Move," *Washington Post,* November 13, 1964.

[207] "The Road Back for the G.O.P.," *New York Times,* November 15, 1964.

[208] "Dirksen Puts Onus on Republican Committee," *Los Angeles Times,* December 13, 1964.

[209] "Burch Quitting Job April 1," *Chicago Tribune,* January 13, 1965.

[210] "G.O.P. Told Why Barry Lost," *Chicago Tribune,* January 24, 1965.

Table 5.1. **Republican National Committee publicity expenses, 1965–1968.**

	1965	1966	1967	1968
Public Relations	221,763	306,160	363,680	600,000
Speakers Bureau	23,249	43,264	45,000	65,000
Minorities	20,467	45,105	101,000	145,000
Senior citizens	3,288	24,145	20,800	27,000
Big cities	1,790	36,990	33,500	75,000
Arts & Sciences	2,861	25,789	92,100	80,000
RCC[a]	47,855	74,944	103,500	95,000
Governor's Association	0	24,799	67,000	90,000
Total budget	1,381,426	1,891,523	2,020,000	3,084,500
Publicity share of budget	23.2%	30.7%	40.9%	38.1%

[a] Republican Coordinating Committee.

Source: Ray C. Bliss Papers, Ohio Historical Society, Series 2, Subseries 2, Box 79, Folder 20; Ray C. Bliss Papers, Ohio Historical Society, Series 2, Subseries 2, Box 121, Folder 8.

publicity, spending up to 40% of its budget on publicity-related divisions in 1967 (see Table 5.1). Most notably, the radio program introduced under Miller was renamed *Comment* and expanded from airing on just 170 radio stations in 1965, to 2,000 by 1968—one-third of all stations in the United States.[211] The concept of *Comment* was that the RNC produced a five-minute radio segment that stations could play in its entirety or use as clips for their news reporting. RNC Director of Public Relations Fred Morrison argued that this allowed the RNC to "give the greatest possible impact to [issues] which the leaders of the party are attempting to drive home on a national scale."[212] According to the committee's own figures, 400 stations played the entire program each week while 1,600 stations regularly used parts of the material.[213] In 1967, the RNC expanded the *Comment* project by creation a television version with the same name and, by 1968, 42% of all TV stations in the country received the program.[214] The RNC also reached out to Republican academics through its new Arts and Sciences

[211] See Kesaris et al., *Papers of the Republican Party*, Series B, Reel 4, Frame 909; Reel 5, Frames 830–831.

[212] Ibid., Reel 5, Frames 456–457.

[213] Ibid., Reel 6, Frames 622–623.

[214] Ibid., Reel 6, Frames 340–341; 624.

division, which distributed literature and recruited university faculty. By 1967, the division distributed its newsletter, *Republican Report,* to more than 11,000 Republican-oriented faculty members.[215]

Bliss used the expanded publicity division to push the GOP's image back toward the center. Within weeks of taking office, Bliss fired a number of Goldwater-era appointees and replaced them with moderates.[216] Under Bliss's leadership the RNC also began providing financial support to the Republican Governor's Association—then the center of moderate Republican power—thereby providing the governors with more direct influence in the national party.[217] In 1966, the RNC announced a new push for Black votes with the appointment of an advisory committee consisting of 12 Black Republican leaders to help "prepare a program to strengthen Republican support among Negroes."[218] Bliss also hired Black businessman and activist Clarence Lee Townes Jr. as a special assistant and three Black staff members at RNC HQ to "recruit Republican voters among the nation's Negro population."[219] Throughout 1966, RNC representatives attended "21 major Negro conventions and meetings" at "which some 15,000 delegates represented more than five million Negro voters."[220] In December 1966, the RNC announced it had hired Junius Griffin, a former aide to Martin Luther King Jr. As an RNC staffer, Griffin would go on to advise Republican candidates on

[215] The Arts and Sciences division was especially focused on political scientists: the RNC had a stand at the APSA and Southern Political Science Association conferences between 1965 and 1968, and Thruston Morton delivered an address at APSA in 1965. See: Report by the Chairman to the Republican National Committee (July 1, 1965—January 31, 1966), Ray C. Bliss Papers, Ohio Historical Society Series 2, Subseries 2, Box 94, Folder 3, p. 20 (hereafter: Ray C. Bliss Papers); The Chairman's Report for 1967 to the Republican National Committee (February 23–24, 1968), Ray C. Bliss Papers, Series 2, Subseries 2, Box 94, Folder 3, p. 23.

[216] "Bliss Starts Shuffle of G.O.P. Staff Jobs," *Chicago Tribune,* March 31, 1965. Bliss also expelled the conservative "Rat Fink" faction of the New Jersey Young Republicans organization and opposed conservative Phyllis Schlafly's attempts at becoming the chairwoman of the National Federation of Republican Women. See: "Supporter of Scranton Given Key GOP Post," *Los Angeles Times,* January 25, 1967; "Bliss Curbs YR Clubs, Acts to Expel 'Finks,'" *Los Angeles Times,* June 21, 1966; Donald T. Critchlow, *Phyllis Schlafly and Grassroots Conservatism. A Woman's Crusade* (Princeton, NJ: Princeton University Press, 2005), 155–162.

[217] "G.O.P. to Give Party Governors $100,000 for Office in Capital," *New York Times,* December 20, 1966; Anthony Sparacino, "The Democratic and Republican Governors Associations and the Nationalization of American Party Politics, 1961–1968," *Studies in American Political Development* 35, no. 1 (2021): 76–103.

[218] "12 Negroes Chosen as G.O.P. Advisers," *New York Times,* February 27, 1966;

[219] "Negro to Get Post on Top G.O.P. Unit," *New York Times,* March 12, 1966; "GOP Moves to Change Image," *Chicago Defender,* May 7, 1966.

[220] "Report by the Chairman 1966," Ray C. Bliss Papers, Series 2, Subseries 2, Box 94, Folder 3, p. 17.

how to appeal to Black voters.[221] The efforts seemed somewhat successful: in the 1966 midterm elections, Black support for Republican candidates increased to 19% (up from 13% in 1964). Townes and the RNC set their goal for 30% Black support in 1968.[222]

As part of the process of moderating the GOP's image, the RNC also created its own version of the DAC. Notably, RNC chairs had a high estimation of the DAC: during an RNC meeting in 1961, Morton praised the DAC as a party institution that "gave [Democrats] a forum for political publicity purposes."[223] And, in January 1965 outgoing chair Burch noted that during the Eisenhower years

> the Democrats had a committee—I don't even recall the name of it. [...] You may further recall that Lyndon Johnson and Sam Rayburn black-balled this particular organization—would not participate in it. Nevertheless, this Advisory Committee did function. It did release its reports and got considerable attention in the press. The press looked at the stature of the people on this committee. As I recall, Eleanor Roosevelt, Adlai Stevenson, people of that nature and they gave a good deal of attention to their deliberations and to their report.[224]

To achieve a similar goal, the RNC voted to create its own policy-setting organization: the Republican Coordinating Committee (RCC). As the *New York Times* reported, the RCC was created to help the party overcome its persistent minority position in American politics:

> [T]he party's whole problem is to broaden its base and give recognition to those states and districts where it did poorly last November. The Republicans must look not inward to the survivors on Capitol Hill—who represent its irreducible hard core—but outward to the independent "swing" voters, who offer its only hope of future recovery.[225]

Unlike with the DAC, Republican congressional leaders were involved in the RCC. Indeed, the RCC—led by Bliss—included major names that reflected the

---

[221] "Civil Rights Aide Offered GOP Position," *Los Angeles Times*, December 16, 1966; "Waner Gets G.O.P. Race Expert's Aid," *Chicago Tribune*, January 21, 1967.

[222] "GOP Designs Blueprint to Snag Negro Vote," *Chicago Defender*, February 4, 1967.

[223] Kesaris et al., *Papers of the Republican Party*, Series B, Reel 1, Frame 95.

[224] Ibid., Reel 4, Frame 647.

[225] "Exit Mr. Burch," *New York Times*, January 13, 1965.

party as a whole: Eisenhower agreed to be involved and was joined by all living former presidential candidates, the party's congressional leadership, several Republican governors, state legislators, and representatives of the RNC.

The RCC's main role was to "moderate the party's image."[226] The RCC produced policy papers that presented moderate policy proposals on issues such as transportation, metropolitan planning, water pollution, poverty, aid for the elderly, and strengthening the United Nations. Notably, many of the positions the RCC took deviated from those the party had taken in 1964. For example, the RCC embraced civil rights legislation[227] and called on all Republicans to "reject membership in any radical or extremist organization."[228] As Mary Brennan has noted, "eliminating the extremist blemish on the party was central to the new image Republicans tried to create."[229] Speaking during a January 1967 meeting, Bliss praised the RCC for helping the public understand "the general direction of movement of our party" and for producing "an image [. . .] around it. So we received tremendous publicity and more and more the papers are starting to pick up and review our papers and editorialize on them [. . .]."[230]

Under both Miller and Bliss, the RNC thus invested in branding, but the image the committee was presenting and the voting groups it targeted changed dramatically. Under Miller, the priority was to appeal White Southerners, and the image the RNC presented was of a conservative party that, if not supportive of Jim Crow, was at least open to letting states determine such issues on their own. After Goldwater's loss, moderates regained control of the RNC. While Ray Bliss in scholarly assessments is often described as a "nuts-and-bolts" party leader with no interest in ideological debates, this ignores the clear moderate slant of the RNC's branding efforts after 1964. Under Bliss, the RNC changed its focus away from the South and tried to repair the damage done to the Republican image during the preceding years. Now, the RNC began to reinvest in reaching out to Black voters and used the RCC to propose moderate, right-of-center policy proposals and promoted these as the party's policies.

[226] Klinkner, *The Losing Parties*, 84.

[227] "Equality in America: A Promise Unfulfilled," Republican Coordinating Committee,. Task Force on Human Rights and Responsibilities, Ray C. Bliss Papers, Series 2, Subseries 2, Box 110, Folder 3.

[228] Cited in Stephen Hess and David S. Broder, *The Republican Establishment: The Present and Future of the G.O.P.* (New York: Harper & Row, 1967), 52.

[229] Mary C. Brennan, *Turning Right in the Sixties: The Conservative Capture of the GOP* (Chapel Hill: University of North Carolina Press, 1995), 109.

[230] See: Kesaris et al., *Papers of the Republican Party*, Series B, Reel 5, Frame 826. After the 1968 election, Bliss also praised the RCC for producing position papers that formed the basis of the party's platform. See: ibid., Reel 7, Frame 148.

Conclusion

In the years between the 1952 and 1968 elections both the DNC and RNC were active participants in major debates about the future of their parties. Specifically, leaders in both parties faced the question of whether to move into a clear ideological direction, or to maintain identities as "big-tent" parties that included politicians and voters from across the political spectrum. In both parties, this question was directly linked to the increased salience of civil rights and the consequences of the position the party would take on its performance in the South.

During the first Eisenhower term, DNC chairs Stephen Mitchell and Paul Butler both followed the strategic belief that the Democratic Party's path back to reliable majorities in Congress and control of the White House required restoring the broad New Deal coalition of the 1930s. With many Southern Whites voting for Eisenhower in 1952, such restoration required placating Southern conservatives in the party. Thus, while the DNC invested heavily in new publicity tools—such as the *Democratic Digest*—the committee avoided civil rights. But while congressional leaders believed the "unity" approach worked, Northern liberals in the party interpreted the 1956 election results as a major warning sign. With Black voters switching to Eisenhower (and with Southern voters failing to return to the Democratic Party) liberals worried that unless a major change in the party image was produced, Republicans would come to dominate in the years to come. And, with Southern conservative Democrats in particularly strong positions of power in Congress, these liberals saw only one party institution able to take on this role of rebranding the Democratic Party: the DNC. Thus, during the second Eisenhower term, the DNC embraced a new task: presenting the national party as being clearly liberal. To achieve this, Butler relied on the expanded publicity division and the newly created DAC, which was given the power to set party policies and produced a series of policy papers embracing civil rights, unions, and other liberal positions.

But once the Democrats were back in the White House after the 1960 election, this wave of branding activity ended. While the DNC engaged in some publicity on behalf of the Kennedy administration, the story of the committee's role during the JFK–LBJ era is one of major decline. The reason for this largely seems to have been that JFK and (in particular) LBJ did not see value in relying on the DNC for branding. LBJ hoped to achieve legislative successes by producing large and bipartisan majorities in Congress and believed that the DNC would not help and might even hurt these efforts. Thus, not only were new DNC initiatives like the *Digest* and DAC ended as soon as the Democrats returned to the White House, but also the DNC's staff and budget were cut dramatically, leaving it unable to provide much of any support to Democratic politicians in the 1966 and 1968 elections.

In contrast, Eisenhower used the RNC extensively to achieve his goal of rebranding the GOP as a right-of-center, moderate political party. Indeed, the RNC's potential as a branding tool was helpful to Eisenhower. However, after the GOP became the out-party due to Richard Nixon's loss in 1960, conservatives and moderates in the party clashed over how the party should move forward. During the first Kennedy–Johnson term, it was the conservative wing of the party that managed to control the RNC and tried to use it to present the Republican Party as a clear conservative party. Crucial in this effort was prioritizing appealing to White Southerners. And, while the RNC never embraced segregation, it did appeal to these voters with a basic "wink-wink-nudge-nudge" message of supporting states' rights. But after Goldwater's dramatic loss to LBJ in the 1964 election, moderates regained control of the RNC and returned to right-of-center messaging of the Eisenhower years. Fundamental to this attempt were major investments in publicity tools (such as the creation of the *Comment* program), increased appeals to Black voters, and the introduction of the Republican version of the DAC to create (moderate) policy papers and restore voters' faith in the GOP as a governing party.

6

Managing Mixed-Ideological Parties, 1969–1980

During the 1950s and '60s both the Democratic and Republic National Committees (DNC and RNC) had, at times, pushed their parties to embrace a (respectively) clearly liberal and conservative party image. But these short-lived attempts at forging ideologically distinct parties were followed quickly by attempts at maintaining broad-ideological and centrist party images. Indeed, by the end of the 1960s, both parties still included a broad range of ideological actors. In the years that followed, both national committees continued emphasizing the importance of maintaining "big-tent" parties as the only way their side could win presidential elections or majorities in Congress. But selling voters on such a party proved complicated.

On the Democratic side, the defeats in the 1968 and 1972 presidential elections set in motion major internal reforms but also attempts by the DNC to produce a party image appealing to Democratic voters supporting liberal politicians like Ted Kennedy or populist conservatives such as George Wallace. While during the first Nixon term, the DNC tried to produce a policy agenda most politicians within the party were comfortable with—including a strategy to get out of Vietnam—after the 1972 election the national committee effectively gave up on trying to produce policy and instead focused on just promoting the party as a unified body, regardless of underlying tensions. However, after Democrats did regain the White House with Jimmy Carter's victory in 1976, the DNC once again declined. With Democrats safely in the majority in Congress, Carter saw little value in "his" national committee, refused to engage in fundraising efforts, and largely let it languish during his time in office.

In contrast, both Richard Nixon and Gerald Ford used the RNC to try to promote themselves and their administrations. During Nixon's first term in office, the RNC used new publicity tools to attack Democrats who opposed Nixon, while after Watergate Ford used the RNC to try to present a new image of a

National Party Organizations and Party Brands in American Politics. Boris Heersink, Oxford University Press.
© Oxford University Press 2023. DOI: 10.1093/oso/9780197695104.003.0006

more open and softer Republican Party to voters. While the RNC faced major financial limitations in this period due to Watergate, it still tried to introduce new major publicity efforts. But while Republicans were successful in winning the White House they remained in the minority in Congress. This problem was exacerbated after the Watergate scandal resulted in congressional defeats in the 1974 and 1976 elections. After the 1976 presidential election, the GOP was also back out of the White House, and the RNC faced what appeared to be an existential crisis of having to reintroduce a deeply unpopular party to voters— and having to do so in the middle of ongoing clashes between moderates and conservatives within the GOP.

After Carter's victory, Bill Brock—a former senator from Tennessee—was elected RNC chair and engaged in a major effort of reaching out to many different voting groups. While this included an early attempt at bringing in (White) evangelical Christians, Brock's chairmanship was focused mostly on the reintroduction of the Bliss-era focus on Black voters. Under Brock, the RNC invested in training Republican politicians on how to appeal to Black voters in their states or districts, and it also tried to improve its broader public image through specific publicity programs and by improving relationships with Black leaders such as Jesse Jackson.

The Age of (Counter-)Reform: The DNC, 1969–1976

As of January 1968, Lyndon Johnson (LBJ) was still the man most likely to be nominated at the Democratic convention in Chicago. Facing only Minnesota senator Eugene McCarthy as his anti–Vietnam War opponent in the primaries, LBJ's renomination still appeared certain. However, a series of events in the beginning of the year, including the Tet Offensive and McCarthy's better-than-expected performance in the New Hampshire primary, pushed New York senator Robert F. Kennedy (JFK's brother and a longtime antagonist of LBJ) to begin his own presidential campaign. In response to this and the increasingly dire situation in Vietnam, LBJ announced in March 1968 he would no longer be a candidate.[1] The subsequent nomination process deeply divided the party. In 1968, delegate allocation to the Democratic convention followed a mixed approach. A minority of states held primaries and pledged their delegates to presidential candidates on the basis of voter preferences. But most delegates were still allocated on the basis of state party leader preferences. After LBJ dropped

---

[1] "LBJ Tells Nation He Won't Run," *Washington Post*, April 1, 1968.

out, Vice President Hubert Humphrey became the de facto administration candidate but waited to announce his candidacy until after registration deadlines for the primaries had passed. As a result, Humphrey focused on swaying party leaders who controlled the majority of unpledged delegates at the convention, while McCarthy and Kennedy ran against each other in the primaries.

While the delegate math was always in favor of Humphrey on this basis, Kennedy's assassination after the California primary guaranteed his nomination. But the Democratic convention was overshadowed by clashes between antiwar protesters and the Chicago police. These clashes followed protests and riots that had already ripped apart American cities after the assassination of Martin Luther King Jr. in April that year. But the Chicago riots underlined just how divided the Democratic Party had become over the war in Vietnam. In Chicago, antiwar protesters were brutally attacked by Mayor Richard Daley's Chicago police department—scenes Senator Abraham Ribicoff (CT) described as "Gestapo tactics"[2] during his convention speech. The convention and the Chicago riots also played into Republican presidential nominee Richard Nixon's law-and-order message in the general election. In November, just four years after LBJ had won one of the biggest presidential election victories in American history, Humphrey went down in defeat.

To be sure, Humphrey's loss was closer than the perfect storm of 1968 might have suggested. In the popular vote, Humphrey and Nixon were less than one percentage point apart. More importantly, Nixon's electoral college majority—301 votes to Humphrey's 191, with former Democratic Alabama governor George Wallace winning the remaining 46 votes as the American Independent Party candidate—came about because Nixon won several states by a small margin, and even a small shift in votes to Humphrey could have denied Nixon a majority of the electoral vote.[3] Additionally, Democrats retained large majorities in Congress (see Figure 6.1). Combined, the results created a complicated assignment for the DNC: on the one hand, the party was in clear need of reform, but, on the other hand, the election was close enough that the party could not afford to alienate any of its current voters, while still needing to improve somewhat among voters who voted for Nixon or Wallace.

[2] Daley reportedly responded from the convention floor by yelling "Fuck you, you Jew son of a bitch! You lousy motherfucker! Go home!" Quoted in: Lawrence O'Donnell, *Playing with Fire: The 1968 Election and the Transformation of American Politics* (New York: Penguin Books, 2017), 368.

[3] For example, Nixon won California (his home state) by around three percentage points. Had Humphrey won California, that alone would have dropped Nixon below 270 electoral votes, and the election would have been decided by the House of Representatives. Nixon also won Alaska, Delaware, Illinois, Missouri, New Jersey, Ohio, and Wisconsin by less than five percentage points. Combined, those states represented 139 electoral votes.

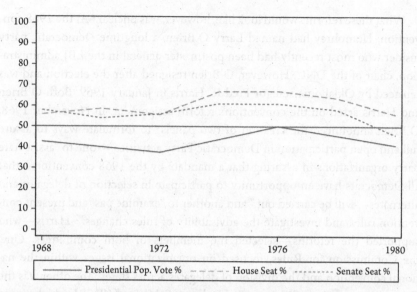

Figure 6.1. Democratic electoral performance in presidential, House, and Senate elections, 1968–1980. *Source: Congressional Quarterly's Guide to U.S. Elections,* 7th ed. (Washington, DC: Congressional Quarterly, 2016).

In the period 1969–1972, the Democratic Party prioritized altering the rules and regulations underlying the selection of delegates to future national conventions as part of its broader goal of reuniting the party for 1972. The origin of these reforms lay in the 1968 convention. Even before delegates met, an ad hoc committee chaired by Iowa governor Harold Hughes had begun assessing the process through which Democratic state parties that did not rely on primaries selected their convention delegates. The resulting report, *The Democratic Choice,* identified numerous problems in the existing system and recommended that the party take action against racial discrimination, set new rules requiring popular input in the selection of convention delegates in all states, and abolish the unit rule, which made it possible to have a state's full delegation vote for the same candidate.[4] At the convention, *The Democratic Choice* was used as the basis for a minority report in the DNC Rules Committee, which subsequently was brought up for a vote on the full convention floor, where it passed with a small majority.[5]

[4] William J. Crotty, *Decision for the Democrats: Reforming the Party Structure* (Baltimore, MD: The Johns Hopkins University Press, 1978), 14–17.

[5] As Philip Klinkner notes, Humphrey—who had a majority of delegates supporting him at the convention—could have stopped the minority report from being endorsed by the convention. However, Humphrey left the vote open to the delegates as an attempt at reaching out to McCarthy and his supporters. See: Philip A. Klinkner, *The Losing Parties: Out-Party National Committees, 1956–1993* (New Haven, CT: Yale University Press, 1994), 91.

What these reforms would look like, however, was unclear.[6] At the 1968 convention, Humphrey had named Larry O'Brien, a longtime Democratic party insider who most recently had been postmaster general in the LBJ administration, chair of the DNC. However, O'Brien resigned after the election and was replaced by Oklahoma senator Fred R. Harris in January 1969. Both O'Brien and Harris acted on the convention's reform assignment. In November 1968, O'Brien announced the creation of two panels "to formulate ways to assure full and open participation in Democratic Party activities"—one to "assist state party organizations in assuring that a mandate by the 1968 convention—that all Democrats have an opportunity to participate in selection of delegates and alternates—will be carried out," and another to "examine past and present convention rules and investigate the advisability of rules changes."[7] Harris—who supported the reforms—selected the members of both committees. One, the Commission for Rules, focused on organizational issues within the national convention and the division of delegates across states. The other was the Commission on Party Structure and Delegate Selection (CDSP), which would come to be known as the McGovern–Fraser committee after its two chairs, South Dakota senator George McGovern and Representative Donald Fraser of Minnesota. The CDSP's proposals would go on to alter presidential selection in the United States radically, calling on state parties to take "affirmative steps" to improve representation of women and minorities among national convention delegates, requiring states to create clear processes underlying their delegate selection, and limiting the number of delegates the state party could appoint.[8]

Harris remained DNC chair for only a year and focused his attentions predominantly on the convention reforms. Notably, Harris believed that one of the key lessons of the 1968 defeat was that supporters of Kennedy and McCarthy were unwilling to support Humphrey in the general election because they believed his nomination to be unfair. By adjusting the structure of delegate selection, Harris hoped the party could unite in 1972. After Harris announced

[6] For more on the rules changes in this period, see: Crotty, *Decision for the Democrats*; William J. Crotty, *Party Reform* (New York: Longman, 1983); Byron E. Shafer, *Quiet Revolution: The Struggle for the Democratic Party and the Shaping of Post-Reform Politics* (New York: Russell Sage, 1983); Klinkner, *The Losing Parties*; David Plotke, "Party Reform as Failed Democratic Renewal in the United States, 1968–1972," *Studies in American Political Development* 10 (1996): 223–288; Sam Rosenfeld, *The Polarizers: Postwar Architects of Our Partisan Era* (Chicago, IL: University of Chicago Press, 2018); Adam Hilton, *True Blues: The Contentious Transformation of the Democratic Party* (Philadelphia: University of Pennsylvania Press, 2020).

[7] "O'Brien Statement," November 23, 1968, Box 176, Folder 1, Democratic National Party Files, 1961–1975, John F. Kennedy Library (hereafter cited as Democratic National Party Files, 1961–1975).

[8] Klinkner, *The Losing Parties*, 95–99.

his desire to resign, Humphrey reached out to O'Brien to suggest he should consider a second stint as DNC chair. While O'Brien initially rebuffed these advances, the executive committee of the DNC unanimously nominated him for the position anyway, and O'Brien relented.[9] While some reformers were concerned that O'Brien—as a longtime Democratic Party insider—would stifle the reform agenda, he largely supported the process for the same reasons Harris had: O'Brien believed that by making the party's internal rules fairer, party unity might be restored.[10] And, under O'Brien, the DNC determined that states would not be able to deviate from the new rules.[11] The result was a notably different delegate body at the 1972 convention: representation of Black, female, and young delegates increased dramatically in comparison with 1968, producing the most diverse convention delegation in the party's history.[12]

Aside from the reform efforts, the DNC engaged in a number of new branding activities during the first Nixon term. But the DNC's role in reframing the party's image occurred within the context of its financial difficulties. With donors unwilling to provide the committee with funding after the disasters that befell the party in 1968, the DNC built up a deficit of $6.2 million by the end of the campaign. Additionally, the committee agreed to take on debts of the Kennedy and McCarthy primary campaigns as a sign of goodwill to the dove wing of the party. With each campaign owing around $1 million, the DNC was thus more than $8 million in debt, separate from its regular monthly expenses.[13] The day after being elected treasurer in March 1970, Bob Strauss was informed that the committee had just $11,000 in the bank, and $31,000 in payroll due the next week.[14] Strauss attempted to reconstruct the DNC's fundraising apparatus, but by the summer of 1970 O'Brien could only report that, while the DNC's debt had now grown to $9.3 million, the committee was at least "maintaining a balance"[15]— that is, it was no longer increasing its debt, but it was not actively paying it off either.

---

[9] O'Brien wrote in his autobiography that this "amused and pleased" Humphrey, who told him, "We've got you on the spot now." See: Lawrence F. O'Brien, *No Final Victories: A Life in Politics from John F. Kennedy to Watergate* (New York: Ballantine Books, 1974), 276.

[10] Shafer, *Quiet Revolution*, 250–251.

[11] Ibid., 255.

[12] By Crotty's measures the average rate of Black representation increased from 5.5% of delegates in 1968 to 15% in 1972. Female delegate representation increased from 13% to 40%. Meanwhile, delegates under 30 years old made up just 4% of delegates in 1968 but in 1972 represented 21% of the delegation. See: Crotty, *Decision for the Democrats*, 143–144.

[13] Klinkner, *The Losing Parties*, 93.

[14] Kathryn J. McGarr, *The Whole Damn Deal: Robert Strauss and the Art of Politics* (New York: Public Affairs, 2011), 83.

[15] Transcript "Issues and Answers," August 30, 1970, Box 228, Folder 6, Democratic National Party Files, 1961–1975.

Despite these difficult circumstances, the DNC did manage to increase its branding role in comparison with its lackluster performance during the Johnson term—a change reflected in the *New York Times* coverage it received during the Harris–O'Brien era. Figure 6.2 shows the results of negative binomial regressions in which the combined term of Harris and O'Brien as DNC chairs is the independent variable, and the lagged monthly *Times* coverage of DNC branding and service activities are the dependent variables. In this model, the data is limited to just those articles covering the DNC that were published between January 1965 and June 1972 (the last full month of O'Brien's term as chair)—thereby comparing *Times* coverage of the DNC under Nixon's first term with that during LBJ's presidency after the 1964 election. While there was no statistically significant change in *Times* coverage of DNC service activities, the coverage of branding activities increased (significant at the 0.05 level). Notably, the results for each individual activity as a separate variable show positive but not statistically significant results—suggesting that the increase in branding was the product of small but, when combined, meaningful increases across all categories.

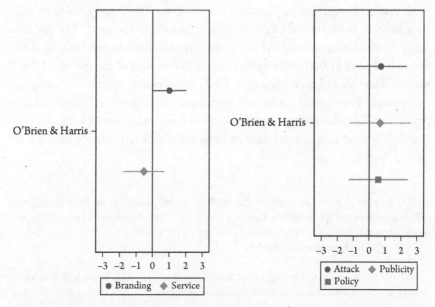

Figure 6.2. Negative binomial regressions of Fred Harris and Lawrence O'Brien's DNC chairmanships on monthly (lagged) *New York Times* coverage of DNC branding and service activities, 1965–1972. *Note:* This model includes variables controlling for presidential and midterm election years, a measure of *New York Times* length, and DNC scandals. The data coverage is limited to articles published between January 1965 and June 1972 covering only the DNC. *Source:* Data collected by author.

After Harris's resignation, O'Brien began reorganizing the DNC—arguing that "we need an organization that can take full advantage of the most up to date campaign and communications technology [...]."[16] O'Brien hired a new press secretary and a director of communications (John Stewart, a former Humphrey staffer).[17] Additionally, O'Brien invested in the DNC's research division, updated its campaign manuals, and organized meetings bringing together DNC and congressional staffers.[18] O'Brien also intended to play an "aggressive"[19] role in setting the tone for the 1970 congressional elections. O'Brien believed that the DNC was "the proper forum, indeed the only forum, through which the party might be united" and that the lack of an obvious spokesperson for the party "demanded that I speak out forcefully for the party, despite the risk of offending some members of Congress."[20] O'Brien did so by attacking Nixon and Vice President Spiro Agnew on their administration's economic policies and their "politics of fear"[21] in response to Vietnam and civil rights protests. O'Brien also made his own policy proposals, including a new plan of revenue sharing between the federal government and states, which included funding for welfare, education, and jobs for the unemployed.[22]

During the 1970 midterm campaign the DNC produced *FACT*—"an economically printed but information-packed newsletter"[23]—as well as a series of other publications intended to help Democratic candidates produce a coherent message, such as "Demo-Quotes," "a compendium of what leading Democrats are saying on key issues,"[24] and materials attacking Nixon and Agnew.

And, similar to the Republican *Comment* project from the 1960s, the DNC created its own series of radio programs. Bill Quinn, a Black reporter who was named DNC publications director in July 1970, became the host of *Black Voices*—a weekly radio show in which he interviewed political figures and which was distributed for free to soul-oriented radio stations across the United States.[25]

[16] "Democrats Shift National Staff," *New York Times*, May 17, 1970.

[17] Ibid.

[18] O'Brien, *No Final Victories*, 277–278.

[19] Ibid., 277.

[20] Ibid., 279.

[21] Ibid.

[22] "O'Brien Proposes Alternatives to Revenue-Sharing Program," *New York Times*, February 21, 1971.

[23] Lawrence F. O'Brien to Members and Friends of the Democratic Party, "A Year's-End Report on the State of the Democratic Party," December 27, 1970, Box 224, Folder 3, Democratic National Party Files, 1961–1975.

[24] Ibid.

[25] "Quinn Named DNC Publications Director," DNC News Release, July 29, 1970, Box 224, Folder 4, Democratic National Party Files, 1961–1975; Memo from Bill Quinn to John Stewart, "Black Communications Machinery," Box 226, Folder 6, Democratic National Party Files, 1961–1975.

The National Action Council, the DNC's youth organization, created a similar radio show called *Student Perspective: Washington*, which provided "weekly, five-minute taped interviews to campus radio stations."[26] Additionally, the National Action Council planned to "utilize campus, labor and underground print media with specially prepared press materials."[27]

With the DNC effectively broke, O'Brien also tried—with limited success— to convince major networks to provide the DNC with free airtime.[28] However, the networks were hesitant to give time to the Democrats in part because the Nixon administration put considerable pressure on them to limit opposition voices. Indeed, the DNC at times found it hard to convince CBS or ABC to even *sell* the committee airtime. In January 1970, two long-term Democratic donors proposed funding a prime time television show created by the DNC that would include a 25-minute documentary and a five-minute appeal for contributions by viewers to the Democratic Party. CBS refused to sell the DNC airtime.[29] Still, in July 1970, CBS provided the DNC with 25 minutes of free airtime for a program called *Loyal Opposition*.[30] The *New York Times* described the program as an "innovative format"[31]: clips of Nixon "making his pledges and predictions on the economy, the war, and other issues—[were] followed by [O'Brien's] factual rebuttals telling what he had actually done."[32] The program tackled a number of issues, including the state of the economy, the unemployment rate, crime, civil rights, pollution, and the extension of the Vietnam War into Cambodia.[33] In response, Republicans appealed to the FCC to rule that the RNC should have the right to create a response program to the DNC broadcast on CBS.[34]

[26] National Action Council—Status Report, September 1971, Box 235, Folder 4, Democratic National Party Files, 1961–1975.

[27] Ibid.

[28] O'Brien, *No Final Victories*, 281.

[29] See: ". . . and Television for Congress," *New York Times*, August 14, 1970; "Democrats Weigh Plea on C.B.S. Ban," *New York Times*, March 22, 1970; "O'Brien Is Gloomy on 1972 Prospect," *New York Times*, March 29, 1970; "Democrats Seek Right to TV Time," *New York Times*, May 20, 1970; "A.B.C. Eases Curb on TV Fund Pleas," *New York Times*, June 16, 1970.

[30] "Democrats Charge Nixon with 'Performance Gap,'" *New York Times*, July 8, 1970; "Democrats Zero in on Their Target: Nixon," *New York Times*, July 12, 1970.

[31] "Democrats Charge Nixon with 'Performance Gap,'" *New York Times*, July 8, 1970.

[32] O'Brien, *No Final Victories*, 281.

[33] "Democrats Charge Nixon with 'Performance Gap,'" *New York Times*, July 8, 1970. Note that "several" CBS stations did not air the program. See: "TV: Changing News Face," *New York Times*, August 3, 1970.

[34] "Reply to 'Loyal Opposition' Appealed," *New York Times*, August 21, 1970. Stewart, during an appearance the National Conference on Citizen's Rights in Broadcasting in October, 1970, described the DNC's attempts at forcing networks to provide free airtime as follows: "Upon assuming the chairmanship of the Democratic National Committee in March, Larry O'Brien set to work on several fronts—probing, proposing, criticizing, and negotiating—in pursuit of greater access and exposure

While the *Loyal Opposition* program was intended to result in at least four more broadcasts, CBS postponed additional episodes until after the November mid-term elections.[35] In April 1971, after a major Nixon speech on the Vietnam War, the DNC was provided with free airtime on ABC, which it used to invite several of the party's presidential candidates to discuss the war with the goal of providing a "thoughtful, low-key treatment of a highly emotional and difficult issue for Democrats" while noting that within the Democratic Party a consensus had formed that the United States would need to set "a time for fixed withdrawal of all U.S. forces"[36] from the region.

This consensus on U.S. withdrawal from Vietnam was in part the product of activities by a new organization formed by the DNC: the Democratic Policy Council (DPC), created in January 1969 to "monitor the Nixon administration's programs" and study "domestic and international problems and issuing reports and recommendations."[37] The DPC was based on the Democratic Advisory Council (DAC), which Harris believed had produced a winning policy agenda for the 1960 election. However, Democratic leaders did not want the DPC to be as antagonistic as the DAC: Humphrey was selected as the council's chair, and Harris expected Democratic congressional leaders to be more open to cooperation as "Senate majority leader Mike Mansfield, and the new Whip, Edward M. Kennedy, have a national outlook that Mr. Johnson and Mr. Rayburn did not have."[38]

In an op-ed published in the *Los Angeles Times*, Humphrey explained that "without a Democratic President in the White House, there should be widespread discussion and debate within our party. What the Democratic Party is trying to do, through its Policy Council, is create new approaches and new

---

on television for the opposition party. Seven months later we have learned a lot; we have kicked up some dust; and we have accomplished very little." See: Remarks by John G. Stewart at the National Conference on Citizens' Rights in Broadcasting, New York, October 26, 1970, Box 224, Folder 3, Democratic National Party Files, 1961–1975.

[35] O'Brien, *No Final Victories*, 282. See also: "C.B.S. Offers Free Time to Critics of White House," *New York Times*, June 23, 1970.

[36] Memo from John Stewart to Lawrence F. O'Brien, Folder 11, Box 188, Democratic National Party Files, 1961–1975; "A.B.C. Gives Democrats Reply Time," *New York Times*, April 10, 1971; "Democrats Get Time on ABC; NBC Refuses," *Washington Post*, April 10, 1971.

[37] "Humphrey Expected to Head Democrat Council," *Los Angeles Times*, January 22, 1969.

[38] "Harris Is Named National Chairman by Democrats," *New York Times*, January 15, 1969; "Humphrey Expected to Head Democrat Council," *Los Angeles Times*, January 22, 1969. Democrats in the Senate formed their own Democratic Policy Committee to "delineate Democratic positions" on topics where there was "a substantial degree of unity among members of the party" in the Democratic caucus. The Senate group was announced after the DNC had voted to create the DPC but before the council was organized. See: "Senate Democratic Unit Moves to 'Delineate' Party Positions," *New York Times*, May 21, 1969.

answers to the challenges of the 1970s."[39] The DNC announced the members of the DPC in September 1969. Harris had previously declared that the DPC would be made up predominantly of self-identified liberals, and among the 20 members of its executive committee only one—South Carolina governor Robert E. McNair—was seen as a conservative. Other members included Senator Edmund Muskie, Hawaii senator Daniel K. Inouye, and Governors John Dempsey (CT) and Forrest H. Anderson (MT). Combined, the DPC members represented, as one Democrat described it, "a frankly liberal group."[40]

The DPC's first policy statement was released in February 1970. In this document, which was presented to the media as "a midterm platform"[41] and was distributed to Democrats across the country, the DPC opposed further antiballistic missile deployment and proposed a ban on missile tests by the United States.[42] The DPC also proposed increasing resources for law enforcement but called on the Senate to reject the Supreme Court nomination of G. Harrold Carswell on the basis of his civil rights record.[43] Additionally, Humphrey endorsed the party reforms—arguing that "the days of racial discrimination, unit rule votes, closed caucuses, and machine controlled selection of delegates are over."[44] Like the DAC before it, the DPC formed a number of subcommittees that were to deal with specific policy issues, such as arms control and economic affairs.[45] The DPC's Committee on National Priorities proposed new welfare programs, including an income maintenance program—which were considerably more liberal than those proposed by Democratic Representative Wilbur Mills (AR), the chair of the Ways and Means committee in the House,[46] and criticized the Nixon administration's "distorted priorities [...] that [...] short-changed education, health care, the fight against crime and other programs."[47] And the Committee

[39] "Report of Democratic Party Death Greatly Exaggerated," *Los Angeles Times*, February 23, 1970.

[40] "Humphrey Will Head Party Rebuilding Effort," *Los Angeles Times*, September 17, 1969.

[41] "Democrat Council Asks for Defeat of Carswell," *Los Angeles Times*, February 11, 1970.

[42] "Statement by Democrats," *New York Times*, February 11, 1970.

[43] "Democrat Council Asks for Defeat of Carswell."

[44] "Report of Democratic Party Death Greatly Exaggerated."

[45] "Democrats Organize Arms Unit," *Washington Post*, November 8, 1969; "Democrats Naming 'Budget Truth' Unit," *New York Times*, January 29, 1970; "Democrats Declare Budget Unrealistic," *New York Times*, February 23, 1970; "Democrats Appoint Environment Panel," *New York Times*, July 20, 1970; "Kennedy-Johnson Economists Blast Nixon's 'Sorry' Record," *Washington Post*, August 16, 1970.

[46] "Harris Proposes Alternative to Nixon's Welfare Plan," *New York Times*, February 11, 1970; "Democratic Policy Council Asks Total Federalization of Welfare," *New York Times*, May 14, 1971; "Big Welfare Boost Asked by Democrats," *Los Angeles Times*, May 14, 1971.

[47] "Democrats Assail Nixon's Priorities," *New York Times*, April 30, 1970. See also: "Nixon Urged to Act on Domestic Needs," *New York Times*, May 21, 1971.

on Economic Affairs attacked Nixon for his fiscal policies, and his failure to curb inflation, calling on the government to increase its spending to help economic development.[48]

Arguably most important among the DPC's subcommittees was the Committee on International Affairs, chaired by Averell Harriman, which produced policies on the Vietnam War. An initial statement adopted in January 1970 sharply criticized Nixon's conduct of the war.[49] The statement represented a major shift from the Vietnam plank included in the 1968 Democratic platform, which had dismissed unilateral withdrawal of American forces in Vietnam. Instead, the DPC called for "a firm and unequivocal commitment" to withdraw all American troops from Vietnam within 18 months.[50] In 1971, the DPC called on Congress to cut off all funding for the Vietnam War by the end of the year.[51] In 1972, in the run-up to that year's Democratic National Convention, the DPC assisted in drafting the convention's platform plank on Vietnam, which stated that "Indochina represents a continuing waste of billions of dollars but even that pales into insignificance when compared to what it is doing to our society, the Vietnamese people and to the respect for our judgment and decency which once pervaded the international community."[52] The DPC also called on an agreement with the Soviet Union to expand the Strategic Arms Limitations Talks (SALT) to include additional types of nuclear missiles that the Nixon administration had excluded.[53]

While the DPC was not as much of a priority as the reform efforts, and—in the assessment of political scientist Philip Klinkner—largely issued "statements that were, for the most part, Democratic party boilerplate,"[54] O'Brien saw the DPC as an important tool to produce a new policy agenda. Stewart, who served as the DPC's executive director, notes that the DPC mostly offered the party "an internal forum for thrashing things out and healing wounds that needed to be healed" and that "the Policy Council gave a lot of groups within the party an opportunity to be heard, but it also represented an attempt to contain and

---

[48] "Democrats Score Fund Bill Vetoes," *New York Times*, August 16, 1970; "Ackley Assails Nixon's Policies to Spur Economy," *New York Times*, February 14, 1971; "Ackley Hits Nixon on Economy," *Washington Post*, July 11, 1971. The DPC also regularly attacked Vice President Spiro Agnew's hostility toward the press; "Democrats Say Agnew Threatens Free Speech," *Los Angeles Times*, November 18, 1969; "Agnew Blasts CBS, Humphrey Differs," *Washington Post*, March 25, 1971.

[49] "Democrats Weigh Shift on Vietnam," *New York Times*, February 8, 1970.

[50] "Democratic Council Asks Pullout within 18 Months," *New York Times*, February 10, 1970.

[51] "Democratic Policy Body Oks Move to Curb War," *Los Angeles Times*, March 25, 1971; "Democratic Council Backs Funds Cutoff for the War by '72," *New York Times*, March 25, 1971.

[52] Quoted in Klinkner, *The Losing Parties*, 101.

[53] Ibid.

[54] Ibid., 100.

channel the debate."[55] While this made the DPC's output less newsworthy than the DAC's clearly liberal policy statements, this was largely by design. After the 1970 midterms, in which Democrats maintained their majorities in both House and Senate, Stewart and O'Brien began to re-conceptualize the DPC's role in the run-up to the 1972 presidential election. With a large and ideologically diverse group of Democrats looking to run for the presidency in 1972, O'Brien feared a contentious presidential nomination fight. O'Brien hoped to use the DNC to "try to keep our party's numerous presidential contenders from tearing the party further apart in the 1972 primaries."[56] Stewart wrote a memo after the 1970 midterms suggesting the DPC should no longer be "a definer of rigid positions" but, rather, function as "a sounding board for varying views"[57] on which "Democrats generally thought to be contenders for the presidential nomination in 1972" that were not already members would join. This, in effect, would make the DPC "a kind of preconvention platform committee."[58] Stewart's proposal argued that the DPC "should strive to avoid procedures that force its membership to establish what purport to be highly refined Democratic 'positions' on a wide range of controversial matters."[59]

In January 1971 O'Brien proposed the idea to Humphrey and Muskie and asked the DPC to "assist in producing this working document on which the Platform Committee will base its decisions at the time of the 1972 National Convention."[60] To ensure success, O'Brien tried to get buy-in from the party's presidential hopefuls. In February 1971, O'Brien brought together Senators Humphrey, Muskie, Harris, McGovern, Ted Kennedy (MA), and Henry "Scoop" Jackson (WA) for a meeting at which he proposed all presidential candidates should be involved in the creation of the party's platform. O'Brien argued that if the major candidates all signed off on the same policies, this would "minimize intraparty bloodletting"[61] in the primaries, creating a stronger position for whoever would win the nomination. The attendees supported the proposal, and Senators McGovern, Birch Bayh (IN), and Harold E. Hughes (IA)—all, at the time, (potential) presidential candidates in 1972—subsequently joined the DPC to help develop new policy issues that "Democratic candidates can use effectively in the primaries, and subsequently, in the general election."[62] To help achieve this, the DPC organized a series of hearings across the country focusing

---

[55] Ibid., 102.

[56] O'Brien, No Final Victories, 290.

[57] "Democratic Policy Unit Seeks Candidate Unity," Los Angeles Times, December 23, 1970.

[58] Ibid.

[59] Ibid.

[60] Ibid.

[61] O'Brien, No Final Victories, 291.

[62] Memorandum, June 14, 1971, Box 233, Folder 4, Democratic National Party Files, 1961–1975.

on specific topics—including issues like pollution and the environment—with Democratic elected politicians, former administration officials, academics, union leaders, and other notables appearing before the Policy Council subcommittees to testify publicly as to what the Democratic Party's policies should be for the 1972 platform.[63] By late spring 1972, the DPC had released 19 policy reports.[64]

Of course, there was only so much the DNC could do to forge unity, in no small part due to George Wallace's ongoing role in the party. After running as a third-party candidate in 1968, Wallace ran for governor as a Democrat in 1970 and barely defeated incumbent Albert Brewer in a primary run-off on the basis of a deeply racist campaign. In January 1972, Wallace announced he would run for the presidency again, but this time in the Democratic primaries.[65] The announcement caused considerable debate within the DNC. Staffer Bill Welsh suggested O'Brien attempt to block Wallace in the Florida primary on the basis that he could not be considered a "bona fide candidate for the Democratic nomination."[66] Welsh also called on O'Brien to publicly dismiss Wallace's candidacy, since

> a statement by the Chairman could be tactically useful in alerting the national party to the duplicity of the Wallace candidacy. He is a racist [. . .] a spoiler [who] boasts that his 1968 candidacy beat [Humphrey] [. . .] and the morality of his politics can certainly be questioned. A strong anti-Wallace statement before the results of the Florida primary are in, would be much better to live with this year, than trying to deal with him after he has won that primary![67]

But while DNC staffers believed Wallace was bad for the party, there was no agreement on how to deal with him, as DNC deputy chair Stan Greigg suggested O'Brien would be better off staying out of the matter entirely.[68] In the end,

[63] For example, the Democratic Party Platform Briefing held in Washington, DC, in May 1972 included testimony from Senator William Proxmire (WI), AFL-CIO president George Meany, former secretary of commerce John T. Connor, and former Budget Bureau director Charles Schultze. See: "Opening Remarks, Democratic Party Platform Briefing, Washington D.C.," May 15, 1972, Box 193, Folder 13, Democratic National Party Files, 1961–1975. See also: Lawrence F. O'Brien to Mrs. Mildred Jeffrey, July 28, 1971, Box 176, Folder 12, Democratic National Party Files, 1961–1975.

[64] "Opening Remarks, Democratic Party Platform Briefing, Washington D.C.," May 15, 1972, Box 193, Folder 13, Democratic National Party Files, 1961–1975.

[65] "Wallace Running, but as a Democrat," *Washington Post,* January 14, 1972.

[66] Memo from Bill Welsh to Lawrence F. O'Brien, January 5, 1972, Box 240, Folder Governor George Wallace 1972, Democratic National Party Files, 1961–1975.

[67] Ibid.

[68] Memo from Stan Greigg to Lawrence F. O'Brien, January 10, 1972, Box 240, Folder Governor George Wallace 1972, Democratic National Party Files, 1961–1975.

O'Brien did not attempt to block Wallace's participation in the primaries but did reject his candidacy, stating that "[no] one, including George Wallace, seriously believes Governor Wallace to be legitimately contending for the Democratic presidential nomination," and that "in the Democratic primaries as well as in the Fall election, a vote for George Wallace is a vote for Richard Nixon."[69]

But the DNC softened its stance toward Wallace after he pledged he would not support anybody but the Democratic nominee during the general election.[70] During the primaries, Wallace performed well, winning Florida, Tennessee, North Carolina, Maryland, and Michigan, and coming in second in Wisconsin, Pennsylvania, and Indiana. However, a failed assassination attempt left Wallace paralyzed and unable to continue his presidential campaign. With the threat of a Wallace nomination gone, O'Brien visited him at the hospital, where he had a "long and delightful visit."[71] In his memoirs, O'Brien expressed his hope at the time that "[Wallace] would return to our party"[72] and at the convention, Wallace—now confined to a wheelchair—was allowed to speak. During his speech, Wallace called on an unsympathetic audience of delegates, to return the Democratic Party to "the average citizen" and abandon "the intellectual super-pseudo snobbery that has controlled it for so many years."[73]

Despite the elimination of Wallace as a potential nominee, the DNC still faced the issue of how to promote a party that nominated George McGovern but also saw Democrats from all ideological wings win support as presidential candidates. This issue is illustrated by the planning the DNC put into a major innovation of the era: the first Democratic Party telethon. As the DNC continued to struggle with raising money, funding the 1972 campaign became a key concern. In the early spring of 1972, entrepreneur John Y. Brown suggested the DNC hold a telethon—which would simultaneously promote the party and bring in new donors.[74] This first DNC telethon was broadcast on ABC before the start of the 1972 convention.[75] During the show, politicians and celebrities—including Andy Williams, Carol Channing, Milton Berle, Lauren Bacall, Burt Bacharach, Groucho Marx, and Shirley MacLaine—presented the Democratic

[69] Statement by Democratic National Chairman Lawrence F. O'Brien, January 13, 1972, Box 240, Folder Governor George Wallace 1972, Democratic National Party Files, 1961–1975. See also: "Wallace Candidacy Scored by Democratic Chairman," *Washington Post*, January 15, 1972.

[70] Lawrence F. O'Brien, *No Final Victories*, 314.

[71] "O'Brien Deplores Attempts to Curb Wallace Delegates," *Washington Post*, May 25, 1972.

[72] O'Brien, *No Final Victories*, 314.

[73] "Unsympathetic Party Hears Wallace," *Washington Post*, July 12, 1972.

[74] John W. Ellwood and Robert J. Spitzer, "The Democratic National Telethons: Their Successes and Failures," *The Journal of Politics* 41, no. 3 (August, 1979): 828–864.

[75] "Democrats Plan Fund-Raising Telethon on Eve of National Convention, DNC Press Release, March 21, 1972, Box 239, Folder 11, Democratic National Party Files, 1961–1975.

party as "the people's party."[76] Though some supporters of George McGovern refused to participate in the program since all the money went directly to the DNC,[77] the telethon was successful, earning the DNC $1.9 million in net profits and providing the party with 19 hours of television time.

But in designing how to fill those hours, the DNC ran into the problem of how to come up with a message that was appealing to all Democratic voters. As Stewart noted in a memo:

> The program's appeal must be as broad as the constituency that will be needed to win in November. [. . .] The program's format and tone are vital in holding together this broad constituency for a simple reason: as soon as specific issues are focused upon, with the exception of the economy, the coalition begins to fragment and dissolve. The surfacing of specific issues will generate a process of exclusion that, little by little, will strip off essential audience segments.[78]

That is, the DNC could not embrace any particular message for fear of alienating at least some of its audience. In a report produced by public opinion researcher Albert Hadley Cantril, the DNC was advised that its telethon should avoid "a hard-line or a soft-line," should not make "a distinctly partisan or anti-Nixon appeal" nor "an ideological appeal," and should not talk about "the party of the people" since this "translated in today's language means "welfare," "handouts," etc.," and that the program should not "create situations in which the divisions within the Democratic Party surface"—meaning, it should "not let the program appear to be a pro-McGovern, or pro-Humphrey program—or anti-Wallace program." With all that off the table, the only remaining option was to center on three, somewhat meaningless, messages: "we are a great people," "it is a time for unity," but also for a "return to individualism."[79]

The 1972 convention itself did not help party unity either. With major battles over policy waged by the delegates, the Democratic platform became one of the most liberal in the party's history. While some of the planks were in line with positions taken by the DNC and DPC—including withdrawal from

[76] "Democrats End TV Fund Appeal," *New York Times,* July 10, 1972.

[77] Strauss had set up the telethon in such a way that the proceeds went into a trust for which he himself was the trustee. The money could not be used to pay for the 1972 general election campaign and, instead, was used to help pay off part of the DNC's debts. See: McGarr, *The Whole Damn Deal,* 98.

[78] Memo from John G. Stewart to Lawrence F. O'Brien, May 22, 1972, Box 245, Folder 13, Democratic National Party Files, 1961–1975.

[79] Memo from Albert H. Cantril to John Stewart, May 22, 1972, Box 245, Folder 14, Democratic National Party Files, 1961–1975.

Vietnam—others, such as guaranteed jobs for all Americans and guaranteed family income, were considerably more left-wing. The convention also proved unpredictable: George McGovern was nominated on the first ballot, but the farcical nomination of Thomas Eagleton as his vice-presidential candidate saw delegates nominate 76 candidates (including a fictional one—*All in the Family's* Archie Bunker).[80] The fall campaign proved not much better. In the days after the convention, news reports revealed Eagleton had received shock therapy as treatment for depression. While McGovern initially promised to keep him on the ticket, mere days later he asked Eagleton to drop out. After being turned down by a number of high-profile Democrats, such as Kennedy, Muskie, and Humphrey, Eagleton eventually was replaced with Sargent Shriver—the former director of the Peace Corps and brother-in-law to John F. Kennedy (JFK).[81]

After all this, Nixon easily defeated McGovern, winning more than 60% of the popular vote and losing only Massachusetts and Washington, DC. Across the country, Nixon's success was remarkable: in all but four of the states he won, his margin of victory was in double digits. The only silver lining for Democrats was that the party maintained its majorities in Congress.

One of the casualties of the 1972 defeat was Jean Westwood, who had been selected by McGovern as DNC chair. Westwood had been active in Democratic party politics in Utah since the 1960s and a member of the DNC since 1968.[82] Westwood was the first female chair of either national committee, but while she was not a liberal hard-liner, she came to represent the failed McGovern presidential campaign and the reform efforts many Democrats blamed for McGovern's nomination and the left-wing platform. As Congressman James O'Hara concluded, the moderate and conservative view was that the "casual Democrat, the uninvolved Democrat"[83] had not been represented at the '72 convention due to the decline of traditional party machines and the lack of influence of organized labor. Another Democratic party regular argued that the McGovern campaign "didn't represent the Democratic party."[84]

In the aftermath of the election the anti-reform forces focused on unseating Westwood. Notably, Westwood did not receive support from McGovern, who later stated that "[it] wasn't that I was unhappy with her—I just didn't think we ought to get into a battle to keep her on after my defeat, and because of that

---

[80] "Democrats Name Western Woman Party's Chairman," *New York Times*, July 15, 1972.

[81] Jules Witcover, *Party of the People: A History of the Democrats* (New York: Random House, 2003), 586.

[82] Jean Westwood, *Madam Chair: The Political Autobiography of an Unintentional Pioneer* (Logan: Utah State University Press, 2007), 5.

[83] Cited in Klinkner, *The Losing Parties*, 107.

[84] Ibid., 108.

she was an easy target for anybody that aspired to that job."[85] That anybody was Strauss, who took Westwood out for lunch after the election to suggest she voluntarily resign—an offer she rejected. Westwood attempted to fight Strauss's candidacy—who was seen by liberals as too conservative. However, at a December 1972 Democratic Governors Association meeting, Strauss received the group's endorsement. Days later, Senate Majority Leader Mike Mansfield also endorsed him.[86] At a mid-December DNC meeting, Westwood voluntarily resigned, as it became clear that she could lose or, at best, beat Strauss only by a handful of votes. Strauss subsequently was elected chair, though with considerable opposition from the reformers on the national committee.[87]

Despite Strauss's lack of popularity with liberals, he was not an ideologue. Strauss had taken on the position of DNC treasurer under O'Brien in no small part because he was simply getting "bored" in his hometown of Dallas and moving to Washington, DC, "was a chance to enlarge my life."[88] From the moment Strauss began working at the DNC he saw his role largely as that of a salesman trying to apply his skill of "[buying] junk and [selling] equipment": "the Democratic party was a piece of junk. And I thought I could make equipment out of it."[89] But, Strauss faced the same problem as his predecessors: How do you sell a party covering the spectrum between segregationist populists like George Wallace and feminist liberals like Representative Bella Abzug (NY)?[90]

Strauss's answer was surprisingly simple. Rather than try to use his position to help one side within the party get the upper hand, Strauss decided to present the Democratic Party as a unified coalition regardless of the major schisms that existed underneath the surface. In the weeks after being elected chair, Strauss appeared in public with liberals like Ted Kennedy and Shirley Chisholm but also traveled to Alabama to meet with Wallace. In the years that followed, Strauss continuously linked liberals and conservatives within the party in the public image.[91] For example, in 1973 Strauss talked Kennedy into appearing with Wallace at a

[85] McGarr, *The Whole Damn Deal*, 112.

[86] "Put Strauss in Mrs. Westwood's Job, Democrat Governors Urge," *Los Angeles Times*, December 4, 1972; "Governors Back Westwood Rival," *New York Times*, December 4, 1972; "Strauss Is Confident, Stresses Party Unity," *Washington Post*, December 8, 1972.

[87] "Strauss Elected Democrats' Head and Vows Unity," *New York Times*, December 10, 1972; "Strauss Heads Democratic Party as Mrs. Westwood Steps Aside," *Los Angeles Times*, December 10, 1972.

[88] McGarr, *The Whole Damn Deal*, 81.

[89] Ibid.

[90] As Strauss colorfully described his task as chair, "it's a little like making love to a gorilla. You don't stop when you're tired. You stop when the gorilla's tired." See: ibid., 131.

[91] "Chairman Strauss's Coalition: A Step Back to Pragmatism," *Washington Post*, December 13, 1972; "Strauss Visits Chisholm on His Unity Campaign," *Washington Post*, December 15, 1972; "Wallace, Strauss Meet Today," *Washington Post*, December 21, 1972.

Fourth of July celebration in Wallace's honor.[92] Similarly, at the 1974 midterm convention, Strauss arranged for Barbara Jordan—a Black Congresswoman from Texas—to introduce Senator Robert C. Byrd (WV), a former member of the KKK, while at the 1976 convention Massachusetts governor Michael Dukakis was tasked with introducing Wallace.[93] Strauss did not try to have these politicians overcome any policy disagreements. Rather, he simply placed them together and hoped voters would accept the fiction of a unified party.

DNC executive director Robert Keefe argued that Strauss viewed the Democratic Party as consisting of "several disputing groups, all important to the party."[94] In Strauss's view, the party could not afford to lose either the conservative or liberal wing and thus concluded that they would need to learn to coexist. During a DNC meeting in 1973, Strauss summarized this view, stating that

> I remain committed to the proposition that our conservatives are not bigots, our business community is not evil, that our young are not irresponsible, that our minorities are not selfish, our liberals are not foolish, and that our Democratic Party is not leaderless or without purpose.[95]

Not all Democrats agreed with Strauss's strategy. In response to the election of Strauss, liberal Democrats formed the Democratic Planning Group (DPG)—an organization independent of the party funded by wealthy backers of McGovern's 1972 candidacy. On the other hand, a group of moderate Democrats formed their own group—the Coalition for a Democratic Majority (CDM).[96] With these two groups battling to drag the Democratic Party toward their ideological preference points, the stage seemed set for a brutal intra-party ideological battle.

Yet, Strauss mostly managed to retain peace within the party. Despite the anti-reform mood after the 1972 election, under Strauss the changes made to the intra-party rules were mostly modest and acceptable to the reformers.[97] Due

[92] "Kennedy Invades South for Wallace Fete Today," *Washington Post*, July 4, 1973; "Kennedy Appears with Wallace, Scores Nixon over Watergate," *Los Angeles Times*, July 5, 1973; "Kennedy Speaks at Wallace Fete," *New York Times*, July 5, 1973; McGarr, *The Whole Damn Deal*, 142–143.

[93] Ibid., 164, 195.

[94] Klinkner, *The Losing Parties*, 111.

[95] McGarr, *The Whole Damn Deal*, 137.

[96] See: Klinkner, *The Losing Parties*, 110–111; Rosenfeld, *The Polarizers*, 148; Crotty, *Decision for the Democrats*, 226–231.

[97] For a more extensive discussion of the post-1972 (counter-)reform activities by the different commissions created by the DNC in this time period, see: Klinkner, *The Losing Parties*; Robert A. Hitlin and John S. Jackson, III, "Change & Reform in the Democratic Party," *Polity* 11, no. 4 (1979): 617–633; Hilton, *True Blues*; David E. Price, *Bringing Back the Parties* (Washington, DC: CQ Press, 1984); Crotty, *Decision for the Democrats*.

to a resolution passed at the 1972 convention, in 1974, the DNC was obligated to organize a midterm convention to set policy and to approve an official party charter that would set rules for future conventions. Strauss did not support such a "mini-convention" (stating he was not the father of this idea and that he "would have practiced a little more birth control"[98] if he had been) and tried to limit its influence. A Charter Commission, chaired by North Carolina governor Terry Sanford, was tasked with preparing a party constitution that would be brought to a vote at the midterm conference. However, the conference itself did not take place until December, *after* the 1974 midterms, so as not to affect any House and Senate campaigns negatively.[99] The Charter Commission agreed on a document that mostly left the reforms of the 1969–1972 era intact, but with some notable changes, such as getting rid of mandatory quotas while still instructing the DNC to ensure full participation of women, racial and ethnic minorities, and other groups in the party.[100]

But Strauss ensured that the midterm convention would be devoid of policy. In a letter to Donald Fraser, Strauss argued that introducing "ideological debate" at the midterm convention was in direct contradiction with his goal of healing "the wounds of the past." Strauss also criticized *Toward a More Responsible Party System*—the American Political Science Association (APSA) report that had inspired Butler in the 1950s. Strauss noted that the report "has been criticized by some over the last several years" and that "political scientists have concluded that many of the suggestions employed in this document are inappropriate and dysfunctional to the American political system."[101] In this spirit, Strauss limited policy debate to only one issue: an economic platform including wage-price controls, tax reform, and public employment that Democrats in Congress already backed.[102] The resolution passed easily and the mini-convention became the Democratic "love-in"[103] Strauss intended it to be. During his address to the convention, Strauss described the Democratic Party as one of

[98] "Democrats' Charter Meeting Faces Pitfalls of Divisiveness, Boredom," *Los Angeles Times*, December 2, 1974.

[99] The DNC estimated in January 1974 that the mini-convention would cost the party $600,000. Strauss's request for suggestions from the DNC on how to pay for this produced two suggestions: a bake sale and canceling the convention. Strauss suggested, "somewhere in between that bake sale and not having the convention, there should be an additional suggestion." See: McGarr, *The Whole Damn Deal*, 157.

[100] See: Klinkner, *The Losing Parties*, 124.

[101] Cited in Rosenfeld, *The Polarizers*, 155.

[102] Price, *Bringing Back the Parties*, 276; "Democrats Chart Sweeping Economic Policy Stand," *New York Times*, December 5, 1974; "'Economic Recovery Plan' Is Offered by Democrats," *New York Times*, December 7, 1974.

[103] Crotty, *Decision for the Democrats*, 249.

pragmatic change, that has learned a lesson from 1968 and 1972. And that lesson, my friends, is that division leads to defeat. That lesson, my friends, is that the reformer and the regular, each attempting to exclude the other from decision making, in the end exclude the Democratic Party from victory, and the American people from decent government.[104]

Despite Strauss's lack of interest in policies, he did create a policy council. In 1973, Strauss announced the creation of the Democratic Advisory Council of Elected Officials (DACEO).[105] The DACEO included Democratic senators (such as Lloyd Bentsen from Texas), members of the House, governors (such as Dale Bumpers from Arkansas), mayors (such as New York City mayor John Lindsay), and longtime party stalwarts (such as Dean Rusk and W. Averell Harriman). The council was chaired by DNC insider Arthur Krim, who, as described by reporter David S. Broder, was an "amiable, elderly motion picture executive best known as a fund-raising crony of Lyndon Johnson" and who approached his role "with all the enthusiasm of a great-uncle asked to arrange a coming-out party for a particularly awkward grandniece [. . .]."[106] The DACEO produced several policy briefs, the most influential of which were a series of statements produced by an economic study group criticizing Republican economic policies and which warned that the country was on a path toward "the worst recession since the Great Depression" due to the Nixon–Ford administrations' policies.[107] As an alternative, the group proposed a series of policies including lowering taxes for low- and middle-income groups, creating public service employment programs to reduce joblessness, and setting government controls on prices, wages, and profits.[108]

But the DACEO was nowhere near as active as the DAC or DPC. The organization did not have staff until early 1974, and Krim mostly tried to ensure that members of the DACEO would not "[spike] the punch with controversy."[109] Broder described members at one of the meetings of the DACEO

---

[104] McGarr, The Whole Damn Deal, 164–165.

[105] "Woodcock Leaves Democratic Post," New York Times, January 21, 1973; "Fight Shaping Up over Future of Democratic Party Reform," Washington Post, March 1, 1973.

[106] "America's Loyal Opposition," Los Angeles Times, November 16, 1973.

[107] "Democrats Criticize GOP on Economy Mismanagement," Washington Post, September 15, 1974.

[108] "Economic Reforms Proposed," Washington Post, November 17, 1974; "Filling the Democratic Policy Gap," Washington Post, February 13, 1974; "The Economy and George Meany," Washington Post, November 14, 1974; "Democratic Plan Favors Controls if All Else Fails," New York Times, November 17, 1974.

[109] "America's Loyal Opposition," Los Angeles Times, November 16, 1973.

as "steadfastly [avoiding] taking clear stands on any of the immediate issues before the country."[110] Other newspapers concluded that Democrats still had "as many internal disputes as they had differences with Mr. Nixon" and noted that a number of study groups within the DACEO had yet to meet.[111] Strauss defended the DNC's activities in terms of policy creation, noting that while much of his attention had thus far been focused on intra-party arrangements, this was necessary because

> until the Democratic Party had begun to function once again with a reasonable degree of unity and mutual cooperation—it was obviously futile to begin with the even more difficult ask of evolving a public ideology [...] I would be the first to admit that we have a long way to go in defining workable approaches and solutions to these problems [...]. But I would also be the first to point out that the Democratic Advisory Council [...] is taking a number of steps to find these answers.[112]

Yet, while DACEO executive director John Stewart announced that the group would meet regularly in 1975, little evidence exists that it achieved much.[113]

In no small part this was due to Strauss's general lack of interest in policy: when asked once what the Democratic Party stood for, Strauss reportedly answered, "Hell, I don't know. That's not my worry."[114] But a lack of interest in policy was not the only reason Strauss limited DNC policy creation. According to DNC staffer Mark Siegel, Strauss believed the DPC had been too liberal in the 1969–1972 period and wanted to limit the extent to which the left wing of the party could use DNC-sponsored organizations to push liberal policies. Thus, Strauss tried to make sure that the DACEO would be as middle of the road as possible by appointing moderate elected officials.[115] Harry McPherson, who had been an LBJ speechwriter, headed the domestic policy group of the DACEO. After complaining to Strauss that nobody appeared to take the group seriously, Strauss reportedly responded that "I thought you, of all people, would understand what I'm trying to do. I'm trying to throw some meat to these silly people so they'll go after it and leave me alone to get something done for this party."[116]

---

[110] "Democrats Ready Plans for Post-Election Effort," *Washington Post,* June 19, 1974.

[111] "Democrats Begin Sharpening Campaign Issues and Introduce New 'Brain Trust,'" *New York Times,* June 19, 1974.

[112] Robert S. Strauss, "Rebuilding the Democratic Party," *Washington Post,* March 2, 1974.

[113] "It's Show Time for Democrats," *Los Angeles Times,* November 19, 1974.

[114] Klinkner, *The Losing Party,* 129.

[115] Adam Hilton, "The Path to Polarization: McGovern-Fraser, Counter-Reformers, and the Rise of the Advocacy Party," *Studies in American Political Development* 33, no. 1 (2019): 104.

[116] McGarr, *The Whole Damn Deal,* 163.

Strauss did regularly attack Nixon (and, later, Ford), particularly on Watergate. Because the DNC had been the victim of the Watergate burglary, the committee sued the Republican Party's Committee to Re-Elect the President (commonly referred to as CREEP) in a civil lawsuit.[117] Through the discovery process, the DNC uncovered new information about the affair until the Senate Watergate committee took over this role.[118] In April, 1973, Strauss suggested a major advertising campaign centered on Watergate and accused Nixon of "[trampling] on our constitutional separation of powers"[119] after the Saturday Night Massacre. After the release of transcripts of recordings of the Nixon tapes, Strauss commented that

I came up through the ranks in politics in Texas. I think I've seen just about everything. [...] But this reading of these tapes has upset me more than anything in my life. I told my wife over the third martini last night, I'm embarrassed to have our kids read this and think it's part of the life I'm in.[120]

More structurally, Strauss continued the telethon format: between 1972 and 1975, the DNC organized an annual telethon following the basic format of the 1972 event. Financially, the telethons were mostly successful. In the first three years, the net profit of the telethon was between $1.9 and $2.8 million each year, but the final telethon in 1975 only raised approximately $900,000 in profit. As political scientists John W. Ellwood and Robert J. Spitzer note, telethons were a "relatively inefficient way to raise political money, with at most two dollars being collected for every dollar it takes to produce a program."[121] According to Strauss, the 1973 telethon cost $2 million—half for airtime, and the other half for the show, publicity, and the phone banks necessary to raise the money—requiring a considerable number of donations to pay for the event itself.[122] However, fundraising was just part of the strategy, as the telethons provided the DNC with an opportunity to promote the party to the American public for many hours in a row on one of the main networks. DNC staffers also saw the telethons as a tool to foster intra-party unity. Partly, this was by providing state parties with a substantial part of the profits. While in 1972, Strauss kept full control of the

---

[117] "O'Brien Sues GOP Campaign," *Washington Post*, June 21, 1972; "Mitchell Linked to Attempts to Settle Suit on Watergate," *Washington Post*, April 19, 1973; "Charges Likely," *New York Times*, April 19, 1973.

[118] "Democrats May Settle Suit," *Washington Post*, August 1, 1973.

[119] "Parties' Chairmen Split on Legality," *New York Times*, October 23, 1973.

[120] "Politicians Call the Transcripts a Crisis for G.O.P.," *New York Times*, May 4, 1974.

[121] Ellwood and Spitzer, "The Democratic National Telethons," 835.

[122] "Democrats' Stars Raise Funds Here," *New York Times*, September 13, 1973.

telethon's profits for the DNC, in subsequent years the DNC shared its profits equally with state party organizations—which in turn inspired the state organizations to invest more resources in promoting the event, with as many as 100,000 Democratic volunteers participating during the 1974 telethon.[123]

The telethons were of particular pride to Strauss, who referred to the annual event as his "baby."[124] The second telethon, which took place in September 1973 and was broadcast on NBC, was a six-hour show combining "appearances by Hollywood personalities and Democratic leaders with film clips" designed to show "what the country is all about."[125] The show was hosted by actor Henry Fonda and TV host Steve Allen, and it featured appearances by stars such as Mary Tyler Moore, Jack Lemmon, and Natalie Wood, and politicians such as Kennedy, Jackson, Senator Walter Mondale (MN), Bentsen, and Wallace.[126] The 1974 telethon proved to be the high point of the tactic. Lasting for 21 hours, the telethon aired on CBS and had 31 million people watching at least part of the event, while nearly 13% of TV households watched the first hour of the show.[127] In this show, Humphrey took on the role of anchorman, discussing policy issues with Democratic mayors and governors.[128] Actors and performers such as Paul Newman, Vincent Price, Rosemary Clooney, Groucho Marx, Robert Vaughn, and Cass Elliott also appeared.[129] The final telethon, which aired in July 1975 for over 20 hours on ABC, mixed celebrity appearances by Alan Alda, Della Reese, Reverend Billy Graham, and Helen Reddy with politicians like Senators Joe Biden (DE) and John Glenn (OH), and all six presidential candidates— including former Georgia governor Jimmy Carter, Bentsen, Jackson, and Harris.[130] Yet, while initial expectations were that the event would equal the $6.9 million pledged during the 1974 telethon, numbers were considerably lower.[131] Given the considerable costs of the event, the 1975 telethon raised less

[123] Ellwood and Spitzer, "The Democratic National Telethons," 839.

[124] McGarr, *The Whole Damn Deal*, 145.

[125] "Democrats to Hold a 7-Hour Telethon," *New York Times*, August 15, 1973.

[126] McGarr, *The Whole Damn Deal*, 147–148; "Democrats Go to the Airwaves in 8-Hour TV Appeal for Funds," *Los Angeles Times*, September 16, 1973.

[127] Ellwood and Spitzer, "The Democratic National Telethons," 830, 842; "21-Hour Telethon to Benefit Democrats," *Los Angeles Times*, May 10, 1974;

[128] "A Chance for the Democrats," *Washington Post*, June 26, 1974.

[129] "Long-Winded Politicians to Get 'The Hook,'" *Los Angeles Times*, June 27, 1974; "Democrats Set Annual Telethon," *New York Times*, June 27, 1974; "The Democrats' Show Must Go On," *Washington Post*, July 1, 1974.

[130] "Democratic Party Telethon Is Set for ABC-TV July 26," *New York Times*, May 15, 1975; "Democrats Will Hit the Telethon Trail Again," *Los Angeles Times*, July 24, 1975; "Demos Set Annual Telethon," *Los Angeles Times*, July 26, 1975; "Democrats Open TV Rush Tonight," *New York Times*, July 26, 1975; "Glenn, 'Hawkeye' Open 4th Democratic Telethon," *Washington Post*, July 27, 1975.

[131] "Democrats' Telethon Is Short of Its Goal," *New York Times*, July 28, 1975.

than one million dollars. In 1976, rather than organize another telethon, the DNC aired a number of commercials during national convention broadcasts appealing for financial contributions.[132]

With the 1976 convention approaching, Mike Barnes, a Democratic staffer from Maryland who had created a new policy discussion group called the Democratic Forum, was invited by Strauss to join the DNC and do "some issues stuff."[133] Barnes became staff director of the DNC's 1976 platform committee, which received input from the DACEO,[134] with the goal of setting a "short, direct, responsive platform [...] but not a laundry list of proposals presented to us by various people,"[135] while Strauss kept his distance.[136] The committee produced a draft platform acceptable to both liberals and conservatives, as well as to Jimmy Carter, the surprise nominee.[137] To ensure that the convention would not descend into anarchy, Strauss required that any debate on minority planks require support from 25% of delegates.[138] At the 1976 convention, Strauss replicated the same unity image setting he had mastered during the previous years, by selecting Barbara Jordan and John Glenn as the two keynote speakers:

> I was trying to give them an image of being in the middle. That's what I wanted. And [Glenn] was a perfect image for me, even though he was dull. We needed somebody dull. You remember, we'd never had a convention in eight years with people who had shoes on, and without people screaming [...]. And we also needed an emotional speaker. A woman. And it didn't hurt that she was black.[139]

Strauss's projection of unity reached its crescendo on the last night of the convention. After Carter finished his acceptance speech and basked in the applause of the delegates, Strauss by name called up almost every Democratic leader—from Hubert Humphrey to George Wallace —to join Carter on stage. And, after Reverend Martin Luther King Sr. delivered the benediction, the crowd joined together to sing "We Shall Overcome."[140]

[132] "Democrats to Make Fund Pleas over TV at July Convention," New York Times, June 11, 1976.

[133] McGarr, The Whole Damn Deal, 187.

[134] "A Party in Search of a Foreign Policy," Washington Post, May 21, 1976.

[135] "Short and Direct Platform Is Predicted by Chairman," New York Times, May 21, 1976.

[136] "Regulatory Agency Appointees Assailed," New York Times, February 1, 1976.

[137] "Democrats Put Moynihan on Platform Subcommittee," New York Times, May 18, 1976; "Democratic Alternative," New York Times, May 24, 1976; "Democrats Start Platform Draft," New York Times, June 12, 1976; "Democrats Adopt a Platform Aimed at Uniting Party," New York Times, June 16, 1976; "No 'Purple' Planks," New York Times, June 18, 1976.

[138] McGarr, The Whole Damn Deal, 187–189.

[139] Ibid., 184–185.

[140] Ibid., 174.

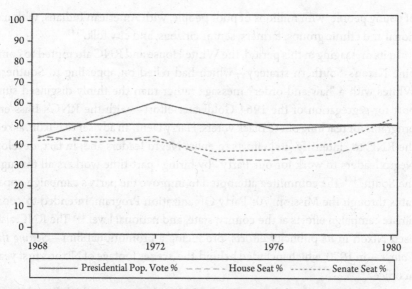

Figure 6.3. Republican electoral performance in presidential, House, and Senate elections, 1968–1980. *Source: Congressional Quarterly's Guide to U.S. Elections,* 7th ed. (Washington, DC: Congressional Quarterly, 2016).

Republican Presidential Control: Nixon–Ford and the RNC

After the massive Goldwater defeat of just four years earlier, the 1968 election pleased most Republican leaders. Nixon, whose political career had seemingly been over after his losses in the 1960 presidential and 1962 California gubernatorial elections, had won the 1968 Republican presidential nomination on the basis of a moderate-conservative coalition at the party's convention. But Nixon's victory was close, and Republicans remained in the minority in Congress (see Figure 6.3). After the election, Nixon adviser Herbert G. Klein announced on *Face the Nation* that the president-elect intended to "develop the Republican Party into a stronger political entity."[141] Part of this project was to continue the RNC's publicity role. With that goal in mind, Nixon replaced Bliss with Rogers Morton, whom Nixon believed to be "an issue-oriented man" and who could function as the "chief Republican spokesman during a period when the party needs promotion rather than consolidation."[142] Morton promised to shed the party's "role as a minority party" by becoming "massively involved with millions

[141] "Klein Says Nixon Will Help Party," *New York Times*, November 18, 1968.
[142] "G.O.P. Governors Cool to Ray Bliss," *New York Times*, December 7, 1968.

of young people, with millions of poor people, with American Indians, with national and ethnic groups, farmers, senior citizens, and city folk."[143]

In its messaging in this period, the White House and RNC attempted to combine Nixon's Southern strategy—which had relied on appealing to Southern Whites with a "law-and-order" message rather than the thinly disguised support for segregation of the 1964 Goldwater effort—with the RNC's Bliss-era programs for reaching out to Black voters. Harry Dent, an adviser to Nixon, asked the RNC to "intensify [its] efforts to enlist Negro leaders and, in fact, develop Negro leaders to work for our Party" by hiring "part-time workers all through the South."[144] The committee attempted to improve the party's campaign apparatus through the Mission '70s Party Organization Program, intended to coordinate campaign efforts at the county, state, and national level.[145] The RNC also used Nixon in its publicity efforts, producing a promotional film—*Setting the Course*—in 1970, which included behind-the-scenes footage of Nixon's first year in office.[146]

But in the wake of the disappointing 1970 midterms—in which Republicans gained two seats in the Senate but lost seats in the House and remained in the minority in both—Nixon replaced Morton as RNC chair. Nixon mostly believed Morton had failed to defend his administration: one Nixon administration insider unfavorably compared Morton with his DNC counterpart, complaining that Lawrence O'Brien "is out there every day slugging" but that Morton failed to play a similar role: "When he is called and it is suggested that maybe he should say something, he always says, 'Well . . . ' and nothing ever happens."[147]

Nixon decided to replace Morton with Senator Bob Dole (KS)—whom White House Chief of Staff H. R. Haldeman described as a "nut cutter"[148] in his diaries. Newspaper reports of the Dole selection interpreted Nixon's choice as an attempt at naming a new "major spokesman for the party."[149] And Dole was indeed more visible than Morton, frequently attacking anti–Vietnam War Democrats and the media for its criticism of Nixon. After 1970, the RNC's

---

[143] "Morton Urges G.O.P. to Shed Stand-By-Role," *Chicago Tribune*, April 15, 1969.

[144] Daniel J. Galvin, *Presidential Party Building: Dwight D. Eisenhower to George W. Bush* (Princeton, NJ: Princeton University Press, 2009), 77.

[145] Ibid., 79.

[146] "GOP Shows Nixon Film: First Year in Office Extolled," *Washington Post*, February 20, 1970.

[147] "Nixon Advisers Reported Irked with Morton—Showdown Due," *Los Angeles Times*, November 7, 1970.

[148] Cited in Galvin, *Presidential Party Building*, 80.

[149] "Dole Is Selected to Direct G.O.P.," *New York Times*, January 6, 1971. Other articles reported that Dole was expected to be the "party's public spokesman," or "the Senate's White House spokesman." See: "Dole Eases into Role as Head of G.O.P. National Committee," *Chicago Tribune*, January 14, 1971; "Dole New GOP Chief," *Los Angeles Times*, January 16, 1971.

main goal—in the assessment of vice chair Thomas Evans—was to "provide Republican leaders [...] with ammunition with which to speak up for the President"[150] and to "get the story of Republican accomplishments out all over America."[151] One of the core tools the committee relied on was *Monday*, a weekly publication distributed to party officials and reporters that became well known for its attacks on (potential) Democratic presidential candidates, including Edmund Muskie, George McGovern, Ted Kennedy, and Hubert Humphrey.[152] The publication was distributed to 285,000 recipients each week by the summer of 1973.[153] Additionally, the RNC produced and distributed over 3,000 video clips for use by television stations.[154]

These continued publicity activities during Nixon's first term in the White House are reflected in *New York Times* coverage of the RNC as well. Figure 6.4 shows the results of negative binomial regressions in which Nixon's incumbency during his first term is the independent variable and the monthly lagged *Times* coverage of RNC branding and service activities are the dependent variables. In this model, the data is limited to articles covering the RNC published between January 1965 and December 1972—thereby comparing *Times* coverage of the RNC under Nixon's first term with that of the committee during the Bliss era between the 1964 and 1968 elections. The results show no significant change in *Times* coverage for combined service activities nor for combined or individual branding activities—suggesting that coverage of the RNC's activities did not change much during Nixon's first term in office in comparison with the Bliss-era RNC when the party was out of the White House.

But the RNC's activities—while potentially helpful to Nixon—did little to boost the party in down-ballot races. In 1972, Nixon won a landslide re-election victory with 60.7% of the popular vote, but Republicans remained in the minority in Congress. In Dole's assessment, the 1972 election was a "sort of a standoff," as "after you take the President's personal landslide, there wasn't

---

[150] Paul Kesaris, Blair Hydrick, and Douglas D. Newman, *Papers of the Republican Party* (Frederick, MD: University Publications of America, 1987), Series B, Reel 8, Frame 512.

[151] Ibid., Frames 513–514.

[152] See: "GOP Assails Democrats on Peace Plan," *Los Angeles Times*, March 21, 1971; "The GOP Newsletter Prepares for '72, Hits at All Possible Foes," *Wall Street Journal*, April 23, 1971; "Hartke Wrong on POW Trade, GOP Declares," *Washington Post*, May 17, 1971; "Muskie's Temper Rapped by G.O.P.," *Chicago Tribune*, October 10, 1971.

[153] "Republicans' Monday Calls It a Day," *Washington Post*, July 31, 1973. Vice-President Spiro Agnew, in December 1972, also lauded the success of *Monday*: "no party organ in my memory has ever been quite as effective as this one, not simply because it is newsworthy, but because it is con-structively partisan. [....] What it does is to try to draw the issues between our political positions and those of the opposition party and it does it in a highly partisan effective sense [...]." See: Kesaris et al., *Papers of the Republican Party*, Series B, Reel 9, Frame 158.

[154] Kesaris et al., *Papers of the Republican Party*, Series B, Reel 9, Frame 95.

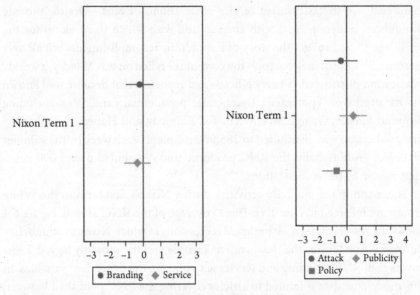

Figure 6.4. Negative binomial regression of Richard Nixon's incumbency as president during his first term on monthly (lagged) *New York Times* coverage of RNC branding and service activities, 1965–1972. *Note:* This model includes variables controlling for presidential and midterm election years, a measure of *New York Times* length, and RNC scandals. The data coverage is limited to articles published between January 1965 and December 1972 covering only the RNC.
Source: Data collected by author.

any landslide at all."[155] Dole argued that the RNC did not have the luxury to "go underground" and would have to "continue a full-time operation aimed at winning the support of disaffected Democrats, primarily blue-collar workers and ethnics who voted for President Nixon, and concentrate on the 1974 election."[156] However, Dole would not lead this effort: after the election, Nixon dropped him as RNC chair in favor of George H. W. Bush, previously ambassador to the United Nations.[157]

Under Bush, the RNC began organizing a set of "New Majority Workshops," aimed at training party activists to convince the Nixon voters, "who came over to us in such great numbers in support of President Nixon"[158] in 1972, to vote in congressional and gubernatorial races as well. During the workshops, the RNC

[155] "Victory Bittersweet for GOP," *Washington Post*, November 9, 1972.
[156] Ibid.
[157] "GOP Chief Dole Getting Set to Leave," *Washington Post*, December 2, 1972; "Bush to Take GOP Post as Dole Quits," *Los Angeles Times*, December 11, 1972.
[158] Galvin, *Presidential Party Building*, 96.

shared "best practices" on how to work with "ethnic voters, Spanish speaking voters, senior citizens, youths, blacks, and the blue collar laborers"[159]—all traditional Democratic voting blocs Nixon and the RNC believed Republicans would need to bring into the party to win majorities in Congress. Crucially, the program also relied on connecting the GOP specifically to Nixon—a logical choice since, as Mississippi RNC member Clarke Reed explained, "the Republican Party is the minority party. The President is the majority president. Let's bridge that gap. […] I say let's sell what's popular. That's the President."[160]

Of course, Nixon's popularity would not last, as the scandal surrounding the cover-up of the 1972 break-in at DNC headquarters in the Watergate Hotel began to spread. The RNC had largely been a sideshow in the Nixon re-election effort—with most of the control of the campaign (as well as its "dirty tricks") centered in the CREEP. Still, the RNC did not escape the scandal: Kenneth Reitz, a Nixon campaign aide hired by the RNC after the election, had to resign after he was implicated in the "spy corps" set up by the Nixon campaign to gather intelligence on Democrats.[161] Watergate also harmed the RNC financially. Traditionally, the Republican Party had been an effective fundraising machine regardless of its electoral fortunes. But Watergate scared off donors: by the middle of 1973, the RNC was $1 million behind in fundraising and had to cut 25% of its staff.[162] *Monday* was no longer published weekly but monthly (thus renamed *First Monday*).[163] The RNC also found itself unable to break through the extensive media coverage of the Watergate scandal with its own messages. Bush told RNC members in September 1973 that "we have cranked out reams of really positive comments, information on programs, but for the last six months a lot of the press has been interested in only you know what."[164]

After Nixon resigned in the summer of 1974, Gerald Ford appointed Bush to be the chief of the U.S. liaison office (effectively, the U.S. ambassador) in China. On Bush's recommendation, Ford selected RNC co-chair Mary Louise Smith as his replacement. Smith—after the short term of Westwood as DNC chair—was the second woman to chair either committee. Smith was a self-described Republican feminist and seen as a moderate, and she made it clear

[159] Ibid.

[160] "Bush Remolds GOP Committee into Adjunct of White House," *Washington Post*, March 19, 1973.

[161] "G.O.P. Aide Resigns," *Chicago Tribune*, April 25, 1973.

[162] "G.O.P. Committee, Facing Deficit, to Cut Staff 25%," *New York Times*, July 18, 1973.

[163] During a September 1973 RNC meeting Bush stressed that the end of the weekly *Monday* publication was purely for financial reasons. See: Kesaris et al., *Papers of the Republican Party*, Series B, Reel 11, Frames 270–271.

[164] Ibid., Frame 271.

that her alliance lied with Ford since "a President of your own party is certainly considered the leader of the party and plays the dominant role, and should."[165]

Before the 1974 election Smith argued that "somewhere the Republican Party is doing something wrong, or else we are not doing enough things right. Either we are being outorganized or we are being outsold and I suspect it is some of both."[166] The midterm results that year were, indeed, disastrous: Republicans now held just 33% of House seats and 38% of Senate seats. Smith concluded that the RNC would need to "reshape the image of the Republican Party and what it stands for in the minds of the American people."[167] To help achieve this, the RNC proposed a $2 million advertising program.[168] During a March 1975 RNC meeting, Smith explained that this program would give "voters a closer look at who we are and where we stand."[169] The plan, which also included training programs and voter registration drives, was a major financial investment given the committee's financial troubles. By the end of 1975, the RNC was so insolvent that it was forced to close its HQ for the month of December to save on heating and electricity.[170] The publicity plan was also unpopular with some Republican politicians. Illinois senator Charles Percy warned that a major advertising push could "lose votes and the money would be better spent for research and for supporting good Republican candidates than for promotional television commercials."[171]

Nonetheless, Smith pushed forward and produced three 30-minute television shows, which were broadcast on NBC and CBS in 1975. Smith described the shows as "a kind of Republican magazine of the air" in which the party presented "an exciting program launched by one of our governors, [...] a legislative report on bills pending in Congress, comments by Republican leaders on current issues [...]." The shows represented "a Republican perspective on the news, on goings on in this country among Republicans and what they are doing"[172] and included "citizen testimonials to individualism, free enterprise, and local government" in an attempt to "combat the widely held misconception that Republicans are rich fat cats unconcerned with the problems of ordinary Americans."[173] One of the shows was titled "Republicans Are People, Too."[174]

[165] Suzanne O'Dea, *Madam Chairman: Mary Louise Smith and the Republican Revival after Watergate* (Columbia: University of Missouri Press, 2012), 71.

[166] Kesaris et al., *Papers of the Republican Party*, Reel 12, Frame 56.

[167] "GOP Seeks to Improve Its Image," *Washington Post*, November 15, 1974.

[168] "Marketing the GOP," *Washington Post*, November 24, 1974.

[169] Kesaris et al., *Papers of the Republican Party*, Reel 12, Frames 392–393.

[170] "Hard-Pressed GOP Unit to Close for 2 Weeks," *Los Angeles Times*, October 25, 1975.

[171] "G.O.P.'s Ad Plan Hit by Percy," *Chicago Tribune*, February 12, 1975.

[172] Kesaris et al., *Papers of the Republican Party*, Reel 12, Series B, Frame 393.

[173] "G.O.P. Plans TV Advertising to Combat Its 'Fat Cat' Image," *New York Times*, June 5, 1975.

[174] Ibid.

Despite these activities, the total quantity of RNC branding efforts in this period declined—a change reflected in *New York Times* coverage of the committee in this period. Figure 6.5 shows the results of negative binomial regressions in which Nixon and Ford's incumbency during the presidential term after 1972 is the independent variable and the monthly lagged *Times* coverage of RNC branding and service activities are the dependent variables. In this model, the data is limited to articles covering the RNC published between January 1969 and December 1976—thereby comparing *Times* coverage of the RNC under Nixon's second term and Ford's presidency with that of the committee during the Nixon's first four years in office. While there is no change in service activity coverage, *Times* reporting on combined branding activities declined (significant at the 0.01 level). In particular, the RNC decreased its attacks on the Democratic Party (significant at the 0.01 level). Combined, these results suggest that the RNC—facing the Watergate scandal and major financial limitations—stepped back its branding activities in comparison with the role it had played promoting Nixon during his first term in office.

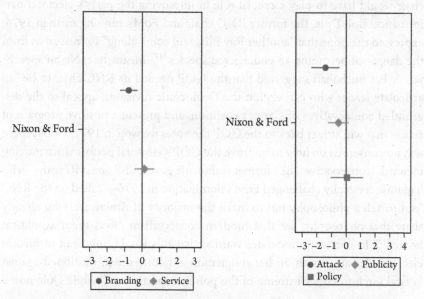

Figure 6.5. Negative binomial regression of Richard Nixon's and Gerald Ford's incumbency as president after the 1972 election on monthly (lagged) *New York Times* coverage of RNC branding and service activities, 1969–1976. *Note:* This model includes variables controlling for presidential and midterm election years, a measure of *New York Times* length, and RNC scandals. The data coverage is limited to articles published between January 1965 and December 1972 covering only the RNC.
Source: Data collected by author.

Four years after Nixon's massive re-election victory, Republicans found themselves out of the White House again. Though the presidential race proved close—with Ford losing the popular vote by around two percentage points and missing an electoral college majority by just two states (Ohio and Wisconsin)—Republicans remained hopelessly in the minority in Congress. Polls conducted in the months after the election underscored just how bad the GOP's position was, as only 20% of Americans self-identified as Republicans.[175] This was not merely a temporary embarrassment but a structural problem facing the party. Smith, who announced she would not run for another term after the election, warned that while it was "almost inevitable that we will make some modest gains over the next two years," the party should not confuse this with a real recovery and "lapse into smug self-satisfaction and be content to remain a minority party forever."[176]

Rebuilding the GOP in the Post-Watergate Era: Bill Brock and the RNC, 1977–1980

After the 1976 election many Republican leaders agreed that the next RNC chair would have to play a crucial role in improving the party's electoral performance. Bob Dole, the former RNC chair and Ford's running mate in 1976, expressed the hope that "another Ray Bliss will come along" to "rescue us from the danger of becoming an endangered species."[177] Meanwhile, Nixon speechwriter Pat Buchanan suggested that the GOP needed its RNC chair to be "an articulate leader who can exploit the Democratic divisions, appeal to the disgruntled conservatives of Carter's coalition, and present a positive program of action that will attract back to the GOP the votes we won in 1972."[178] But there was no consensus on how to improve the GOP's electoral performance moving forward. Conservatives, like former California governor Ronald Reagan—who had unsuccessfully challenged Ford's nomination in 1976—called on the RNC "not to sell a philosophy but to make the majority of Americans who already share that philosophy, see that modern conservatism offers them a political home."[179] In contrast, moderates warned that this would only lead to further electoral defeats. Smith, in her resignation announcement, cautioned against "a fatal lurch to either extreme of the political spectrum,"[180] while Dole noted

---

[175] "20% of Voters Found Affiliated to G.O.P.," *New York Times*, August 21, 1977.

[176] Kesaris et al., *Papers of the Republican Party*, Series B, Reel 14, Frame 616.

[177] "Dole: GOP Needs a Strong Leader," *Washington Post*, November 29, 1976.

[178] "GOP Heads for Another Blunder," *Chicago Tribune*, December 28, 1976.

[179] "A 'Shadow Cabinet' Suggested by Ford," *New York Times*, January 16, 1977.

[180] "GOP Chairman to Resign; Warns against Extremes," *Los Angeles Times*, November 22, 1976.

that the GOP faced an "anti-people image"[181] and that overcoming this image
required the Republicans to expand their voter coalition:

> We need the women, the young, the blacks, the Hispanics, the ethnics,
> the Indians. We need working men and women. [. . .] If we sit idly by in
> the complacent belief that Gov. Carter will make a botch of things and
> give us a new lease of life, we may not have a comeback.[182]

The person who had to figure out how to move the GOP forward was Bill Brock,
a senator from Tennessee who lost his re-election in 1976. Brock was not a favorite of conservatives or moderates, but benefited from a failed attempt by
Ford, Reagan, Vice President Nelson Rockefeller, and former secretary of the
treasury John Connally to unite behind one candidate.[183] This left Brock as the
most acceptable candidate to most RNC members, including conservatives
who—like Mississippi RNC member Clarke Reede—concluded that Brock
was "the most conservative candidate who can get elected."[184] Brock had been
seen as a conservative during his time in the Senate, but he mixed moderates
and conservatives in appointments at the RNC. For example, he hired Peter
Teeley—the former press secretary to New York senator Jacob Javits—and
Charles R. Black—special assistant to North Carolina senator Jesse Helm—to
important positions in the RNC.[185]

But the party image Brock promoted as chair was in line with the one favored
by moderates. Brock believed the challenge facing the RNC was changing "the
perception of this party."[186] To achieve this, the RNC would need to "identify
with the majority of the American people and they, in turn, identify with our
goals."[187] Part of Brock's approach was to invest in party building: in 1977, Brock
announced a "very ambitious $1.7 million plan" to "hire, train, and pay a full-time
organizer for each state, with the specific responsibility of rebuilding the party's

---

[181] "Dole: GOP Needs a Strong Leader," *Washington Post*, November 29, 1976.

[182] "GOP Governors Hear Dole Plea for Unity," *Los Angeles Times*, December 1, 1976.

[183] "Top Republicans Unable to Agree on Filing Two Major Party Posts," *New York Times*, January 7, 1977.

[184] "Brock Elected GOP Chairman," *Los Angeles Times*, January 15, 1977.

[185] "GOP Communications Post Goes to Aide of Sen. Javits," *Washington Post*, February 14, 1977; "Brock Picks Attorney as GOP Campaign Chief," *Washington Post*, April 20, 1977.

[186] Kesaris et al., *Papers of the Republican Party*, Series B, Reel 14, Frame 735.

[187] Ibid., Frames 738–739. Similarly, the Advisory Committee on Outreach, installed by Brock, concluded in a 1979 report that the party would need to seek actively "to bring non-Republicans into the party structure, a kind of political affirmative action. We cannot continue to approach non-Republicans at election time, soliciting their votes and their dollars for the candidates we have selected for them and ignoring them inbetween [sic] times" ("Steve Bull to William Brock," August 2, 1979, Brock Papers, Box 38, Folder 18).

badly eroded base."[188] Brock hoped this plan would help restore "the roots, the foundations of our party at the local level" by creating a bench of Republican talent: "[if] we don't start electing people to City Hall and courthouses and state legislatures, we have no foundation on which to build."[189]

Brock also created a series of advisory committees to set party policy positions.[190] During Brock's term as RNC chair, the advisory committees weighed in on a number of issues, including economic affairs, natural resources, "human concerns" (that is, welfare reform and urban policy), national security, and international affairs.[191] The RNC brought in Republican leaders and thinkers, such as Alan Greenspan, Herbert Stein, Robert Bork, Caspar Weinberger, George Romney, and Hugh Scott as chairs of the different (sub) committees.[192] As part of this process, the RNC began publishing a journal, Commonsense, to promote the findings of the Advisory Committees.[193] The journal also provided space for Republican academics and politicians to write about welfare, international relations, party reforms, and inner-city politics. In the first issue, Brock wrote that "the contest for votes must also be a contest of ideas" and that Commonsense would introduce "ideas into the policy debate; for testing and refining those ideas; and for accommodating them to the diverse desires of a pluralistic people."[194] Contributors included political scientists Jeane Kirkpatrick, Aaron Wildavksy, and John F. Bibby.

More importantly, the RNC invested heavily in promotional projects aimed at a broader public. In the spring of 1980, the RNC spent more than $5 million—20% of its budget for the year—on a media project consisting of, among others, a series of TV broadcasts in 50 media markets. The aim of the project was to provide "campaign education—educational television" focused "primarily, on the fact that Democrats are the majority in Congress, that Congress has created our problems, it is the source of inflation, that Republicans would commit to reduction in federal spending, a reduction in taxes, and increase in our defense."[195]

---

[188] "The New National Chairman of GOP Is a True Believer," Los Angeles Times, January 31, 1977.

[189] "GOP Leader Calls Energy Plan Ripoff," Chicago Tribune, April 30, 1977.

[190] "Chairman's Memo," March 26, 1977, Brock Papers, Box 38, Folder 38.

[191] "Compendium of Reports, Work in Progress and Recourse Material," Brock Papers, Box 40, Folder 1.

[192] "Republican National Committee Advisory Councils Committees Directory," January 1979, Brock Papers, Box 44, Folder 4.

[193] "Memorandum from Mike Baroody to Bill Brock," September 21, 1977, Brock Papers, Box 66, Folder 15. The research division spent a considerable part of its budget on Commonsense: in 1978, the division budgeted $300,452 out of its total request of $894,337 for the journal. See: "Memorandum from Mike Baroody to Arlene Triplett," September 14, 1977, Brock Papers, Box 66, Folder 15.

[194] Bill Brock, "Introduction to a Republican Journal of Thought and Opinion," Commonsense 1, no. 1 (1978): iv.

[195] Kesaris et al., Papers of the Republican Party, Series B, Reel 18, Frames 226–227.

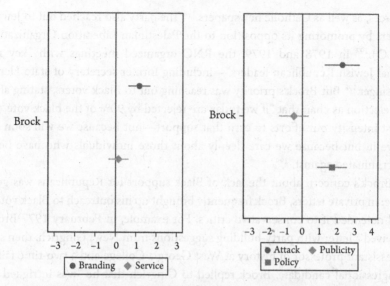

Figure 6.6. Negative binomial regression of Bill Brock's RNC chairmanships on monthly (lagged) *New York Times* coverage of RNC branding and service activities, 1973–1980. *Note:* This model includes variables controlling for presidential and midterm election years, a measure of *New York Times* length, and RNC scandals. The data coverage is limited to articles published between January 1973 and October 1980 covering only the RNC.
Source: Data collected by author.

The RNC's increased branding efforts after the Ford administration are reflected in *New York Times* committee coverage. Figure 6.6 shows the results of negative binomial regressions in which Brock's incumbency as RNC chair is the independent variable and the monthly lagged *Times* coverage of RNC branding and service activities are the dependent variables. In this model, the data is limited to articles covering the RNC published between January 1973 and October 1980 (the last month before Ronald Reagan's presidential election victory)—thereby comparing *Times* coverage of the RNC under Brock with that of the committee during the Nixon–Ford term. Coverage of all RNC branding activities combined increased during the Brock era (significant at the 0.001 level), while coverage of RNC service activities did not change. In terms of specific branding activities, *Times* coverage increased for attacks by the committee against the Democratic Party and of the RNC taking on policy positions (both significant at the 0.001 level).

Since Republicans had seen such a decline since the 1972 Nixon landslide, the number of voting groups the party could appeal to was considerable—and the RNC relied on something of a scattershot approach in doing so. The RNC targeted Chinese, Polish, Russian, Italian, Spanish, and German language media sources, as well as Catholic newspapers.[196] The party also reached out to Jewish voters by promoting its opposition to the Palestinian Liberation Organization (PLO).[197] In 1978 and 1979, the RNC organized meetings with "key national Jewish Republican leaders"—including former secretary of state Henry Kissinger.[198] But Brock's priority was reaching out to Black voters, stating after his election as chair that "if we today are rejected by 90% of the black vote, we must intensify our efforts to earn that support—not because we will soon receive it, but because we care deeply about those individuals who have been discriminated against."[199]

Brock's concern about the lack of Black support for Republicans was genuine: in private letters, Brock frequently brought up his outreach to Black voters and defended it to conservative critics. For example, in February 1977 Brock received a letter with party-building suggestions from Newt Gingrich, then still an assistant professor of history at West Georgia College and a two-time failed congressional candidate. Brock replied to Gingrich that he "was intrigued by what you did not [underline in original] mention, especially in light of the large amount of press on this particular subject. I am, of course, referring to the added emphasis on Blacks."[200] To be sure, Brock's interest also came from a direct personal understanding of the electoral consequences of having GOP candidates underperform with Black voters: in 1976, Brock lost his own re-election to the Senate by 78,000 votes, while his Democratic opponent received an estimated 130,000 Black votes.[201] And Brock's fate was not unique in this regard: according to an analysis of the Joint Center for Political Studies, Black votes were pivotal to Carter's victories in Alabama, Florida, Louisiana, Maryland, Mississippi, Missouri, North Carolina, New York, Ohio, Pennsylvania, South Carolina, Texas, and Wisconsin.[202] Thus, in close elections, even a relatively modest switch in

---

[196] See: "Memorandum from Cheryl Davis to William Brock, Ben Cotton and Jean Hawkins," February 7, 1980, Brock Papers, Box 38, Folder 4; "Memorandum from Cheryl Davis to William Brock, Ben Cotton, and Jean Hawkins," February 1, 1980, Brock Papers, Box 39, Folder 4; "Memorandum from Cheryl Davis to William Brock, Ben Cotton, and Jean Hawkins," May 1, 1980, Brock Papers, Box 39, Folder 4; "Memorandum from Don Shea to Pete Teeley," January 10, 1979, Brock Papers, Box 40, Folder 4.

[197] "Report on the Outreach Program of the Republican National Committee for Increased Support from the Jewish Community," October 23, 1978, Brock Papers, Box 39, Folder 14.

[198] "Lawrence Y. Goldberg to William Brock," January 19, 1978, Brock Papers, Box 57, Folder 14; "H. David Weinstein to Carol Browning," November 13, 1979, Brock Papers, Box 57, Folder 2; "William Brock to John Trubin," December 3, 1979, Brock Papers, Box 57, Folder 11.

[199] Kesaris et al., Papers of the Republican Party, Series B, Reel 15, Frame 4.

[200] "William Brock to Newt Gingrich," February 21, 1977, Brock Papers, Box 35, Folder 18.

[201] Leah Wright Rigueur, The Loneliness of the Black Republican (Princeton, NJ: Princeton University Press, 2016), 264.

[202] "The GOP Knows It Has a Problem," Chicago Tribune, March 27, 1977.

Black support could increase the probability of a GOP win. The RNC therefore produced a variety of programs aimed at reaching out to Black voters. In 1978, the National Black Republican Council (the RNC's official body representing Black Republicans) organized five regional workshops to train Black Republican party workers to reach out to voters in their communities.[203] The RNC also bought advertising space around Black television shows, including a set of one-minute commercial spots around *America's Black Forum*, a weekly television news show.[204]

Most notably, Brock extended an $800,000 contract to the Black-owned political consulting firm Wright-McNeill & Associates.[205] Wright-McNeill had become known in the Republican Party after its successes in the 1976 election: as historian Leah Wright Rigueur has noted, while across the country Black voters supported Democratic candidates by large margins, in Georgia—the firm's home state—White Republican clients that had hired Wright-McNeill had won over half of the Black vote. Meanwhile, Black Republican candidates that had hired the firm won more than 90% of the Black vote.[206] The RNC hoped to replicate these successes at a national level by having Wright-McNeill produce national "campaign strategies geared toward the Black community."[207] During the Carter administration, Wright-McNeill advised a considerable number of Republican candidates and campaigns in at least 16 states, predominantly (but not exclusively) in the South.[208] And, with dissatisfaction with the Carter administration on the rise, the GOP hoped the Wright-McNeill approach would help the party. As Robert Wright wrote to Brock, "Black dissatisfaction with Jimmy Carter is obvious and growing," with several civil rights leaders (including Jesse Jackson, Vernon Jordan of the Urban League, and Ben Hooks of the NAACP) expressing "displeasure of the Carter administration."[209]

[203] "Third Force Seminar and Leadership Conference," Brock Papers, Box 39, Folder 3.

[204] "Ben Cotton to America's Black Forum, Inc.," March 27, 1978, Brock Papers, Box 57, Folder 22.

[205] Brock described the amount as an "enormous" expenditure, indicating the importance he placed on this project ("Republicans Courting Black Voters in South after Years of Inactivity," *New York Times*, August 1, 1978).

[206] Wright Rigueur, *The Loneliness of the Black Republican*, 267.

[207] Cited in ibid.

[208] Based on staff reports, Wright-McNeill representatives worked with campaigns in Texas, Georgia, Tennessee, Ohio, Illinois, Virginia, Florida, Connecticut, Pennsylvania, Massachusetts, Mississippi, Arkansas, Alabama, Kansas, New York, and Kentucky in 1978 and 1979. See: "Wright-McNeill and Associates Field Reports," Brock Papers, Box 40, Folder 23.

[209] "Memorandum from Bob Wright to William Brock and Charlie Black," August 11, 1977, Brock Papers, Box 40, Folder 23.

But the firm was also clear that "the greatest barrier to the Republican Party in making a significant, indelible impact on the Black electorate's voting pattern was the negative image the Republican Party has in the Black community."[210] The Wright-McNeill playbook thus relied on having local (White) Republicans build connections with local Black leaders and reaching out to voters through specialized publicity efforts. For example, in May 1979, Thelma Duggin, a field coordinator in the Wright-McNeill program, provided the Republican Party in Montgomery, Alabama, with an outline of a proposed plan consisting of three phases: research, public relations and education, and voter education. Local Republicans were encouraged to inform themselves about Black community leaders in local clubs and churches and connect with them. Once they had created such working relationships, their next task was to set up speaking engagements with local Black organizations, schools, and churches and distribute literature on the necessity of creating a two-party system in the South. Leaders were also urged to "constantly [prepare] news releases for the press on activities and stands on issues of concern to the Black community," and to invite famous Black speakers "such as Alex Haley, Jesse Jackson, [and] Black Republican elected officials" to visit their towns.[211]

Not all Republican candidates proved compatible with the Wright-McNeill strategy. One example was former congressman Ron Paul (TX), who had lost his reelection in 1976 but was planning another run for the House. Duggin recounted that Wright

> informed [Paul] that if he [...] wanted the Black vote, it would be necessary for him to moderate his stand on issues. Paul vehemently refused, saying that he was right and would not moderate his stands. [...] I talked to about 20–30 Blacks, both by phone and in person. I received very negative responses and at times had to defend my "helping" Ron Paul. Ron Paul was, overall, described as an insult to Black voters. [...] They described him as being extremely conservative with racist tendencies.[212]

Based on this visit, Duggin and Wright concluded that Paul's positions on welfare, the minimum wage, and healthcare were too conservative to convince Black voters to support him.

---

[210] "Robert L. Wright to William Brock," February 1, 1979, Brock Papers, Box 40, Folder 23.

[211] "Thelma Duggin to Jack Crittenden," May 29, 1979, Brock Papers, Box 50, Folder 17; "Jack P. Crittenden to Bill Brock," June 7, 1979, Brock Papers, Box 50, Folder 17.

[212] "Field Report Form," April 6, 1978 (Texas), Brock Papers, Box 40, Folder 23.

Wright-McNeill also pushed Brock to improve relations with Black leaders,[213] and to do so Brock invited Jesse Jackson to address the RNC. In his invite, Brock explained that

the RNC has embarked on a program to open the Republican Party to greater participation by black Americans. [. . .] We Republicans must listen to and be responsive to blacks, but it is equally important that blacks truly participate in the Republican party and become deeply involved in the making of our Party's decisions and policies.[214]

Brock saw Jackson's appearance as a major turning point and invited Republican leaders—including Senate Minority Leader Howard Baker—to be present to "show Reverend Jackson, his supporters and others that the leadership of the Republican Party is unified in its effort to bring blacks into our Party, to encourage them, help them and listen to them."[215] During his speech, Jackson called for an alliance between Black Americans and the GOP, arguing that "black people need the Republican Party to compete for us so that we have real alternatives for meeting our needs. The Republican Party needs black people if it is to ever compete for national office or, in fact to keep it from becoming an extinct party."[216] Such an alliance was possible because of Carter's performance in office: "the priorities that we voted for Mr. Carter on have changed. The President would have gotten far fewer black votes if he had run on a platform of energy and government reorganization."[217]

Many Republicans were pleased with Jackson's message. Dole thought it was "a breakthrough just having him here," while Brock wished "we had Republicans who speak like that."[218] And the RNC continued its relationship with Jackson in 1979, when it sponsored a fundraiser for Jackson's Push EXCEL educational scholarship program.[219] Brock addressed the NAACP's annual conference in

---

[213] "Memo from Phyllis Berry to William Brock," December 13, 1977, Brock Papers, Box 38, Folder 31.

[214] "Bill Brock to the Reverend Jesse Jackson," December 23, 1977, Brock Papers, Box 57, Folder 27.

[215] "Bill Brock to Howard H. Baker," January 10, 1978, Brock Papers, Box 56, Folder 33. Similar invitations were sent to House Minority Whip Robert H. Michel, National Republican Senatorial Committee (NRSC) chair Bob Packwood, House Minority Leader John Rhodes, Assistant Minority Leader in the Senate Ted Stevens, and National Republican Congressional Committee (NRCC) chair Guy Vander Jagt.

[216] "Blacks and GOP Need Each Other—Jesse Jackson," *Los Angeles Times*, January 21, 1978.

[217] Ibid.

[218] Ibid.

[219] "Memorandum from Robert Wright to William Brock," June 25, 1979, Brock Papers, Box 40, Folder 23. NAACP executive director Benjamin Hooks also spoke at an RNC meeting in 1978. See: "Benjamin L. Hooks to Bill Brock," August 24, 1978, Brock Papers, Box 57, Folder 29.

1978, stressing that Black voters were "extremely important" to the Republican Party and that he hoped his legacy would be that "no political party in America will ever again take black voters for granted or write them off as a captive of the opposition."[220] Later that year, the RNC organized an urban conference in Detroit during which Michigan governor William Milliken warned that the GOP could not "use tax limitation as the current euphemism for the anti-black, anti-Spanish-speaking and anti-poor sentiments of some segments of the population."[221] The efforts to appeal to Black and other minority voters thus saw a major expansion. In 1979, Brock reported that programs centered on "people who had not had an adequate voice in the Party" had been "multiplied about threefold" since 1976.[222]

In January 1979, the RNC made its most public declaration in its outreach to Black voters by selecting Detroit as its 1980 convention city, despite opposition from conservatives who dismissed Detroit as a "crummy"[223] city. Brock believed the selection said "something about the party's commitment, not only to minorities, but to ethnic groups, workers, and the urban community."[224] The selection, in the assessment of the New York Times, vindicated the "kind of leadership [Brock] has tried to give the party, a combination of nuts-and-bolts technical work and the insistence that the party must reach out, not merely try to further please those voters it pleases already."[225] Brock believed his approach was paying off in the form of the GOP's strong performance in the 1978 midterms.[226]

---

[220] "Can't Take Your Vote for Granted, GOP Chairman Tells NAACP," *Chicago Tribune*, May 8, 1978.

[221] "GOP Launches Bid for Blacks, Ethnics," *Washington Post*, July 20, 1978.

[222] Kesaris et al., *Papers of the Republican Party*, Series B, Reel 17, Frame 95. Representatives of the National Republican Heritage Groups and the Republican National Hispanic Assembly complained that their organizations were underfunded—especially in comparison with the amount of money the RNC spent on Black outreach (see: "Bill Brock to Benjamin Fernandez," April 7, 1977, Brock Papers, Box 57, Folder 16; "Edward J. Derwinski to Bill Brock," March 27, 1977, Brock Papers, Box 57, Folder 16). Meanwhile, the RNC's reliance on Wright-McNeill caused frustration among the leadership of the National Black Republican Council (NBRC)—which accused Brock of hiring "[his] Blacks" ("James C. Cummings, Jr. to Bill Brock," December 12, 1979, Brock Papers, Box 58, Folder 4) instead of relying on the NBRC. After the NBRC decided to boycott Republican candidates who received support from Wright-McNeill, Brock cut its funding (see "James C. Cummings, Jr. to Ben Cotton," December 31, 1979, Brock Papers, Box 58, Folder 4).

[223] "Republicans Reach Out to a Wider Audience," *New York Times*, January 28, 1979.

[224] Ibid. See also: "Detroit Picked by GOP as 1980 Convention Site," *Los Angeles Times*, January 24, 1979. Notably, William McLaughlin, the chairman of the Michigan Republican State Committee, in his bid to convince the RNC to choose Detroit as the convention city also connected Detroit to the Equal Rights Amendment: "It is important to note that Michigan was one of the first states in the nation to ratify the ERA" (Kesaris et al., *Papers of the Republican Party*, Series B, Reel 16, Frame 135).

[225] "Republicans Reach Out to a Wider Audience," *New York Times*, January 28, 1979.

[226] Kesaris et al., *Papers of the Republican Party*, Series B, Reel 17, Frame 95.

Additionally, polling conducted in 1979 showed that the party's image had improved, particularly on economic issues.[227] And, while after the 1976 election polls had been so dire that some Republicans wondered whether the party should change its name altogether, by 1980 RNC pollster Bob Teeter concluded, "the word Republican [...] ceased to be such a millstone as it has been around the neck of many of our candidates."[228]

However, the convention that was supposed to reflect the GOP's breakthrough in courting minority voters instead solidified the conservative takeover of the GOP through the nomination of Reagan and the most conservative party platform since 1964. Brock's actions as chair had not fundamentally altered the power division within the party, nor had he convinced conservatives his approach was working. Columnists Evans and Novak reported that several RNC members considered Jackson's RNC appearance "an irrelevant exercise."[229] One anonymous RNC member shared that he had told "[Brock] when he started on this that it was okay so long as it didn't detract from our main chance at getting more blue-collar workers. He told me it wouldn't, but he was wrong."[230] Buchanan also dismissed Brock's attempts:

> the reality is that Bill Brock can no more deliver a platform satisfactory to Jesse Jackson than can Jesse Jackson deliver a black precinct to the Republican Party of Goldwater, Nixon, Reagan, and Ford. The road to Republican recovery does not lie through Harlem or Watts.[231]

While Brock largely promoted an image of the GOP that would be displaced by the emergent conservative wing, he was ahead of the conservative curve in one crucial way: his attempts at bringing evangelical Christian leaders into the party. The Christian right had begun in earnest as a political movement following the attempts at ratification of the Equal Rights Amendment (ERA) in the early 1970s. The ERA passed Congress in 1970 with large bipartisan majorities

---

[227] Ibid., Reel 18, Frames 173–174.

[228] Ibid., Reel 18, Frame 194.

[229] "The GOP's Curious Quest for Black Votes," *Washington Post*, January 26, 1978.

[230] Ibid.

[231] "Jesse, GOP Still Far Apart," *Chicago Tribune*, February 7, 1978. To be sure, Reagan himself reached out to Black voters in the 1980 election. Reagan met with Black Republicans during the 1980 convention and received their support. During the fall campaign, Wright-McNeill helped produce a campaign strategy for Reagan to attract Black support and attack Carter. Reagan himself met with Jackson and campaigned in the South Bronx to appeal directly to Black and Latino voters, but this appearance was mostly a failure that "quickly deteriorated into a shouting match between the politician and about seventy demonstrators." See: Wright Rigueur, *The Loneliness of the Black Republican*, 286.

and the (token) support of Nixon.[232] However, the process of ratification ended in failure in 1979, in part because of a movement of (mostly) Christian women organized by longtime Republican activist Phyllis Schlafly. Under pressure of Schlafly and other anti-ERA groups, several states that had previously ratified the amendment undid their support. The failure of the ERA inspired a host of evangelical Christian leaders to become politically active, and to push social issues such as abortion, feminism, and homosexuality to the center of the political sphere.

While opposition to the ERA had been a conservative movement, it had not been a purely Republican one. Republican support for the ERA was robust: Republican members of Congress supported the ERA in 1970, and the party reiterated its support in its 1972 and 1976 platforms. Meanwhile, some of the strongest opponents of the ERA had been conservative Democrats, such as Senator Sam Ervin (D-NC).[233] White evangelical Christian voters also were not yet a Republican voting group: in 1976 most White evangelicals voted for Carter, a born-again Southern Baptist.[234] Yet, the Christian evangelical leaders became frustrated with Carter's policies, and Republicans took advantage of this gap in 1980 with a platform tailored to their demands. Reagan, at a convention of 15,000 ministers in August, summarized the GOP's embrace of the Christian right by telling the crowd that "I know this is nonpartisan, so you can't endorse me, but I want you to know that I endorse you."[235]

But the RNC had begun wooing evangelical leaders well before Reagan's nomination. In 1979 and 1980 the RNC organized a series of meetings between Brock and high-profile evangelical leaders and provided them with advice on how to organize into a political force. Ben Cotten, Brock's deputy at the RNC, explained during an RNC meeting in 1980 that the match between the GOP and White evangelicals was a natural one: "it was our belief [. . .] that not to participate and become involved with people who had never before been involved in the political process would have been to abandon an opportunity to expand the party" because the "issues that motivate them—faith, freedom, and family—[. . .] [are] precisely why the Republican Party and the evangelicals should go hand in hand."[236] Brock made a similar appeal to evangelical leaders.

---

[232] Robert Mason, *Richard Nixon and the Quest for a New Majority* (Chapel Hill: The University of North Carolina Press, 2004), 155.

[233] Ruth Murray Brown, *For a "Christian America": A History of the Religious Right* (Amherst, NY: Prometheus Books, 2002), 85.

[234] See: Sidney M. Milkis, Daniel Tichenor, and Laura Blessing, "'Rallying Force': The Modern Presidency, Social Movements, and the Transformation of American Politics," *Presidential Studies Quarterly* 43, no. 3 (2013): 658.

[235] Cited in ibid., 659.

[236] Kesaris et al., *Papers of the Republican Party*, Series B, Reel 18, Frames 560–562.

In letters sent in the fall of 1979, Brock expressed his concern that "the assault upon our spiritual heritage is awesome and growing" and explained that the "Republican Party is seeking advice on the necessary content of the 1980 RNC Party Platform as to reflect those basic values which have contributed so much to the strength of this nation."[237]

The evangelical leaders Brock was appealing to included Jerry Falwell, Bob Jones, Pat Robertson, Tim LaHaye, and Jim Bakker. To assist Christian conservatives in bringing out voters for the GOP, the RNC created a "Program for Political Participation of Church-Going Christians"—made available to ministers to reach out to their congregation. The program proposed three steps for ministers to take: First was ensuring that the members of their congregation were registered to vote. Second was that

> an effective method of communication must be developed so they will know without question, for all positions on the ballot, not just President or U.S. Senator, which candidates support the values they themselves support and which ones on the basis of their record or their public statements do not.[238]

Finally, ministers were urged to ensure that their flock actually turned out to vote on election day.

To be sure, the RNC did not expect the evangelicals to become influential in the party fast. While the RNC was hopeful Christian conservative voters could help the party in 1980, the committee's staff had a poor impression of the evangelical leaders. Ahead of a May 1980 meeting with Falwell, LaHaye, and James Robison, RNC staffers briefed Brock that "the degree of political sophistication amongst this group is very low"[239] and advised him to stress that, while the RNC wanted them to "be a part of the decision-making process, i.e. that their voices will be heard and they will be part of the action,"[240] they should not expect any big changes in party policies in the short term: "It would not be wise to try and suggest to them that if Republicans are elected that all their concerns will be dealt with an all the problems will go away."[241] This

---

[237] "William Brock to leaders in the evangelical community (form letter)," November 19, 1979, Brock Papers, Box 44, Folder 19.

[238] "A Program for Political Participation of Church-Going Christians," 1980, Brock Papers, Box 38, Folder 10.

[239] "Memorandum from Eddie Mahe, Jr. to Bill Brock," May 19, 1980, Brock Papers, Box 38, Folder 10.

[240] Ibid.

[241] Ibid.

turned out to be a major miscalculation. With Reagan controlling a majority of delegates at the convention he also controlled the platform writing process. And Reagan's delegates produced a platform tailored to White Christian voters, rejecting both the ERA and abortion rights. The language of the platform came as a shock to moderate Republicans: for example, Mary Dent Crisp, co-chair of the RNC and a supporter of the ERA and abortion rights, resigned in protest at the convention.[242]

While some moderate Republicans warned that the clearly conservative candidate and platform in 1980 would doom the party's chances in the general election, Reagan's dramatic victory against Carter managed even to include some congressional success for a change, as Republicans (for the first time since 1952) won a majority in the Senate. After the election, Brock, in a letter to Governor Lamar Alexander (TN), celebrated the party's successes and took credit for the RNC's role in them. "The excitement to me," Brock wrote,

> came in the breadth and depth of our success. The attraction of Democrats, blue collar workers, Catholics, over 35% of the Jewish voters, and twice the anticipated level of black support reflected in not just a Presidential landslide, but Senate, Gubernatorial, Congressional and legislative races as well.[243]

But the 1980 election also fundamentally shifted the balance of power within the Republican Party. While conservatives had been a major force within the GOP before, they had never succeeded in fully controlling the national party for long. Previously, the nomination of Barry Goldwater as the party's presidential candidate in 1964 had been a high point for the movement, but his subsequent dramatic defeat led to a resurgence of moderate control immediately after. And each Republican president since the New Deal—Eisenhower, Nixon, and Ford—had combined conservative and moderate policies. Crucially, the RNC—with the exception of the period 1961–1964—had consistently supported a moderate, centrist image of the GOP. Reagan's nomination and victory fundamentally changed the intra-party political landscape.

---

[242] Kesaris et al., *Papers of the Republican Party*, Series B, Reel 18, Frame 974. Brock, himself a supporter of the ERA as well, defended the Republican platform in letters to concerned Republicans: "At no point does [the platform] oppose the Equal Rights Amendment. [. . .] In my own view, our Platform in no way inhibits those of us who support the Equal Rights Amendment from proceeding to seek its adoption" ("Bill Brock to Dorothy B. Ward," July 21, 1980, Brock Papers, Box 55, Folder 18).

[243] "Bill Brock to Lamar Alexander," November 15, 1980, Brock Papers, Box 63, Folder 26.

The Carter Years: Presidential Neglect and DNC Decline

Jimmy Carter's close victory in 1976 may have left Democratic leaders cautiously optimistic in that they finally figured out a way to bridge their own intra-party divisions. But any such optimism did not last: Carter proved to be an alienating figure to voters, as well as to Democrats in Congress. And, as party leader, Carter proved to have little to no interest in managing the DNC. To be sure, the Carter team—led by political strategist Hamilton Jordan, who had worked at the DNC during the Strauss era—initially showed some support for reorganizing the national committee. Carter selected Kenneth Curtis, the former governor of Maine, as the next DNC chair. Curtis claimed he had been promised "very direct access to the White House"[244] and expected to handle "some of the political activity that's been in the White House"[245] during previous administrations and began his tenure as DNC chair by creating a set of plans to reorganize the committee. These plans centered on providing training to campaign workers and more financial and research assistance for candidates. For any of this to be achieved, the committee would need to raise money, as it was $4 million in debt and faced $3 million in payments for debt relief and operating expenses in the first months of 1977 alone. Curtis hoped that Carter would appear at a series of fundraising dinners to help pay off these debts.[246]

However, as Daniel Galvin notes, the White House never replied to Curtis and "there is no record that Carter's team even discussed Curtis's party-building plans."[247] Curtis submitted a second, and more detailed, proposal, which was also ignored. Carter did appear at a fundraiser in New York in June 1977 and reportedly attended a second event later in the year but refrained from the kind of major fundraising Curtis had hoped he would do.[248] With the White House also unwilling to work with the DNC on patronage issues,[249] the relationship between the new president and "his" national committee had quickly become toxic. DNC members were described as feeling "unloved, and more importantly, unrewarded"[250] by the Carter White House. In October 1977, Carter appeared

---

[244] Galvin, *Presidential Party Building*, 207.

[245] "Carter Campaign Aides Leading Democrats' Staff," *New York Times*, January 19, 1977.

[246] Galvin, *Presidential Party Building*, 207–208.

[247] Ibid., 208.

[248] "Carter Attends Democratic Dinner at Waldorf That Raises $1 Million," *New York Times*, June 24, 1977.

[249] "National Committee Scolds Carter for Bypassing State Party Chiefs," *New York Times*, April 2, 1977.

[250] "It's Carter Folks vs. Regular Democrats," *New York Times*, December 11, 1977.

at a DNC meeting and called on the committee to support his attempts at ratifying the Panama Canal Treaty. Instead, the committee only passed a "slightly watered-down resolution of support" for Carter's treaty—a "hollow victory,"[251] as it did not actually endorse the specific treaties Carter had negotiated.

By the end of 1977, Curtis had enough and announced his resignation, describing being chair of this DNC as "not the sort of job that you lay down in the street and bleed to keep [...]."[252] Curtis stressed the financial difficulties of the DNC, asking reporters, "Did you ever try to meet a payroll every two weeks for a bankrupt organization?"[253] Curtis also criticized Mark Siegel, a former DNC executive director who was now the liaison between the Carter administration and the committee. The White House criticized Curtis in turn, with anonymous political advisers to Carter telling the New York Times that Curtis had "simply presided over the competing constituencies within the party rather than molding them into an effective, unified political apparatus."[254]

Why this rocky start between Carter and the DNC? As David E. Price has noted, Carter and his team won the Democratic nomination as outsiders and largely viewed the DNC and state party organizations as "potential antagonists to be neutralized" rather "than as potential allies to be nurtured."[255] Galvin, on the basis of internal memos from within the Carter White House, comes to a similar conclusion: Jordan believed investing in the DNC was not in Carter's best interest as a "DNC operation that requires a lot of time and supervision from here is more of a problem than a help."[256] Price concluded that "no modern president [...] has made less use of his national party organization than Carter."[257] To be sure, Carter himself blamed the learning curve he faced as a new president. During a January 1978 DNC meeting, at which the committee voted to elect John C. White—a longtime party insider and Carter's selection—as Curtis's

[251] "Carter Asks Democratic Leaders to Help Him on Panama Treaties," New York Times, October 8, 1977.

[252] "Democratic Leader Denies White House Forced Him to Quit," New York Times, December 9, 1977.

[253] Ibid.

[254] "Curtis to Step Down as Democrats' Chief," New York Times, December 8, 1977.

[255] Price, Bringing Back the Parties, 78. While Carter's rise as a political outsider may have explained part of his lack of support for the DNC, both Carter and Jordan had directly been involved with the DNC in the run-up to the 1976 primaries to increase Carter's stature within the party. See: McGarr, The Whole Damn Deal, 140–142.

[256] Galvin, Presidential Party Building, 209.

[257] Carter did have the DNC pay for 150,000 Christmas cards to be sent to people who had supported his campaign in 1976. Additionally, Chip Carter—one of the president's adult children—worked at the DNC for a period of time in 1977. See: Price, Bringing Back the Parties, 78; "It's Carter Folk vs. Regular Democrats"; "Mrs. Carter Says She Tells the President 'What I Think,'" New York Times, March 10, 1977; "Notes on People," New York Times, August 12, 1977.

replacement, Carter gave a speech to the committee members.[258] In this address, Carter explained that he had to do

> hundreds of hours of personal study about the history and present circumstances concerning the Middle East, Africa, Latin America, Panama, SALT, comprehensive test bans, domestic programs. And I have to admit to you that in many instances, I put those responsibilities ahead of my responsibilities to the Democratic National Committee. I don't think you've had the support that was needed from the White House. […] This year, there will be a much closer allegiance and alliance from the White House toward the Democratic National Committee.[259]

Carter agreed to appear at five fundraising dinners, which the DNC hoped would help retire its remaining debt (now reported to be between $1.9 and $2.8 million).[260] Under White, the DNC stepped up its direct mail fundraising efforts and used these appeals to promote some of Carter's policies on energy and tax reform.[261] Carter also promised to campaign extensively for Democratic candidates in the 1978 midterm elections, and members of the DNC were invited to a June "candlelight-and-champagne" reception at the White House to further mend fences.[262]

But despite Carter's rapprochement, little changed. Several of the fund-raising dinners Carter agreed to were postponed for various reasons.[263] When the White House did work with the DNC they found the experience frustrating because the committee lacked staff.[264] Of course, this was in part because the committee's chronic money problems meant White had to fire 30 (out of 80) DNC staff members and cut payroll by one-third.[265] Within the White House, a collective understanding had developed that the DNC simply was not

---

[258] "Headliners," *New York Times*, January 1, 1978; "Carter, Apologizing for Neglect, Makes Up with Party Committee," *New York Times*, January 28, 1978.

[259] Quoted in Galvin, *Presidential Party Building*, 209.

[260] "Democratic Chief Says First Goal Is Funds for Debts and Campaign," *New York Times*, January 4, 1978; "Carter, Apologizing for Neglect"; "Lance in His Element at Salute to Carter," *New York Times*, January 21, 1978; "Notes on People," *New York Times*, April 27, 1978.

[261] "For the Democrats, a Need to Catch Up," *New York Times*, May 28, 1978.

[262] "Carter, Apologizing for Neglect"; "Carter Seeks to Improve Ties with Party Leadership," *New York Times*, June 7, 1978.

[263] The official reason generally was "scheduling problems," though local Democratic leaders blamed Carter's policy of selling jet fighters to Saudi Arabia and Egypt as having alienated Jewish donors. See: "Carter Seeks to Improve Ties."

[264] Galvin, *Presidential Party Building*, 215.

[265] Ibid., 211; "Interest Groups Gaining Influence at the Expense of National Parties," *New York Times*, March 26, 1978.

important. And, as Jordan explained in a memo to Carter in December 1977, incumbent members of Congress didn't necessarily "want or need technical help from the party [...]"[266] either. As Democrats already had large majorities—in the assessment of the *New York Times*, the Democrats after the 1976 election were a "party that has no place to go but down"[267]—prioritizing the DNC was considered pointless.

The one exception to the Carter administration's disinterest for the DNC appears to have been a "public relations offensive"[268] proposed by White with the goal of promoting to different groups in the Democratic Party the administration's policies and achievements. The program would mimic the way Kennedy used the DNC in "Operation Support," and how later presidents—like Reagan and Clinton—would also use their national committees to promote their government's policies, and themselves. But it is not entirely clear to what extent this program was actually implemented, and—if it was—whether it achieved much. White and the DNC did engage in some branding activities on behalf of Carter in 1978.[269] And the *New York Times* described White as "flying in tourist class [...] touring the country to speak at party gatherings" while "the rest of the Democratic program consists of using the mails to get the word around."[270] But beyond these reports there is no evidence this "offensive" amounted to much.[271]

The dramatic decline of the DNC under Carter is reflected in the type of *New York Times* coverage the DNC received. Figure 6.7 shows the results of negative binomial regressions in which Carter's incumbency is the independent variable and the lagged monthly *Times* coverage of DNC branding and service activities are the dependent variables. In this model, the data is limited to just those articles covering the DNC that were published between January 1973 and December 1980—thereby comparing *Times* coverage of the DNC under Carter with that during Strauss's chairmanship. In terms of service coverage, there was no change between the Carter and Strauss years. But in terms of branding, *Times*

---

[266] Galvin, *Presidential Party Building*, 216.

[267] "New Democratic National Chairman," *New York Times*, January 22, 1977.

[268] Galvin, *Presidential Party Building*, 211.

[269] In December of that year, the DNC created a 12-minute film celebrating Carter's presidency to be shown at that year's midterm convention. The DNC also opposed the G.O.P. proposals to cut taxes. See: "One-Third of Footage in Film for Democrats Supplied by the Navy," *New York Times*, December 8, 1978; "President Is Moving to Combat Antitax Sentiment," *New York Times*, June 22, 1978; "Middle Class Thinks Itself Hit Most by Taxes and Inflation," *New York Times*, August 1, 1978.

[270] "Democrats Seeking to Stem G.O.P. Tax-Cut Moves," *New York Times*, August 1, 1978.

[271] Galvin, who is one of the few scholars to discuss the program, bases his discussion on a series of internal memos proposing this program, but there is no further discussion of its implementation. To the extent that the DNC actually engaged in an offensive, it did not produce much media coverage.

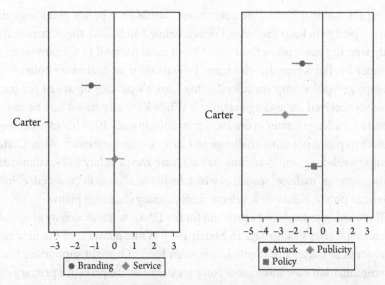

Figure 6.7. Negative binomial regression of Jimmy Carter's presidency on monthly (lagged) *New York Times* coverage of DNC branding and service activities, 1973–1980.
Note: This model includes variables controlling for presidential and midterm election years, a measure of *New York Times* length, and DNC scandals. The data coverage is limited to articles published between January 1973 and December 1980 covering only the DNC.
Source: Data collected by author.

coverage declined markedly (significant at the 0.001 level). This decline affected coverage of all types of branding activities, with coverage of DNC attacks on the GOP (significant at the 0.001 level), publicity activities (0.01 level), and policy position taking (marginally significant at the 0.10 level) all decreasing.

A major DNC-organized activity that did occur in 1978 was the second midterm national convention. As in 1974, there was little institutional enthusiasm for the event. The White House "gently [prodded]"[272] the DNC to reduce the number of delegates to the convention, and, as the convention neared, Carter's advisers became concerned it would spotlight growing discontent within the party with the president. The DNC organized the convention after the midterms to minimize its impact and tried to limit debate by requiring 25% of delegates to undersign a policy plank for it to be considered. However, liberal groups coordinated and were able to achieve the required number of signatures on several issues, including inflation, national health insurance, and energy monopolies.[273] At the convention itself, White had to include language in a healthcare plank

[272] "Democratic Leaders Vote to Cut Size of '78 Midterm Conference," *New York Times,* June 11, 1977.
[273] "Liberals Press Floor Fights before Democratic Parley," *New York Times,* December 8, 1978.

calling for national healthcare insurance,[274] while on a policy plank regarding Carter's pledge to keep the federal deficit below $30 billion, the administration easily won the convention floor vote.[275] But most harmful to Carter was an appearance by Ted Kennedy, who turned a workshop on healthcare policies into a campaign-style stump speech rejecting Carter's policies on social programs. Kennedy received a standing ovation.[276] While Kennedy stated that he did not intend to challenge Carter in the 1980 primaries, in early 1979 his advisers began to meet to plot a potential challenge to Carter's renomination.[277] After Carter's peculiar week-long soul-searching stay at Camp David in July 1979, culminating in his infamous "malaise" speech in which he noted a "crisis of confidence" in the American public, Kennedy accelerated his primary challenge plans.[278]

This challenge produced a problem for the DNC, as it was already involved in organizing Carter's campaign. In March 1979 White announced the new coordinator of the Carter Presidential Campaign Inc.[279] Outright supporting Carter for renomination now was a more complex situation. To prevent a primary challenge, White privately presented party leaders with a series of "harsh lectures" urging them to close ranks.[280] Publicly, White tried to dissuade Kennedy from challenging Carter and demanded Kennedy make a "categorical statement taking himself out of the 1980 Presidential race to enable President Carter to be re-elected," as there "is no question the single most important advantage in a political race is incumbency" and it would be "suicidal to throw it away."[281]

But by August, White had accepted that a primary challenge was likely, predicting that "the nomination of this party is not going to be given to anyone without a fight, including the President. [. . .] The President is going to have to run for it."[282] That turned out to be a bit of an overstatement. While Kennedy

---

[274] The latter meant overriding a decision made by the Strauss-installed Winograd Commission, which had investigated the increasing number of presidential primaries and the enactment of the different intra-party rules since the 1968 convention. See: Price, *Bringing Back the Parties*, 153.

[275] Rosenfeld, *The Polarizers*, 238–241; "Democrats, under Pressure, Vote to Praise Carter Budget Priorities," *New York Times*, December 11, 1978.

[276] "Kennedy Presses for Health Plan," *New York Times*, December 10, 1978.

[277] "Kennedy Assails Carter on Budget at Midterm Meeting of Democrats," *New York Times*, December 10, 1978; Witcover, *Party of the People*, 606.

[278] Witcover, *Party of the People*, 606–608.

[279] "New Director in Carter Drive," *New York Times*, March 9, 1979.

[280] Galvin, *Presidential Party Building*, 212.

[281] "White Holds Kennedy Must Bar Own Race if President Is to Win," *New York Times*, June 6, 1979. The DNC also ended its contract with a fundraising company in July 1979 after it became known that the company had also been sending out letters seeking support for a Draft Kennedy movement. See: "Party Drops Company Tied to Kennedy Draft," *New York Times*, July 24, 1979.

[282] "Energy Program Risks Losing Momentum as Congress Poses Obstacles," *New York Times*, July 26, 1979.

did indeed become an active candidate for the Democratic presidential nomination, Carter avoided campaigning after the beginning of the Iran hostage crisis in November 1979. With Kennedy's campaign off to a rough start due to a mangled television interview, and with Carter now a de facto wartime president, the Kennedy challenge largely fizzled.[283] While Kennedy performed well in later primaries, Carter won more states, votes, and—crucially—delegates and was renominated at the convention on the first ballot.[284]

In the 1980 presidential election, the Carter campaign relied on the DNC and largely limited the committee's activities on behalf of congressional candidates. But money again proved a major limitation, in part because the DNC had delayed major fundraising efforts while the Carter–Kennedy primary fight was ongoing.[285] As Price notes in 1979–1980, the DNC and Democratic congressional campaign committees combined raised nearly $19 million. But the RNC and its congressional campaign committees raised six times that. While the DNC did some publicity work—such as creating radio "actualities"—and engaged in campaign activities, its role was "at best a pale reflection of the RNC's."[286] While the RNC spent $3 million on state legislative campaigns alone, the DNC had "no sustained national effort, primarily because of financial limitations"[287] for those races. Looking back in 1982, Carter concluded that "the way the Democratic National Committee has been structured in recent years, it has been of very little help, either to an incumbent President or to the nominee of our Party" and that the DNC "quite often is more of a burden on a nominee than it is an asset to him."[288] By then, the feeling was mutual: former chair White replied to Carter's attack, saying, "I can't even get mad, all I can do is laugh about it. [. . .] The White House got everything it ever asked for in financial and political support and Carter expressed gratitude to me for what we did. I'm just amazed he'd say anything different from that now."[289]

---

[283] Witcover, *Party of the People*, 608–612.

[284] White announced on May 2 that the primary race was effectively over and that the DNC would start working to re-elect Carter. See: "Chief of Democrats Declares Race Over," *New York Times*, May 3, 1980.

[285] "Carter, in a Partisan Speech, Urges Election of All Democrats This Fall," *New York Times*, March 27, 1980.

[286] Price, *Bringing Back the Parties*, 43; "Candidate Grooming Isn't Left to Chance," *New York Times*, February 10, 1980.

[287] "Fight for Legislatures Stirs National Action," *New York Times*, November 3, 1980.

[288] "Carter Assails Party Panel, Calls It Burden to Nominee," *Los Angeles Times*, October 28, 1982.

[289] Ibid.

Conclusion

Scholarly assessment of national committee activity in the late 1960s and 1970s has—for understandable reasons—focused mostly on the DNC's reform efforts. The DNC committees that reformed and, later, counter-reformed the party's convention rules radically changed the process of presidential selection in the United States. But while reform was certainly central to the DNC's activities in this era, both committees also engaged in party-branding efforts. In fact, in the minds of DNC chairs, the reform efforts were a fundamental part of this process, aimed not just at changing the party as an institution, but also at healing the major divide within the Democratic Party on Vietnam and the controversial nomination of Hubert Humphrey in 1968.

During the Nixon–Ford years, the DNC tried to mend this divide while keeping both liberals and conservatives in the party. The approach it relied on to achieve this changed somewhat: during the first Nixon term, the DNC tried to appease liberals through reforms and succeeded in helping negotiate a party-wide consensus on withdrawal from Vietnam. After McGovern's defeat in 1972, DNC chair Bob Strauss changed tactics. Strauss was not in the business of producing an ideological or even policy-based message for his party and blamed the 1972 loss on an ideological wing within the party overextending itself and dominating in a way that alienated moderate voters. His solution was to steer the party back to a middle-of-the-road, centrist image. In practice, this meant Strauss simply projected the idea of unity. The result was a national party representing no clear policy agenda. Indeed, political commentator Richard Reeves in 1975 concluded that the "Democratic party, in fact, stands for very little these days except being against Republicans."[290] But while Strauss did not provide voters with clarity on the party's ideological or issue direction, it allowed for a coexistence of very different Democrats within the same party. And while the approach produced criticism from both liberals and conservatives, the mirage of a unified party culminated in Jimmy Carter's close victory against Ford, and Democrats back in unified control of the government. But with Carter in the White House, the DNC once again became sidelined: neither Carter nor his White House staff saw much value in the national committee and mostly ignored it during his four years as president.

While the financial consequences of the Watergate scandal limited the RNC's activity after the 1972 election, both Richard Nixon and Gerald Ford used the RNC to promote themselves and their administration. Under Nixon's first term, the RNC—particularly under chair Bob Dole—focused on defending

---

[290] "Nationally, the Democrats Are a Fiction," *New York Times*, June 1, 1975.

the president against criticism from Democrats. After Nixon's resignation, Ford used the RNC to try to present a new, kinder, image of the GOP. Still, after Ford's defeat in 1976, the RNC saw a major jolt in activity. Under RNC chair Bill Brock, the party not only saw new investments in its organization and publicity division; it also saw energetic attempts at reaching out to voting groups. The most important in this regard was a major effort to appeal to Black voters. Brock's interest in prioritizing the Black vote was a product of his genuine belief that the GOP could not ignore Black interests, as well as an understanding that the lopsided Democratic support among Black voters hurt the GOP electorally. Indeed, Brock himself lost his Senate seat in part due to the overwhelming support his Democratic opponent had received from Black votes in Tennessee. Throughout his four years as chair, the RNC under Brock thus invested heavily in appealing to Black voters—both through nuts-and-bolts candidate training by the Black-owned Wright-McNeil & Associates, and broader publicity efforts. The latter even included publicly connecting the RNC to Black leaders such as Jesse Jackson, who were increasingly dissatisfied with Carter's leadership.

Brock's focus on appealing to Black voters connected him more to the moderate wing of the GOP than to the ascendant conservative side, which would soon come to control the party. The one exception in this regard concerns Brock's attempts at bringing evangelical Christian leaders into the party. However, even there Brock's RNC underestimated the influence these evangelicals would soon have in the party. Indeed, the nomination and election of Ronald Reagan in 1980 fundamentally shifted the power within the Republican Party between moderates and conservatives. With Reagan's victory, the party's leader was now a conservative, and the long-standing argument from moderates that the conservative wing could not win the party elections and would lead to defeats similar to the 1964 loss by Barry Goldwater was proven wrong by Reagan's massive electoral college victory. The GOP now had a new party leader who would go on to dominate the GOP both during his own terms in office and in those that followed. Hereafter, the Republican Party become a clearly conservative political party. And the RNC would follow suit, while the DNC would face 12 years in the wilderness trying to reinvent the Democratic Party brand.

7

"Reagan's Party" versus "Recapturing the Center of American Politics," 1981–2000

Ronald Reagan's landslide victory in 1980 had a major effect on both parties. On the Republican side, Reagan's presidency represented the victory of the party's conservative wing. Dismissed in the 1950s and '60s by GOP moderates as a fringe group that would lead the party to electoral ruin, Reagan's victory concluded the long-term conservative project of taking over the Republican Party. Moving forward, Reagan's political message of constraining the federal government, a hawkish foreign policy, and socially conservative positions would become the new standard within the GOP. While the Republican National Committee (RNC) had long been one of the main proponents of a moderate political strategy, with Reagan as party leader, the committee now embraced these new policies. And the committee began centering Reagan in its messaging to voters: from 1981 forward, the RNC consciously and consistently presented the GOP as "Reagan's party."

Meanwhile, Reagan's 1980 victory initiated a 12-year Democratic exile from the White House, as well as six years of minority status in the Senate. In response to each lost election, the Democratic National Committee's (DNC's) response was roughly consistent: committee chairs blamed each loss on the party's inability to appeal to White voters because the party was seen as being controlled by "fringe" groups. As a result, the DNC tried to change the public image of the Democratic Party by supporting more conservative policies and openly dismissing the influence of Black leaders in the party. This strategy of downplaying the liberal image of the party included the DNC embracing a more aggressive approach on foreign policy, supporting fiscally conservative proposals on Social Security and taxation, and a tough-on-crime agenda (with, generally, implied racial connections).

National Party Organizations and Party Brands in American Politics. Boris Heersink, Oxford University Press.
© Oxford University Press 2023. DOI: 10.1093/oso/9780197695104.003.0007

After Democrats regained control of the White House in the 1992 election, Bill Clinton extensively used the DNC to promote his administration's policies (including its ill-fated attempt at healthcare reform) and his own re-election efforts. Indeed, the DNC's prioritization of Clinton often frustrated Democrats in Congress, who felt the committee neglected their needs. And the excessive spending the committee engaged in on behalf of Clinton also produced one of the biggest financial scandals in national committee history when it was revealed that the DNC had accepted extensive donations from foreign nationals in the run-up to the 1996 election. Meanwhile, the RNC used its time as an out-party in the 1990s to invest in its publicity division—including building a new TV studio, and entering the Internet age with a variety of programs. But with competitive presidential primary elections beginning earlier each cycle, both the RNC and the DNC in out-years also began to see limits to their ability to try to produce a coherent party message. While still engaging in many of the same strategies they relied on in the past—including policy-setting organizations and new publicity innovations—out-committees in this period increasingly began to cede the spotlight to their party's presidential contenders.

The DNC during the Reagan–Bush Era

The 1980 election represented a particularly bitter pill for Democrats. Jimmy Carter became the first elected president since Herbert Hoover to lose re-election and won only 41% of the popular vote and six states plus the District of Columbia. Additionally, Republicans—for the first time since 1954—won a majority in the Senate, leaving Democrats only majority control in the House (see Figure 7.1). In the days after the election, leading Democrats told the *Wall Street Journal* that the election results required them to "sit back and try to figure out what the party really stands for."[1] The *Los Angeles Times* reported that "many Democrats believe their basic problem cannot be solved until they go through the tortuous process of finding a new identity for themselves."[2] Democratic strategist Harold M. Ickes concluded that "when you say 'I'm a Democrat' now, people don't know what you stand for."[3] Even outgoing Vice President Walter Mondale suggested that "one of the virtues of losing is that it gives you time to think again, and to refresh yourself" and that, given the size of the loss, 1980 had provided the party with "a priceless opportunity" to focus on the "central questions"[4] of what the party

---

[1] "Licking Wounds," *Wall Street Journal*, November 6, 1980.
[2] "Democrats Seek Formula for Regrouping in 1980s," *Los Angeles Times*, December 22, 1980.
[3] Ibid.
[4] Ibid.

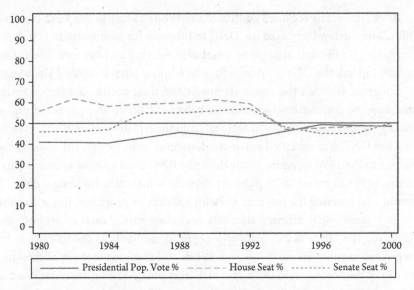

Figure 7.1. Democratic electoral performance in presidential, House, and Senate elections, 1980–2000. *Source: Congressional Quarterly's Guide to U.S. Elections*, 7th ed. (Washington, DC: Congressional Quarterly, 2016).

actually stood for. To reform the party's brand, those same Democrats looked to the DNC. In part, this was based on the recent role the RNC had played in the GOP, as "even Democrats agree that GOP chairman Bill Brock should be given much of the credit for the Republican landslide,"[5] and the DNC was advised to copy "the Republicans by setting down some basic themes and promoting them through a national advertising campaign."[6]

DNC chairman and Carter appointee John White announced he would not seek to remain in office, and in the contest for his replacement—a position White described as not "all that swell a job [. . .] but right now the only bone in the yard"[7]—several elected officials who had lost their races in the 1980 election considered running for the chairmanship, including Arkansas governor Bill Clinton and Indiana senator Birch Bayh.[8] In the end, however, only one serious contender emerged: Charles Manatt, chair of the Democratic Party in California and of the DNC's national finance council. Manatt campaigned extensively, reportedly spending between $48,000 and $72,000 to win the job.[9] By the time the DNC met in February 1981, Manatt had secured majority support among

[5] "Licking Wounds."
[6] "In Era of Permanent Campaign, Parties Look to 1982," *New York Times*, January 26, 1981.
[7] "The Democrats Look for New Ideas and Jobs," *New York Times*, November 9, 1980.
[8] Ibid.
[9] "Manatt Working to Win Party Post," *Los Angeles Times*, January 24, 1981.

committee members, and his opponents dropped out of the race. In his acceptance speech, Manatt described the DNC as having been "out-conceptualized,
out-organized, out-televised, out-coordinated, out-financed, and out-worked"[10]
in the 1980 election. While the RNC had stated $67 million in receipts in
Federal Election Commission (FEC) filings for the period 1979–1980, the
DNC over the same period reported only $14.7 million.[11] Indeed, to illustrate
how dire the DNC's condition had become, the *Wall Street Journal* reported that
the committee had in its headquarters "15 IBM Selectric typewriters [. . .] but
only three 'elements' (those little round typing balls) to operate them."[12] Manatt
promised he would have the committee "recapture the initiative in ideas and organization and planning."[13]

Manatt's core strategy in this regard was based on the understanding that the
1980 disaster was the consequence of White blue-collar voters abandoning the
party due to the (perceived) influence of "interest groups"—that is, Black, feminist, and other liberal activists—in the party. This perception was not unique to
Manatt: speaking in February 1981, then-still-DNC-chair White explained that

> the political needs of our traditional supporters—white ethnics, urban
> dwellers, labor, blue-collar workers, small businessmen—have changed
> but we haven't changed with them. [. . .] Blue-collar workers have
> moved into the same middle-class bracket as white-collar workers and
> have the same concerns about taxes, the environment, schools. [. . .]
> We have to capture the center. But that doesn't mean we have to be less
> compassionate or progressive.[14]

Manatt attempted to boost the role of the blue-collar faction by adding union
leaders as new at-large DNC members, and at the same time decreasing the
overall strength of Black members.[15] The DNC also created the Democratic
Labor Council—an organization combining representatives of the DNC with
20 unions.[16] Black Democrats interpreted these actions as an attack: California

[10] "Manatt Takes Over as New Democrat Chief," *Los Angeles Times*, February 27, 1981.

[11] "DNC Services Corp / Democratic National Committee: 1979–1980," (FEC ID: C00010603),
https://www.fec.gov/data/committee/C00010603/?tab=summary&cycle=1980; "Republican
National Committee: 1979–1980" (FEC ID: C00003418), https://www.fec.gov/data/committee/
C00003418/?cycle=1980.

[12] "The Democrats Now Search for Solutions," *Wall Street Journal*, July 27, 1981.

[13] "Manatt Takes Over as New Democrat Chief," *Los Angeles Times*, February 27, 1981.

[14] Cited in Philip A. Klinkner, *The Losing Parties: Out-Party National Committees, 1956–1993*
(New Haven, CT: Yale University Press, 1994), 156.

[15] "Democrats Bicker over Black Seats," *Los Angeles Times*, February 27, 1981; "Democrats
Entangled in Dispute over Party Positions for Blacks," *New York Times*, February 27, 1981.

[16] "Democrats, Labor Formally Become Allies," *Chicago Tribune*, January 6, 1982.

assemblywoman and DNC member Maxine Waters called on "Chuck Manatt [to] stop his one-man effort to disrespect blacks and minorities."[17] Around the same time, the DNC introduced unpledged delegates (commonly referred to as "superdelegates") to the 1984 Democratic National Convention. On the advice of a commission led by North Carolina governor James Hunt, the DNC agreed to decrease the power of interest groups by reserving delegate spots for elected officials. With 548 new delegates added for the 1984 convention, this meant that "members of Congress, governors, mayors, state chairmen, and other officials" would make up slightly more than 14% of the total delegation. As Hunt explained, the introduction of superdelegates was intended to "make the convention more representative of the mainstream of the party."[18]

In addition to trying to downplay the influence of Black leaders, the DNC largely relied on attacking Reagan and the GOP as the party of wealthy, out-of-touch, right-wing extremists who were looking to undermine core government programs. Much of this approach centered on Reagan representing, as Manatt wrote in a letter to two million Democratic voters, a "small fringe group" intent on weakening Social Security.[19] Some of the DNC's attacks came in the form of a series of television ads in the summer of 1982. This included one ad featuring images of "Republican tax cuts filling champagne glasses but trickling only a few drops into a coffee mug" and closed with the slogan "It isn't fair, it's Republican." Another ad featured a Baltimore factory worker who had appeared in a Reagan ad in 1980 but now blamed Republicans for "unemployment [being] the highest since the Great Depression," while another featured a rampaging elephant in a china shop.[20] As reporter David Broder wrote in February 1983, the DNC played an important role in "orchestrating an effective Democratic propaganda attack on such issues as Social Security and the recession"[21] during the first two years of the Reagan administration.

The DNC also innovated its publicity outreach efforts. Some of these followed the GOP's example. In 1983, the DNC announced that it now had the capacity to provide members of Congress with the ability to record interviews

[17] See: "Blacks Issue Election Warning," *Chicago Tribune,* April 21, 1984; "Black Mayors Criticize Democratic Committee," *Washington Post,* April 21, 1984.

[18] "Democrats' Unit Votes to Relax '70s 'Reforms,'" *Washington Post,* January 16, 1982.

[19] "Democrats Assail Reagan in Mailings," *New York Times,* September 3, 1981. See also: "Reagan Addresses Union Convention," *New York Times,* September 4, 1981; "Democratic Convention May Vote on Nuclear Freeze," *Washington Post,* June 13, 1982; "Democrats Open Parley by Assailing Reagan," *New York Times,* June 26, 1982.

[20] "Democrats Plan New Set of TV Ads," *New York Times,* July 28, 1982; "Democrats Slate Radio-TV Blitz on GOP Policies," *Los Angeles Times,* September 14, 1982.

[21] "Manatt Rebuilding Democrats, Step by Step, for 1984 Battles," *Washington Post,* February 5, 1983.

with home television stations and transmit the video by satellite. While an important new tool for Democratic legislators, Republican members of Congress had been using this technology for more than a year.[22] The DNC also produced the party's responses to Reagan's State of the Union addresses. In 1982 the party created a pre-taped program showcasing politicians and voters, including "man-in-the-streets and woman-in-the-unemployment-line interviews" in which one elderly woman concluded that she preferred Herbert Hoover over Reagan as "he was blunt and he was what he seemed, and this one is charming and he beguiles you."[23] The 1983 program featured Democratic members of Congress presenting a series of Democratic alternatives to Reagan's agenda aimed at middle-class voters, such as simplification of the tax code, federal budgets on a pay-as-you-go basis, investments in the modernization of industries, and being "tough on trade."[24]

Manatt also brought back the telethon format. Airing on NBC in 41 states in May 1983, the DNC created a 17-hour program described as a "political Woodstock." During this show, the DNC aimed to add 300,000 new donors and raise $8 million while simultaneously promoting the party.[25] The broadcast combined appeals by politicians with a plethora of celebrities, including Jane Fonda, Paul Newman, Mary Tyler Moore, Gregory Peck, Jack Lemmon, Kris Kristofferson, Willie Nelson, and Waylon Jennings.[26] However, the telethon was a bust in terms of financial gain: initially scheduled to cost just $1 million when the project was announced, the budget ballooned to between $5 and $6 million, and local party leaders warned that the show would never be able to recoup this amount. On top of this, the RNC called on Republicans to call in to the show and keep the lines busy so that Democrats would be unable to get through and donate. While Manatt initially announced that the show made $20 million, in reality only $3 million was raised and 100,000 new donors added.[27]

In terms of policy, Manatt created a new—though unsuccessful—version of the Democratic Advisory Council (DAC). Shortly after the 1980 election,

[22] "Briefing," *New York Times*, August 5, 1983.

[23] "Democrats Hold Reagan's Theme Has Been Unfairness to the Needy," *New York Times*, January 27, 1982.

[24] "Democrats Answer Reagan with Fistful of Solutions," *Los Angeles Times*, January 26, 1983.

[25] "Democrats Plan a 17-Hour 'Political Woodstock' on TV to Raise Campaign Funds," *Los Angeles Times*, January 28, 1983.

[26] "Celebrate America Display Ad 19," *New York Times*, May 28, 1983.

[27] "Democrats Plan a 17-Hour 'Political Woodstock.'"; "Telethon Assailed in New Mexico by Leading Democrats," *Washington Post*, May 21, 1983; "Democratic Head Assails Bid by G.O.P. to Disrupt Telethon," *New York Times*, May 24, 1983; "TV Highlights: Stars Are Out for Democrats," *Chicago Tribune*, May 28, 1983; "Party Is Deep in Red: Democrats Must Stump for Dollars," *Wall Street Journal*, July 3, 1984.

the *New York Times* reported that leading Democrats believed the party needed "a new kind of instrument, similar to the old Democratic Advisory Committee [sic] of the 1950's, to help develop and publicize [...] new ideas about governing and new means of pursuing the traditional Democratic goals [...]."[28] In 1981, Manatt announced the creation of the National Strategy Council (NSC), charged with shaping "new ideas for the party."[29] In October 1981, Ted Kennedy, Mondale, Byrd, California governor Edmund G. Brown, New York mayor Ed Koch, and members of Congress such as Barney Frank (MA) and Charles Rangel (NY) gathered at the council's first meeting. While the members had no trouble criticizing Reagan, identifying an alternative proved complicated. Koch charged the Democratic Party with being too closely aligned with liberal lost causes and called on it to "[recapture] the center of American politics" by becoming more critical of welfare fraud, crime, busing, and racial quotas.[30] Other participants just noted a lack of ideas: Boston mayor Kevin White concluded that "we have no idea of what forward is, as distinguished from just winning."[31] In 1982, the NSC met again to discuss "Reaganomics" and Democratic economic alternatives. The main conclusion of this session was that while "Reagan is slipping [...] our party hasn't recovered as much as Ronald Reagan has failed. What we have to say now is 'Here are our ideas. . . .' "[32] A midterm platform created by the DNC in 1982 suffered from the same flaws and—in the assessment of the *New York Times*—was "pretty specific on charges of what President Reagan has done wrong and pretty general about what the Democrats would do differently."[33] After the 1982 midterms, the NSC met infrequently, had limited staff, and was perceived as a low priority within the DNC.[34]

Meanwhile, in Congress, conservative (mostly Southern) Democrats proved willing to work with Reagan and the Republicans on a number of issues, to the frustration of liberals in the party. The DNC tried to put pressure on these conservatives, but with little success. In June 1981, the executive committee of the DNC unanimously called on House Democrats to oppose proposed legislation that would cut taxes and future Social Security benefits. DNC vice chairman Richard G. Hatcher warned Democratic elected officials that "we are watching very, very closely" and that "those who present themselves to the electorate

---

[28] "Democrats in Search of Ideas," *New York Times*, January 25, 1980.

[29] "Democrats, Mood Optimistic, Plan Election Moves," *New York Times*, February 7, 1982.

[30] "Top Democrats Bid Party Panel Develop Issues," *New York Times*, October 18, 1981.

[31] Ibid.

[32] "Democrats, Mood Optimistic, Plan Election Moves," *New York Times*, February 7, 1982.

[33] "Democrats Starting a Platform Two Years Early," *New York Times*, June 20, 1982.

[34] David E. Price, *Bringing Back the Parties* (Washington, DC: Congressional Quarterly Press, 1984); Caroline Arden, *Getting the Donkey out of the Ditch: The Democratic Party in Search of Itself* (Westport, CT: ABL-CIO, 1988), 53–60.

as Democrats [. . .] are expected to support the principles of the Democratic Party."[35] The DNC announced it would engage in "grass-roots politicking" in six Southern states to put pressure on conservative "boll weevil Democrats" to oppose Reagan's proposed tax cuts.[36] The one area where the DNC was successful in producing a party-wide policy position concerned support for a nuclear weapons freeze. After debating the issue in the run-up to writing its 1982 midterm platform, Manatt in 1983 announced that the party now strongly supported arms control, placing the Democratic Party "and its presidential candidates on record in favor of a mutual and verifiable nuclear freeze."[37]

Despite these difficulties, the DNC was able to recover from the slump it experienced during the Carter era. A year after Manatt's election, the DNC was "awash in Republican-style task forces and targeting committees, strategy councils and study groups, programs for recruitment and programs for direct mail fundraising and workshops where they tell each other how to put it all together."[38] This revitalization is reflected in *New York Times* coverage of the DNC under Manatt. Figure 7.2 shows the results of negative binomial regressions in which Manatt's chairmanship is the independent variable and the lagged monthly *New York Times* coverage of DNC branding and service activities are the dependent variables. In this model, the data is limited to just those articles covering the DNC published between January 1977 and December 1984— thereby comparing coverage of the Manatt-led DNC with that during Carter's presidency. Coverage of the DNC's branding and service activities increased markedly during the Manatt era (significant at, respectively, the 0.001 and the 0.01 level). However, while coverage of the DNC's publicity efforts and attacks on the GOP increased (both significant at the 0.001 level), coverage of policy position taking did not. Indeed, much like it had under Strauss, Manatt's DNC thus was mostly branding the Democratic Party in opposition to the GOP, without setting a clear positive policy agenda for the party.

But a more active DNC with no clear alternative to the Reagan-led GOP did not restore the Democratic Party to electoral success. The 1982 midterms were only a moderate success, with gains in the House but a continuation of the status quo in the Senate. And the 1984 election proved an even bigger disappointment than 1980, as Democratic nominee Walter Mondale won only one

[35] "Panel of Democrats Makes Loyalty Plea," *New York Times*, June 5, 1981.

[36] "Democrats Seek Public's Support to Counter Reagan Tax Proposal," *New York Times*, July 7, 1981.

[37] "Party Chairman Puts Democrats behind a Freeze," *Washington Post*, September 21, 1983. See also: "Democrats to Address Atom Arms Freeze at Parley," *New York Times*, June 14, 1982; "Democrats Facing Test on Unity Goal," *New York Times*, June 24, 1982.

[38] "Why Can't Democrats Be More Like Republicans? They're Trying," *Washington Post*, March 23, 1982.

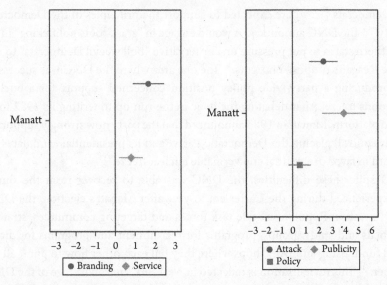

Figure 7.2. Negative binomial regressions of Charles Manatt's DNC chairmanship on monthly (lagged) *New York Times* coverage of DNC branding and service activities, 1977–1984. *Note:* This model includes variables controlling for presidential and midterm election years, a measure of *New York Times* length, and DNC scandals. The data coverage is limited to articles published between January 1977 and December 1984, and covering only the DNC. *Source:* Data collected by author.

state.[39] While Manatt tried to put a positive spin on the outcome—noting that Democrats would "never, ever have to face Ronald Reagan again"[40]—others predicted a "long and agonizing appraisal of how they can renew their appeal to the white majority in Presidential elections."[41] Shortly after the election, Manatt

[39] Manatt's term ended in a clash between himself and Mondale. After winning the nomination, Mondale attempted to replace Monatt with Bert Lance, the Georgia Democratic party chairman, to appeal to Southern voters. However, Monatt refused to resign and a majority of DNC members opposed the selection of Lance (a strong supporter of Carter), so Mondale had to back off. As a result, Manatt was retained for the duration of the campaign and told to focus on raising money for the ticket. Notably, the Manatt–Mondale dust-up represented the first time that a presidential candidate was denied the right to select and replace his party's national committee chair. While presidents would remain in charge of their committees, moving forward this shift meant that failed presidential candidates no longer had the ability to shape their party's national committees through their choice of chair after their defeats. See: Leon Epstein, *Political Parties in the American* Mold (Madison: The University of Wisconsin Press, 1986) 225; "Mondale Requests that Manatt Quit Party's Top Post," *New York Times,* July 15, 1984; "Manatt Retained as Party Chairman," *Los Angeles Times,* July 16, 1984; "Chairman's Job Said Secure through Fall," *Washington Post,* July 16, 1984.

[40] "The Democrats: Numb and Dazed," *Washington Post,* November 7, 1984.

[41] "Party Looks Inward for Ways to Regain Majority," *New York Times,* November 8, 1984.

announced he would not run for a second term but urged the party to focus on "appeals to working people and independents, one that will win back white voters in California, New York, and Alabama [. . .]."[42]Arizona governor Bruce Babbitt argued that the problem "of the Democratic Party is not the lack of a messenger but the incoherence of our message,"[43] while Tennessee Democratic Party chair Dick Lodge claimed, "the problem is the public's perception of the Democrats. The perception is that we are the party that can't say no, that caters to special interests and that does not have the interests of middle America at heart."[44]

The race to replace Manatt came down to three candidates: Paul Kirk, a former adviser to Ted Kennedy, former North Carolina governor Terry Sanford, and Nancy Pelosi, then the former chair of the California Democratic Party and a member of the DNC. Despite criticism from Pelosi that he was too close to Kennedy and organized labor, Kirk won the election comfortably.[45] Kirk announced that his core goal would be to help the Democratic Party "earn anew the intellectual and political respect of mainstream Americans."[46] Some reporters noted that Kirk's selection represented a rejection of the party's Black caucus and 1984 presidential candidate Jesse Jackson. Indeed, Kirk's election coincided with the rejection of Jackson's preferred candidate for DNC vice chair.[47] Other reports noted that some Democrats were "deeply ambivalent about its growing dependence on its allies in organized labor."[48] Combined, the atmosphere in the committee was fraught, with one DNC member summing up the experience by saying that after "one more meeting like this [. . .] I'm going home and hang myself."[49]

In 1985 centrist Democrats skeptical of Kirk created their own organization: the Democratic Leadership Council (DLC), under the direction of Al From, the former executive director of the House Democratic Caucus.[50] As Clinton, an early participant, explained in his memoirs, the DLC tried to forge "a winning message for the Democrats based on fiscal responsibility, creative

[42] "Manatt Urges TV Training for Nominee," *Los Angeles Times*, November 13, 1984. See also: "Democrats Voice Future Concern," *New York Times*, November 10, 1984; "Democrats Focus on Party Chief," *Washington Post*, November 9, 1984.

[43] "Democrats Need a Message as Much as a Messenger," *Washington Post*, December 26, 1984.

[44] "Democrats Chart the Way Back," *Washington Post*, November 19, 1984.

[45] "Democrats Pick a Kennedy Ally as Party's Chief," *New York Times*, February 2, 1985.

[46] "Party Elections Angers Jackson," *Chicago Tribune*, February 2, 1985.

[47] Klinkner, *The Losing Parties*, 183; "Democrats Pick a Kennedy Ally as Party's Chief," *New York Times*, February 2, 1985.

[48] "Democrats Remain in Doldrums," *Washington Post*, February 3, 1985.

[49] Ibid.

[50] Klinkner, *The Losing Parties*, 182.

new ideas on social policy, and a commitment to a strong national defense."[51] Although liberals in the party dismissed the DLC (Jesse Jackson referred to it as "Democrats for the Leisure Class"[52]) and the DNC and DLC had an openly hostile relationship, in terms of policy preferences the organizations were not particularly different. Indeed, Kirk's attempts at setting a policy agenda for the party generally revolved around the same perspective as the DLC, such as his proposal to eliminate Social Security for those who had "no real need for" it and an across-the-board budget freeze.[53]

Indeed, the DNC issued a remarkable mea culpa for abandoning "mainstream" American politics shortly after Kirk took control of the committee. The DNC's response to Reagan's 1985 State of the Union address (narrated by Clinton) included testimonials from Democratic voters crediting Reagan with improving the economy and criticizing Mondale's proposal to raise taxes. Clinton promised viewers that Democrats would

> work for a government that will go beyond the prison of past thinking, a government that will work in partnership with the private sector to foster economic growth, a government that will operate its own programs with a commitment to excellence and accountability and independence [from] narrow interests [...].[54]

The program received pushback from some Democrats—who described it as "defensive," "depressing," and "defeatist"[55]—but the program sent a clear message of the DNC's policy strategy moving forward.

As part of this process, the DNC also withdrew its recognition of caucuses—minority group organizations within the national committee. Kirk had opposed caucuses even before he was elected, arguing that their presence led "white male Americans [saying], 'Do we have to have a caucus to have a vote in the party?' "[56] After becoming chair, Kirk described the caucuses as "political nonsense"[57] and argued that "the proliferation of caucuses makes diversity a weakness. And if caucuses are a reflection of politics by separation, that is a formula for defeat."[58]

[51] Bill Clinton, My Life (New York: Alfred A. Knopf, 2004), 319.

[52] Klinkner, The Losing Parties, 186.

[53] "Top Democrat Draws Fire on Social Security," Los Angeles Times, April 18, 1985; "Democrats Trying to Contain Damage from Kirk Remark," New York Times, April 19, 1985.

[54] "Democrats Defensive in Response," Washington Post, February 7, 1985.

[55] "Democrats: No Emmy, Please," New York Times, February 8, 1985.

[56] "Democrats Chart the Way Back," Washington Post.

[57] "Democratic Party Starts to Get Its Act Together," Los Angeles Times, February 7, 1985.

[58] "New Democratic Chairman Meets with the Party's Southern Leaders," Washington Post, February 17, 1985..

In May 1985, the DNC executive committee voted to revoke the official recognition of the party's minority caucuses representing Black, women, Hispanic, Asian-Pacific, liberal-progressive, lesbian and gay, and business and professional groups within the DNC.[59] While the revocation still allowed the groups to hold informal meetings, they were no longer part of the party's organization. Unsurprisingly, the move was unpopular with Black leaders: Representative Mickey Leland (TX), a Black member of the DNC, described the decision as "an abomination. The caucuses have been a means for blacks and Hispanics to participate and generate interest in the party, and this is going to stifle them."[60] Similarly, Jesse Jackson dismissed Kirk's leadership as "a scheme" to prove the party's "manhood to whites by showing its capacity to be unkind to blacks."[61]

A few months later, Kirk announced a new DNC policy institute intended to "update the party's message to voters."[62] Kirk hoped this would pre-empt DLC attempts at replacing the DNC as "the 'true' voice of the party."[63] The Democratic Policy Commission (DPC) was led by Utah governor Scott Matheson and included members such as House Majority Leader Jim Wright (TX), Senator Al Gore (TN), and governors Richard Riley (SC) and Mark White (TX). The DPC's goal was to produce a "definitive set of proposals" to "set a tone" for the 1986 midterms.[64] Kirk limited membership to elected officials to signify that "the larger interests and broader agenda of the Democratic Party and the nation have superseded the singular agenda of elite groups"[65] in the party. The commission held a series of public sessions across the country to help shape its final report. In doing so, the commission's larger goal was to help "convince disaffected Democrats in the South and the West that the party has broken the grip of such interest groups as organized labor."[66]

DNC polls supported the strategy: a 1985 survey found that when "party leaders talk about fairness, middle-class voters see it as a code word for giveaway."[67] As Philip Klinkner concludes, the poll suggested that middle-class White

[59] Klinkner, *The Losing Parties*, 188.

[60] "DNC Withdraws Recognition of 7 Caucuses," *Washington Post*, May 18, 1985.

[61] "Kirk Mollifies Blacks," *Washington Post*, June 30, 1985.

[62] "Democrats Pick a Kennedy Ally as Party Chief."

[63] Quoted in Kenneth S. Baer, *Reinventing Democrats: The Politics of Liberalism from Reagan to Clinton* (Lawrence: The University Press of Kansas, 2000), 88.

[64] "Democratic Panel Is Formed to Lure Voters Back to Party," *New York Times*, May 16, 1985.

[65] "From Biden to Babbitt to Nunn," *New York Times*, May 18, 1986.

[66] For example, in the Midwest, the commission gathered to discuss the Reagan administration's lack of assistance for farmers. In Boston, the commission discussed the future of the industrial economy, while in New Orleans it gathered to assess Democratic military and foreign policy. Finally, in its Salt Lake City meeting, the commission focused on issues related to "family and community." See: "Panel of Democrats Studies Policy Directions," *New York Times*, May 4, 1986; "Democrats Focus on Farm Crisis in Midwest," *New York Times*, February 16, 1986.

[67] "Voters Wary of 'Fairness' Theme," *Washington Post*, November 23, 1985.

voters "interpreted politics through the prism of race" and that they viewed "the Democratic party as controlled by blacks, minorities, and fringe social groups."[68] The DPC report *New Choices in a Changing America*, released in September 1986, focused on providing "pragmatic" public-private responses to economic change and domestic economic reforms and mostly ignored issues like entitlement programs or civil rights.[69] The report was notably hawkish on foreign policy—attacking the Soviet Union as a "totalitarian society"—and supportive of increased defense spending.[70] As one unnamed Democrat described the report, it reflected an attempt "get out from under the false image that Democrats are weak on defense, have weird life styles and are big taxers and spenders."[71]

In the 1986 midterm results, Kirk saw evidence that his approach was paying off. In the House, Democrats won five seats while in the Senate they won eight seats and regained majority control. Kirk argued that these successes were evidence the party had regained its "psychological edge and shattered the thesis that the electorate was undergoing a fundamental change in party allegiance"[72] toward the GOP. In the wake of the midterms, party strategists called on the DNC to help produce a set of "goals and themes that would attract enough voters to give [the Democrats] an electoral college majority" and "replace the tarnished liberal image of the past [. . .]."[73] However, the DNC faced a relatively new obstacle in its ability to play such a role: the early start of the presidential primary campaigns. In the pre-reform era, presidential candidates generally waited until the start of the presidential election year to announce their campaigns. But the spread of primaries and caucuses since 1972 introduced the concept of the "invisible primary"—a time period of campaign activity in which presidential hopefuls began campaigning months before the first primary or caucus.[74] Presidential hopefuls now announced their candidacies in the spring of 1987, and this early start of the campaign limited the DNC's branding role—both because presidential candidates dominated political news coverage, and because

[68] Klinkner, *The Losing Parties*, 187.

[69] Ibid.; "A Modest First Step for the Democrats," *Washington Post*, July 30, 1986; "Democrats Elect Pragmatism over Ideology," *Washington Post*, September 23, 1986.

[70] "Special Panel's Report Assails Soviet 'Empire' and Stresses Family," *New York Times*, September 21, 1986; "Democratic Panel Shifts Foreign Policy Emphasis," *New York Times*, July 3, 1986.

[71] "Special Panel's Report Assails Soviet 'Empire' and Stresses Family," *New York Times*, September 21, 1986.

[72] "Oh What the New Year Might Bring," *New York Times*, January 1, 1987.

[73] "Parties Face Challenges as They Gear Up for '88," *Los Angeles Times*, December 26, 1986.

[74] William G. Mayer and Andrew E. Busch, *The Front-Loading Problem in Presidential Nominations* (Washington, DC; Brookings Institution Press, 2004); Marty Cohen, David Karol, Hans Noel, and John Zaller, *The Party Decides: Presidential Nominations before and after Reform* (Chicago, IL: University of Chicago Press, 2008).

the focus on intra-party debates between the candidates made it more difficult for the committee to take positions without taking sides in the primaries.

Nonetheless, the DNC attempted to manage the primary process. Kirk called for a positive campaign that should avoid "self inflicted political wounds," "campaigns devoting considerable expense and effort to tearing down the opposing Democratic candidates," and "bashing the party itself and to bickering about nominating rules and internal procedures."[75] Kirk established the Democratic Unity Task Force to monitor the tone of the primary campaigns and "advise, admonish, and—if necessary—publicly bring a political pressure to bear upon any candidate, campaign, or constituency group, indulging in negative campaigning."[76] Kirk also advocated for the 1988 platform to be short, concise, and devoid of "legislative laundry lists." Instead, the 1988 platform was to be "an open letter to the American people"[77] that should avoid "potentially damaging stances on specific, complex issues such as taxes, abortion or gay rights [. . .]."[78] A platform lacking specifics would deprive Republicans of targets for easy attacks and would not force Democrats in the South to campaign against their own party's policies.[79] Indeed, the DNC commission rejected inclusion of specific proposals favored by Jackson (the runner-up in the primaries to Michael Dukakis, the governor of Massachusetts) calling for higher taxes on corporations, a freeze in military spending, and a "no first use" rule for nuclear weapons.[80]

The 1988 election, however, proved to be another disappointment as Dukakis went down to defeat against Vice President George H. W. Bush. A silver lining was that Democrats in Congress fared much better: in both House and Senate, Democrats expanded their already comfortable majorities. But Dukakis's loss indicated that the Democratic Party continued to face the major question of how to gain back voter support at the presidential level—or, as a DNC member summarized the conundrum, "why is it we can elect people to every office in the land except for President?"[81]

Kirk announced he would not run for a second term, and the contest to replace him quickly centered on Ron Brown, a lawyer and Jackson's manager at the 1988 Democratic National Convention. Brown self-identified as an "independent, mainstream, progressive"[82] Democrat and would be the first Black

[75] "Democrats to Clean Up Act for '88," *Chicago Tribune*, March 12, 1987.

[76] Ibid.

[77] "Top Democrat Asks Platform of Few Words or Promises," *New York Times*, December 4, 1987.

[78] "Kirk Wants Platform to Be Brief, Simple," *Los Angeles Times*, December 5, 1987.

[79] "Kirk Wants '88 Platform to Be Brief," *Washington Post*, December 5, 1987.

[80] "Democratic Panel Passes Platform," *New York Times*, June 26, 1988.

[81] "Democrats Begin Quadrennial Debate," *New York Times*, November 11, 1988.

[82] Steven A. Holmes, *Ron Brown: An Uncommon Life* (New York: John Wiley & Sons, 2000), 166.

chair of either party. Brown reportedly spent $250,000 on his campaign and received support from Jackson, Kennedy, New York governor Mario Cuomo, and the AFL-CIO. Even Babbitt supported Brown, arguing that he had "credibility with the liberal wing to bring the party to the center. [. . .] It's the Nixon-to-China effect."[83] But Brown also inspired opposition: From opposed him because "we have been trying to move the party in a new direction for four years and that is not the direction of Jesse Jackson and Ted Kennedy."[84] Similarly, the Louisiana Democratic Party opposed Brown because his election would send "a message to the electorate in this state [. . .] that we are going away from the middle," and the Alabama party chair claimed that "Brown's selection will say that Ted Kennedy, Mario Cuomo and the other northeast liberals are back in control."[85] Despite such opposition, Brown lined up majority support in the DNC weeks before the chairmanship election in February 1989.[86]

Brown announced he would use the DNC as a "campaign organization" and the party would "have to send a different kind of message"[87] and that Democrats would present voters with a "tougher" image: "We need to say flat out: There is no one tougher than Democrats when it comes to protecting our children from drugs, when it comes to protecting our cities against crime, and when it comes to protecting our nation against aggression and terrorism."[88] Strengthening the Democratic Party's reputation was crucial because Democrats "don't have a real strong identity," and, as a result, "all the garbage, trash and nonsense our opponents throw at us stick."[89] As chair, Brown continued to embrace the kind of centrist policies Kirk had supported during his term. For example, Brown supported legislative plans to roll back Social Security payroll taxes—plans the DLC also supported—as "it just makes sense for us Democrats to be on the side of cutting payroll taxes for working people [. . .]."[90] Brown also attacked Bush for not being strong enough in his efforts to fight drug use: "everyone knows that

---

[83] "Jones, Barnes Join Race to Head DNC," *Washington Post,* December 15, 1988. See also: "Kirk to Quit Top Democratic Party Job," *New York Times,* December 6, 1988; "Kennedy Endorses Ex-Aide," *New York Times,* December 8, 1988; "The Jackson Problem," *Washington Post,* December 11, 1988; "Cuomo and Bradley Back Jackson Aide to Lead Democrats," *New York Times,* December 22, 1988; "Labor Leaders Back Brown for DNC Chair," *Washington Post,* January 12, 1989; Baer, *Reinventing Democrats,* 128.

[84] "Front-Runner Ron Brown Raises Doubts for Democrats Choosing New Chairman," *Los Angeles Times,* December 26, 1988.

[85] "Brown's DNC Rival Bows Out," *Washington Post,* January 26, 1989.

[86] "Ex-Jackson Aide Confident of Winning Top Party Post," *New York Times,* January 26, 1989; "Brown's Path Clear for Leader of Party as Contender Quits," *New York Times,* January 31, 1989.

[87] "Ron Brown: Party's Image Is on the Line," *Los Angeles Times,* February 9, 1989.

[88] "New Chairman Tells Democrats to Be Tough," *New York Times,* February 16, 1989.

[89] "Democrats: Let's Get On with It," *Chicago Tribune,* June 19, 1989.

[90] "Moynihan Plan Gets Big Backer," *Chicago Tribune,* March 24, 1990.

drug violence in this country is getting worse, not better. Cocaine addiction is up, the murder rate is the highest ever, our prisons and courts are overflowing and overwhelmed."[91] Brown promised that Democrats would fight a "real" drug war by increasing the number of prosecutors and police officers.

But Brown's attempts also faced pushback, some of which was connected to his own race. While Brown himself shrugged off the historic nature of his election—noting that "this isn't the first thing I've done that was previously for whites only"[92]—Black Democratic leaders at times seemed particularly disappointed in Brown's role as DNC chair. In March 1989, Brown endorsed Richard M. Daley in the Chicago mayoral election while Jackson had expressed his support for Black independent candidate Timothy C. Evans.[93] In response to Brown's support for Daley, Representative Gus Savage (IL) told Black voters in Chicago that "when Ron Brown brings his Oreo you-know-what into Chicago, I'll guarantee I'm going to help organize a reception party for him at the airport and to follow him all the way to some white hotel to denounce his coming in [to Chicago]."[94] Meanwhile, Jackson criticized Brown's campaign visits as intended "not to garner votes for Daley" but as Brown passing "a litmus test for his unconditional loyalty to the party."[95]

At the same time, the DLC continued to challenge the DNC. In 1990 alone, the DLC added new chapters in Kentucky, North Carolina, South Carolina, Alabama, Mississippi, and Texas.[96] By 1991 the DLC's membership included over 400 elected officials, with chapters in 20 states.[97] Despite the DNC embracing largely the same goals, the DLC's hostility toward the committee continued: From dismissed the DNC as "a disaster" that played "the very kind of politics that brought us down to landslide defeats [. . .],"[98] while Clinton— gearing up for his presidential campaign—stated that he would "like [the

[91] "Ron Brown Blasts Bush's Drug War Efforts," *New Pittsburgh Courier*, September 28, 1991.

[92] "Ron Brown Declares Independence," *New York Times*, January 29, 1989.

[93] Steven A. Holmes, *Ron Brown: An Uncommon Life* (New York: John Wiley & Sons, Inc., 2000), 201.

[94] "For Democrat Brown, Warmth Turns to Chills," *Washington Post*, March 12, 1989. See also: "Democratic Leader, Bowing to Pressure, to Stump in Chicago," *New York Times*, March 14, 1989. Brown and Savage clashed again in 1990 after the latter criticized his (White) primary opponent for accepting contributions from Jewish donors. As a result, Brown decided the DNC would no longer fund Savage's re-election campaign. See: "Democratic Leader Scolds Savage," *Chicago Tribune*, March 25, 1990; "Ron Brown Cuts Funds from Savage Campaign," *New Pittsburgh Courier*, April 7, 1990.

[95] "Jackson Urges Unity to Help Evans," *Chicago Tribune*, March 20, 1989. See also: Holmes, *Ron Brown*, 201–203.

[96] "Moderate Democrats Trying to Grow Grass Roots," *Washington Post*, December 12, 1990.

[97] Rae, *Southern Democrats*, 117.

[98] Quoted in ibid., 121.

DLC] to be what people think of when they think of the Democratic National Committee."[99]

With the Democratic primary contest starting in 1991, Brown announced that the DNC would focus on raising money, plotting general election strategy, and conducting research while allowing presidential candidates to fight among themselves. As it became clear in 1992 that Clinton was going to be the nominee, Brown began to work on identifying a way to "sell" him to Democratic voters. This was particularly necessary because the Clinton campaign was almost out of money and running third in the polls—behind Bush and third-party candidate Ross Perot. The DNC paid for a Q & A session between undecided voters and Clinton, which aired on NBC.[100] Finally, Brown ensured that the Democratic National Convention focused solely on promoting Clinton: only those who had endorsed Clinton were provided with speaking slots, and Brown worked behind the scenes to make sure that the platform reflected Clinton's positions and was not challenged on the convention floor.[101]

While Brown did not produce major new publicity initiatives or new party organizations to help set party policies, the Democratic Party was more successful than it had been in previous years. In the 1990 midterms, Democrats strengthened their majorities in both House and Senate. Two years later, Democrats not only maintained their congressional majorities but also, finally, regained the White House. Commentators credited Brown for this victory by helping shape the party's criticism of Bush's economic record. The *Washington Post* argued that Brown changed the DNC "from a political backwater into a significant force in developing party and presidential campaign strategy."[102] Similarly, *Chicago Tribune* columnist Steve Daley noted:

> Brown was the guy on television telling giggling interrogators that, yes, a Democrat could win in 1992. [. . .] Brown kept pushing the idea that if Democrats could stop the ideological self-immolation they performed every four years, they might be able to organize themselves to beat the Republican ticket. [. . .][103]

[99] "'Mainstream' Democratic Group Stakes Claim on Party's Future," *Washington Post*, May 3, 1991.

[100] "Clinton Discusses Policy, Not Perot, in TV Forum," *New York Times*, June 13, 1992; "Lagging in the Polls, Clinton Also Faces a Cash Shortage," *New York Times*, June 19, 1992; "Democrats Use Experts to Seek Data on Bush," *New York Times*, July 2, 1992; "Democrats Hire Firms to Investigate Bush," *Washington Post*, July 2, 1992; "Contest Set by Democrats," *New York Times*, May 18, 1992.

[101] Baer, *Reinventing Democrats*, 201.

[102] "Clinton Team Assumes Control of DNC Today," *Washington Post*, January 21, 1993.

[103] "Some Advice for Next GOP Chairman: Learn from Democrats' Ron Brown," *Chicago Tribune*, November 15, 1992.

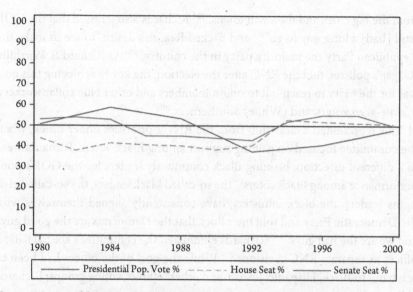

Figure 7.3. Republican electoral performance in presidential, House, and Senate elections, 1980–2000. *Source: Congressional Quarterly's Guide to U.S. Elections,* 7th ed. (Washington, DC: Congressional Quarterly, 2016).

And, after three disastrous performances, Brown's prediction of Democratic success finally paid off in 1992: despite sky-high approval ratings during the Gulf War, Bush went down in defeat against Clinton. With Democrats maintaining their majorities in Congress, the party was now—for the first time since 1976—back in unified control of government.

The RNC during the Reagan–Bush Years, 1981–1992

The 1980 "Reagan Revolution" not only placed Reagan in the White House with a comfortable electoral vote majority but also saw Republicans win control of the Senate for the first time since 1952 (see Figure 7.3). After the election, Reagan selected Oklahoma GOP chair Richard Richards to lead the RNC. Richards was the first state chairman to endorse Reagan in his 1976 challenge against Gerald Ford. While he represented the victorious conservative wing, he argued that Reagan's 1980 victory had been the product of a broad coalition of voters and that, as chair, his goal would be "to make this a party of opportunity for everyone—for Hispanics, blacks and whites, rich and poor, young and old, from the big cities and the small towns."[104] Richards also stressed that the GOP "still [had] a long way to go"[105] and backed Reagan's desire "to see us make the Republican Party the majority party in the country."[106] As Richard B. Wirthlin, Reagan's pollster, told the RNC after the election, the key to achieving this goal was for the party to reach out to union members and other blue collar workers, middle-aged voters, and (White) Southerners.[107]

This represented a clear shift from the RNC's priorities under Brock, when the committee focused on gaining support among Black voters. Richards went in a different direction, blaming Black community leaders for the GOP's poor performance among Black voters: "the so-called black leaders, the so-called civil rights leaders, the black ministers, have consistently aligned themselves with the Democratic Party and told their flock that the Democrats are the good guys and we are the bad guys."[108] Richards eliminated the committee's special liaison offices as separate RNC divisions.[109] While the goal of the offices had been to reach out to Black, Hispanic, Jewish, and other "ethnic" voting groups, Richards believed that

> [the liaison offices] became very exclusive groups. They haven't reached out. They haven't expanded. [. . .] What happens when you form groups like this is that they talk to themselves. The effort we made toward blacks and Hispanics was in error. It didn't work.[110]

Using Reagan's victory as a blueprint, the RNC in 1981 produced a new report outlining a strategy to provide unified Republican control of the federal government before the year 2000. The strategy largely relied on RNC publicity efforts, including "new magazines and television productions to spread

---

[104] "New GOP Chief Says Right Is Overstating Its Influence," *Los Angeles Times*, January 18, 1981; "Utah Lawyer Is Said to Be Reagan Choice as G.O.P. National Chairman," *New York Times*, December 17, 1980.

[105] "Party's Organizational Man," *New York Times*, January 18, 1981; "New GOP Chief Seeking to Gain Majority Status," *Washington Post*, January 18, 1981.

[106] "G.O.P. Is Urged to Work Harder to Build Up Party at Local Level," *New York Times*, March 28, 1981. Both Richards and Reagan referred to their goal of turning the GOP into a "majority party" frequently throughout 1981. See, for example: "GOP to Be Majority Party, Chief Predicts," *Washington Post*, June 9, 1981; "The G.O.P. Bid for Majority Control," *New York Times*, June 14, 1981; "Make GOP Majority, Reagan Urges Party," *Los Angeles Times*, June 13, 1981.

[107] "G.O.P. Is Urged to Work Harder."

[108] "Black Leaders Criticized by G.O.P. Chairman," *New York Times*, September 20, 1981.

[109] Daniel J. Galvin, *Presidential Party Building: Dwight D. Eisenhower to George W. Bush* (Princeton, NJ: Princeton University Press, 2009), 126.

[110] "GOP Chairman Is Abolishing Ethnic Liaison Groups," *Washington Post*, February 19, 1981. See also: "Republican National Committee 'Desegregated,'" *Los Angeles Times*, June 9, 1981.

the party's message,"[111] and spending five percent of its annual budget on research and development in political technology. The RNC proposed embracing the computer age by establishing a "futurist desk" at its headquarters to reach out to voters.[112] More practically, the RNC began using its publicity division to promote Reagan's legislative agenda. For example, the committee sent 200,000 postcards to Republican voters pre-addressed to Speaker of the House Tip O'Neill urging him to support Reagan's proposed budget cuts. The committee also used FEC data to create a list of voters that had donated to Reagan and conservative Democrats, and it contacted those donors to put pressure on the Democrats they had also supported. And the RNC encouraged voters to write op-ed pieces in hometown newspapers of conservative Democratic members of Congress and distributed nearly one million copies of a special edition of *First Monday* in support of Reagan's first budget.[113]

The RNC and RCCC also consistently aired TV and radio ads supporting Reagan and his policies. In spring 1981, the committees spent $500,000 on radio ads backing Reagan's tax cuts,[114] and the RNC's TV ads represented the longest and most expensive national advertising campaign in the history of either party—$12 million worth of TV ads between fall 1981 and spring 1982.[115] The ads promoted the GOP as the party that would "make America tough again"[116] and defended Reagan's policies on the economy, taxation, and Social Security. One ad featured a "grandfatherly mail carrier" describing Reagan's successes thus far and urging voters to "give the guy a chance!"[117]

To be sure, the RNC had money to spend: while the DNC reported only $10 million in total receipts during Reagan's first two years in office, the RNC reported receiving (and spending) $78.7 million.[118] But despite these efforts,

---

[111] "G.O.P. Sees Good Works as Good Politics," *New York Times*, April 19, 1981.

[112] "Republicans Look at the Future and See High Technology and Tight Discipline," *Washington Post*, July 2, 1981.

[113] "Planning an Avalanche," *New York Times*, March 10, 1981; "GOP Going to Bat to Get 62 Democrats on Base with Reagan Budget," *Washington Post*, May 2, 1981.

[114] "G.O.P. Radio Tax-Cut Ads Set," *New York Times*, July 24, 1981.

[115] "GOP Launches Ad Blitz 13 Months before Vote, Aims to Deflect Griping," *Washington Post*, September 29, 1981; "G.O.P. Fund Goals Set for '82 Races," *New York Times*, October 29, 1981; "Weepy TV Ad Could Give GOP Something to Really Cry about," *Washington Post*, May 18, 1982; "G.O.P. Ad Crediting Reagan for Pension Rise Is Attacked," *New York Times*, July 7, 1982.

[116] "G.O.P. Hoping Joggers Will Reach the Voters," *New York Times*, September 29, 1981; "G.O.P. Campaign Official Says a TV Ad Had Run Its Course," *New York Times*, June 17, 1982.

[117] "G.O.P. to Focus Campaign on 'Give Him a Chance,'" *New York Times*, September 3, 1982.

[118] "DNC Services Corp / Democratic National Committee: 1981–1982" (FEC ID: C00010603), https://www.fec.gov/data/committee/C00010603/?tab=summary&cycle=1982; "Republican National Committee: 1981–1982" (FEC ID: C00003418), https://www.fec.gov/data/committee/C00003418/?cycle=1982.

the 1982 midterms were disappointing: Republicans maintained their Senate majority but lost 26 seats in the House, putting them back near pre-1980 numbers. Richards had announced his retirement before the election and Reagan selected longtime RNC member Frank Fahrenkopf as the next chair.[119] Under Fahrenkopf, the RNC focused on re-electing Reagan. The committee unanimously endorsed Reagan for re-election in January 1983, well before Reagan had announced he would even run.[120] The RNC was then integrated into the Reagan–Bush campaign organization and aided in organizing voting registration drives and providing campaign publicity.[121] In the spring of 1983, the RNC began a $1 million television advertising campaign crediting Reagan with economic improvement—a remarkably early start for a presidential re-election campaign. The committee put on more TV ads in the early months of 1984 during the Democratic primary campaign to counter criticism of the administration's achievements by Democratic presidential candidates.[122]

The RNC also attempted to overcome the gender gap that had emerged in 1980. While Reagan had won a plurality of support among women, for the first time there was now a considerable gap between men and women supporting the Republican presidential candidate. Fahrenkopf announced he would work on "the steps we need to end discrimination"[123] on the basis of gender, and the RNC produced a series of mailers in which it stressed Reagan's record in appointing women, and his "wholehearted commitment toward insuring equal opportunities for women."[124] The RNC also trained women in the party to help convince other women to (re)join the GOP, by focusing on the effect economic growth had on working women.[125] In 1984, the RNC announced it would put significant funding behind female Republican candidates, and would "get the message out that [Reagan] is a strong support of women's rights and issues"[126] through another advertising campaign.[127]

[119] Additionally, Nevada senator Paul Laxalt was appointed "general chairman" of the party— a previously nonexistent job. See: "White House Puts Its Own Man on GOP Committee," *Los Angeles Times*, December 10, 1981; "White House Tightens Its Control over GOP," *Washington Post*, December 11, 1981; "Laxalt and Political Ally Chosen for G.O.P. Posts," *New York Times*, January 29, 1983.

[120] "Reagan Unanimously Endorsed for '84," *Los Angeles Times*, January 29, 1983.

[121] Galvin, *Presidential Party Building*, 131–132.

[122] "GOP to Spend up to $4 Million on TV Ads," *Los Angeles Times*, December 22, 1983.

[123] "GOP Chief Prods Reagan for Early Candidacy 'Signal,'" *Washington Post*, February 4, 1983.

[124] "Male-Female Split on Politics Found a Key Factor in Polls," *New York Times*, October 27, 1982.

[125] "G.O.P. Starts Training in 'Gender Gap' Politics," *New York Times*, June 6, 1983.

[126] "Republican Party Makes an Effort to Close a Perceived 'Gender Gap,'" *Los Angeles Times*, February 17, 1984.

[127] "G.O.P. Starting Campaign to Show 'Reagan Is Terrific on Women's Issues,'" *New York Times*, April 6, 1984.

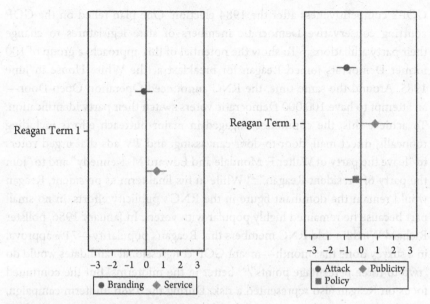

Figure 7.4. Negative binomial regression of Ronald Reagan's first term as president on monthly (lagged) *New York Times* coverage of RNC branding and service activities, 1977–1984. *Note:* This model includes variables controlling for presidential and midterm election years, a measure of *New York Times* length, and RNC scandals. The data coverage is limited to articles published between January 1977 and December 1984, and covering only the RNC.
Source: Data collected by author.

The continuation of the RNC's branding activities under Reagan is evident in the *New York Times* coverage the RNC received during his first term in office. Figure 7.4 shows the results of negative binomial regressions in which Reagan's incumbency during his first term in office is the independent variable and monthly lagged *Times* coverage of RNC branding and service activities are the dependent variables. In this model the data is limited to articles covering the RNC published between January 1977 and December 1984—thereby comparing *Times* coverage during Reagan's first term as president with that during Brock's time as out-party chair. While *Times* coverage of service activities increased during Reagan's first term (significant at the 0.05 level), combined branding coverage did not change—suggesting a continuation of the type of efforts that existed under Brock. In terms of specific branding activities, coverage of the RNC under Reagan increased with regard to publicity activities (marginally significant at the 0.10 level) but decreased in terms of RNC attacks on Democrats (significant at the 0.01 level).

With Reagan easily re-elected in a massive landslide but Republicans still far from a House majority, Fahrenkopf announced a series of plans to improve the

GOP's competitiveness after the 1984 election. One plan relied on the GOP courting conservative Democratic members of state legislatures to change their party affiliation.[128] To show the potential of this approach, a group of 100 former Democrats joined Reagan for breakfast at the White House in June 1985. Around the same time, the RNC announced Operation Open Door— an attempt to have 100,000 Democratic voters switch their party identification. To achieve this, the committee engaged in major outreach efforts including robocalls, direct mail, door-to-door canvassing, and TV ads that urged voters to "leave the party of Walter F. Mondale and Edward M. Kennedy" and to "join the party of President Reagan."[129] While in his final term as president, Reagan would remain the dominant figure in the RNC's publicity efforts, in no small part because he remained highly popular with voters. In January 1986, pollster Richard Wirthlin told RNC members that Reagan's popularity—74% approval in a survey done that month—meant GOP congressional candidates would do "two to three percentage points"[130] better in the midterms. But the continued focus on Reagan also represented a risk. During the 1986 midterm campaign, Republican strategists complained that the RNC lacked a message separate from support for the administration.

The 1986 midterms proved a setback in the path toward Republican unified government: Republicans lost seats in the House and their majority in the Senate. In response, Fahrenkopf announced the RNC would try to produce a new GOP message, abandoning antigovernment rhetoric and instead presenting it as the party of compassion:

> Compassion [is] a word we should never be afraid to use. Despite what the Democrats think, compassion doesn't belong just to them. [...] Concern over budget deficits will not override the concern of even the most conservative voter worried about losing the family farm, sending a child to college, or the need to clean up a toxic-waste site [...].[131]

However, despite Fahrenkopf's intentions the RNC became notably less active in 1987 and 1988 as the committee was facing the same issue confronting the DNC: the rise of long presidential primary campaigns. In 1987–1988, the GOP

---

[128] Kenneth W. Thompson, ed., *Leadership in the Reagan Presidency, Part II: Eleven Intimate Perspectives* (Lanham, MD: University Press of America, 1993), 35.

[129] "Republicans in 4 States Try to Lure 100,000 Voters from Democrats," *Washington Post*, July 27, 1985.

[130] "Reagan Pollster Says President's Popularity Bodes Well for G.O.P.," *New York Times*, January 25, 1986.

[131] "GOP Leaders Compose a New Song," *Washington Post*, January 24, 1987.

saw a clash between two former RNC chairs: Senate Minority Leader Bob Dole and Vice President George H. W. Bush. With the party also facing a decline in fundraising the RNC was forced to lay off 15% of its staff in July 1987, and little came from the "compassion" rebranding effort.[132]

After his victory, Bush selected his campaign manager Lee Atwater as the next RNC chairman.[133] Atwater announced the committee would concentrate resources on contesting a small group of winnable but rarely challenged seats in the House—races RNC spokesman Mark Goodin described as "seats where these guys have had free rides, where they're vulnerable on issues."[134] Additionally, Atwater argued that the RNC would aim to translate the party's electoral success in the South in presidential elections into down-ballot Republican success.[135] Atwater's other major project as RNC chair was a new attempt to reach out to Black voters, particularly "a kind of 45-and-under black [. . .] who is prone to listen to our message and is tired of being considered of being in the hip pocket of the Democratic Party."[136] Atwater was arguably not the most effective person to make this argument, as he had been held responsible for an advertisement in 1988 in which Dukakis was attacked for prison furlough policies in Massachusetts. The ad centered on a Black man, William Horton, who had kidnapped, raped, and tortured a couple while on furlough. Democrats such as Jesse Jackson dismissed the ad as racist.[137] Still, Atwater argued that reaching out to Black voters was "more than just a political necessity; it is a moral imperative" and increasing Black GOP support would result in "a strong representative party [. . .]."[138]

In the first months of his chairmanship, Atwater gave a speech at Atlanta's Ebenezer Baptist Church, promised he would recruit more Black Republican candidates and conceded that "affirmative action has worked" and that Black

---

[132] "GOP Committee Lays Off 40, Blames Lack of Funds," *Los Angeles Times*, July 15, 1987.

[133] "Despite Criticism Bush Picks Sununu as Chief of Staff," *New York Times*, November 18, 1988; "Fierce G.O.P. Partisan," *New York Times*, November 18, 1988; "Atwater Elected Chairman of G.O.P.," *New York Times*, January 19, 1988.

[134] "House and Local Seats to Be Targets of G.O.P.," *New York Times*, December 11, 1988.

[135] Ibid.

[136] "Atwater Tells GOP Governors of Plans to Attract Blacks," *Washington Post*, November 22, 1988.

[137] For more on the Horton advertisement and its racial implications, see: Tali Mendelberg, *The Race Card: Campaign Strategy, Implicit Messages, and the Norm of Equality* (Princeton, NJ: Princeton University Press, 2001), 134–165.

[138] "Atwater Is Elected Chief of RNC, Outlines Goals," *Washington Post*, January 19, 1989. In February 1989, Atwater was elected to the board of trustees of Howard University, Washington, DC's, major historically Black college. After student protests, Atwater resigned again a month later. See: "Atwater Resigns from Howard Board, Yields to Student Protest," *Los Angeles Times*, March 8, 1989.

voters should join the GOP since there now "is a large Black middle class and we are the party of the middle class."[139] After former KKK leader David Duke won a seat in the Louisiana state legislature as a Republican, Atwater dismissed him as "a pretender, a charlatan, and a political opportunist who is looking for any organization he can find to legitimate his views of racial and religious bigotry and intolerance,"[140] and the RNC provided Black radio stations across the country with a recording of Atwater's repudiation.[141] But, as under Brock, outreach to Black voters did not result in a change in Republican Party policies. During a May 1989 meeting with Black business leaders, Atwater acknowledged that the GOP had "a bad image on civil rights" and the party would "have to be very aggressive on knocking that image problem down" by "[opening] the party [up] and [showing] people that they are welcome." But Atwater also stressed he did not believe the party would have to make "any great changes"[142] in its policies to be successful.

Reviews of the Bush-era RNC were initially positive. With Atwater as its media-savvy leader, the RNC played an active role in promoting the party and attacking Democrats, especially on a series of financial scandals surrounding members of Congress. Some Republicans pointed to Bush's background as a former RNC chair as a particular benefit: Republican consultant Edie Mahe noted that while "Reagan didn't understand anything about the Republican Party, it was purely a vehicle for him. Bush is heart and soul part of the party."[143] But there was no doubt that the RNC's priority was supporting Bush. Atwater stressed in interviews that he saw himself as "the chief political operative of the Republican Party. I do not consider myself the leader of the Republican Party. President Bush is."[144] Bush's control was reflected in the RNC's positioning on abortion: while conservative Christians within the party called for a clear pro-life position, Atwater supported pro-choice candidates and called on Republicans to support "Republican candidates regardless of their position on abortion."[145]

[139] "GOP Chairman Will Reach for Blacks," *New York Amsterdam News*, February 11, 1989; "Atwater's Speech Makes Him a Target Again," *New York Times*, June 21, 1989.

[140] "Ex-Klansman's Victory Poses Hard Questions for G.O.P. Head," *New York Times* February 25, 1989.

[141] Ibid.

[142] "Republicans under Bush Reach Out to Minorities," *Los Angeles Times*, May 29, 1989.

[143] Ibid.

[144] "Man as Symbol: Atwater's First Year as the Republican National Chairman," *New York Times*, December 29, 1989.

[145] "Atwater Urges Softer Abortion Line," *New York Times*, January 20, 1990. See also: "The GOP's Abortion Travail," *Washington Post*, January 15, 1990; "G.O.P. Blurs Focus on Abortion, to Dismay of

But the RNC's role began to decline from 1990 onward. In no small part this was due to Atwater's declining health: in March 1990 Atwater was diagnosed with a terminal brain tumor. While he remained the party's "general chairman" until his death the next year, his illness left the RNC without leadership.[146] And Bush had a difficult time finding a replacement: in November 1990, Bush announced that Bill Bennett—the former secretary of education under Reagan—would become RNC chair in January 1991. But by December, Bennett announced he would decline the position due to concerns about whether he would be able to keep payments regarding a book he was under contract for. In January 1991, Bush instead selected Clayton K. Yeutter, his secretary of agriculture, as the new chair,[147] though conservative activist Paul M. Weyrich concluded that the choice showed "how far down in the Rolodex they had to go."[148]

Under Yeutter there did not appear to be any major RNC publicity operations, and his time at the RNC proved short-lived as he moved back into the administration as domestic policy director after just one year.[149] Bush next selected Richard Bond, a longtime adviser and lobbyist.[150] Under Bond, the RNC helped coordinate Bush's re-election activities. Notably, the RNC did so even though Bush faced a primary challenge from Pat Buchanan. An RNC spokesman left no doubt that the committee's focus was on re-electing its president: "The chairman is 100% behind George Bush and so is the committee."[151] But the RNC's role was

Some Party Faithful," *New York Times*, January 18, 1990; "G.O.P. Chiefs Meet to Plan a Strategy on Abortion," *New York Times*, January 19, 1990.

[146] "GOP Leader Hospitalized after Collapse," *Chicago Tribune*, March 6, 1990; "Republican Chairman Is Hospitalized Again," *New York Times*, March 24, 1990; "Atwater's Surgeon Says Brain Tumor Is 'Aggressive and Dangerous,'" *Washington Post*, April 5, 1990.

[147] See: "Yeutter Picked for Top GOP Post, Sources Say," *Los Angeles Times*, January 5, 1991. See also: "Bennett Said in Line for Top GOP Post," *Washington Post*, November 18, 1990; "Revamping the RNC," *Washington Post*, November 25, 1990; "Bennett Declines Republican Party Post," *Los Angeles Times*, December 13, 1990; "Lee Atwater, Master of Tactics for Bush and G.O.P., Dies at 40," *New York Times*, March 30, 1991.

[148] "Yeutter Picked for Top GOP Post, Sources Say," *Los Angeles Times*, January 5, 1991.

[149] RNC fundraising also proved to be lackluster during the 1989–1990 period: while the Republicans remained comfortably ahead of the DNC (which received only $14.5 million across this period), the RNC reported its lowest two-year receipt total since 1980 at $69 million (nearly $15 million less than during the comparable pre-midterm period of 1985–1986). See: "DNC Services Corp / Democratic National Committee: 1989–1990" (FEC ID: C00010603), https://www.fec.gov/data/committee/C00010603/?tab=summary&cycle=1990; "Republican National Committee: 1989–1990" (FEC ID: C00003418), https://www.fec.gov/data/committee/C00003418/?cycle=1990.

[150] "New Chairman Installed to 'Invigorate' G.O.P.," *New York Times*, February 2, 1992.

[151] Bond also accused Buchanan of having hijacked David Duke's message on race and religious tolerance and put a jacket and tie on it and try to clean it up." See: "Buchanan Calls for Ouster of GOP Chairman Bond," *Los Angeles Times*, March 11, 1992.

also subservient to that of the political team in the White House and in his own campaign organization. Indeed, as early as February 1991, Bush's Chief of Staff John H. Sununu had made it clear that he intended to control Bush's schedule of appearances, policy development, and speech writing during the campaign—leaving relatively little influence to the RNC.[152]

The RNC and the Clinton Administration, 1993–2000

The 1992 election ended the GOP's three-term winning streak. Bush's poor performance (he received only 37.5% of the popular vote) was partly the product of third-party candidate Ross Perot's strong showing but was bad enough that many Republican politicians anticipated a period of intra-party infighting. Rep. Jim Leach (IA) predicted that "the first verbal assault will come from the right, which will argue that if the Republicans were just purer, they'd be in no trouble" while "the second assessment, from the more mainstream and the public at large, will be that the party has become too co-opted by narrow groups."[153] Indeed, conservatives blamed the results on Bush's backtracking on his "no new taxes" pledge made during the 1988 campaign. Meanwhile, moderates in the party—such as Peter Smith, a former House member and head of the Ripon Society—noted that "the country finally got a look" at the "right wing extremists" in the GOP during the 1992 Republican national convention, during which conservatives like Pat Buchanan were given a prime time spot, "and the country turned its back on them."[154]

Several prominent Republicans considered a run for the chairmanship of the RNC—including former governors John Ashcroft (MO) and Pete DuPont (DE). Meanwhile, Senate Minority Leader Bob Dole (KS) proposed appointing Senator Mitch McConnell (KY) as general chairman.[155] In the end, Haley Barbour (an aide in the Reagan administration who had later become a lobbyist) won the election.[156] Barbour's victory seemed motivated at least in part by the RNC's need to have a chair "who could sit across from Bryant Gumbel and not

---

[152] "Amid Silence, Portents of Bush's 1992 Campaign," *New York Times*, February 13, 1991.

[153] "At Dawn of New Politics, Challenges for Both Parties," *New York Times*, November 5, 1992.

[154] "Looking to the Future, Party Sifts through Past," *New York Times*, November 11, 1992.

[155] "Republicans' Next Contest Is Strictly Internal as Party Fights to Avoid Democrats' Fate in '70s," *Wall Street Journal*, November 5, 1992; "Dole Wades into Republican Battle, Urges Sen. McConnell for New Post," *Washington Post*, January 8, 1993; "Rarity for Republicans: Party Leadership Race," *New York Times*, January 13, 1993.

[156] "Lobbyist Takes Over GOP," *Washington Post*, January 30, 1993.

let Bryant Gumbel get the best of him."[157] But the new chair was also expected, as Dole put it, to "sit down and find some common ground"[158] within the party. What that common ground should look like was not immediately clear. Indeed, Dole himself added that he did not have a remedy. Meanwhile, Bond urged the party to abandon the anti-abortion position it had taken in the 1992 platform and to "not cling to zealotry masquerading as principle."[159]

As chair, Barbour—who listed Bliss and Brock as his models—successfully reinvigorated the RNC's fundraising apparatus, and the committee reported receipts of $105.8 million in the 1993–1994 cycle.[160] Barbour used part of these donations to make major investments in the RNC's publicity division. This included building a new TV studio in RNC headquarters paid for by a $2.5 million donation from household cleaning products company Amway.[161] The committee used this studio to produce daily 15-minute news feeds it broadcast to 750 television affiliates and news services. Additionally, the RNC produced *Rising Tide*, a weekly news show that ran on 2,000 cable systems with a potential reach of as much as 55 million viewers. The show (described by *New York Times* columnist Frank Rich as "slick and well financed" and also "less irritating than some of its Sunday morning counterparts"[162]) was promoted by Reagan and Bush, and early episodes had Dole host a Larry King–style call-in show.[163] Later, during the 1996 Republican National Convention, the RNC relied on the format to air 30-minute morning programs hosted by Barbour on the USA Network.[164] The expanded publicity division also joined the Internet age: beginning in 1994, the GOP maintained an outlet on the CompuServe online service called *Republican Forum*. In the first two years that the service was active, more than 100,000 people used CompuServe to download information about the party. These investments put the RNC at a considerable advantage in comparison with their Democratic counterparts during the Clinton years: Democratic Senator Tom Daschle (SD) concluded that Republicans were "years ahead" of Democrats in political communication during the 1990s.[165]

[157] "G.O.P. Seeks Identity and a Message," *New York Times*, January 31, 1993.

[158] Ibid.

[159] "G.O.P. Seeks Identity and a Message"; "Departing Chairman Scolds Republicans Over 'Zealotry,'" *New York Times*, January 30, 1993.

[160] "Republican National Committee: 1991–1992" (FEC ID: C00003418), https://www.fec.gov/data/committee/C00003418/?cycle=1992; "Republican National Committee: 1993–1994" (FEC ID: C00003418), https://www.fec.gov/data/committee/C00003418/?cycle=1994.

[161] "Amway Contributes $2.5 Million to G.O.P.," *New York Times*, November 24, 1994.

[162] "Tin Cans and String," *New York Times*, April 13, 1995.

[163] "G.O.P.-TV: New Image in Appeal to Voters," *New York Times*, January 30, 1994.

[164] "From Convention, G.O.P. Cable Show," *New York Times*, June 16, 1996.

[165] "Leading the Political Communications Race," *Washington Post*, April 24, 1995.

Unsurprisingly, the RNC used its new publicity tools to attack Clinton. Indeed, Clinton's presidency provided Republicans with an easy target. In the spring of 1993, as a series of scandals and negative press stories were surrounding the administration, Barbour noted that, "[Clinton] has done more to unify the Republican Party in 120 days than I'll do in four years."[166] Early in the administration, Barbour attacked Clinton for focusing on the issue of whether gay and lesbian service members could serve openly by dismissing this as "a political payoff [to] a very powerful special interest group of the Democratic Party."[167] The RNC also put pressure on members of Congress to keep them from supporting Clinton's legislative proposals. In response to Clinton's 1993 budget, the committee sent mailings to donors urging them to reach out to their members of Congress and threatening them with political repercussions if they supported the plan.[168] Simultaneously, the committee put pressure on conservative Democrats in Congress. Throughout 1993, the RNC aired radio ads in Democratic districts criticizing Clinton's tax policies and House Democrats who voted for tax increases but against $90 billion in spending cuts.[169] After the passage of Clinton's economic plan, the RNC changed its focus to the next major piece of Clinton's domestic legislative program: healthcare reform. Notably, the healthcare effort was partly funded by Perot, who offered $1 million of his own money for the RNC to air a nationally televised TV program criticizing the Clinton plan.[170] The RNC's ads warned viewers that the Clinton plan would add "100 new Government bureaucracies" and "Government price fixing, rationing, and delays" while its "mandates on small business" would cost "up to 3 million American jobs."[171] The healthcare plan stranded after congressional Democrats decided not to bring it up to a vote.

While opposing Clinton was a core element of the RNC's branding efforts, Barbour warned that "our success will not be guaranteed by [Clinton] messing up. We have to be seen as a party of ideas. [In 1992], a lot of people didn't

---

[166] "As Clinton's Problems Grow, So Do Hope and Unity of the Republican Party," *New York Times*, May 23, 1993.

[167] "Hearings Could Sway the Debate on Gay Troops," *New York Times*, February 1, 1993.

[168] See: "A Threatening Letter from GOP Draws Apology," *Los Angeles Times*, May 2, 1993.

[169] "At G.O.P. Meeting, an Uninvited Guest," *New York Times*, July 9, 1993; "For Some House Freshmen, Supporting Clinton Is Balancing Act," *Washington Post*, August 5, 1993; "G.O.P. Ads Attack Democrats on Tax Rise," *New York Times*, December 9, 1993.

[170] "G.O.P. Sees Crime as a Major Issue," *New York Times*, January 22, 1994; "GOP Works to Retain Its Best Issues," *Washington Post*, January 25, 1994; "Still Seeking an Alternative, GOP Launches Ads against Clinton Health Plan," *Washington Post*, May 21, 1994; "G.O.P. Studies Offer by Perot," *New York Times*, July 1, 1994; "Texan's Cash Will Finance TV Program for G.O.P.," *New York Times*, July 2, 1994.

[171] "Local Governments May Pay More in Health Plan," *New York Times*, October 20, 1993.

have a sense the Republican Party was for anything except to win the next election."[172] To help produce new policy ideas, the RNC created the National Policy Forum (NPF), consisting of 14 councils dealing with a variety of policy issues—including the economy, healthcare, family issues, and foreign policy. Each council included 50–80 members and held meetings between late 1993 and early 1994 to gather information and present Republican ideas to a broader audience.[173] The idea was that, in the words of NPF president Michael E. Baroody, the "Republican Party has a pretty strong understanding of what it believes and is secure in its convictions. So it can go out to the grass roots to test ideas."[174] While some Republicans expressed concerns that this would only spotlight internal disagreements, others—including former RNC chair Bond— praised the idea as providing the party with a chance of getting "new ideas on the record" but sparing it "something like the fractious mid-term conventions that the Democrats stopped having in the mid-80s. It basically puts a very smart distancing mechanism in place to prevent divisiveness."[175]

Despite these efforts, the center of such activity was in Congress where House Minority Leader Newt Gingrich produced his Contract with America. After its publication, the RNC quickly embraced this plan—installing an office at the committee HQ focused exclusively on promoting it.[176] The RNC also spent $1.9 million in TV ads in the last days of the midterm campaign attacking Democrats for cutting Social Security and Medicare.[177] And in the 1994 election the GOP's long congressional hopes were finally realized: whether through the Contract with America, slow economic recovery, or Clinton's scandals having Democratic congressional candidates (in Barbour's assessment) run from their president "like scalded dogs,"[178] Republicans won eight seats in the Senate and 54 seats in the House, and, for the first time in 40 years, the GOP held majority control in both houses of Congress.

With Republicans in control in Congress, the RNC began promoting its legislation. In February 1995, the RNC paid for TV ads supporting the GOP's balanced budget amendment to the Constitution in seven conservative-leaning states with Democratic senators.[179] Barbour was directly involved in promoting

[172] "GOP Chief Says Party Can't Just Be Negative," *Chicago Tribune*, July 8, 1993.

[173] "GOP Opens Hunt for New Ideas, Consensus," *Washington Post*, September 29, 1993.

[174] "G.O.P. Hopes New Group Can Attract Support from Outsiders," *New York Times*, November 15, 1993.

[175] Ibid.

[176] "Democrats Find a Target in G.O.P. 'Contract,'" *New York Times*, October 19, 1994.

[177] "New Attack by G.O.P. Lifts Democrats' Spirits," *New York Times*, October 28, 1994.

[178] "Democrats See Voters Lashing Out at Clinton," *New York Times*, June 9, 1994.

[179] The ads had limited to no effect: the constitutional amendment failed in the Senate by one vote, with only one Democratic senator in the targeted states—Senator J. James Exon (NE)—voting

the GOP's plans on Medicare reform, acting as "a vigorous field general in the rhetorical war" between Democrats and Republicans.[180] The RNC also attempted to influence media coverage of the plan, in part by trying to prevent reporters from referring to Republican proposals as incorporating "cuts" in the program. Barbour contacted the nightly news anchors of NBC and ABC, and a correspondent of CBS, chiding them for using the term in their reports.[181] The committee also backed Republican tax cuts vetoed by Clinton, spending $1.5 million on a tax season ad campaign aired in 22 states.[182]

Around the same time, the RNC began spotlighting immigration. In a March 1996 press release, entitled "America: Welcome Mat or Doormat," the RNC argued immigration (both legal and undocumented) was responsible for half of the decline in real wages for the lowest-skilled American-born workers. While the *Wall Street Journal* dismissed this as "nativist,"[183] Barbour responded that

> Republicans believe America must continue to be the land of opportunity, but that does not mean that everyone in the world can come live here. [...] While anyone has a right to advocate open borders, it is inaccurate to label as nativists those who support high, but limited levels of immigration. Nor is it nativist to protect our borders against the flood of illegal immigration that places an unfair burden on American taxpayers.[184]

In June 1996, the RNC used a $1.5 million ad buy—mostly in California—to air TV commercials criticizing the Clinton administration for "[supporting] illegal immigrants."[185] However, in contrast, Barbour continued the RNC strategy of refusing to take sides on abortion, arguing that "it doesn't do any good to say bad things about each other. It's silly to think everybody's going to agree on every issue."[186]

in favor. See: "GOP Ads Push Budget Amendment," *Washington Post*, February 14, 1995; "Budget Plan Fails in Senate, Setting Back GOP Agenda," *Wall Street Journal*, March 3, 1995.

[180] Barbour had advised congressional leaders to postpone changes to Medicare until after the 1996 elections. Once the decision was made to move on the issue earlier, Barbour came on board. See: "Republican Leaders Win Battle by Defining Terms of Combat," *Washington Post*, October 29, 1995.

[181] "2 Political Parties Turn to Airwaves for Medicare Debate," *New York Times*, August 16, 1995; "Republican Leaders Win Battle by Defining Terms of Combat," *Washington Post*, October 29, 1995.

[182] "GOP Ad Campaign Hits Clinton for Vetoing Tax Relief," *Washington Post*, April 10, 1996.

[183] "Nativist RNC," *Wall Street Journal*, March 20, 1996.

[184] "We're for Immigration: But There Are Limits," *Wall Street Journal*, April 2, 1996.

[185] "The Republicans Attack on Spending for Illegal Immigrants," *New York Times*, June 22, 1996.

[186] "GOP Leaders Urge End to Party Squabbles," *Washington Post*, May 6, 1996.

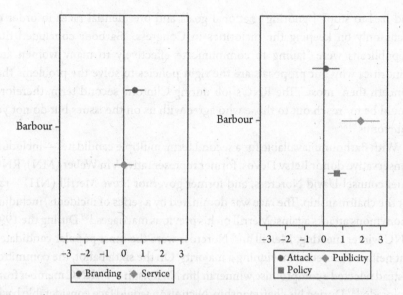

Figure 7.5. Negative binomial regression of Haley Barbour's RNC chairmanship on monthly (lagged) *New York Times* coverage of RNC branding and service activities, 1989–1996. *Note:* This model includes variables controlling for presidential and midterm election years, a measure of *New York Times* length, and RNC scandals. The data coverage is limited to articles published between January 1989 and December 1996, and covering only the RNC. *Source:* Data collected by author.

Combined, the RNC under Barbour saw a clear jolt of activity, reflected in *New York Times* coverage. Figure 7.5 shows the results of negative binomial regressions in which Barbour's incumbency as chair is the independent variable and monthly lagged *Times* coverage of RNC branding and service activities are the dependent variables. In this model the data is limited to just those articles covering the RNC that were published between January 1989 and December 1996—thereby comparing coverage during Barbour's time as chair to that during George H. W. Bush's term as president. *Times* coverage of RNC branding activities increased under Barbour (significant at the 0.05 level), while coverage of service activities remained constant. In terms of coverage of specific branding activities, the results show increased coverage of publicity activities (significant at the 0.001 level) and RNC policy position taking (significant at the 0.01 level)—reflecting the major investments in the RNC's publicity tools, and its promotion of the Contract with America.

While Republicans managed to maintain their congressional majorities in 1996, the election nonetheless was a disappointment, as Clinton easily beat Republican nominee Bob Dole. After the election, Barbour warned Republicans the party would need to improve its standing with women and minority voters and had to stop "[ignoring] national goals and presidential races in order to focus only on keeping the majorities in Congress." Barbour concluded that Republicans were "failing to communicate effectively to many women and minorities why our proposals are the right policies to solve the problems that concern them most." The RNC's job during Clinton's second term, therefore, would be to "reach out to those who agree with us on the issues but do not yet vote for us."[187]

With Barbour unavailable for a second term, multiple candidates—including conservative donor Betsy DeVos, former representative Vin Weber (MN), RNC chief counsel David Norcross, and former governor Steve Merrill (NH)—ran for the chairmanship. The race was dominated by a series of incidents, including anonymous attacks against Merrill on his previous marriages.[188] During the 1997 RNC winter meeting, Merrill and Norcross were the most popular candidates, but neither succeeded in winning a majority. On the sixth ballot, the committee instead selected a compromise winner in Jim Nicholson—an RNC member from Colorado.[189] During his chairmanship, Nicholson would face considerable backlash, as GOP insiders often criticized his lack of experience and underwhelming public role. Former Colorado state chair Don Bain described Nicholson as "a political rookie,"[190] while a GOP strategist complained in the summer of 1997 that Nicholson was "never seen, he's never quoted, he's excluded."[191]

To be sure, Nicholson's performance was constrained by the RNC's financial entanglements after the 1996 election. During the presidential campaign reports revealed that the DNC had accepted major donations from noncitizens, resulting in a multi-year criminal investigation. While the DNC was the main focus of these investigations, the RNC had also accepted donations from foreigners and had to return money as well.[192] The scandal involved Barbour's NPF, which had provided donors who contributed more than $100,000 with active involvement in the organization. Additionally, Barbour convinced a Hong Kong businessman to put up $2.1 million in collateral allowing the NPF to get a

[187] "Some Parting Advice," *Washington Post*, January 16, 1997.

[188] "Top GOP Post Could Attract Many Contenders," *Washington Post*, November 12, 1996; "List of Aspirants Grows for Top RNC Job Opening," *Washington Post*, December 13, 1996; "Reach Out, Barbour Tells RNC," *Washington Post*, January 17, 1997.

[189] "Republicans Pick Coloradan as Their New Party Chairman," *New York Times*, January 18, 1997.

[190] "New Leader for Republicans," *New York Times*, January 18, 1997.

[191] "RNC Chairman Trying to Move into Spotlight," *Washington Post*, July 20, 1997.

[192] "Clinton Announces New Limits on Fund-Raising by Democrats," *New York Times*, January 22, 1997; "U.S. Subsidiaries of Foreign Companies Gave Heavily to G.O.P.," *New York Times*, February 21, 1997; "GOP Groups Will Return Foreign Funds," *Washington Post*, May 9, 1997.

commercial bank loan that was used by the RNC to fund campaign expenses in the 1994 midterms.[193]

The RNC still found itself thrown into policy debates on abortion. While Nicholson tried to present the GOP as a "big tent," in 1998 antiabortion advocates attempted to pass a resolution banning the RNC from backing GOP candidates who opposed a ban on late-term abortions.[194] Nicholson (himself pro-life) urged RNC members not to make abortion a litmus test. Other former RNC chairs, including Bond, Barbour, and Fahrenkopf, backed him—as did Representative Henry Hyde (IL), a major figure in the party's pro-life movement. Meanwhile, Massachusetts Governor Bill Weld, a pro-choice Republican, described the resolution as a "litmus test worthy of Lenin."[195] While the RNC voted the resolution down, it did vote for a separate resolution rejecting partial birth abortion—though RNC member Tim Lambert, who wrote the original resolution, rejected this as "not a compromise" but "capitulation" to pro-choice Republicans.[196]

On other social issues, the committee had no problem taking positions. Nicholson attacked comedian Ellen DeGeneres, who had recently come out as gay, as a poor model "for a family kind of life."[197] And, as the scandal surrounding Clinton's affair with a White House intern broke in January 1998, the RNC leaped on the issue.[198] One RNC ad featured two women talking about the problem they faced explaining Clinton's behavior to their children. The ad linked Clinton's moral failings with criticism of Democrats for producing "higher taxes and more government," while praising Republicans for supporting tax cuts, balanced budgets, "putting people on welfare back to work, and having a plan to save Social Security."[199] But the GOP did not benefit from the scandal

---

[193] "GOP Tool to Revive Party Instead Results in Scrutiny," *New York Times*, June 2, 1997; "RNC Papers Detail Close Ties with Big Donors, Policy Forum," *Washington Post*, July 3, 1997; "Democrats Get to Scrutinize G.O.P. Asian Connection," *New York Times*, July 22, 1997.

[194] "GOP Abortion Foes to Seek Fund Ban," *Washington Post*, October 19, 1997; "GOP Facing New Abortion Debate," *Washington Post*, December 30, 1997.

[195] "Who Is a Republican?," *New York Times*, January 14, 1998. See also: "Chairman of the Republican National Committee Fights 'Litmus Test' on Abortion," *New York Times*, January 7, 1998; "Abortion Proposal May Dominate RNC Meeting," *Washington Post*, January 7, 1998; "RNC Is Warned against Antiabortion Tactic," *Washington Post*, January 13, 1998.

[196] "Republicans Reject Abortion Litmus Test," *New York Times*, January 17, 1998.

[197] "Disney's Homosynergy," *New York Times*, May 4, 1997.

[198] "Republican Party Chief Enters Fray with Attack over Clinton Scandal," *New York Times*, February 13, 1998; "Republicans End Silence on Troubles of President," *New York Times*, March 1, 1998.

[199] "The Republican Ad That Revisited the White House Scandal," *New York Times*, October 29, 1998. See also: "Republican Party Chief Enters Fray with Attack over Clinton Scandal," *New York Times*, February 13, 1998; "Lewinsky Issue Inspires Theme for G.O.P. Ads," *New York Times*, September 2, 1998.

in the 1998 midterms: for the first time since 1934, the incumbent party did not lose in a midterm election. In the aftermath of the underwhelming results, party insiders criticized Nicholson. Top GOP donors attacked him for failing to "articulate a clear message" to voters and focusing on "scandal and impeachment."[200] Nicholson promised that the RNC would "have a better message discipline about taxes, about improving our national defense" and was re-elected to a second two-year term.[201]

While generally less visible than under Barbour, Nicholson did continue to invest in online activities. Most notable in this regard was the RNC's announcement in 1999 that it was beginning its own Internet service. For a subscription fee of $19.95 a month, GOP donors and subscribers of Republican publications were invited to join a GOP Internet access service. Subscribers would receive direct online communications from the national committee. Larry Purporo, deputy chief of staff of the RNC, was the director of the "e-GOP" program and noted that it would allow the committee to respond to political events instantly: "when Al Gore double-speaks on his record on the nuclear test ban treaty, we'll get our response in [subscribers'] hands the same minute as it reaches a state party chairman."[202] The e-GOP program also played up the Republican Party's home for Christian evangelicals, as it came with an "anti-smut filter" blocking pornography. During the 2000 convention, the GOP provided a prime time Internet broadcast each night "without intrusion from Democratic attacks and spin—not to mention the intrusion of editorializing journalists."[203]

In 1999, with the presidential primary campaigns in full swing, the RNC switched to attacking Gore. The RNC produced a regular feature called "The World According to Gore," which it distributed by fax and through email.[204] As Gore tried to distance himself from Clinton in the wake of the impeachment scandal, the RNC put up a billboard outside of Gore's campaign headquarters in Tennessee showing Clinton and Gore hugging.[205] Nicholson also attacked Gore's support for gay and lesbian members of the military serving openly, accusing him of "pandering to the far left" and "[compromising] U.S. security to

[200] "Big Donors Say G.O.P. Leaders Lack Direction," New York Times, January 16, 1999.

[201] Ibid. See also: "Engler Claims No Wish for RNC Job," Washington Post, November 16, 1998; "RNC Chief Lobbies to Keep Job," Washington Post, November 19, 1998; "G.O.P. Chairman Overcomes Challenge to His Re-Election," New York Times, January 23, 1999.

[202] "Republicans Plan to Offer a Party Line to the Internet," New York Times, November 8, 1999.

[203] "GOP Web TV: An Unconventional Airing of the Republican Gathering," Washington Post, July 30, 2000.

[204] "House Republicans, in a Shift of Focus, Begin a Public Campaign against Gore," New York Times, May 19, 1999; "In Bush-Gore Race, 3 Words For Media: 'You've Got Mail,'" New York Times, June 1, 2000.

[205] "Flashback Courtesy of the G.O.P.," New York Times, November 23, 1999.

socially engineer the military."[206] But with Republican nominee George W. Bush building up an extensive campaign organization of his own, independent from the RNC, the committee's role in the general election appears to have been limited. Indeed, the victorious 2000 election campaign was mostly masterminded by Bush's adviser Karl Rove, with only a limited role for Nicholson's RNC.[207]

Presidential Promotion and Scandal: The DNC in the Clinton Years

Bill Clinton entered the White House in peculiar electoral conditions: while his victory in the electoral college was comfortable, the three-person race left Clinton with only 43% of the popular vote. Stanley Greenberg, Clinton's pollster, in a presentation to the DNC in January 1993, warned that Clinton's victory was largely the result of intra-party disagreement within the GOP and that while "the Republican coalition collapsed in 1992, but we have not yet formed a new Democratic coalition."[208] Therefore, Democratic leaders—including Clinton himself—did not view the 1992 presidential election victory as an indicator of a party that had permanently solved its electoral problems of the 1970s and 1980s. Indeed, as Greenberg argued, "this election was not in any way a realigning election. [...] We have [...] to bring [Ross Perot supporters] over. I believe that is our primary task if we are going to turn this election from a Republican collapse into a genuine Democratic victory."[209]

Clinton selected his campaign manager David Wilhelm as DNC chair. Wilhelm was expected to be a regular participant in daily White House briefings, and Clinton administration officials promised that the relationship between White House and committee would be better than they had been under Carter.[210] Wilhelm predicted "the [DNC] will emerge as the principal vehicle for how President Clinton can communicate outside the Beltway."[211] In this spirit, he began his chairmanship with a set of major initiatives. As Paul Herrnson notes, Wilhelm "created a new public relations function" for the DNC intended

---

[206] "Gore Meets with Gay Leaders before Homestretch in Iowa," *New York Times*, January 21, 2000.

[207] "Revisiting Several Moments That Have Embarrassed Gore," *New York Times*, September 1, 2000; "Bush Defends Ad That Assails Gore," *New York Times*, September 2, 2000.

[208] "Democrats Get a New Chairman, and a Warning," *New York Times*, January 22, 1993.

[209] "New Democratic Party Chief Named," *Los Angeles Times*, January 22, 1993.

[210] "Chicago Political Veteran to Lead Democratic Party," *Chicago Tribune*, January 15, 1993; "Clinton Taps Wilhelm as Party Chief," *Washington Post*, January 15, 1993.

[211] "New Party Chairman Is Planning to Look beyond Washington," *New York Times*, January 16, 1993.

to "generate public support for Clinton and his policies to help the president convince members of Congress to vote for his legislation."[212] In February 1993, Wilhelm announced that

> we're in the process of contacting a million people. We have sent out a half-million pieces of mail; we're on the phones to another half million. We're encouraging them to get engaged in the debate, call their congresspeople, call radio talk shows, write letters to the editor, to help make a reality what the campaign was all about—which was fundamentally economic change.[213]

Indeed, New York Times coverage of the DNC's activities during the first Clinton term showed an increase in publicity efforts in comparison with the Brown era. Figure 7.6 presents the results of negative binomial regressions in which Clinton's presidency during his first term is the independent variable and the lagged monthly Times coverage of DNC branding and service activities are the dependent variables. In this model the data is limited to just those articles covering the DNC published between January 1989 and December 1996—thereby comparing coverage of the DNC during Clinton's first term in office with that during Brown's time as DNC chair. New York Times coverage of all branding and services activities combined increase (respectively significant at the 0.01 and 0.10 level). Crucially, the coverage increased particularly with regard to the Times mentioning DNC publicity efforts (significant at the 0.001 level) and policy position taking (significant at the 0.01 level).

The increase in DNC policy position taking under Clinton is not surprising. After 12 years of the committee being very careful about the policies it promoted to maintain party unity, with Clinton in the White House, in control of the DNC, and concerned about building support among voters for his agenda, the committee now had a clear assignment to promote the administration's legislative agenda. Additionally, with Clinton engaging in fundraising activities on behalf of the DNC, the committee also had more financial resources than before: during the Reagan and Bush administrations the DNC's midterm cycle fundraising maxed out at $17.2 million, but in the 1993–1994 cycle, the DNC reported receipts of $63 million (see Table 7.1). While the RNC still easily outraised the DNC, this nonetheless meant a clear improvement for the Democrats.

[212] Paul S. Herrnson, "Bill Clinton as a Party Leader: The First Term," in The Clinton Presidency: The First Term, 1992–96, ed. Paul S. Herrnson and Dilys M. Hill (New York: St. Martin's Press, 1999), 71.

[213] "David Wilhelm: Charting a Permanent Campaign for a Changing Democratic Party," Los Angeles Times, March 8, 1993.

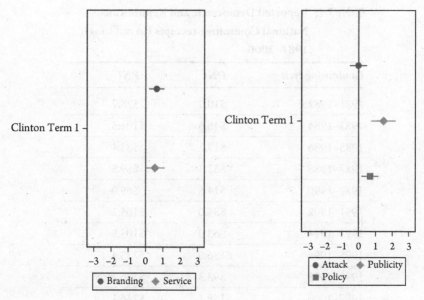

Figure 7.6. Negative binomial regressions of Bill Clinton's first term as president on monthly (lagged) *New York Times* coverage of DNC branding and service activities, 1989–1996. *Note:* This model includes variables controlling for presidential and midterm election years, a measure of *New York Times* length, and DNC scandals. The data coverage is limited to articles published between January 1989 and December 1996, and covering only the DNC. *Source:* Data collected by author.

During the first two years of the Clinton administration, much of the DNC's publicity efforts involved promoting its healthcare plan.[214] Led by First Lady Hillary Clinton, healthcare reform was a priority for the administration, and the DNC hired a new campaign manager with the purpose of organizing grassroots support for the legislation.[215] However, the rollout of the program faced problems. The DNC abandoned an attempt to use an independent foundation to raise money from corporations and unions for a public relations campaign after criticism that the organization was not, as advertised, bipartisan. Subsequently, a planned "National Health Care Awareness Day" was canceled because of a lack of planning and the likely absence of media attention since it had been scheduled to occur on the same day as the signing of a peace treaty between Israel and the PLO. The DNC did, however, support the healthcare reform effort by airing

[214] See: Galvin, *Presidential Party Building*, 226–229.

[215] "David Wilhelm: Charting a Permanent Campaign"; "DNC-Backed Lobby to Push Health Plan," *Washington Post*, June 3, 1993.

Table 7.1. **Reported Democratic and Republican National Committee receipts (in millions), 1981–2000.**

Fundraising cycle	DNC	RNC
1981–1982	$10.0	$78.7
1983–1984	$46.6	$104.5
1985–1986	$17.2	$83.4
1987–1988	$52.3	$89.5
1989–1990	$14.5	$69.0
1991–1992	$84.0	$105.2
1993–1994	$63.0	$105.8
1995–1996	$136.0	$233.4
1997–1998	$98.3	$136.1
1999–2000	$158.1	$246.1

Note: The reported receipts include contributions from donors as well as transfers from other political committees, loans, and offsets. The DNC and RNC filings submitted to the Federal Election Commission (FEC) do not consistently differentiate between these different types of income; thus, total receipts are the most consistent way to compare the committees' financial resources across time and with each other.

Source: "DNC Services Corp / Democratic National Committee" (FEC ID: C00010603), https://www.fec.gov/data/committee/C00010603/; "Republican National Committee" (FEC ID: C00003418), https://www.fec.gov/data/committee/C00003418/.

TV ads targeting senior citizens—including a spoof of the infamous "Harry and Louise" ad put forward by insurance companies opposing the legislation.[216]

Not all Democrats were happy with Clinton's use of the DNC. Some members of Congress criticized the DNC for not providing them political cover on the Clinton economic plan.[217] Others were unhappy with the DNC's activities promoting healthcare: Senator Richard H. Bryan (NV) complained that

[216] "The Health Care Speech, Closely Watched," *Washington Post*, September 23, 1993; "Democratic Party Chief Scorches Clinton Agenda's Foes," *Los Angeles Times*, October 10, 1993; "Democrats' Ad for Health-Care Reform Distorts Governor's Position, GOP Says," *Wall Street Journal*, February 16, 1994; "Getting Even with Harry and Louise," *New York Times*, July 10, 1994. See also: Jacob Hacker, *The Road to Nowhere: The Genesis of President Clinton's Plan for Health Security* (Princeton, NJ: Princeton University Press, 1997) 139.

[217] "House Democrats Tell Wilhelm DNC Is 'Inept,'" *Washington Post*, June 23, 1993; Bob Woodward, *The Agenda* (New York: Simon and Schuster, 1994), 119.

the DNC's TV ads sent the wrong message and that "those of us who know our states" should "have been consulted in what was the most effective way to craft a message."[218] Senator Bob Kerrey (NE) outright urged "all my friends for the moment not to give money to the Democratic National Committee."[219] In the first two years of the administration, the *New York Times* concluded that the DNC had "devoted itself, and millions of dollars, to fighting for Mr. Clinton's programs rather than promoting the prospects of individual Democrats [...]."[220] Indeed, Harold Ickes, Clinton's Deputy Chief of Staff, described Wilhelm as "the president's agent" and joked that "if we asked [Wilhelm] to drop himself off a bridge, he might raise a modest objection. At least he might ask for a low bridge."[221]

In the run-up to the 1994 midterm elections, the DNC criticized the Republican religious right and spent $2 million on advertisements attacking the GOP's Contract with America.[222] But with Democrats losing their majorities in Congress, the results were, as Wilhelm summarized, catastrophic: "Call it what you want: an earthquake, a tidal wave, a blowout. We got our butts kicked."[223] Press assessments placed part of the blame on the DNC. Reporter David Broder argued that the DNC "diverted much of its focus to support efforts—mainly misguided TV campaigns masterminded by White House consultants—for the embattled Clinton legislative program. The fundamentals of precinct-level organizing were given short shrift."[224] Wilhelm had announced he would resign before the midterms, and Clinton selected Connecticut Senator Chris Dodd and Donald Fowler, a veteran DNC member from South Carolina, to lead the DNC together. In this new setup, Dodd would promote the party while remaining in the Senate, and Fowler was to deal with managing day-to-day affairs at the party's HQ.[225]

Dodd believed the 1994 defeat was "due to the fact that we did a miserable job as a party in letting people know exactly what had been done"[226] but the DNC's priority remained Clinton. As early as March 1995, the DNC sent out

---

[218] "New DNC Health Ads Wind Up Offending Senate Democrats," *Washington Post,* July 15, 1994.

[219] Ibid.

[220] "Clinton Moving to Avoid Losses in '94 Elections," *New York Times,* February 22, 1994.

[221] "Man on a Tightrope," *Washington Post,* April 20, 1994.

[222] "Democrats Struggle to Build Damage-Control Strategy for Fall Elections," *Washington Post,* June 26, 1994; "Democrats' New Ads Attack G.O.P. 'Contract,'" *New York Times,* October 13, 1994.

[223] "Democrats Name Director Acting Party Chairman," *Washington Post,* November 15, 1994.

[224] "The Road Back," *Washington Post,* November 20, 1994.

[225] "Aides Say Clinton Will Choose Dodd to Lead Democrats," *New York Times,* January 10, 1995; "Clinton Seeks to Have Dodd, Fowler Share Party's Chairmanship," *Wall Street Journal,* January 10, 1995.

[226] "New Democratic Chief Declares that Party Will Recoup," *New York Times,* January 20, 1995.

a mailer advocating for Clinton's re-election, and between August 1995 and January 1996 the DNC spent more than $15 million on Clinton re-election ads. In addition to this, the committee also scheduled another $10 million in ad buys for the spring and summer of 1996. This advertising campaign was part of a scheme designed by Clinton's pollster Dick Morris, who had been brought on board after the midterms and was now on the DNC payroll. The ads aired in more than 20 states and presented Clinton as a centrist by spotlighting his crime policies and support for tax cuts and welfare reform.[227] Clinton himself was personally involved in their creation—reportedly going through proposed ads and "[offering] suggestions and even [editing] some of the scripts."[228]

But the DNC's extravagant spending on behalf of Clinton's re-election would come back to haunt the committee. While Clinton easily won re-election, the DNC's fundraising became a major political scandal. Due to its massive spending, the DNC was projected to have a deficit of $7 million before the election. In trying to close its budget gap the DNC accepted major financial donations from noncitizens.[229] In October 1996, the Dole campaign first suggested that the DNC might have broken the law in accepting a donation from an Indonesian couple. Further news reports indicated that the DNC received donations from non–U.S. citizen donors, some of which were collected during a fundraiser at a Buddhist temple in California at which Vice President Al Gore had been present.[230] In response, the DNC fired finance Vice Chairman John Huang and began returning suspect donations.[231] The scandal continued throughout 1997 and 1998—including revelations that the DNC accepted donations from impoverished Native American tribes in exchange for participation in a White House lunch. The tribes donated the money in the hope that it would provide their leaders with the opportunity to talk with Clinton about regaining 7,500

---

[227] "Dick Morris, Burning His Bridges," *Washington Post*, February 3, 1999; "Democrats Aim Straight at Heart on Reelection," *Washington Post*, March 29, 1995; "2 Political Parties Turn to Airwaves for Medicare Debate," *New York Times*, August 16, 1995; "Attacking the G.O.P.'s Plan for Medicare," *New York Times*, November 4, 1995; "Party Spends $15 Million on Ads to Burnish Clinton," *Washington Post*, February 7, 1996.

[228] Bob Woodward, *The Choice* (New York: Simon and Schuster, 1996), 236, 344.

[229] See: "Gore Was 'Solicitor-in-Chief' in '96 Reelection Campaign," *Washington Post*, March 2, 1997; "Clinton Told of Need to Make Fund-Raising Phone Calls in '95," *Washington Post*, March 29, 1997.

[230] The Buddhist temple fundraiser was also controversial because as a religious institution it was tax exempt.

[231] "Dole Aide Suggests 'Potentially Criminal Actions' in DNC Gift," *Washington Post*, October 15, 1996; "DNC Donor Controversy Widens as Republicans Step Up Criticism," *Washington Post*, October 18, 1996; "Democrats Relieve Top Fund-Raiser," *Washington Post*, October 19, 1996; "DNC Acknowledges Inadequate Checks on Donors," *Washington Post*, November 2, 1996; "DNC Returns More Big Donations with Foreign Ties," *Washington Post*, November 8, 1996.

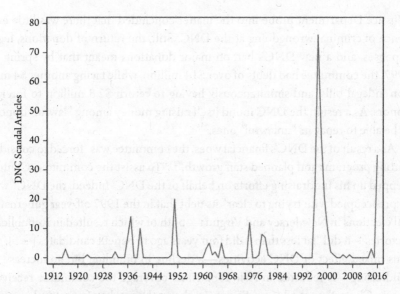

Figure 7.7. Annual number of *New York Times* articles reporting on DNC scandals, 1913–2016. *Source:* Data collected by author.

acres of tribal land seized by the federal government a century earlier, but the land was not returned.[232] The financial scandal would go on to dominate the DNC's activities during much of Clinton's second term. Indeed, as can be seen in Figure 7.7, which shows the number of annual *New York Times* articles covering DNC scandals between 1913 and 2016, the fundraising scandal received by far more *Times* coverage than any DNC-related scandal before or since.

As the DNC's financial scandal unfolded, Clinton named a new duo team to lead the committee: Colorado Governor Roy Romer and Steve Grossman, the former chair of the Massachusetts Democratic Party and of the American Israeli Public Affairs Committee (AIPAC). Romer and Grossman identified "restoring the DNC's public image" and "instilling a heightened appreciation for fund-raising laws"[233] in the committee as their core priorities. But the financial scandal continued to reverberate. For example, the DNC's decision to transfer donations intended for the committee to Clinton's presidential campaign in 1996 meant several of the party's major donors found out they inadvertently gave more to Clinton's re-election effort than they were legally allowed to.[234] By summer 1998,

---

[232] "A Tribal Shakedown," *New York Times*, August 13, 1997.

[233] "Gov. Romer Is Tapped for DNC," *Washington Post*, January 14, 1997.

[234] See: "DNC Bars Foreign Donations," *Washington Post*, January 22, 1997; "'Mistakes Were Made,' Clinton Says of Gifts," *Washington Post*, January 29, 1997; "Chinese Embassy Found to Direct Money to Democrats, Paper Says," *New York Times*, February 13, 1997; "$2 Million Diverted by Party to Candidates, Records Say," *New York Times*, September 10, 1997.

a Justice Department probe into the matter concluded that there was little evidence of criminal wrongdoing at the DNC. Still, the return of donations, legal expenses, and a new DNC's ban on major donations meant that by spring of 1997, the committee had debts of over $14 million, while facing another $4 million in legal bills, and simultaneously having to return $2.8 million to foreign donors. As a result, the DNC found itself raising money among "lawful" donors to be able to repay its "unlawful" ones.[235]

As a result of the DNC's financial woes, the committee was "forced to consider cutting programs and planned staff growth."[236] To assist the committee, Clinton stepped up his fundraising efforts on behalf of the DNC. Indeed, the DNC "was so preoccupied with trying to clear" its debt that in the 1997 off-year gubernatorial elections in New Jersey and Virginia—both of which resulted in Republican victories—it did "far less than it did four years ago to benefit candidates [...]."[237] This mixed effect of DNC activities—a decline in branding but an increase in fundraising—is reflected in New York Times coverage the committee received during Clinton's second term. Figure 7.8 shows the results of negative binomial regressions in which Clinton's incumbency after the 1996 election is the independent variable and the lagged monthly Times coverage of DNC branding and service activities are the dependent variables. In this model, the data is limited to just those articles covering the DNC published between January 1993 and December 2000—thereby comparing coverage of the DNC during Clinton's second term with that in his first term. Times coverage of combined branding activities decreased while its coverage of DNC service activities increased (though both coefficients are significant only at the 0.10 level). With regard to specific branding activities, coverage of publicity activities and policy position taking by the DNC declined (significant at, respectively, the 0.10 and 0.05 level).[238]

In early 1998, as Clinton's affair scandal began to receive major media attention, the DNC did step in to defend him by creating an office of damage control to distribute new information to media surrogates. The DNC also urged Democratic voters to express their support for Clinton by calling into talk radio stations, or even in "coffee break conversations at the office," and Romer and

---

[235] "Democratic Party Unable to Pay Debts from Last Year's Elections," New York Times, March 27, 1997; "Owing $14 Million, DNC Can't Refund $1.5 Million in Questionable Gifts," Washington Post, April 13, 1997; "Democrats Return $1.4 Million in Questionable Donations," Washington Post, June 28, 1997; "Campaign-Finance Probe Finds Little Evidence of Criminal Wrongdoing at DNC, White House," Wall Street Journal, June 26, 1998.

[236] "DNC Considers Plans to Contain Financial Crisis," Washington Post, May 19, 1997.

[237] "Democrats' Big Debt Hurts Efforts in 3 Races," New York Times, October 30, 1997.

[238] On the other hand, Clinton also stepped up his fundraising efforts during his second term: coverage of DNC fundraising efforts increased in Clinton's second term (an effect that is significant at the 0.001 level).

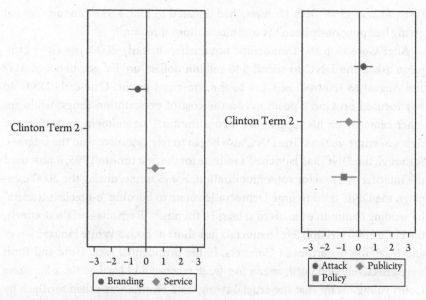

Figure 7.8. Negative binomial regressions of Bill Clinton's second term as president on monthly (lagged) *New York Times* coverage of DNC branding and service activities, 1993–2000. *Note:* This model includes variables controlling for presidential and midterm election years, a measure of *New York Times* length, and DNC scandals. The data coverage is limited to articles published between January 1993 and December 2000, and covering only the DNC.
Source: Data collected by author.

Grossman stressed that Clinton "is doing a great job [. . .] and the American people want him to go on doing the job they elected him to do."[239] After the 1998 midterms, Grossman resigned as DNC chairman due to health issues in his family.[240] In January 1999, Clinton selected Indiana Democratic Party chair Joseph Andrew as the new DNC chair. With the presidential primaries in full swing, Andrew mostly focused on attacking the likely Republican nominee, Texas governor George W. Bush.[241] In September 1999, Romer also stepped down and was replaced with Philadelphia Mayor Ed Rendell, who focused on fundraising. Nonetheless, his selection was notable because Rendell had already endorsed Gore for the 2000 Democratic presidential nomination. While Rendell "un-endorsed" Gore upon becoming DNC chair, the DNC's core leadership now consisted of a strongly pro-Gore group, as Andrew had been recruited by

[239] "Democratic Chiefs Urge Faithful to Go on Offense for Clinton," *New York Times*, February 20, 1998.

[240] "Democratic Chairman Grossman to Step Down," *Washington Post*, December 3, 1998.

[241] "Bush Sets No Litmus Test for Judges," *Washington Post*, June 15, 1999.

Gore, finance chair Beth Dozoretz had donated to him, and senior adviser Pat Ewing had previously been his communications director.[242]

After Gore won the Democratic nomination in early 2000, the Gore campaign asked the DNC to spend $30 million dollars on TV ads between May and August to reintroduce Gore to the American public. One early DNC ad buy focused on Gore's positions on the cost of prescription drugs, while another centered on his support for a constitutional amendment protecting the rights of crime victims. The DNC also began to rely extensively on the Internet. Although the DNC had launched a website for the first time in 1995, it now used the Internet as a tool for voter mobilization. For example, during the 2000 campaign the DNC tried to urge Democratic voters to become "e-precinct leaders" by sending committee emails to at least 10 friends.[243] Regardless of these efforts, the close 2000 election left Democrats just short of both a White House victory and regaining majorities in Congress. In the presidential race, Gore and Bush were effectively tied until, after a five-week recount and legal battle, a Supreme Court ruling meant that the crucial swing state Florida was called for Bush by just 537 (out of nearly 6 million) votes. With this close defeat, the DNC—after eight years of supporting Clinton and a series of major financial scandals— found itself back in the opposition.

Conclusion

Between Reagan's landslide 1980 victory and George W. Bush's razor-edged win in 2000, the competitive dimensions of the American party system changed dramatically. Reagan's first victory was followed by additional presidential election successes, but the Republican Party was never fully able to translate this dominance to congressional races. This political reality affected both national committees. In the GOP, the RNC fully embraced Reagan as the leader of the party. While the committee had been under nearly continuous moderate control from the 1950s onward, it now embraced Reagan's policy agenda and explicitly presented the GOP as "Reagan's party." The RNC continued its

---

[242] "Democrats' New Chairman Is Sign of Al Gore's Power," *New York Times*, September 24, 1999; "DNC's Upper Echelon Is Dominated by Gore Supporters," *Wall Street Journal*, September 27, 1999; "Party Chief Changes Mind on Gore," *New York Times*, September 28, 1999; "Top Democratic Fund-Raiser Resigns," *New York Times*, October 5, 1999.

[243] "Crossing the Finish Line: The Democrats," *Washington Post*, July 23, 1995; "Gore Aides Seek Huge Party TV Ad Buy," *Washington Post*, May 23, 2000; "Gore as Defender of Drug Benefits for Elderly," *New York Times*, June 8, 2000; "NC Issue Spot Touts Gore's Medicare Plan," *Washington Post*, June 8, 2000; "Gore Backs an Amendment for Crime Victims' Rights," *New York Times*, July 13, 2000; "Campaign Briefing: The Internet," *New York Times*, September 16, 2000.

president-centered approach after George H. W. Bush won the 1988 election—though less actively after the death of RNC chair Lee Atwater. During this same period, DNC chairs tried to move the Democratic Party to the center. They did so because they believed they had lost White voters who saw the Democratic Party as controlled by "interest groups." Black groups in particular were blamed for the party's poor performance, and DNC chairs tried to "toughen" up the image of the Democratic Party by moving to the right on social policies, welfare, crime, and taxation.

Bill Clinton's victory placed the DNC back under presidential control for the first time since the Carter administration. Despite his criticism of the DNC in the 1980s, Clinton did not ignore the committee as most of his predecessors had. Instead, Clinton relied extensively on the DNC to promote his policies and his re-election. The DNC engaged in major promotion efforts on behalf of the administration's legislative agenda—including its economic plan and the failed attempt at a major healthcare overhaul. After the dramatic 1994 midterms, the DNC immediately pivoted toward supporting Clinton's re-election campaign: starting in the summer of 1995, the DNC spent millions of dollars on ads supporting Clinton. This extensive spending on behalf of the president frustrated many congressional Democrats and appears to have pushed the DNC into highly questionable fundraising tactics. After Clinton's 1996 victory, the DNC found itself ensnared in a major scandal regarding its acceptance of donations from foreign nationals, limiting the committees' effectiveness during his second term. The DNC's financial scandal notwithstanding, the Clinton era did represent a major step forward for the DNC as a fundraising organization: DNC receipts jumped from an average of $34.2 million per two-year cycle during the Reagan–Bush years to an average of $113.9 million for each two-year cycle during the Clinton administration.[244] While the RNC retained its massive financial advantage, the DNC's long period of being practically on the brink of bankruptcy throughout the 1970s and '80s had ended.

With the RNC out of the White House after 1992, the committee returned to its core branding role and made major investments in its publicity infrastructure—including building a new TV studio in its headquarters, creating a series of cable TV shows, and stepping into the Internet age with several new programs aimed at communicating directly with voters. But the RNC in the 1990s largely left policy positioning to leaders in Congress and happily embraced Newt Gingrich's Contract with America. The committee did take two clear positions in the 1990s: on the one hand, despite the increasing influence of conservative Christians in the party, the RNC continued to insist that the GOP

---

[244] "DNC Services Corp / Democratic National Committee" (FEC ID: C00010603).

was a "big tent" on abortion. And, under RNC chair Barbour, the committee began to take on a more critical position on immigration.

The period 1981–2000 thus shows some consistent changes in both parties. On the one hand, both national committees' publicity divisions were used extensively by incumbent presidents. And, while out of the White House, both the DNC and RNC tried to use their (now) traditional strategies of major publicity efforts and creating policy-setting organizations within the party to (re)shape their party's brands—both in terms of spotlighting specific policies and trying to update voters' broader views of the party. But the DNC and RNC also clearly were becoming less central to these attempts. In particular, the rise of presidential primaries and the increasingly early start of presidential campaigns began to limit the ability of (out-party) national committees to play the kind brand-setting role they previously had. And, with presidential candidates now building massive campaign organizations independent of the national committees, the value of the DNC and RNC to presidents would also be in doubt.

"Near Obscurity"

The Deterioration of National Committee Branding, 2001–2016

While already facing constraints in the 1980s and 1990s, the branding role of both national committees continued to decrease after the 2000 election. In part, this was the product of incumbent presidents in both parties seeing little value in relying on their national committees for publicity support. While both George W. Bush and Barack Obama would occasionally use their committees for these purposes, both came into office with political operations independent from the national committees, and, during their presidencies, neither committee engaged in the kind of massive publicity efforts they had designed and executed in the past. Obama in particular had little interest in the Democratic National Committee (DNC): instead, he prioritized his own campaign organization (Obama for America [OFA]) and even turned it into an independent competitor to the DNC after the 2012 election.

But the fading relevance of national committee branding efforts is not just the product of presidential disinterest. Indeed, previous presidents ignored their party's national committee and let them decline institutionally only for the organization to re-emerge after a lost presidential election. Once back out of the White House, these committees would invest heavily in their publicity divisions and engage in major publicity and policy efforts aimed at reintroducing their party to voters. But even out-committees in the post-2000 era find it hard to play such a role. One cause of this is the previously discussed rise of presidential primaries: with presidential candidates dominating intra-party debate and news coverage as early as two full calendar years before the next presidential inauguration, national committee chairs lack the time and political freedom to produce the kind of major branding efforts their predecessors used to engage in.

A second and more recent limitation to the committees' ability to engage in major branding effort is the rise of political communication tools that make it easier for other actors in the party to present alternative messaging. While national committees never had a monopoly on political communication, their strength within their parties was in no small part based on the fact that communicating with voters on a national basis required money and technological resources unavailable to most politicians and political organizations. Both the DNC and Republican National Committee (RNC) regularly invested heavily in their publicity divisions to produce up-to-date communication technology at a cost few other actors or groups in the party would be able to afford. But starting in the 1990s access to such political communication technology became more independent from political parties themselves (in the form of talk radio and ideological news networks) and much more easily accessible to partisan actors independent from the DNC and RNC (the Internet). As a result, branding efforts from the DNC or RNC can now easily be countered by equally loud voices from in (or even outside of) the party.

Finally, the 2000 election solidified an electoral system in which both parties have at least a chance at being able to win the presidency and majorities in Congress in each election. And, in doing so, both parties rely on a base of voters rather than on the dwindling number of voting groups that can actually be persuaded to vote for either side in future elections. To be sure, voters reliably supporting their party is nothing new, but the combination of parties that are more homogenous ideologically, that fight each other in a series of very close elections, and that rely mostly on unmovable voters to provide them with victory raises questions about the necessity of national committee-style branding efforts. As shown in previous chapters, throughout the 20th century both national committees consistently attempted to use party branding efforts to convince voters who did *not* vote for their party in previous elections to join them in the future—often by trying to introduce new policy positions. While committees still attempted to engage in such efforts after 2000, persuading voters through updated party brands is a less appealing strategy when doubling down on the existing base may be a surer bet for electoral success.

Combined, the DNC and RNC in the period after the 2000 election play much less of a branding role than they had in the decades before. Even in cases where the committees did try to set new party brands—for example, the DNC under Howard Dean after the 2004 election or the RNC's efforts at reshaping the party's image after 2012—the efforts were short-lived, heavily criticized within the party, or both.

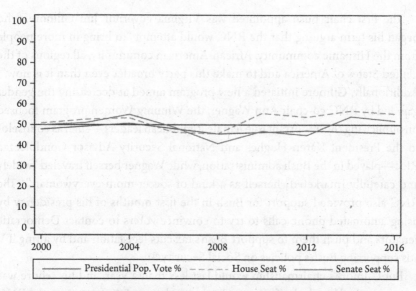

Figure 8.1. Republican electoral performance in presidential, House, and Senate elections, 2000–2016. *Source: Congressional Quarterly's Guide to U.S. Elections, 7th ed.* (Washington, DC: Congressional Quarterly, 2016).

George W. Bush and the RNC

George W. Bush's 2000 election victory was the closest in American history: while Al Gore won the popular vote, in the decisive electoral college state—Florida— the two candidates were just a few hundred votes (out of nearly six million votes cast there) apart. After weeks of recounts and court cases, the Supreme Court's decision in *Bush v. Gore* effectively decided the election in Bush's favor. At the congressional level, the confusing election results also reverberated: while Republicans retained control of the House, in the Senate the parties were tied at 50-50 each—though, with Vice President Dick Cheney as the deciding vote, Republicans held the majority, at least temporarily (see Figure 8.1). After the election, Bush and his top political adviser Karl Rove set themselves the goal of building a "long-lasting GOP majority"[1] but placed their political team in the White House. As a result, the RNC played a limited and subservient role. Indeed, one of the most notable characteristics of the RNC under Bush was its number of different committee chairs: between 2001 and 2008, Bush appointed six individual RNC chairs—some serving as little as a few months.

[1] Cited in Daniel J. Galvin, *Presidential Party Building: Dwight D. Eisenhower to George W. Bush* (Princeton, NJ: Princeton University Press, 2010), 255.

The first chair Bush appointed was Virginia governor Jim Gilmore, who began his term arguing that the RNC would attempt "to bring in more people from the Hispanic community, African-American community, all regions of the United States of America and to make this party broader even than it is now."[2] Additionally, Gilmore initiated a new program aimed at decreasing the gender gap: led by RNC co-chair Ann Wagner, the Winning Women program focused on publicizing the important role female Republican leaders—such as counselor to the President Karen Hughes and National Security Advisor Condoleezza Rice—played in the Bush administration, while Wagner herself traveled "widely and carefully [marketed] herself as a kind of soccer-mom everywoman."[3] The RNC also provided support for Bush in the first months of his presidency by using automated phone calls to try to convince voters to contact Democratic senators and push them to support Bush's tax cuts legislation and by airing TV ads supporting Bush's policies on Social Security.[4]

But Gilmore's chairmanship would last less than a year, and his tenure was mostly marked by a lack of communication and cooperation between the RNC and the administration. While the RNC and Bush worked together in coordinating fundraising, Gilmore rarely communicated directly with the president.[5] Meanwhile, White House advisers complained that Gilmore was not "suitably aggressive in pitching the president's agenda," and Representative Thomas M. Davis (VA), chairman of the GOP's congressional campaign committee, argued that "[Gilmore] needs to understand that he's the president's guy. It's not his committee. He's the president's eyes and ears."[6] While the 9/11 attacks limited political activity from both national committees, the GOP faced two short-term political setbacks when it lost both the New Jersey and Virginia gubernatorial elections in November. In December, Rove canceled a planned RNC publicity campaign supporting a post-9/11 economic stimulus bill, and Bush replaced Gilmore with another governor: Marc Racicot of Montana.[7] Bush promised that under Racicot the RNC would "reach out to members of the labor unions and the minorities" and "continue to take our positive, optimistic message to all neighborhoods around the country."[8] Reporters noted that Bush was

[2] "G.O.P. Chief Is Seeking More Diversity," New York Times, December 23, 2000.

[3] "G.O.P. Tries to Counter Lack of Support among Women," New York Times, August 1, 2001.

[4] "Bush Pushes Hard to Woo Democrats Over to Tax Plan," New York Times, March 5, 2001; "Study in Congress Sees Need to Tap Social Security," New York Times, August 28, 2001.

[5] "Bush and His Cabinet Stepping in as Chief Fund-Raisers for G.O.P.," New York Times, April 19, 2001; "Bush Gala Expected to Net $15 Million," New York Times, May 20, 2001.

[6] "Tensions Touch G.O.P. Chief's Tenure," New York Times, July 20, 2001.

[7] "GOP Leader Is Criticized over Party's Election Losses," New York Times, November 9, 2001; "Ex-Governor Weighs Top Republican Post," New York Times, December 4, 2001; "White House Scuttles Plan for G.O.P. Ad Campaign," New York Times, December 20, 2001.

[8] "Party Chairman, Presidential Friend," New York Times, December 6, 2001.

a longtime friend of the new RNC chair—suggesting a closer relationship between president and national committee. However, once elected chair, Racicot and Bush rarely met in person and Rove remained the RNC's main source of contact at the White House.

Under Racicot, the RNC did actually introduce a new outreach program aimed at Hispanic voters. The RNC had already begun such efforts in 1999 after polling suggested that many Hispanics were dissatisfied with the Democratic Party. As Bush had won nearly half of Hispanic votes in his re-election in Texas in 1998, the RNC began airing Spanish language ads. Under Racicot, the RNC created a half-hour weekly television program in Spanish called *Abriendo Caminos* ("forging paths"). The RNC broadcast the program in electoral battleground states with high concentrations of Hispanic voters, and the show regularly provided information about the Bush administration's proposals while criticizing Democrats. Around the same time, the RNC also began offering Spanish language classes to members of Congress.[9]

With the war in Afghanistan ongoing and the Bush administration gearing up for an attack against Iraq, public sentiment shifted toward Republicans who won seats in House and Senate in the 2002 midterms, thereby ending the Democratic Senate majority that had followed the defection of Vermont senator Jim Jeffords from the Republican caucus in spring 2001. After the 2002 midterms, Bush moved Racicot into his independent re-election campaign organization and selected lobbyist Ed Gillespie as the next RNC chair.[10] Gillespie mostly engaged in fundraising and attacking Democrats for their opposition to the Iraq War,[11] but the RNC postponed major media buys until the end of 2003. When the committee did begin airing ads, it focused on terrorism and called on voters to contact their member of Congress and "tell them to support the president's policy of pre-emptive self-defense."[12]

[9] "The Party of George 'Doble Ve,'" *New York Times*, June 24, 2002; Leslie Sanchez, *Los Republicanos: Why Hispanics and Republicans Need Each Other* (New York: Palgrave MacMillan, 1997), 162–172; Zachary W. Oberfield and Adam J. Segal, "Pluralism Examined: Party Television Expenditures Focused on the Latino Vote in Presidential Elections," in *The Mass Media and Latino Politics: Studies of U.S. Media Content, Campaign Strategies and Survey Research: 1984–2004*, ed. Federico A. Subervi-Vélez (New York: Routledge, 2008), 291–308.

[10] "Bush Names Lobbyist as Leader of G.O.P.," *New York Times*, June 17, 2003.

[11] "Bush's Speech Offers Focus for Democrats' Attacks," *New York Times*, September 11, 2003. See also: "New G.O.P. Chief Hammers Democrats," *New York Times*, July 26, 2003; "Instant Response, by Committee," *New York Times*, November 30, 2003.

[12] This part of the ad frustrated Republican foreign policy experts in the State Department and White House because they argued that the Bush doctrine relied on preemptive self-defense only as a last option. See: "When Foreign Policy Aims and Campaign Needs Clash," *New York Times*, November 28, 2003. See also: "G.O.P. to Run an Ad for Bush on Terror Issue," *New York Times*, November 21, 2003.

After Massachusetts senator John Kerry became the likely Democratic nominee in March 2004, the Bush campaign and RNC produced a 90-day media strategy aimed at defining Kerry as "indecisive and lacking conviction" through "a coordinated blitz of advertisements, speeches, and sound bites."[13] The RNC also played up social issues, in the hope of increasing turnout among Christian conservatives—both to win competitive states and to provide Bush with a majority of the popular vote. These tactics including sending mailers to voters in Arkansas and West Virginia that warned them that Democrats were seeking to ban the Bible.[14]

While the RNC did not engage in any major publicity efforts on behalf of Bush, it is important to remember that the organization was already less active during the second Clinton term. Indeed, New York Times coverage of the RNC did not change much between the first George W. Bush term and the chairmanship of Jim Nicholson. Figure 8.2 shows the results of negative binomial regressions in which Bush's incumbency during his first term as president is the independent variable and lagged monthly Times coverage of RNC branding and service activities are the dependent variables. In this model, the data is limited to just those articles covering the RNC published between January 1997 and December 2004—thereby comparing coverage during Bush's first term with that of Nicholson's preceding term as RNC chair. While the coefficients for service coverage and every measure of branding coverage are all negative, none are statistically significant.

Bush's re-election saw him win yet another close race while in Congress Republicans increased their majorities. After the election, Bush replaced Gillespie with his former campaign manager, Ken Mehlman. Mehlman celebrated the Republican electoral performance in 2002 and 2004 as the party winning "a majority, not a plurality twice" but stressed that "one of our goals now needs to be to take these gains and make them more durable."[15] Mehlman acknowledged that "we're certainly not in the position that F.D.R. Democrats were in the 1930s and 40s. We're not the overwhelming favorite. There are going to be challenges. [...] But it does mean we're in a very strong position."[16] Under Mehlman, the RNC regularly attacked Democratic critics of Bush and helped strategize the party's (failed) attempt at overhauling Social Security and the nomination process of Supreme Court nominees John Roberts and Samuel

[13] "90-Day Strategy by Bush's Aides to Define Kerry," New York Times, March 20, 2004.

[14] "Republicans Admit Mailing Campaign Literature Saying Liberals Will Ban the Bible," New York Times, September 24, 2004.

[15] "Bush Picks Campaign Chief to Head G.O.P.," New York Times, November 16, 2004.

[16] "Some See Risks for G.O.P. as It Revels in New Powers," New York Times, January 24, 2005.

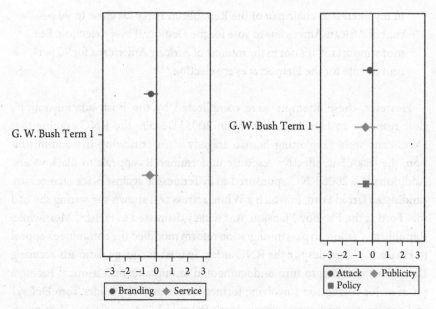

Figure 8.2. Negative binomial regression of George W. Bush's presidency on monthly (lagged) *New York Times* coverage of RNC branding and service activities, 1997–2004.
Note: This model includes variables controlling for presidential and midterm election years, a measure of *New York Times* length, and RNC scandals. The data coverage is limited to articles published between January 1997 and December 2004, and covering only the RNC.
Source: Data collected by author.

Alito.[17] Mehlman also returned to the party's persistent lack of support among Black voters. According to news reports, Mehlman spent considerable time and energy raising money for Black Republican candidates and promoted a religion-based program as a way of creating a relationship between the RNC and Black churches. Mehlman appeared at the NAACP's 2005 conference, and used his speech there to apologize for the GOP's reliance on the Southern strategy while criticizing the Democratic Party for taking Black voters for granted:

> Some Republicans gave up on winning the African-American vote, looking the other way or trying to benefit politically from racial polarization. I am here today as the Republican chairman to tell you we were wrong. [. . .] If my party benefited from racial polarization in the past, it is the Democratic Party that benefits from it today. I know it is not

---

[17] "Pressure by White House Is Being Applied with Care," *New York Times*, May 19, 2005; "G.O.P. Chief Says Democrats Play Politics on Court Nominee," *New York Times*, August 6, 2005; "After Miers Failure, White House Begins Aggressive Effort to Sell New Court Choice," *New York Times*, November 2, 2005.

in my interest as chairman of the Republican Party for close to 90 percent of African-Americans to vote for the Democrat every election. But more important, it's not in the interest of African-Americans for 90 percent to vote for the Democrat every election.[18]

However, these attempts were complicated by the Bush administration's slow response to Hurricane Katrina in 2005. Despite the RNC arguing that Democrats were "exploiting human tragedy"[19] in criticizing the administration, the lack of an effective response undermined its appeals to Black voters. Additionally, a 2006 RNC-sponsored ad in Tennessee against Black Democratic candidate Harold Ford, in which a White actress was shown suggesting she had met Ford at the Playboy Mansion, was widely dismissed as racist.[20] Meanwhile, Republicans' failure to pass immigration reform muddled the committee's appeal to Hispanic voters, despite the RNC airing Spanish language radio ads accusing Democrats of trying to turn undocumented immigrants into felons.[21] Facing a set of major corruption (involving former House majority leader Tom DeLay) and sex (involving Representative Mark Foley [FL]) scandals, the Katrina aftermath, and voter opposition to the Iraq War, the RNC limited its activities in 2006 to just six states.[22] Despite reassurances that the RNC could rely on a well-financed Get Out the Vote Project, Republicans faced major defeats in the 2006 midterms, resulting in Democratic majorities in both the House and Senate for the first time since the 1992 election.[23]

In the wake of this defeat, Mehlman announced that he was not available for a second two-year term, and Bush selected Senator Mel Martinez of Florida as his fifth RNC chair.[24] Martinez, who had been born in Cuba and moved to the United States as a child, had been Secretary of Housing and Urban Development in the Bush administration and successfully ran for the Senate in 2004. While Martinez announced that under his leadership the RNC would reach "out to

[18] "Bush and Party Chief Court Black Voters at 2 Forums," New York Times, July 15, 2005. See also: "Republican Party Is Backing Black Candidates in Bid to Attract Votes," New York Times, July 1, 2005; "G.O.P. Courts Blacks and Hispanics on Social Security," New York Times, March 20, 2005.

[19] "Democrats Looking to Use New Orleans".

[20] "In Tight Senate Race, Attack Ad on Black Candidate Stirs Furor," New York Times, October 26, 2006.

[21] "G.O.P. Risking Hispanic Votes on Immigration," New York Times, March 30, 2006; "The Immigration Impasse," New York Times, April 25, 2006.

[22] "Rove's Word Is No Longer G.O.P. Gospel," New York Times, September 3, 2006; "In House Races, More G.O.P. Seats Are Seen at Risk," New York Times, October 7, 2006.

[23] "Democrats Have an Intensity, but G.O.P. Has Its Machine," New York Times, October 15, 2006.

[24] "Republican Party Chairman Will Not Seek Another Term," New York Times, November 10, 2006; "Hispanic Is Expected to Be Next Public Face of the G.O.P.," New York Times, November 14, 2006.

all Americans, speaking to their hopes and aspirations and dreams,"[25] he was largely invisible during his short time in office. Attempts at promoting the party to minority voters largely stalled—with Republican presidential candidates refusing to participate in a September 2007 PBS debate on minority issues,[26] and Martinez resigned only 10 months into his term as chair. As Martinez' replacement, Bush named Mike Duncan, then the RNC's general counsel.[27] However, with media attention focused squarely on the presidential candidates, Duncan predominantly focused on raising money in his single year in office.

While the RNC engaged in some publicity and branding efforts—and, at least in terms of newspaper coverage, remained roughly at its rate of activity during Nicholson's out-party chairmanship—it is clear Bush did not see the RNC as a particularly important political tool. The national committee did invest in outreach to Hispanic and—immediately after the 2004 election—Black voters, but both efforts appear to have faded as Bush's second term continued. And, with the GOP facing major losses in 2006 and 2008, the Republican Party found itself exiting the Bush era not just out of the White House but far outnumbered in the House and Senate. While in the past this would have likely inspired major expansion of the RNC's branding role, moving forward from the 2008 election the RNC would find itself limited in its ability to try to create a new image for the party.

The DNC during the George W. Bush Administration

After Al Gore's concession to Bush in December 2000, a clear favorite quickly emerged to take over as the new DNC chair: Terry McAuliffe, party fundraiser and close personal friend to Bill Clinton. And, with the endorsement of Clinton, Gore, and the party's congressional leaders, McAuliffe successfully fought off a last-minute challenge for the chairmanship by former Atlanta mayor Maynard H. Jackson.[28] Despite this easy victory, to many in the party McAuliffe represented "the wretched excess of the Clinton years," raising questions as to whether he could function as "a principal party spokesman."[29] An early example

[25] "Outgoing Chief Warns G.O.P. on Outlook for 2008 Races," *New York Times*, January 18, 2007.

[26] "The G.O.P.'s Candidate-Free Debate," *New York Times*, September 20, 2007.

[27] "Senator Steps Down as a Top G.O.P. Official," *New York Times*, October 20, 2007.

[28] "Clinton Confidant Gains Support to Lead the DNC," *New York Times*, December 16, 2000; "Clinton Ally Set to Lead DNC," *Washington Post*, December 16, 2000; "Black Democrats to Contest Party Leadership," *New York Times*, December 22, 2000

[29] "Democrats Shift into Reverse," *New York Times*, February 2, 2001.

of the potential issues related to McAuliffe's close connections to Clinton was the revelation that he had successfully lobbied him during the last days of his presidency for a pardon on behalf of James H. Lake, who had been convicted for providing illegal campaign contributions.[30] Additionally, McAuliffe's political persona—"more full of Barnum than ballast"[31]—rubbed many Democrats the wrong way.

But, while McAuliffe came with limitations, he also had an undeniable strength: a proven ability to raise a lot of money for a party organization that traditionally had been bad at doing so. This was a particularly helpful skill in the early 2000s, as both the DNC and RNC engaged in a last-minute fundraising dash before the passage of new campaign finance laws. With the parties facing the possibility that new restrictions would constrain their ability to raise money, both committees prioritized fundraising in 2001 and 2002.[32] And McAuliffe succeeded: by July 2001, the DNC raised more than $23 million—a Democratic record in a non-election year. And, in March 2002, just one day after the Senate voted to abolish soft money contributions, the DNC received the highest single donation in American history: a $7 million check from billionaire Haim Saban.[33]

McAuliffe used these funds to help the DNC catch up to the RNC. After his election as chair, McAuliffe stated that "without a Democratic president and White House podium, we must change how the D.N.C. does business" and announced that he would follow the RNC's example from the Clinton era: "The Republicans [expanded the RNC's PR apparatus] from the day Bill Clinton took office [. . .] George Bush is about to taste that same medicine."[34] To deliver on that, McAuliffe argued for major investments in the DNC's infrastructure. Most notably, McAuliffe built a new headquarters for the national committee, which—at a cost of $32 million—included a variety of new technological tools, such as state-of-the-art radio and TV studios.[35] McAuliffe explained in his autobiography that

---

[30] "Access Proved Vital in Last-Minute Race for Clinton Pardons," New York Times, February 25, 2001.

[31] "McAuliffe Still Wants to Send a Message to Republicans," New York Times, March 5, 2004.

[32] "Race Is under Way for Campaign Cash before New Limits," New York Times, February 11, 2001.

[33] "Democratic Donations Reach a Record for a Nonelection Year," New York Times, July 7, 2001; "Pocketing Soft Money till Pocket Is Sewn Up," New York Times, March 4, 2002; "Soft Money Lives: Democrats Take in $12 Million (2 Gifts)," New York Times, March 22, 2002.

[34] "Democrats Choose Close Friend of Clinton to Lead Party," New York Times, February 4, 2001.

[35] "Soft Money Lives," New York Times. Notably, Democrats in Congress were not all supportive of these investments in a new DNC HQ, arguing that the money should be spent instead on their re-election efforts in the 2002 midterms. See: Terry McAuliffe and Steve Kettmann, What a Party! My Life among Democrats: Presidents, Candidates, Donors, Activists, Alligators, and Other Wild Animals (New York: Thomas Dunne Books, 2007), 277.

You get what you pay for. The Republicans had invested heavily in developing their infrastructure, dating back to Ray Bliss's groundbreaking work with direct mail in the 1960s, and they had been well rewarded for their foresight. [. . .] The issue was not how much you spent, but what that money bought you.[36]

But in terms of publicity, McAuliffe's DNC did not become much more active than the committee had been during Clinton's second term. In no small part, this was a direct result of the 9/11 terrorist attacks—which left Democrats effectively unable to criticize Bush. The DNC had funded attack ads against Bush throughout the spring and summer of 2001, and McAuliffe had been "on TV and in the press every day jabbing Bush with reminders to the country that he had not been elected President."[37] After 9/11, Bush's approval ratings skyrocketed, and McAuliffe and other Democrats scaled back their criticism of the president as the war on terror unfolded. This lack of major publicity efforts during the McAuliffe era also reflected to some extent in *New York Times* coverage of the DNC in this period. Figure 8.3 shows the results of negative binomial regressions in which McAuliffe's incumbency as DNC chair is the independent variable and the lagged monthly *Times* coverage of DNC branding and service activities are the dependent variables. In this model, the data is limited to articles covering the DNC published between January 1997 and December 2004—thereby comparing coverage of the DNC from the McAuliffe era with that under Clinton's second term in the White House. Note that, as discussed in the previous chapter, the DNC was considerably less active during this second Clinton term. A reinvigorated DNC should see *more* branding coverage. Instead, the results show that there was no statistically significant change in *Times* coverage across any of the variables—indicating that the committee was at the same level as when the party still held the White House.

But while McAuliffe described himself as a chair who focused on "mechanics, not message,"[38] and his clear strength was in fundraising (as the DNC reported a record haul of over $400 million in receipts for the 2003–2004 cycle), McAuliffe nonetheless was one of the first Democratic party leaders to try to reignite political debate about Bush's leadership. Initially, he tried to do so by focusing on domestic issues, such as the state of the economy, and the importance of "a safe retirement benefit, access to affordable prescription drugs, and a reassuring sense that children will be well educated and that the environment will be protected."[39] McAuliffe also attempted to link the Bush administration

---

[36] McAuliffe and Kettmann, *What a Party!*, 279.

[37] Ibid., 274; "Ads Brawl in a Never-Ending Political Season," *New York Times*, July 3, 2001.

[38] "McAuliffe Still Wants to Send a Message to Republicans," *New York Times*, March 5, 2004.

[39] "Facing Wartime President, Democrats Focus on Home Front," *New York Times*, April 22, 2002.

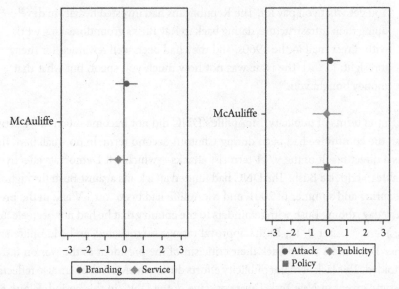

Figure 8.3. Negative binomial regression of Terry McAuliffe's DNC chairmanship on monthly (lagged) *New York Times* coverage of DNC branding and service activities, 1997–2004. *Note:* This model includes variables controlling for presidential and midterm election years, a measure of *New York Times* length, and DNC scandals. The data coverage is limited to articles published between January 1997 and December 2004, and covering only the DNC. *Source:* Data collected by author.

to the Enron scandal—which saw a Texas energy corporation bankrupted after presenting fake earnings—arguing that Bush relied on "risky investments, mountains of debt, accounting shenanigans and a little fuzzy math, then the folks at the top cash in while innocent working people are left holding the bag."[40] In the summer of 2002, McAuliffe also began criticizing Bush's handling of the war on terror. McAuliffe argued that Bush had squandered an "extraordinary opportunity" to take the nation through difficult times:

> All this trust, all this support—what an opportunity to lead. But in the end, to what end? A White House that even Republicans call the most political ever. An administration adrift, with polling numbers as their only compass and high approval ratings as their only destination.[41]

[40] "Democrats Say Bush Aide Uses War for Political Gain," *New York Times*, January 20, 2002.

[41] The *New York Times* noted that "historically, leaders of political parties have more flexibility in making these kinds of attacks" than elected officials. See: "With Eye to 2004, Democratic Party Chief Reproaches Bush," *New York Times*, August 11, 2002.

Despite these attempts, terrorism—reignited by the potential of a new war in Iraq—remained a top voter priority, and Republicans expanded their majority in the House and regained it in the Senate.[42] In the wake of the midterm results, several Democrats called for McAuliffe's resignation: Reverend Al Sharpton—a civil rights activist gearing up for his own 2004 presidential campaign—attacked McAuliffe's management of the party, and a Democratic fundraiser concluded he was not "ready to be the image and the spokesman for the Democratic Party."[43] But, with presidential candidates announcing their campaigns in February 2003, the DNC ceded the stage, and McAuliffe's role as a public spokesman mostly ended after the midterms.

In the 2004 election, Democrats again failed to regain control of the White House and Congress as presidential nominee John Kerry lost the crucial swing state Ohio by nearly 119,000 votes. McAuliffe announced he would not run for a second term and noted that the Bush campaign had been "much more sophisticated in their message delivery, very specific targeted niche. Which is what we now need to do as a party."[44] Although there were eight candidates running to succeed McAuliffe, one was particularly prominent: Howard Dean, the former governor of Vermont.[45] Dean had become a favorite of liberals and antiwar activists in the party during his presidential primary campaign in 2003–2004. Dean expected his campaign to play mostly an agenda-setting role by focusing on healthcare and his opposition to the Iraq war. But in the summer of 2003, Dean found himself the surprise front runner. However, after back-to-back defeats in Iowa and New Hampshire (and a media storm surrounding his "scream" at the end of his Iowa concession speech), Dean quickly dropped out of the race. With Kerry losing the presidency, Dean now saw an opportunity to take control of the DNC and use it to promote an agenda that "reflect[s] the socially progressive, fiscally responsible values that bring our party—and the vast majority of Americans—together."[46]

A crucial selling point of Dean's DNC chair campaign was his promise of producing a "50-state strategy." In this program, the DNC would provide funding and hire executive directors for each state.[47] Dean developed the concept in the summer of 2004 after he met with party leaders from 18 states on the

---

[42] "Daschle Sharply Attacks Bush's Economic Policies," *New York Times*, September 19, 2002; "Democrats' Ad Has Bush Mistreating Elderly," *New York Times*, October 4, 2002.

[43] "Stung by Losses, Party Buzzes about Its Leader," *New York Times*, November 12, 2002.

[44] "Democratic Leader Analyzes Bush Victory," *New York Times*, December 11, 2004.

[45] "Democrats Hear from 8 Who Want to Lead Party," *New York Times*, December 12, 2004.

[46] "Dean Enters Race for Democratic Chairman," *New York Times*, January 12, 2005.

[47] "Dean Looks at Party Chairmanship," *New York Times*, November 9, 2004; "Howard Dean Runs Again. But for What? Stay Tuned," *New York Times*, December 9, 2004; "Democrats Hear from 8".

"untargeted" list from the Kerry campaign and the DNC. As these states were considered unwinnable, they would receive no funding from the campaign or the national committee. Dean believed this approach to be a mistake:

> the best window we have to talk to Democrats [...] is in the presidential campaign, and we were just saying to the people of those 18 states, "We're not interested in you." You cannot be a national party if you say that to anybody. *Anybody* [italics in original].[48]

Dean was by no means a consensus candidate, as many elected officials were concerned that he was too liberal or too unpredictable to be an effective spokesperson for the party.[49] But Dean was popular with state party leaders, who believed he had the potential of exciting donors and volunteers. Scott Maddox, the chairman of the Democratic Party in Florida explained that

> The only knock against Howard Dean is that he's seen as too liberal. I'm a gun-owning pickup-truck driver and I have a bulldog named Lockjaw. I am a Southern chairman of a Southern state, and I am perfectly comfortable with Howard Dean as D.N.C. chair. What our party needs right now is energy, enthusiasm and a willingness to do things differently. I think Howard Dean brings all three of those things to the party.[50]

Dean was elected by voice vote and without opposition.[51]

But despite Dean's unanimous election by the DNC, some of the party's leaders remained concerned that he would alienate voters. Congressional leaders Harry Reid and Nancy Pelosi tried, but failed, to get Dean to agree he would refrain from presenting himself as the party's public face. Instead, as chair, Dean enthusiastically attacked Republicans.[52] And, given the many scandals the GOP faced during Bush's second term in office, he was given plenty to work with. Dean regularly criticized the Iraq War, claimed Republican legislators had "never [...] made an honest living in their lives,"[53] and spotlighted the Bush administration's

---

[48] "Is Howard Dean Willing to Destroy the Democratic Party in Order to Save It?," *New York Times*, October 1, 2006.

[49] "Dean Emerging as Likely Chief for Democrats," *New York Times*, February 2, 2005.

[50] "Florida Democrats Back Dean as Leader," *New York Times*, January 18, 2005.

[51] "Democrats Elect Dean as Committee Chairman," *New York Times*, February 13, 2005.

[52] "Is Howard Dean Willing to Destroy the Democratic Party?.

[53] "Dean, Feisty and Unbowed, Stands by Words on DeLay," *New York Times*, May 23, 2005; "Dean's Remarks Draw Fire from Both Sides of Aisle," *New York Times*, June 10, 2005; "Democrats Still Search for Plan on How to Deal With Iraq," *New York Times*, December 8, 2005.

failings in the wake of the devastation left by Hurricane Katrina.[54] To illustrate the importance of Katrina, the DNC held its 2006 spring meeting in New Orleans, with Dean spending time visiting areas hit hardest by the hurricane. While helping clean up debris, Dean described the administration's failing as a "searing, burning" issue and predicted that "it's going to cost George Bush his legacy, and it's going to cost the Republicans the House and the Senate and, maybe very well the presidency in the next election. People will never forget this."[55]

For all the concerns about Dean's image as a liberal—mostly due to his opposition to the Iraq war and support for same-sex partnership registration—his strategic agenda was more complex. Indeed, one of Dean's priorities was reaching out to (Southern) White working-class voters—the same group the DNC had prioritized in the 1980s and early 1990s. During his presidential campaign, Dean had famously claimed he wanted "to be the candidate for guys with Confederate flags in their pickup trucks,"[56] and, while dismissed as a gaffe, this comment reflected a conviction on Dean's side that Democrats would need to adjust how they appealed to White, rural, blue-collar voters who "ought to be voting with us and not them [...]."[57]

One important part of this strategy was an increased effort by the DNC to reach out to Christian voters. Dean's assessment of the 2004 election was that many Christian voters prioritized other considerations over economic issues: "People weren't scared about losing their jobs. They were scared about losing their kids, about what was on television, and about the methamphetamine lab the local sheriff had just found."[58] Dean argued Democrats would have to reach out to these voters by relying on a message that incorporated religious appeals: "We have done it in a secular way, and we don't have to."[59]

This perspective included a "big-tent" approach to the issue of abortion. During an appearance on *Meet the Press* in December 2004, Dean stated that "we ought to make a home for pro-life Democrats"[60] in the party. As chair, Dean placed Leah Daughtry, his chief of staff at the DNC and a Pentecostal minister,

[54] "Democrats Intensify Criticism of White House Response to Crisis," *New York Times*, September 8, 2005.

[55] "Democrats Looking to Use New Orleans as G.O.P. Used 9/11," *New York Times*, April 22, 2006; "In New Orleans, Dean Criticizes G.O.P. on Lack of Aid," *New York Times*, April 23, 2006.

[56] "Rivals Attack Dean for Wooing 'Guys with Confederate Flags,'" *New York Times*, November 2, 2003.

[57] Ibid.

[58] "Helping Democrats Find a Religious-Friendly Voice," *New York Times*, October 20, 2007.

[59] "Democrats in 2 Southern States Push Bills on Bible Study," *New York Times*, January 27, 2006.

[60] Amy Sullivan, *The Party Faithful: How and Why Democrats Are Closing the God Gap* (New York: Scribner), 159.

in charge of the committee's new Faith in Action (FIA) program. FIA existed of seven staff members at DNC HQ, as well as a 60-person faith advisory board, and its core goal was to provide Democratic candidates with advice on how to articulate Democratic values to Christian voters.[61] The program financed faith outreach programs in several Southern states by promoting Democratic candidates' life stories as framed around religious narratives. Although Daughtry herself was pro-choice, the FIA program was catholic in terms of the religious arguments and policy positions it paid for state parties to promote.[62] In Alabama, the local Democratic Party used FIA support to present a "covenant for the future" that promoted mandatory Bible literacy courses in public schools, a constitutional amendment banning abortion, and opposition to same-sex marriage.[63] In the DNC's assessment, these efforts were successful as in 2006 the "religion gap" had decreased from 30 points to just 10.[64]

Dean also enacted his 50-state strategy. After the successful 2006 midterms—in which Democrats won majorities in House and Senate—many Democrats praised Dean and the DNC for these investments, and newly elected Representatives Tim Walz (MN) and Nancy Boyda (KS) explicitly credited the 50-state strategy with their victories.[65] But prior to the midterms, congressional leaders were skeptical of Dean's approach: Representative Rahm Emanuel (IL) and Senator Chuck Schumer (NY)—chairs of the Democratic Congressional Campaign Committee (DCCC) and the Democratic Senatorial Campaign Committee (DSCC)—believed Dean squandered money in states where Democrats would never win.[66] One example of Dean's approach was presented in a profile in the New York Times in October 2006. Traveling with Dean to Alaska, reporter Matt Bai described how Dean, after realizing the entire Democratic state party organization existed of just one full-time organizer, promised the DNC would pay for additional staff to be hired there. The exchange, as Bai recounts, reflected "why so many leading Democrats in Washington wish [Dean] would spend even more time in Alaska—preferably hiking the tundra for a few months, without a cellphone."[67]

---

[61] "Helping Democrats Find a Religious-Friendly Voice."

[62] Note that the DNC's FIA was not operating in a vacuum in this regard: as Amy Sullivan has noted, after the 2004 election a broader debate existed within the Democratic Party regarding its positions on abortion and the potential of reaching out to pro-life voters. See: Sullivan, The Party Faithful, 157–158.

[63] "On Sunday She Is a Pentecostal Preacher. During the Week She Is Planning the Democratic Convention," New York Times, July 20, 2008.

[64] "Helping Democrats Find a Religious-Friendly Voice."

[65] "Democratic Leader Reminds Party that Victory Is No Mandate."

[66] "Dean and Party Leaders in a Money Dispute," New York Times, May 11, 2006.

[67] "Is Howard Dean Willing to Destroy the Democratic Party?"

After the midterms, Dean warned that Democrats "must not squander opportunities to keep building the party"[68] and should strengthen efforts at reaching out to evangelical voters. However, like Kirk, Brown, and McAuliffe before him, the presidential primaries—and in particular the matchup between Senators Barack Obama (IL) and Hillary Clinton (NY)—meant Dean's public role receded. As one *New York Times* profile from October 2007 noted, Dean now conducted "business in near obscurity, rarely appearing on television or at public events."[69] And, with Obama having built his own massive campaign operation during the primaries, the DNC's role in the general election was limited as well. Dean announced after the 2008 election that he would not serve a second term, but in a memorandum sent to members of the DNC, he asserted that the extent of Obama's victory and Democratic gains in House and Senate were a direct effect of his 50-state strategy.[70] Indeed, one of the Senate gains came in Alaska—one of the "unwinnable" states Dean insisted the party should invest in—where Democrat Mark Begich unseated incumbent Ted Stevens by less than 4,000 votes.

Obama and the DNC: Benign Neglect

After two close losses for the Democrats in 2000 and 2004, Barack Obama won the popular vote with the highest percentage for a Democrat since LBJ in 1964 and a comfortable electoral college majority. Crucially, Democratic success also extended to Congress. In the House, Democrats won a substantial majority while in the Senate, they (temporarily) held a filibuster-proof majority of 60 seats (see Figure 8.4).[71] As the new administration had no lack of crises to deal with—the global economic crash in the fall of 2008 reached its depths in the spring of 2009, and the United States remained militarily involved in both Iraq and Afghanistan—it is unsurprising that the DNC was no priority to Obama early on. But during his eight years as party leader, the 2008 success was followed by dramatic losses in election cycles that did not have Obama on the ticket. And despite these major setbacks, Obama failed to invest in the

[68] "Democratic Leader Reminds Party that Victory Is No Mandate."

[69] "His Meteoric Days behind Him," *New York Times*, October 21, 2007.

[70] "Dean Won't Seek New Term as D.N.C. Chief," *New York Times*, November 11, 2008; "Dean Seeks a Share of Credit in Obama Victory," *New York Times*, November 12, 2008.

[71] The extremely close Minnesota senate race remained undecided for months. After Al Franken was declared the winner in that race, Ted Kennedy's death and eventual replacement by Republican Scott Brown meant the supermajority was not fully in place through much of Obama's first two years in office.

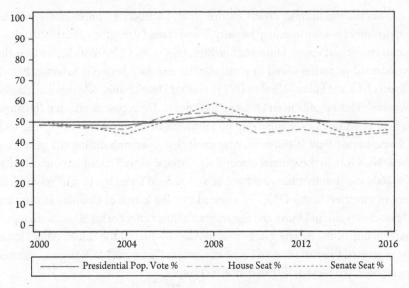

Figure 8.4. Democratic electoral performance in presidential, House, and Senate elections, 2000–2016. *Source: Congressional Quarterly's Guide to U.S. Elections,* 7th ed. (Washington, DC: Congressional Quarterly, 2016).

DNC: indeed, Obama's approach as party leader was described by his aides as one of "benign neglect."[72]

Of course, Obama is far from the only (Democratic) president to have shown little interest in the DNC and, much like Jimmy Carter before him, may simply not have seen much value in the committee as an organization. Obama's dealings with the DNC prior to winning the presidency were limited: while he ran in several races in Illinois, his only statewide race for the Senate in 2004 saw him quickly become the frontrunner due to his electrifying speech at the 2004 Democratic convention and a weak Republican opponent. During his 2008 presidential primary campaign, Obama had been forced to build up a formidable campaign organization of his own to help him beat Hillary Clinton. While brutal, Obama's campaign manager David Plouffe credited the Obama–Clinton contest with forcing the campaign to create a significant campaign presence in nearly every state.[73] As a result, OFA became a highly developed, well-funded, independent body with major technological and data capacities, and considerable volunteer support across the country.[74] In the 2008 general election, OFA

[72] Edward-Isaac Dovere, *Battle for the Soul: Inside the Democrats' Campaigns to Defeat Trump* (New York: Viking, 2021), 15.

[73] "Dean Seeks a Share of Credit in Obama Victory."

[74] "Democrats Take Page from Their Rival's Playbook," *New York Times,* November 1, 2008.

"effectively subsumed all the responsibilities of the DNC through its own fund-raising, voter turnout efforts and opposition research."[75]

As Sidney Milkis and John York note, the OFA became a defining feature of Obama's relationship with his party.[76] Initially, Obama and his campaign managers agreed to place OFA within the DNC as a semiautonomous organization. The goal was to use the 2008 campaign contact lists and resources to help the administration promote and pass policies. In this regard, OFA had clear potential: the Obama campaign had gathered email addresses of 13 million supporters and three million donors. Additionally, two million supporters had been active participants in the campaign efforts in some form.[77] If the DNC and OFA could activate these supporters on behalf of Obama's legislative program, they could form an important force in American politics.

Indeed, during the long process of crafting and passing the Affordable Care Act (commonly referred to as Obamacare) in 2009 and 2010, the administration hoped to activate "an army of supporters talking, sending e-mail and texting to friends and neighbors as they try to mold public opinion."[78] But while OFA invested in its ability to reach supporters in a smart way—that is, micro-targeting its appeals "based on gender, race, age, voting history, magazine subscriptions, car registrations, property values, and hunting licenses"[79]—its grassroots network languished. Still, the OFA component of the DNC at times produced notable shows of support for the healthcare bill. For example, in October 2009, it prompted 315,000 supporters to call members of Congress and demand their support for the healthcare overhaul.[80]

The DNC—under leadership of then Virginia governor Tim Kaine—also provided more traditional support—airing national and local TV spots defending the healthcare proposals and attacking Republican and conservative opponents like radio host Rush Limbaugh, RNC chair Michael Steele, and South Carolina senators Lindsey Graham and Jim DeMint for their opposition to Obamacare.[81] Part of the DNC strategy was targeting Republican-held congressional districts that voted for Obama in the 2008 election.[82] But the DNC also targeted states with Democratic senators on the fence about supporting the

---

[75] "Dean Won't Seek New Term as DNC Chief," *New York Times*, November 11, 2008.

[76] Sidney M. Milkis and John Warren York, "Barack Obama, Organizing for Action, and Executive-Centered Partisanship," *Studies in American Political Development* 31, no. 1 (April 2017), 1–23.

[77] Ibid., 4.

[78] "Melding Obama's Web to a YouTube Presidency," *New York Times*, January 26, 2009.

[79] Milkis and York, "Barack Obama, Organizing for Action, and Executive-Centered Partisanship," 5.

[80] Ibid.

[81] "Two Sides Take Health Debate outside Capital," *New York Times*, August 3, 2009.

[82] "Taking the Campaign Home," *New York Times*, November 11, 2009.

healthcare overhaul: pro-Obamacare DNC ads were broadcast in North Dakota (the home state of Kent Conrad), Indiana (Evan Bayh), Florida (Bill Nelson), Nebraska (Ben Nelson), and Louisiana (Mary Landrieu).[83]

Nonetheless, the DNC was caught off guard by the intensity of the push-back against the legislation. In the summer of 2009, Democratic lawmakers faced highly hostile town halls with participants attacking them mostly on their support of the healthcare overhaul. DNC communications director Brad Woodhouse noted that "we all had a good sense that some of this was going to take place," but "I think we were a little surprised [...] at the use of swastikas and the comparisons to Adolf Hitler and the Third Reich [...] and [...] the mob mentality."[84] The DNC tried to use these town hall attacks in their pro-Obamacare ads, warning viewers that "the right-wing extremist Republican base is back [and is] organizing angry mobs, just like they did during the election."[85] After the successful passage of Obamacare, the DNC continued to match the GOP and its more radical Tea Party wing.[86] As one Democratic strategist told the *New York Times*, the party's strategy was to remind voters "that it's now really dangerous to re-empower the Republican Party."[87] The DNC prioritized energizing Black voters—spending $3 million on targeted advertising, including an ad featuring civil rights leader Joseph Lowery, who reminded voters that after the election of "our first African American president [...] there are those doing everything in their power to block the president's agenda."[88]

The 2010 midterms produced a major backlash as Republicans gained a whopping 63 seats (and with it, the majority) in the House. The damage was even worse at the state legislative level, where Republicans gained majorities in 14 states and now held unified control of state government in 15. Kaine remained chair after the midterms but announced in April 2011 that he would resign to run for a senate seat in Virginia. As Kaine's replacement, Obama selected Florida Representative Debbie Wasserman Schultz. Unlike Kaine, who had been close to Obama, Wasserman Schultz had no preexisting relationship with the president. Indeed, Wasserman Schultz had been a supporter of Clinton during the 2008 primary races and was one of the "last of the Mohicans"[89] backing Clinton

---

[83] "Competing Ads on Health Plan Swamp Airwaves," *New York Times*, August 16, 2009.

[84] "White House Adopts New Playbook in Debate on Health Care Overhaul," *New York Times*, August 11, 2009.

[85] "Competing Ads on Health Plan Swamp Airwaves," *New York Times*, August 16, 2009.

[86] "Democrats Try to Make Tea-G.O.P. Connection," *New York Times*, July 29, 2010; "Democratic Ad Casts Boehner in a Central Role," *New York Times*, September 14, 2010; "Obama Says the G.O.P. Is Beholden to Interests," *New York Times*, October 11, 2010.

[87] "Obama Advisers Weigh Offensive against the G.O.P.," *New York Times*, September 20, 2010.

[88] "Threat Response," *New York Times*, October 16, 2010.

[89] "Democratic Party's Chairwoman Was Seen as Loyal to a Fault," *New York Times*, July 25, 2016.

after Obama's nomination was all but assured. As reporter Edward-Isaac Dovere argues, however, Obama chose Wasserman Schultz with the 2012 election in mind: as a female member of Congress from a crucial swing state, and as a Jewish politician, the Obama team hoped the selection of Wasserman Schultz as chair would be well received by voting groups important to Obama's re-election chances.[90]

With OFA taken out of the DNC again to function as Obama's independent re-election campaign organization, the DNC engaged in supportive publicity activities in the run-up to 2012. In the fall of 2011, the DNC began airing an ad in five swing states attacking Republican frontrunner Mitt Romney as a serial flip-flopper on issues abortion and healthcare.[91] Additionally, the DNC focused on securing Obama's support among specific voting groups by airing Spanish language ads and created a new outreach program toward Jewish voters.[92] The DNC also supported state party organizations: for example, it provided the Ohio Democratic state party with a little over $800,000, "including substantial cash and payments covering phones and computer equipment."[93] But the Obama administration constrained the DNC when it believed it was acting against its interests: after West Wing officials found out the DNC had been using OFA to support protests against Wisconsin governor Scott Walker's anti-union policies, "they angrily reined in the staff at the party headquarters."[94]

Combined, the DNC during Obama's first term engaged in basic support activities on behalf of an incumbent president—in no small part because OFA was incorporated into the committee for most of this period. Indeed, in comparison with the Dean era, *New York Times* coverage of the DNC during Obama's first term does not show a change in combined branding activities. Figure 8.5 shows the results of negative binomial regressions in which Obama's incumbency as president is the independent variable and the lagged monthly *Times* coverage of DNC branding and service activities are the dependent variables. In this model,

[90] Dovere, *Battle for the Soul*, 17.

[91] "Democrats Take Aim at Romney's Shifts," *New York Times*, November 29, 2011; "Waiting for Mitt the Moderate," *New York Times*, January 5, 2012; "The Flub Watch Never Stops for Obama's Team," *New York Times*, February 6, 2012; "For Romney's Trusted Adviser, 'Etch a Sketch' Comment Is a Rare Misstep," *New York Times*, March 22, 2012; "Obama and Democrats Ready to Pressure Republicans on 'Buffett Rule,'" *New York Times*, April 7, 2012; "In Strategy Shift, Obama Team Attacks Romney from the Left," *New York Times*, April 21, 2012; "Obama's Camp Makes Aggressive Push for Romney to Disclose Offshore Finances," *New York Times*, July 10, 2012.

[92] "Arizona Sees a Boom in Voting-Age Hispanics," *New York Times*, December 2, 2011; "Seeing Ripple in Jewish Vote," *New York Times*, September 15, 2011; "Democrats Have Session on Reaching Out to Jews," *New York Times*, September 10, 2011.

[93] "Fund-Raising for Romney Eats into Obama's Edge," *New York Times*, May 22, 2012.

[94] "With a Change in Top Aides, the West Wing Quiets Down," *New York Times*, March 4, 2011.

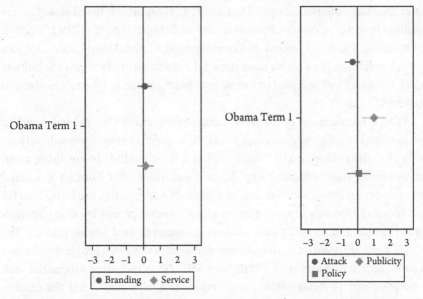

Figure 8.5. Negative binomial regressions of Barack Obama's presidency on monthly (lagged) *New York Times* coverage of DNC branding and service activities, 2005–2012.
Note: This model includes variables controlling for presidential and midterm election years, a measure of *New York Times* length, and DNC scandals. The data coverage is limited to articles published between January 2005 and December 2012, and covering only the DNC.
Source: Data collected by author.

the data is limited to articles covering the DNC published between January 2005 and December 2012—thereby comparing coverage of the DNC under Obama's first term with that under Dean. The only statistically significant result shows an increase in publicity efforts under Obama (significant at the 0.01 level), reflecting some of the efforts the DNC engaged in to support Obama's legislative goals and re-election campaign.

But after Obama's re-election, the relationship between president and party organization deteriorated. In January 2013, Obama announced that OFA—now renamed Organizing for Action—would continue not as a part of the DNC but as an independent organization.[95] In announcing the shift, Obama argued that OFA "has always been about more than just winning an election [...]. Organizing for Action will be a permanent commitment to this mission."[96] Obama thus turned his campaign organization into a de facto competitor of the DNC. As the *New York Times* noted after the announcement, "Democratic donors may

---

[95] "Obama to Turn Campaign Machinery to Promoting Policy," *New York Times,* January 18, 2013.
[96] Milkis and York, "Barack Obama, Organizing for Action, and Executive-Centered Partisanship," 6.

choose to contribute"[97] to OFA rather than the DNC. Indeed, in February 2013 Obama's political team engaged in a campaign to raise $50 million for OFA, with large donors promised access to quarterly meetings with Obama himself at the White House.[98] To be sure, Obama still appeared at fundraisers for the DNC, and OFA eventually shared its email contact lists with the DNC.[99] But, given that the DNC was left with a considerable deficit after the 2012 campaign, and remained $7 million in debt by December 2015, the independence of OFA undeniably hurt the committee.[100] Indeed, the DNC's income dropped dramatically in the 2013–2014 cycle: while the DCCC and the DSCC reported record receipts, the DNC reported $60 million less in receipts than in the previous midterm cycle.[101]

During the 2014 midterms, Democrats faced dramatic losses—resulting in a Republican takeover of the Senate as well. While a shake-up of the DNC might have been warranted given these results, Obama kept Wasserman Schultz in office, Dovere argues that

> Obama was so uninterested in the party organization that he didn't care enough to have the fight [Wasserman Schultz] was suggesting if he fired her, threatening to imply that the White House had problems with women and with Jews. [...] No one, aides would eventually admit, had the energy to really do anything about the situation—as if they were talking about getting a roommate to do the dishes, and not taking responsibility for what was happening to their party.[102]

And, after the midterms, attention shifted back to yet another presidential primary battle—this time between now-former secretary of state Hillary Clinton and Vermont senator Bernie Sanders. The Clinton camp, assuming they would

[97] "Republican Committee Begins Midterm Election Cycle in the Black," *New York Times*, January 31, 2013.

[98] "Obama's Backers Seek Big Donors to Press Agenda," *New York Times*, February 22, 2013.

[99] "Obama Pauses from Fray to Raise Money for 2014," *New York Times*, April 3, 2013; "Obama Vows Aggressive Campaign for Party's Congressional Candidates," *New York Times*, February 28, 2014; Milkis and York, "Barack Obama, Organizing for Action, and Executive-Centered Partisanship."

[100] Dovere, *Battle For the Soul*, 16; "Hillary Clinton Fortifies Ties and Fund-Raising with Democratic Committee," *New York Times*, December 3, 2015.

[101] See: "DNC Services Corp / Democratic National Committee: 2013–2014," (FEC ID: C00010603), https://www.fec.gov/data/committee/C00010603/?tab=summary&cycle=2014; "DCCC: 2013–2014" (FEC ID: C00000935), https://www.fec.gov/data/committee/C00000935/?tab=summary&cycle=2014; "DSCC: 2013–2014" (FEC ID: C00042366), https://www.fec.gov/data/committee/C00042366, https://www.fec.gov/data/committee/C00000935/?tab=summary&cycle=2014.

[102] Dovere, *Battle for the Soul*, 17.

easily win the nomination, showed early interest in the state of the DNC. In fall 2015, Clinton campaign manager Robby Mook requested a review of the DNC's capacities and concluded that its communications department had become "skeletal."[103]

The biggest publicity effort the DNC engaged in during the 2015–2016 primaries proved to be controversial. In May 2015, the DNC announced it would co-sponsor six debates with all Democratic presidential candidates. Crucially, if candidates attended unsanctioned debates, they risked being excluded from the official debates.[104] Wasserman Schultz claimed the debates would "give all Americans a chance to see a unified Democratic vision of economic opportunity and progress—no matter whom our nominee may be."[105] But the number of debates was quickly criticized by Clinton's opponents, who argued that the DNC had "rigged" the debate schedule to benefit Clinton.[106] Representative Tulsi Gabbard (HI)—a vice chair of the DNC—subsequently claimed she was disinvited from the first debate after she agreed with the criticism.[107] As the primary race between Clinton and Sanders dragged on, the DNC approved more debates but then received pushback for scheduling them at unpopular times: two of the 2015 debates were on Saturday night, while GOP debates were on weeknights when they were more likely to attract viewers.[108]

Relations between the DNC and the Sanders campaign were already tense: in its early stages, the Sanders campaign had requested office space at DNC HQ since Senate rules precluded them from using their own space in the Capitol. Wasserman Schultz denied the request.[109] Given that Clinton's campaign wasn't requesting space either, this may have been an understandable decision, but it created suspicion in the Sanders camp that the DNC supported Clinton. The DNC–Sanders feud continued after it was discovered that Sanders campaign

---

[103] "Hillary Clinton Fortifies Ties and Fund-Raising with Democratic Committee."

[104] "Calls Intensify for More Debates on the Democratic Side," *New York Times*, September 3, 2015; "Bernie Sanders's Campaign Says He Would Sit Out Unsanctioned Debate," *New York Times*, January 26, 2016.

[105] "Democrats Plan Six Presidential Debates, Starting This Fall," *New York Times*, May 5, 2015.

[106] "Martin O'Malley Accuses D.N.C. of Favoring Hillary Clinton," *New York Times*, August 5, 2015; "Hillary Clinton's Rivals Critical of Democratic Party Politics," *New York Times*, August 28, 2015;

[107] Gabbard resigned as DNC vice chair in 2016 to endorse Sanders. See: "Two D.N.C. Officials Call for Adding More Debates," *New York Times*, September 9, 2015; "D.N.C. Officer Says She Was Disinvited from Debate after Calling for More of Them," *New York Times*, October 12, 2015; "Tulsi Gabbard, Rising Democratic Star, Endorses Bernie Sanders," *New York Times*, February 28, 2016.

[108] "The Invisible Democratic Debates," *New York Times*, December 17, 2015; "Martin O'Malley and Bernie Sanders Bristle at Holding Debates on Weekends," *New York Times*, December 18, 2015.

[109] Jonathan Allen and Amie Parnes, *Shattered: Inside Hillary Clinton's Doomed Campaign* (New York: Crown, 2017), 46.

staffers accessed Clinton campaign data through a shared DNC voter database, while a Clinton agreement with the DNC to cooperate in fundraising added further suspicions about the DNC's independence.[110]

While Sanders endorsed Clinton before the start of the national convention, the toxic relationship between the DNC and his campaign soon returned to the headlines. In June 2016, the *Washington Post* reported that the DNC's computer systems had been infiltrated by Russian hackers.[111] The FBI had flagged suspicious activity in 2015 and informed the DNC about it, but its leadership was not made aware of the breach until April 2016. By then, hackers had had access to intra-committee communications—including opposition research on GOP presidential nominee Donald Trump—for months. In July, the Friday before the start of the Democratic convention, WikiLeaks released around 20,000 DNC emails accessed through the Russian hack. Among these were emails critical of the Sanders campaign: in one, a communications official suggested that the DNC could urge reporters to focus more critically on Sanders and "that his campaign is a mess."[112] In another email, DNC CFO Brad Marshall suggested attacking Sanders (or one of his campaign surrogates) on their religious beliefs.[113] While these revelations did not prove the DNC's activities cost Sanders the nomination, it certainly showed that DNC staffers preferred Clinton.[114] In response to the outrage, Wasserman Schultz resigned.[115]

Despite the rough election year, many Democrats believed Clinton would win the 2016 election against Trump. But election night turned into an increasingly

[110] Sanders was given the same proposal to work together in fundraising but rejected the opportunity. See: "Sanders vs. Party: Why Voter Data Can Be So Important," *New York Times*, December 18, 2015; "Democratic Party Defends Actions over Data Breach as Bernie Sanders's Campaign Suspends Two Aides," *New York Times*, December 19, 2015; "Hillary Clinton Reaches Deal with Democratic Party on Fundraising," *New York Times*, August 27, 2015; "Hillary Clinton Fortifies Ties and Fund-Raising with Democratic Committee," *New York Times*, December 3, 2015.

[111] "Russian Government Hackers Penetrated DNC, Stole Opposition Research on Trump," *Washington Post*, June 14, 2016.

[112] "Released Emails Suggest the D.N.C. Derided the Sanders Campaign," *New York Times*, July 22, 2016.

[113] The email read, "It might may no difference, but for KY and WVA can we get someone to ask his belief. Does he believe in a God. He had skated on saying he has a Jewish heritage. I think I read he is an atheist. This could make several points difference with my peeps." The email did not define who this "he" referred to. After the leak, Marshall suggested it was more likely he was referring to a Sanders campaign surrogate than to Sanders himself but provided no additional evidence. See: "Released Emails Suggest the D.N.C. Derided the Sanders Campaign."

[114] Boris Heersink, "No, the DNC Didn't 'Rig' the Democratic Primary for Hillary Clinton," *Washington Post*, November 4, 2017.

[115] "Debbie Wasserman Schultz to Resign D.N.C. Post," *New York Times*, July 24, 2016; "Debbie Wasserman Schultz Is Met with Jeers at Pre-Convention Breakfast," *New York Times*, July 25, 2016; "The Democrats' Damaging Damage Control," *New York Times*, July 25, 2016.

dark surprise: while Clinton won the popular vote by a considerable margin, Trump won the electoral college through close victories in three battleground states. In the aftermath of the 2016 election, Democrats linked Clinton's defeat to the decline of the DNC under Obama. One DNC consultant concluded that "the Democratic Party now is left literally at zero—zero dollars in the bank, zero infrastructure as the Clinton campaign closes up shop, and, most importantly, zero majority control in Washington and in thirty-three of the states."[116] And Nebraska Democratic Party Chair Jane Kleeb directly blamed OFA, arguing that

> OFA was created as a shadow party because Obama operatives had no faith in state parties. [. . .] OFA had no faith or confidence in the state parties so they created a whole separate organization, they took money away and centralized it in D.C. They gave us a great president for eight years, but we lost everywhere else.[117]

Toward the Party of Trump: The RNC, 2009–2016

The 2008 election left the Republican Party with the seeming necessity of reinventing its party image. Not only did Obama win the White House; Democrats expanded their majorities in Congress. The end of the second Bush term left Republicans with few bright spots: the quagmire in Iraq, the botched response to Hurricane Katrina, and the massive economic crash in the fall of 2008 left the party little in terms of policy achievements to build on. In the wake of the 2008 election, former speaker of the House Newt Gingrich called on Republicans to "be honest about the level of failure for the past eight years and why Republican government didn't succeed. Otherwise, we'll get back in power again and do the same things again."[118]

In the run-up to the RNC meeting in January 2009, committee chair Duncan indicated he would be open to a second term, arguing that he could return the party to its "core conservative principles."[119] But Duncan was challenged by other candidates, including Chip Saltsman (the Tennessee GOP chair), J. Kenneth Blackwell (the former secretary of state of Ohio), and Michael Steele (the former lieutenant governor of Maryland).[120] Race played an important part in the chairmanship campaign: Saltsman distributed a CD at a holiday party

[116] Dovere, *Battle for the Soul*, 10.

[117] "Obama's Party-Building Legacy Splits Democrats," *Politico*, February 9, 2017.

[118] "Sparring Starts as Republicans Ponder Future," *New York Times*, November 11, 2008.

[119] "A Bid to Keep G.O.P. Reins," *New York Times*, December 11, 2008.

[120] "Republicans Receive an Obama Parody to Mixed Reviews," *New York Times*, December 28, 2008.

that included the racist song "Barack the Magic Negro"—originally played on Rush Limbaugh's show. On the other hand, two of the candidates—Steele and Blackwell—were Black, which, in the assessment of Florida GOP chair Jim Greer, introduced the potential "advantage of a credible message of inclusion if you have a minority as chairman."[121] During the RNC's 2009 winter meeting Steele was elected as the RNC's first Black chairman after six ballots.

Steele believed the GOP faced "an image problem," the solution to which required "defining ourselves to the people of this country"[122] but appears to not have introduced any major new publicity programs during his two-year term as chair. The RNC did regularly criticize Obama and congressional Democrats and aired nationwide ads opposing Obama's policies—most notably, the Affordable Care Act.[123] Steele defended Republicans when they were accused of bigotry after criticizing Obama. After Republican member of Congress Joe Wilson was accused of racism after he interrupted a speech Obama gave in Congress by yelling "You lie" at the president, Steele responded that "characterizing Americans' disapproval of President Obama's as being based on race is an outrage."[124]

But while Steele was known for his "feisty public presence and television skills"[125] as a talking head on cable news, his goal of applying GOP values to "urban and suburban hip-hop settings"[126] and using related vernacular produced mostly ridicule. Steele argued that Democrats were wrong to include too much "bling bling"[127] in their economic stimulus bill and initially titled his blog on the RNC's website "What Up." Matters did not improve when Steele argued in July 2010 that the ongoing war in Afghanistan—which had started under the Bush administration in response to 9/11—was "a war of Obama's choosing."[128] A number of Republicans, including Senators John McCain and Lindsey Graham, criticized Steele. The satirical news program *The Daily Show* saw host Jon Stewart ridiculing Steele by speaking with a Sesame Street–type puppet of his liking. "Puppet Michael Steele," voiced by comedian Wyatt Cenac, mocked both Steele's Afghanistan gaffe and his "urban hip hop" persona:

---

[121] "At Defining Moment for G.O.P., a Diverse Choice of Leadership," *New York Times*, January 11, 2009.

[122] "Seeking New Path, Republicans Pick First Black as National Chairman," *New York Times*, January 31, 2009.

[123] "New Poll Finds Growing Unease on Health Plan," *New York Times*, July 30, 2009; "A Last-Minute Surge," *New York Times*, December 15, 2009.

[124] "White House Is Sitting Out Race Debate," *New York Times*, September 17, 2009.

[125] "Seeking New Path, Republicans Pick First Black as National Chairman."

[126] "The Right Way to Make Fun of Michael Steele," *New York Magazine*, December 17, 2010.

[127] "Trillion Dollar Baby," *New York Times*, February 11, 2009

[128] "Republican Senators Denounce Steele's Remarks," *New York Times*, July 5, 2010.

Puppet Michael Steele: Fourth of July at the cribble, baby. I'm feeling the thrill of the grill, 'cause you know I likes to chill!

Jon Stewart: I must say I didn't expect you to be so upbeat. Your comments about Afghanistan are very controversial.

Puppet Michael Steele: I nailed it! I hibbled that bibble like a jibble on the dribble!

Jon Stewart: I'm not sure what that means, but people in your own party are blasting you. Here's Senator Lindsey Graham.

Lindsey Graham [in video clip, on *Face the Nation*]: "Dismayed, angry, upset. It was an uninformed, unnecessary, unwise, untimely comment."

Puppet Michael Steele [frowning, wounded, wiping eye]: Lindabale Grahibble?[129]

Steele's concern with the GOP's inability to win support among non-White voters reflected a similar assessment many of his predecessors had made before. Steele believed the GOP should be reaching out to Black voters and acknowledged that

> we have offered [non-White Americans] nothing! And the impression we've created is that we don't give a damn about them or we just outright don't like them. And that's not a healthy thing for a political party. I think the way we've talked about immigration, the way we've talked about some of the issues that are important to African-Americans, like affirmative action [. . .] I mean, you know, having an absolute holier-than-thou attitude about something that's important to a particular community doesn't engender confidence in your leadership by that community—or consideration of you for office or other things—because you've already given off the vibe that you don't care.[130]

However, in terms of what the GOP actually should do to convince these voters, Steele's solution was largely similar to the choices his predecessors made. That is, while he aimed to "open up" the party, he noted that this did "not mean that I need to backslide on what I believe or what values we hold."[131] Thus, while Steele's campaign tour in a bright-red "Fire Pelosi" bus in the run-up to the 2010 midterm elections included stops in Democratic strongholds like Harlem, the RNC did not combine outreach to Black voters with policy change.[132]

[129] Quoted in Chris Smith, *The Daily Show (The Book): An Oral History* (New York: Grand Central Publishing, 2016), 292–293.

[130] Lisa DePaulo, "The Reconstructionist," *GQ Magazine*, March 11, 2009.

[131] Ibid.

[132] "A Republican Leader Visits a Democratic Stronghold," *New York Times*, October 27, 2010.

At the same time, the GOP did connect with the widespread Tea Party protests against Obama-era economic spending and healthcare reform bills. To be sure, as Theda Skocpol and Vanessa Williamson have shown, the Tea Party mostly represented an intra-GOP phenomenon among older, White, conservative Republicans.[133] Crucially, the Tea Party was also inherently linked to race. In part this was through countless examples of activists and elected officials questioning Obama's religion and nationality (most notably, the birther movement as championed by then-still-reality-TV-host Donald Trump). But Obama's race also affected policy perception: White conservatives with high levels of racial resentment believed Obama was trying to benefit Black Americans through his policies, such as Obamacare—regardless of the fact that these polices were not about race.[134] Thus, as the GOP embraced the Tea Party in 2009 and 2010 any attempts by the RNC to also appeal to minority voter support were almost certain to fail.

Steele's time in office proved to be short-lived. While the Republican Party saw major successes in the 2010 midterms—winning six seats in the Senate and regaining a massive 63 seats and the majority in the House—Steele had become an increasingly contentious figure in the party due to his gaffes. But the bigger issue appears to have been a lack of success in fundraising, which became particularly controversial when it was discovered that Steele had also been engaging in paid speeches. Additionally, in April 2010 it was revealed that the RNC had paid a $2,000 bill for expenses by committee staff and donors at a strip-and-bondage club in Los Angeles, suggesting both poor expense management and an image not consistent with the Republican "family values" brand.[135] Katon Dawson, who had been one of Steeles's competitors in the 2009 RNC chairmanship race, criticized him for failing to understand the difference between good and bad publicity: "Lee Harvey Oswald had 100 percent name ID and none of it was any good. The bad press hurts us on the ground."[136]

---

[133] Theda Skocpol and Vanessa Williamson, *The Tea Party and the Remaking of Republican Conservatism* (New York: Oxford University Press, 2013).

[134] Antoine J. Banks, *Anger and Racial Politics: The Emotional Foundations of Racial Attitudes in America* (New York: Cambridge University Press, 2014).

[135] RNC reported that receipts for the 2009–2010 electoral cycle were down in comparison with the previous midterm cycle ($196.3 million vs. $243 million), though the RNC's share of the total receipts by the three main Republican committees (RNC, the National Republican Congressional Committee, and the Republican Senate Campaign Committee) was roughly comparable— reflecting a general decline in donations between the two cycles. See: "Republican National Committee" (FEC ID: C00003418), https://www.fec.gov/data/committee/C00003418/; "NRCC" (FEC ID: C00075820), https://www.fec.gov/data/committee/C00075820/; "Republican Senate Campaign Committee" (FEC ID: C30002026), https://www.fec.gov/data/committee/C30002026/.

[136] "G.O.P. Squirms as an Unwelcome Spotlight Focuses on Its Leader," *New York Times*, April 7, 2010.

After the midterm elections, RNC member Henry Barbour (the nephew of former RNC chair and, by then, governor of Mississippi, Haley Barbour) began reaching out to possible candidates to challenge Steele, including Reince Priebus, the chair of the Wisconsin GOP.[137] Days later, RNC political director Gentry Collins resigned and criticized Steele's leadership—suggesting the RNC was insolvent and would not play a meaningful role in the 2012 election unless a new leader was elected.[138] Steele still ran for re-election, but Priebus defeated him and other candidates after seven ballots.[139] With presidential nominees announcing their candidacies in spring 2011, Priebus initially focused on fundraising.[140] By the summer of 2012, the RNC had recovered well enough that the committee assisted the Romney campaign with as much as $21 million worth of attack ad buys in July and August 2012 alone.[141] But the campaign largely relied on its own operations and support from Super PACS in the fall. Despite the Republican high expectations after the 2010 midterm successes, the 2012 election proved to be a major disappointment. Obama easily defeated Romney and Democrats gained seats in Congress.

After the election, Priebus announced an RNC-sponsored investigation into the causes of the party's defeat. As Tim Miller, an RNC staffer at the time, recalls, this project came about in response to

> pressure [. . .] from donors and committee members to assess what had gone wrong, determine why the party had lost the popular vote in five of the last six elections, and figure out what needed to be done to win back the White House the next time around.[142]

The team behind this project—dubbed the Growth and Opportunity Project—included mainstream Republicans such as Henry Barbour and former George W. Bush spokesman Ari Fleischer as well as RNC staffers such as Sean Spicer and Elise Stefanik.[143] The team engaged in extensive interviews with Republican

[137] "Republicans Maneuver to Oust Their Leader," *New York Times*, November 10, 2010.

[138] "Top Republican Official, Breaking with Party Chairman, Resigns," *New York Times*, November 17, 2010.

[139] "Embattled GOP Chief Is Seeking Second Term," *New York Times*, December 14, 2010; "Steele Faces His Rivals in Gentle G.O.P. Debate," *New York Times*, January 4, 2011; "G.O.P. Elects New Chairman as Steele Drops Out," *New York Times*, January 15, 2011.

[140] "R.N.C. May Sponsor Debates in Exchange for Help on Debt," *New York Times*, April 3, 2011.

[141] "Strong July for GOP," *New York Times*, August 17, 2012.

[142] Tim Miller, *Why We Did It: A Travelogue from the Republican Road to Hell* (New York: Harper, 2022), 79.

[143] "RNC Launches Election Post-Mortem," *Washington Post*, December 10, 2012; Tim Alberta, *American Carnage: On the Front Lines of the Republican Civil War and the Rise of President Trump* (New York: HarperCollins, 2019), 138–139; McKay Coppins, *The Wilderness: Deep*

activists and released its conclusions in March 2013.[144] The report was quickly dubbed the "autopsy" of the 2012 election and presented a variety of suggestions on how the RNC should adjust its activities. These suggestions included improving fundraising, investing in data harvesting, and changing the presidential selection process by shortening the primaries and limiting the number of primary debates. In the years that followed, Priebus followed through on many of these suggestions. After the 2014 midterms (which saw the GOP win control of the Senate), Priebus reported that the RNC expanded its grassroots campaign operations and had invested a reported $175 million in its data gathering and analysis capabilities.[145] By the 2016 campaign, the RNC had 6,000 full- or part-time staff members working in battleground states and worked with "the largest voter file in RNC history."[146]

But the autopsy report also spotlighted the need for a radical change in the GOP's public image. The report noted that

> public perception of the Party is at record lows. Young voters are increasingly rolling their eyes at what the Party represents, and many minorities wrongly think that Republicans do not like them or want them in the country. When someone rolls their eyes at us, they are not likely to open their ears to us. At the federal level, much of what Republicans are doing is not working beyond the core constituencies that make up the Party.[147]

To alleviate this, the report recommended Republicans "need to campaign among Hispanic, black, Asian and gay Americans and demonstrate that we care about them too."[148] And, while the Growth and Opportunity Project did not identify many specific policies the GOP should follow, it did support comprehensive immigration reform as a necessary step.

The Growth and Opportunity Project's vision of a kinder, gentler Republican Party was clearly not achieved. In no small part, this failure followed the strong

inside the Republican Party's Combative, Contentious, Chaotic Quest to Take Back the White House (New York: Little, Brown and Company 2015), 66; Miller, *Why We Did It*, 80.

[144] Coppins, *The Wilderness*, 68.

[145] Reince Priebus, "Two Years Later, GOP Shows Growth and Opportunity," *Real Clear Politics*, March 18, 2015; Bob Woodward, *Fear: Trump in the White House* (New York: Simon and Schuster, 2018), 23.

[146] Major Garrett, *Mr. Trump's Wild Ride: The Thrills, Chills, Screams, and Occasional Blackouts of an Extraordinary Presidency* (New York: All Points Books, 2018), 53–54.

[147] Republican National Committee, *Growth and Opportunity Project* (2013), 4. Accessed online at https://online.wsj.com/public/resources/documents/RNCreport03182013.pdf.

[148] RNC, *Growth and Opportunity Project*, 75.

rejection of the "autopsy" report's conclusions from conservatives in the party.[149] After the report was released, Limbaugh argued the GOP had been "totally bamboozled"[150] by the report. Still, other leading Republicans—including Speaker of the House John Boehner and Majority Leader Eric Cantor—expressed support for the project, and Priebus promoted it in a series of appearances, including in Black churches.[151] Notably, in the spring of 2013 it seemed as though a major overhaul of immigration legislation—combining amnesty for undocumented immigrants with updated rules and restrictions for the future—would be achieved. With Republicans in the Senate working with Democrats on immigration legislation, even Kentucky senator Rand Paul (a Tea Party favorite) called for a path to legal status for undocumented immigrants.[152] However, while the Senate successfully passed a bipartisan immigration bill with considerable Republican support, the bill was not considered in the GOP-controlled House due to disapproval in the caucus and massive opposition against the plan in conservative media.[153] Instead, in the run-up to the 2014 midterms, the RNC's branding focused on attacking the Obama administration on issues such as the roll-out of the Obamacare health exchanges, minor scandals surrounding the Secret Service, a small number of cases of the Ebola virus, and the rise of the Islamic State in the Middle East.[154]

This general lack of influence of the RNC in branding is also reflected in New York Times coverage during the Priebus era. Figure 8.6 shows the results of negative binomial regressions in which Priebus's incumbency as RNC chair is the independent variable and the lagged monthly Times coverage of RNC branding and service activities are the dependent variables. In this model, the data is limited to articles covering the RNC published between January 2009 and December 2016—thereby comparing coverage of the RNC from the Priebus era with that under Steele. The results show a decrease in Times coverage of combined RNC branding activities under Priebus (significant at the 0.05 level), and specifically decreases in attacks on the Democrats (significant at the 0.01 level) and policy position taking (marginally significant at the 0.1 level).

As the GOP entered 2015 and the race for the next presidential nomination began, any moderation in immigration policy would remain off the table.

[149] Coppins, The Wilderness, 70.

[150] "Blunt Report Says G.O.P. Needs to Regroup for '16," New York Times, March 19, 2013.

[151] Ibid.; Coppins, The Wilderness, 71.

[152] "Administration Official Defends Release of Detainees," New York Times, March 20, 2013.

[153] Alberta, American Carnage, 160–163.

[154] "Cry of G.O.P. in Campaign: All Is Dismal," New York Times, October 10, 2014. "See also: "Glitches in State Exchanges Give G.O.P. a Cudgel," New York Times, February 2, 2014; "Sebelius Resigns after Troubles over Health Site," New York Times, April 11, 2014."

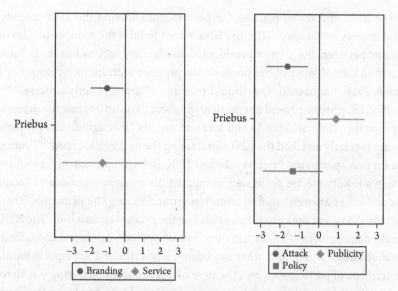

Figure 8.6. Negative binomial regression of Reince Priebus's RNC chairmanship on monthly (lagged) *New York Times* coverage of RNC branding and service activities, 2009–2016. *Note:* This model includes variables controlling for presidential and midterm election years, a measure of *New York Times* length, and RNC scandals. The data coverage is limited to articles published between January 2009 and December 2016, and covering only the RNC.
Source: Data collected by author.

Donald Trump, during his campaign announcement in June 2015, notoriously criticized Mexican immigrants as "bringing drugs. They're bringing crime. They're rapists. And some, I assume are good people."[155] Priebus attempted to have Trump tone down his comments on immigration and explained to him that "You can't talk like that. We've been working really hard to win over Hispanics."[156] But neither Trump nor some of the other candidates in the race (such as Ben Carson, who referred to Muslims as "rabid dogs"[157]) did.[158] Several RNC insiders—including Communications Director Spicer—encouraged Priebus to undermine Trump's campaign. But Priebus believed there was no real chance Trump would win the nomination and it would be better to have him lose on his own.[159]

[155] "Here's Donald Trump's Presidential Announcement Speech," *Time*, June 16, 2015.

[156] Bob Woodward, *Fear: Trump in the White House* (New York: Simon and Schuster, 2018), 11.

[157] "After 2012, the GOP Set Out to Be More Inclusive. What Happened?," *Politico*, November 21, 2015.

[158] "GOP Leaders Fear Damage to Party's Image as Donald Trump Doubles Down," *Washington Post*, July 8, 2015.

[159] Alberta, *American Carnage*, 244.

The RNC did try to manage the processes underlying the 2016 presidential primaries. In January 2015, the RNC voted to limit the number of televised debates between the party's presidential candidates, and to use its influence in setting the calendar of the primaries to produce a presumptive nominee by March 2016. Combined, this should produce a "short, orderly process."[160] In practice, the process proved not particularly short (Trump became the presumptive nominee only on May 3) and far from orderly. Throughout the primaries, Trump regularly attacked the RNC for framing the race against him.[161] Fearing a Trump third-party run, Priebus asked all 17 Republican presidential candidates to sign a loyalty pledge promising to support the eventual nominee.[162] Despite this and other attempts to find common ground during the primaries, Trump continued bashing the committee as biasing the process against him. The RNC's debate management—under the direction of Spicer—produced considerable pushback from Trump and other candidates, who criticized attempts at limiting the number of participants, and the type of questions asked during one debate on CNBC.[163] Meanwhile, as the primaries continued into April, and the Trump campaign failed to get some of its delegates appointed at the state level, Trump described the nomination system as "absolutely rigged. It's a phony deal."[164]

Regardless, as a Trump nomination became all but assured, Priebus declared him the presumptive nominee and pledged the committee's support.[165] And,

---

[160] "Republicans Like Their 2016 Options, Assuming They Avoid Chaos," *New York Times*, January 18, 2015.

[161] Among Trump's comments were his reference to Priebus as "not [...] a five-star Army general" after the RNC chair called him to ask him to tone down his comments on immigrants, calling the RNC "foolish" for how it handled him in general, and accusing the RNC of packing debate audiences with anti-Trump donors. See: "Can't Fire Him: Republican Party Frets over What to Do with Donald Trump," *New York Times*, July 9, 2015; "Donald Trump Threatens Third-Party Candidacy," *New York Times*, July 23, 2015; "R.N.C. Disputes Donald Trump's Claim on Being Stacked with Donors," *New York Times*, February 15, 2016.

[162] "Republican Party Asks Candidates to Sign Loyalty Pledge," *New York Times*, September 2, 2015; "A Pledge for Republican Togetherness, on Donald Trump's Terms," *New York Times*, September 3, 2015; "Donald Trump Signs Loyalty Pledge to Republican Party," *New York Times*, September 3, 2015.

[163] "G.O.P. Seeks Debate Strategy for Expanding Candidate List," *New York Times*, May 14, 2015; "Fox News to Streamline G.O.P. Field for Debate," *New York Times*, May 21, 2015; "Fox News Whittles Field for the First G.O.P. Debate," *New York Times*, August 5, 2015; "CNBC Sets Higher Bar to Enter Next Republican Debate," *New York Times*, October 1, 2015; "A G.O.P. Stalwart's Task: Retooling Candidate Debates," *New York Times*, October 27, 2015; "Ratings Winner for CNBC Is Ammunition for G.O.P.," *New York Times*, October 30, 2015; "G.O.P. Drops Debate on NBC Citing 'Gotcha,'" *New York Times*, October 31, 2015.

[164] "Donald Trump, Losing Ground, Tries to Blame the System," *New York Times*, April 12, 2016.

[165] "Indiana Primary Takeaways: For Donald Trump, Now Comes the Hard Part," *New York Times*, May 4, 2016.

Trump would need it: unlike other recent presidential nominees, Trump had run a bare-bones primary campaign—relying on free media coverage rather than a well-designed campaign organization. Indeed, according to Trump campaign manager Steve Bannon, the Trump campaign existed of "a few people in a room—a speechwriter, and an advance team of about six people that scheduled rallies in the cheapest venues [...]."[166]

After Trump was officially nominated at the Republican convention in July, the campaign used the RNC's updated data and campaign tools extensively, despite the fact that leading Republicans like Senate Majority Leader Mitch McConnell were urging Priebus to divert all Republican resources to the party's congressional candidates instead.[167] After the release of the *Access Hollywood* tape—which included audio footage of Trump in 2005 bragging about sexually harassing women—Priebus reportedly pushed Trump to drop out of the race.[168] But Trump did not, and the RNC continued to support him, despite internal polls showing Trump behind consistently in all swing states.[169] But to the surprise of nearly all operatives involved in the Trump campaign and RNC, Trump won by around 80,000 votes across three states. And, while Republicans lost seats, they retained their majorities in Congress as well. While the RNC's branding efforts between Obama's victory in 2008 and Trump's in 2016 had contributed little to nothing to reshaping the GOP's brand, the committee was given credit for its considerable investments in its service role. With Priebus prioritizing building up the RNC's voter data capacity, the committee was able to support Trump in a way his own campaign would have never been able to do. Even Trump himself was (uncharacteristically) appreciative of Priebus and the RNC: at his victory party, the new president-elect singled out Priebus as "a superstar. Amazing guy. Our partnership with the RNC was so important to the success and what we've done."[170]

Conclusion

Under Presidents George W. Bush and Barack Obama both parties' national committees were largely on the sidelines: both Bush and Obama came into the

---

[166] Woodward, *Fear*, 9.

[167] Ibid., 11.

[168] Ibid., 31; Garrett, *Mr. Trump's Wild Ride*, 62–63; Alberta, *American Carnage*, 373. In contrast, Miller argues that Priebus merely told Trump *other actors* in the party wanted him to drop out and withheld his own assessment. See: Miller, *Why We Did It*, 137.

[169] Garrett, *Mr. Trump's Wild Ride*, 54.

[170] Woodward, *Fear*, 46–47.

White House with a well-developed personal campaign organization and political team and saw little value in investing time and energy into their national committees. In the case of Bush, this meant that the RNC faced a revolving door of chairs—some of whom remained in office just one year or less—with few new branding operations. Meanwhile, Obama's disinterest in the DNC went even further. During his first term, Obama agreed to incorporate his own personal organization OFA into the DNC and used the combined organization to a moderate extent to support his attempts at passing healthcare reform. But from 2011 onward, with the DNC now under the leadership of Debbie Wasserman Schultz, the national committee was rarely on Obama's agenda. Crucially, OFA was again taken out of the DNC to function as Obama's personal re-election campaign organization and after 2012 was kept separate. Indeed, Obama decided to use OFA as an independent political organization—functioning effectively as a competitor to the DNC.

But presidential neglect—while harmful to parties as national organizations—is not a new phenomenon: in the past, whenever national committees faced a period of decline as the in-party, they would generally reinvigorate their organization after a lost election. In terms of financial investments, this remained true in both parties: after the 2000 election, DNC chair Terry McAuliffe raised large amounts of money and used them to invest in the DNC's infrastructure—including by building new headquarters for the party and expanding on the fundraising machine created during the Clinton era. Similarly, after the 2012 loss, the RNC under Reince Priebus invested heavily in the committee's "nuts-and-bolts" organization. What was lacking in out-party committee behavior in this period were the kind of systematic branding efforts that would have followed such investments in the past. Part of the cause of these limited branding efforts was the shortened time span available due to long presidential primary campaigns. For example, DNC chair Howard Dean—who took office with a clear idea of how to rebrand the Democratic Party and aggressively engaged in such efforts in the first two years of his term—saw himself overshadowed and ignored as his party's presidential hopefuls began their campaigns in early 2007. With the candidates dominating intra-party debate and media coverage there was little space for chairs like Dean, McAuliffe, or Priebus simultaneously to try to promote a specific new brand for the party.

Additionally, the committees were functioning in a new media environment. While in the past, national committees had some level of monopoly on major national publicity efforts within their parties, with the rise of the Internet, talk radio, and ideological news networks, this space became much more crowded. A clear example of this new reality was the RNC's attempt at rebranding the GOP after the 2012 election. While the RNC's own report explaining Republican losses in that election stressed a need for a gentler, more open party that embraced immigration reform, any attempts by the RNC at presenting this as a new image of the GOP was overshadowed by criticism from conservative critics—including talk radio host Rush Limbaugh, Fox News presenters, and activists and politicians in the party who could now much more easily reach large audiences and counter whatever message the RNC might be promoting.

As a result, both national committees by the 2016 election had seemingly run out of opportunities to play the kind of major branding roles they had in the past. To presidents, the national committees' value was increasingly limited. Unlike Eisenhower, Reagan, or Clinton, more recent presidents generally did not need to rely on their national committee for organizational support or publicity efforts. And, even out of the White House, both the opportunity and space available to national committees to engage in major rebranding efforts seem increasingly limited.

9

Conclusion

The Past and Future of National Committees

In this book, I have argued that the Democratic National Committee (DNC) and Republican National Committee (RNC) play a complex but important role in American politics due to their goal of trying to (re)shape their respective parties' national brands. Such party branding activity is important to the party, as politicians believe voters rely on the party's brand as a core heuristic in elections. For such a heuristic to work, the image voters have of a party needs to be somewhat consistent, which is difficult to achieve in a political system in which both parties often include political actors with very diverse preferences, and in which party leaders lack the ability to force members outright to follow their orders. National committees form an imperfect solution to this problem: as the sole national organizations of each party, the DNC and RNC have at least some credibility when they speak on behalf of the party as a national institution. Additionally, both committees were able to invest heavily in their publicity divisions, providing them with tools often unavailable to other actors or organizations within their party. Thus, throughout the 20th century, the DNC and RNC regularly engaged in major publicity operations with the goal of providing voters with a clear understanding of the party's brand.

As the historical cases in this book have shown, the committees tried to achieve this by creating a plethora of political communication tools such as magazines, TV and radio shows, Internet services, and advertisements in all types of media formats. Additionally, both national committees over time began to claim the right to set party policies on behalf of their parties through a long series of organizations tasked with designing new policy agendas. In doing so, national committees used their available agency to determine what *type* of brand to promote—that is, what policies to center, what politicians to spotlight, and which voting groups to target. As a result, the DNC and RNC have found themselves in the center of each major intra-party conflict in the 20th century.

National Party Organizations and Party Brands in American Politics. Boris Heersink, Oxford University Press.
© Oxford University Press 2023. DOI: 10.1093/oso/9780197695104.003.0009

But while party branding is a fundamental goal of national committees as political institutions, success in shaping that brand is not guaranteed. National committees cannot make voters embrace their preferred party image: they can only try to reach out to voters with informational cues and hope they incorporate them into their assessment of the party. As the history presented here shows, voters often are not persuaded. To be sure, this is not a flaw unique to the national committees and their branding efforts. Rather, it reflects the complicated nature of party branding as a political goal: there is no easy way to convince voters they should support one party over the other. Thus, while the DNC and RNC may not necessarily succeed in their branding efforts, their value to politicians in the parties is that they *try*. And, when they fail, the answer is simply to engage in different and/or more branding efforts moving forward.

But this book has also shown that the extent to which national committees engage in branding is not consistent. One crucial barrier to branding is whether a party is in the White House or not. 'In-parties' have presidents with de facto control over their party's national organization. Their use (or disuse) of national committees differs based on the political context in which they find themselves but generally falls in two categories: either presidents see value in using the committees as branding tools and instruct them to promote their administration's policies and themselves, or they see no use in them and let them decline as organizations. While presidential neglect hurts national committees as organizations, they often rebound after the next presidential election loss. But over time, the committees' ability to play a central role in setting the tone on behalf of their party has become more complicated: with the rise of long presidential primaries, easier access to mass political communication tools, and more ideologically homogenous parties, the space for national committees to engage in major rebranding efforts has become more limited. As a result, the DNC and RNC in recent years appear to have become less relevant in terms of their branding roles.

In the following sections, I discuss the main conclusions of this book. I focus specifically on three core areas: the branding role of out-party national committees, the effects of presidential leadership on national party organizations, and the future of the DNC and RNC in a radically different era of partisanship and political communication.

Out-Party National Committees

The cases in this book show remarkable consistency in the way partisan actors respond to defeat in a presidential election. Often, politicians explicitly blame losses on voters' perception of their party's brand. From William G. McAdoo's assessment that Democratic defeat in 1920 was caused by a "failure to get the Democratic side before the people through proper publicity"[1] to John D. M. Hamilton's conclusion after the 1936 election that "when you talk to the average man about the Republican Party, he asks you what the Party stands for,"[2] politicians believe electoral success or failure is directly linked to voters' image of the party. After a loss, those partisan actors equally consistently identified a solution to this branding problem: have their national committee work at producing a more successful brand for future elections. After all, these politicians believed that—as Everett Dirksen stated in 1964—it is the national committee's "business [. . .] to project the true"[3] image of its party to voters. And, when the previous brand has failed to convince voters, it is the DNC or RNC's job to be— in Franklin Delano Roosevelt's terminology—"the body which should guide"[4] the party toward an electorally more effective version of the brand.

In executing this role, national committee chairs invest heavily in their organization's publicity divisions and/or create new political communication tools to reach out to voters. In the pre-television era, the DNC and RNC used radio broadcasts, which allowed politicians selected by the committees to make speeches to a national or regional audience, and both committees used their publicity offices to distribute party materials to news media outside of Washington, DC, to have their party's message reflected in local media. With technological advances in political communication, the committees updated their approaches as well. Both the DNC and RNC began to invest in television in the 1940s, '50s, and '60s by creating TV ads and building an infrastructure at their headquarters allowing politicians in their party to connect with local stations in their districts or states. In doing so, committees often came up with new communication tools they controlled—such as the DNC's popular magazine *Democratic Digest* or the RNC's radio and TV format *Comment*. The goal of these communication tools was to reach a large audience of voters and present them directly with the topics and politicians the national committee believed best represented their party. These investments did not end with the TV era. Indeed, in the early 1990s the RNC invested in the Internet as a new communication tool—going so far as to start its own Internet access service (complete with "anti-smut" filter). And, in the early 2000s when, under Terry McAuliffe, the DNC invested in new

[1] "McAdoo on Party's Needs," *New York Times,* January 9, 1921; "Envy the Elephant," *Los Angeles Times,* January 9, 1921.

[2] Paul Kesaris, Blair Hydrick, and Douglas D. Newman, *Papers of the Republican Party* [microform] (Frederick, MD: University Publications of America, 1987), Reel 5, Frame 435.

[3] "Dirksen Puts Onus on Republican Committee," *Los Angeles Times,* December 13, 1964.

[4] Cited in Jurdem, *Return to the Arena,* 137.

headquarters, one of the selling points was that the building came with state-of-the-art publicity production facilities.

In creating these tools, both committees frequently copied each other's (and their own) previous branding attempts. The clearest example is the long series of sub-national committee organizations given the power to set party policies. Both the RNC and DNC had attempted to define their party's positions on important policies in the first half of the 20th century—such as the DNC's attempts to embrace opposition to Prohibition in the 1920s or the RNC's role in forging a Republican consensus position on post–World War II international relations. But the DNC's attempts under Paul Butler's leadership to use the Democratic Advisory Council (DAC) to set party policies after the 1956 election reflected a dramatic expansion of national committee influence. For the first time, a national committee claimed to have the institutional power to determine its parties' policies. While the DAC was dismissed by political analysts at the time (and political scientists afterward) as ineffective, politicians believed the council had clear value for the Democratic Party. Indeed, after the DAC, national committees in both parties created new versions of the DAC in response to presidential election losses in 1964 (the Republican Coordinating Committee), 1968 (the Democratic Policy Council), 1972 (the Democratic Advisory Council of Elected Officials), 1976 (the RNC's advisory committees), 1980 (the DNC's National Strategy Council), 1984 (the Democratic Policy Commission), and 1992 (the RNC's National Policy Forum).

Fundamentally, each of these organizations had the same goal. What this goal was *not* was to achieve immediate policy outcomes through legislation. Indeed, this would have been close to impossible given the conditions under which each organization was founded: the DAC and its many successors were generally formed at a time when its party would be unable to pass legislation easily, as it did not have control of one or multiple veto points in the legislative process. Instead, the goal for these organizations was to shape voters' image of what policies the party supported at the time and convince them to vote for the party in future elections. Indeed, RNC chair Dean Burch, in discussing the DAC, did not focus on the organization's inability to have its proposals taken up in Congress but instead stressed the "considerable attention in the press"[5] the DAC's reports received as evidence for why the RNC should create its own similar organization.

The goal of engaging in party branding efforts was consistently present in out-party national committees across the cases presented here, and the quantitative results presented in Chapter 2 support the argument that national committees

[5] Kesaris et al., *Papers of the Republican Party*, Series B, Reel 4, Frame 647.

of out-parties are more engaged in branding efforts than those "in" the White House. But there were exceptions: in some cases, out-party committees did not see major branding efforts for reasons that appear to be connected to individual national committee chairs who (for varying reasons) were not interested in encouraging and managing such activities—including chairs such as Clem Shaver (DNC, 1925–1928, who seemed generally uninterested in running the organization) and Everett Sanders (RNC, 1932–1934, who faced considerable health issues throughout his period as chair). But when committee chairs like Shaver or Sanders fell short, others in the party often criticized the national committee for not expanding its branding role. For example, FDR criticized Shaver for having "very frankly declined to assume any responsibility whatever."[6] for producing a coherent Democratic message. Financial limitations often also were a core explanation for national committee chairs being unable to expand the branding activities to the extent demanded by other party leaders. Yet, even in those years, national committee chairs often did try to work with the limited resources they had to create publicity on behalf of their party. For example, Larry O'Brien and Bob Strauss—who served as chairs of the DNC between 1968 and 1976 in a period in which the organization was effectively insolvent—were still able to introduce new branding-related communication tools and party organizations, including Strauss's DNC telethon format. And, after the Watergate scandal resulted in a notable decrease in donations to the RNC, chair Mary Louise Smith prioritized spending money on a major publicity campaign to reintroduce the GOP to voters.

What type of image did out-party committees use these publicity tools to promote? In some specific cases, committee chairs tried to use their position to alter existing policy positions within the party dramatically. And when they did, this often resulted in backlash from other politicians within the party who disagreed with those attempts. John Raskob tried to use his control over the DNC to push the Democratic Party to embrace opposition to Prohibition. In return, he received major pushback from Southern Democrats and FDR and his allies. Similarly, Paul Butler's attempts at repositioning the Democratic Party as a clearly liberal party after the 1956 election caused major upset among conservative Democrats. And attempts by Bill Miller and Dean Burch to rebrand the GOP as a clearly conservative party in the 1960s was condemned by moderates in the party, who warned that the RNC's Southern strategy required effectively condoning segregation and would hurt the GOP outside of the former Confederacy.

[6] Cited in Jurdem, *Return to the Arena*, 137.

Mostly, however, both the DNC and RNC attempted to moderate their party's images. That is, party chairs attempted to find ways to appeal to what they believed to be the median voter in future elections by downplaying what they perceived to be the extremists in their party pushing those voters away. In the case of the Republican Party, for much of the 20th century this meant the RNC was trying to limit the influence of its party's conservative wing on voters' perception of the Republican party brand. During the New Deal era, this included the RNC's central role in ending the GOP's policy of isolationism. In between the 1952 and 1980 elections, the RNC was nearly continuously (with the exception of the Miller–Burch era) on the side of the Eisenhower wing of the GOP. That is, the RNC tried presenting the Republican Party as a reasonable, centrist party that voters could trust to manage—but not dismantle—the post–New Deal expanded federal government. Crucially in this period, the RNC also often prioritized reaching out to Black voters—particularly under the leadership of Ray Bliss (1965–1968) and Bill Brock (1977–1980)—as part of this attempt at moderating the party's image. And, even after the Reagan Revolution, the RNC's political strategy remained centered on appealing to moderates by stressing the "big tent" nature of the Republican Party with regard to abortion or embracing immigration reform after the 2012 election.

The DNC's goals were largely similar. After its long period of White House control ended in 1952, Stephen Mitchell embraced a "unity" strategy aimed at keeping Southern conservatives in the party. While under his successor Butler this approach was replaced with the attempt of rebranding the Democratic Party as a clearly liberal institution, after losses in 1968, 1972, 1980, 1984, and 1988 the DNC returned to Mitchell's goal of producing unity within a still ideologically broad party. However, embracing "unity" in practice meant the DNC promoted a set of policy choices that generally went against preferences of liberals in the party. DNC chairs, facing the question of how to reconfigure their voting coalition, concluded that there was no path to victory without support from voters it perceived as being more conservative than its party image. As a result, these chairs worked to move the Democratic brand away from liberal policies. This meant the committee in the 1970s forged a working relationship with George Wallace, while in the 1980s the DNC tried to downplay the influence of "liberal groups" in the party—most importantly, Black leaders. Meanwhile, these chairs focused on presenting the Democratic Party as "tough" on crime, drugs, welfare, and in international relations. Even Howard Dean—a hero of the liberal wing of the Democratic Party due to his early opposition to the Iraq War—as DNC chair centered his 50-state strategy on appealing to White Republican voters and embracing (some) socially conservative messaging.

But "moderation" still reflects taking on policy positions. Indeed, as the historical cases presented here show, national committees of out-parties have perpetually placed themselves in major intra-party debates about the future direction of their party. When they did, they often alienated those in the party who disagreed with their proposed image of the party—whether that was conservatives in the Democratic or Republican parties opposing committee attempts to produce a liberal or moderate party brand, Republican moderates challenging a conservative RNC's Southern strategy, or Black leaders criticizing DNC chairs for prioritizing outreach to White conservative voters. The reason these partisan actors opposed their national committee is that they believed they would face negative consequences from the "wrong" party brand. And, because they believed that their national committee was part of the process of shaping such brands, they were deeply invested in their activities. As a result, throughout the history covered in this book, out-party national committees were not mere service providers on the periphery of party politics: their branding role placed them in the center of their parties.

In-Party National Committees

The same is not consistently true for in-party national committees. Because presidents have de facto control over their national committee while they are in office, national committee chairs (selected by those presidents and serving at their pleasure) understand the national committee's role to be fundamentally different when the party controls the White House. Indeed, political actors in and outside of national committees identify in-party committee chairs as—in the words of Bill Clinton's Deputy Chief of Staff Harold Ickes—being "the president's agent."[7] Indeed, RNC chair Smith—who served under President Gerald Ford—argued that "a President of your own party is certainly considered the leader of the party and plays the dominant role, and should,"[8] while RNC chair Lee Atwater (serving under President George H. W. Bush) stressed that "I do not consider myself the leader of the Republican Party. President Bush is."[9]

The case studies presented in this book only show one clear exception to the understanding that an in-party national committee is expected to support its incumbent president: the peculiar case of RNC chair John T. Adams, who served under Warren G. Harding and Calvin Coolidge. During the Wilson administration, the RNC had begun to expand its organization and policy-setting role.

[7] "Man on a Tightrope," *Washington Post*, April 20, 1994.

[8] Suzanne O'Dea, *Madam Chairman: Mary Louise Smith and the Republican Revival after Watergate* (Columbia: University of Missouri Press, 2012), 71.

[9] "Man as Symbol: Atwater's First Year as the Republican National Chairman," *New York Times*, December 29, 1989.

After the 1922 midterms increased the power of progressives in the Republican Party, Adams—a conservative—began openly to oppose both progressive Republicans in Congress and certain positions taken by the Harding administration. But Adams was a clear outlier: throughout every other administration, in-party national committees followed the incumbent president's commands.

How do presidents use their control? In some cases, presidents relied on their national committees to continue their branding activities but center them on messages supportive of their own political goals. Often, this includes national committees supporting a president's legislative agenda. During the first years of the Kennedy administration, the DNC engaged in Operation Support to back bills Kennedy tried to get through Congress. Under Reagan and Clinton, the RNC and DNC spent millions of dollars on television advertisements and other promotional activities backing their respective president's legislative priorities. But in-party committees also use their branding tools to promote the presidents themselves—most notably, in support of upcoming re-election efforts. For example, while the DNC had dramatically declined during the New Deal, it was temporarily revitalized in the run-up to Harry Truman's 1948 campaign. The RNC remained active during Nixon's first term in the White House but mostly used its publicity tools to promote Nixon and attack Democrats who disagreed with him. Under Reagan, the RNC purposely connected its broader publicity to the president personally, consistently presenting the GOP as "Reagan's party." And as early as the summer of 1995, the DNC began spending millions of dollars on ads supporting Clinton's re-election effort.

In some conditions, connecting the party to the president and their policies can be a positive for the party as a broader institution. In the Republican Party in the period 1952–1992, incumbent presidents practically always outperformed the GOP in down-ballot races: Eisenhower, Nixon, Reagan, and George H. W. Bush won landslide election victories while the Republican Party underperformed in comparison in congressional, gubernatorial, and state legislative races. Trying to produce an image of a party in connection to its most visible and most popular national politician under those conditions is quite sensible. That is, national committees can make the rational decision that they—to use a description of the RNC's strategy after Nixon's 1972 landslide—should "sell what's popular. That's the President."[10]

But presidents may not always be popular, and their policies may not necessarily have broad support within the party. Despite his overwhelming victory in 1972, Nixon's decline during the Watergate scandal hurt the RNC's ability to

[10] "Bush Remolds GOP Committee into Adjunct of White House," *Washington Post*, March 19, 1973.

"sell" the GOP to voters. Even the RNC's choice to place Reagan at the core of its branding strategy in the 1980s eventually produced a messaging vacuum toward the end of his second term. The DNC's promotion of Kennedy's legislative agenda at times clashed with Democratic opponents—particularly in the South. And Clinton's use of the DNC to promote his own policies and re-election campaign angered many Democrats in Congress, who argued that the DNC not only was not helping their re-election efforts but also was even outright hurting them. Thus, presidential control of national committee branding can come at a cost to other actors in the party—both figuratively (when the messages national committees prioritize are not benefiting other members of the party) and literally (when the committees spent extraordinary amounts of money on promoting its president but failed to invest in lower-ballot races).

But while many presidents see value in relying on their national committees for branding purposes, not all do. Presidents may have multiple reasons for why they might believe that party branding by a national committee is unlikely to benefit them. One concern—which played into Lyndon Johnson's decision to ignore and shrink the DNC—might be that partisan branding efforts could complicate a president's ability to build bipartisan legislative majorities. In other cases, presidents may simply conclude that their national committee is not necessary to achieve their political goals—such as FDR's assessment that Democratic victories in presidential and congressional elections could be achieved without an active DNC. While this is certainly not true for all presidents, the analysis presented in Chapter 2 shows that on average in-party national committees do see fewer branding activities covered in the *New York Times*. Notably, this does not apply to coverage of service activities—suggesting that the change does not reflect a complete rejection of national committees by presidents or a lack of news media interest in covering in-party national committees.

Indeed, the case studies presented in this book confirm that presidents such as Coolidge, Hoover, FDR, Johnson, Carter, George W. Bush, and Obama frequently had little interest in their national committees. The result of such presidential neglect is the decline of national committees as organizations. Thus, while the DNC as an out-party during the Hoover administration had built a massive publicity division, the organization declined dramatically during FDR's long presidency. John F. Kennedy, before he was even inaugurated, ordered the DNC to end both the *Democratic Digest* and the DAC (two of the most important party branding innovations introduced during the Eisenhower years), and Jimmy Carter neglected the DNC from the beginning of his presidency. In recent years, George W. Bush and Barack Obama had little interest in managing their respective national party organizations—with the latter going so far as to set up his former personal campaign organization as a direct competitor to the DNC after the 2012 election.

To be sure, such neglect can reflect an understandable choice from the perspective of the president. Presidents face complex and daunting issues that require much of their time and attention. As Daniel Galvin has argued, it is mostly presidents of minority parties (like Eisenhower and Reagan) who invest some of their time in party-building activities—reflecting their concern with their party's inability to win congressional majorities and their belief that national party organizations are crucial to solving this problem. But presidents who believed (rightly or wrongly) that their parties were in a relatively strong electoral position may reasonably have decided that focusing on managing their national committees is a poor investment. As a result, national committees (but, given the Democratic Party's consistent success in maintaining congressional majorities for much of the 20th century, particularly the DNC) often found themselves stuck in a rather inefficient cycle: an out-party committee may invest heavily in its publicity division with the goal of promoting an appealing version of its party's brand, but those investments can dissolve once their party wins the White House, only to have the committee rebuild it all again after the next presidential election defeat.

The Future of National Committees: The End of Branding?

The case studies presented in this book show that both the DNC and RNC throughout the 20th century saw producing and shaping their party's national brand as a core role. But executing this role has become increasingly difficult for the committees. In recent decades, the political space available for national committees to try to engage in major (re)branding efforts has decreased, and the competition in such messaging has expanded dramatically.

One change has been the extension of the presidential primary process. Due to frontloading, primaries themselves have started earlier—though as of now, they have remained within the actual presidential election year. But the invisible primary process has stretched the primary season to a nearly two-year event. As a result, throughout that period, media and voters are focused largely on presidential candidates fighting over the nomination, and national committees' pronouncements are less likely to gain interest. Additionally, the nature of presidential primaries as intra-party contests also undermines the national committees' ability to engage in branding efforts. The committees—through their publicity efforts—try to send signals to voters about the "correct" image they should have of the national party. But during presidential primaries, individual candidates are also engaged in debates about what that image should be. While both the DNC and RNC in the past have tried to manage such debates, the reality appears to be that, if national committees were to continue with major branding operations during the primaries, they are likely to be seen as taking sides in the primaries and run the risk of being accused of trying to "rig" the contest in favor of a candidate. Indeed, the major controversies regarding the RNC in 2016 and the DNC in the 2016 and 2020 primaries suggest that national party organizations would like to avoid finding themselves in such a position.

This expansion of presidential primaries in the political calendar is particularly problematic for the committee's branding efforts since such long primaries are all but guaranteed to occur when the party is out of the White House. That is, an in-party with a president in their first term generally does not see a primary contest since presidents often are all but assured of being renominated.[11] But out-parties practically always have a competitive primary for their presidential nomination. This means out-parties—those with committees that historically would try to engage in major rebranding efforts for their parties—see the amount of time to engage in such efforts essentially cut in half. Prior to the expansion of the primary timetable in the 1980s, out-party national committees would have close to four years to try to build up their branding operations and then use those tools to promote an image they believed would increase their party's electoral viability. But, in the modern primary system that period effectively ends after the midterm elections. This leaves national committees very little time to invest in their resources, devise a new message, and promote it to voters.

A good illustration of this is the chairmanship of Howard Dean, who became chair of the DNC after the 2004 election and had a clear strategy for how the Democratic Party should be rebranded. In 2005 and 2006, Dean worked at implementing this strategy by promoting an image of the Democratic Party as reaching out to voters that the party had "forgotten" about in recent years (i.e., White, working-class, and religious voters). The highly successful 2006 midterm results were interpreted by many—including Dean himself—as evidence that his strategy was paying off, and one would imagine Dean had every incentive to continue playing an active role in promoting his version of the Democratic Party in the remaining years of his term. But with presidential candidates like Hillary Clinton, Barack Obama, and John Edwards announcing their candidacies as early as January 2007, Dean effectively disappeared from the political stage.

While the invisible primary has been part of the American political system since the 1980s, more recent changes in political communication have further undermined the DNC and RNC's branding role. Historically, national committees were particularly well positioned to engage in party branding

---

[11] During the modern era of primaries only presidents Gerald Ford (in 1976) and George H. W. Bush (in 1992) faced serious opposition to their (re)nomination.

because doing so required major financial investments and innovation in publicity tools. That is, the DNC publishing a magazine like the *Democratic Digest* or the RNC creating a TV and radio program like *Comment* were valuable to actors in the party because they themselves generally had no easy way to promote a vision of the party in anything close to the same quality or range. In this regard, things have fundamentally changed through the introduction of ideological (and, to a large extent, partisan) news sources in the form of talk radio and cable news networks which cater to specific audiences that largely overlap with voters in the parties. As a result, the hosts and pundits that appear on its programs may brand on behalf of a party of which they are not officially members.[12] On the Republican side in particular, activities of figures like Rush Limbaugh, Sean Hannity, Bill O'Reilly, or Tucker Carlson have had a clear effect on what voters understand the Republican Party to stand for. To be sure, this often is in line with the broad image that actors within the GOP would like voters to have. But at other times—such as the RNC's failed attempt at centering immigration reform after the 2012 election—actors outside of the party can successfully override efforts by the national committee.

An even bigger change has been the introduction of the Internet and social media in political communication. While initially both committees saw the Internet as yet another new communication tool that they could easily co-opt into their existing publicity divisions, it is clearly different from radio or television. Unlike these other communication tools, the Internet has made it easier and cheaper than ever before for individual political actors to reach millions of voters without having to rely on national party organizations. A good illustration of how social media usage by individual politicians has diminished the influence of the national committees is a simple comparison of the number of followers the DNC and RNC accounts and specific politicians have on Twitter. In the summer of 2021, the main DNC Twitter account had only around 130,000 followers. The main Twitter account of the RNC did better, with 2.5 million followers. But both those numbers are dwarfed by those of individual politicians within their parties. For example, Senator Ted Cruz's (R-TX) campaign account alone had 4.5 million followers, while Democratic Representative Alexandria Ocasio-Cortez (NY)—a particularly social media–savvy politician—had 12.7 million followers. Cruz and Ocasio-Cortez are perhaps especially appealing to hyper-partisan social media users, but even the considerably less "hip" Twitter account for Nancy Pelosi as Speaker of the House had 7.1 million followers. And

---

[12] To be sure, as Hans Noel has argued, pundits of all types (or "academic scribblers") functioning outside of the official party organizations have always played a role in defining the changing components of political ideologies. See Hans Noel, *Political Ideologies and Political Parties in America* (New York: Cambridge University Press, 2014).

presidents easily beat all those numbers: Joe Biden's personal Twitter account had 31.3 million followers, while Donald Trump, at the time that his account was suspended after his encouragement of the failed insurrection of January 2021, had 88.7 million followers. Meanwhile, his predecessor Barack Obama had around 130 million followers.

While some of these followers may be foreign accounts, inactive users, or bots, and most Americans are not active on Twitter, it nonetheless signifies how much social media has changed political communication. This has had many effects on American politics—not the least of which is the dramatic proliferation of political misinformation about everything from Obama's birthplace, the "Big Lie" regarding Trump's loss in the 2020 election, and conspiracy theories regarding QAnon and Covid. But it also dramatically undermines the DNC and RNC's ability to play a leading branding role in their parties. In the 1950s, the DNC's *Democratic Digest* was considered an important and major new communication tool for the party, which started at a run of 100,000 copies. Reaching these voters required investment and a sophisticated publicity division. But today, many politicians can easily reach many more than 100,000 people within seconds of posting on Facebook or Twitter. An appearance on a prime time show on Fox News or MSNBC can reach millions of viewers, with potentially millions more watching clips in the hours that follow on social media. While national committees never had a monopoly on political communication on behalf of their party, their ability to be a dominant voice in the way that they used to seems increasingly unrealistic in today's political communication era.

Final Thoughts: The Future of National Committees

Where does this leave the national committees and their parties moving forward? Ironically, given this book's framing of branding in contrast to the traditional perspective of the DNC and RNC, the path both committees appear to be taking is to focus more on service activities. While the RNC very quickly abandoned its attempts at pushing the GOP to embrace policies that would bring in minority voters after the 2012 election, it invested heavily in expanding its campaign operations. In particular, the RNC built up an extensive voter database, which it allows Republican candidates to use in elections. Increasingly, it appears that such data is becoming a core argument for the continuing value national party organizations provide to their parties.

The national committees have become more aggressive in challenging other organizations aiming to replace their role in this regard. In 2018, after the political network of Charles and David Koch—which is nearly exclusively supportive of Republican candidates but external to its party organization—announced its intentions of building up a similar information system independent of the RNC. In response, RNC chair Ronna Romney McDaniel warned donors not to support the Koch effort because the RNC "is the only entity which can be trusted with the data Republicans candidates need to win up and down the ballot."[13] That same year, the DNC proposed combining splintered voter databases that existed across the national committee, state parties, and other organizations.[14]

It is, of course, possible that a future national committee chair might be able to navigate this new reality and be more visible than recent DNC and RNC chairs like Tom Perez or Romney McDaniel. But it seems undeniable that the kind of major branding operations both national committees engaged in during the 20th century are unlikely to exist in the 21st. It is debatable to what extent this is a positive or negative development for political parties and American politics more broadly. With both parties now strongly ideologically polarized and voters increasingly reliant on negative partisanship in making political decisions, perhaps there is simply little value to the type of branding efforts national committees used to engage in.[15] Throughout most of the period covered in this book, national committee chairs functioned under the assumption that different voting groups were persuadable and that their job was to convince them to support the party in future elections. In terms of electoral strategy, given the competitiveness of American elections since 2000, that approach is now less appealing than simply doubling down on energizing the party's base. And, given that the national committees often were unsuccessful in achieving the goals underlying their rebranding efforts (think only of the RNC's inability to convince Black voters to rejoin the party), one could argue that the demise of national committee branding efforts may not be a great loss.

But what national committees were trying to achieve through their branding efforts reflected a core underlying feature of party competition: that is, party leaders believed their ability to win elections relied on convincing voters that they were a better choice than the opposite party. This also encouraged parties to innovate and reinvent themselves. Martin Van Buren—one of the strongest early defenders of political parties as permanent fixtures in American politics— argued that permanent competition between political parties forces them to

---

[13] "RNC Warns Donors to Steer Clear of Kochs," *Politico*, August 2, 2018.

[14] "'We Have a Crisis': Democrats at War over Trove of Voter Data," *Politico*, December 6, 2018.

[15] Alan I. Abramowitz and Steven W. Webster, "Negative Partisanship: Why Americans Dislike Parties but Behave Like Rabid Partisans," *Political Psychology* 39, no. S1 (2018): 119–135; Steven W. Webster, *American Rage: How Anger Shapes Our Politics* (New York: Cambridge University Press, 2020).

engage in "a fair and open contest for the establishment of principles in the administration of government."[16] Such a contest requires parties not just to articulate but also to adjust those principles as electoral conditions change. The DNC and RNC branding efforts throughout the 20th century reflected this necessity: when parties underperformed, the national committees attempted to identify and promote a new version of the party that voters would find appealing. But if parties merely need to excite an already convinced base, they may not have much need to update or even identify what their governing principles are. Indeed, the Republican Party in 2020—for the first time in the existence of the GOP—failed to pass a platform at its national convention, replacing it with a mere expression of support for Donald Trump instead.[17] The disappearance of national committee branding activities thus not only reflects a change in the core role that two major institutions play in American politics; it also illustrates the potential broader disappearance of parties' attempts at managing the process of producing a national brand to compete genuinely for support from different voting groups.

---

[16] Quoted in James W. Ceaser, *Presidential Selection: Theory and Development* (Princeton, NJ: Princeton University Press, 1979), 135.

[17] "The G.O.P. Delivers Its 2020 Platform. It's from 2016," *New York Times*, August 25, 2020.

INDEX

For the benefit of digital users, indexed terms that span two pages (e.g., 52–53) may, on occasion, appear on only one of those pages.
Tables and figures are indicated by *t* and *f* following the page number

Black voters
  Democratic National Committee and, 127–28,
    130–31, 138–39, 140–41, 160–61, 183–84,
    200, 230, 233–34, 239, 240–41, 274–75,
    296, 319–20
  disenfranchisement of, 15n.32, 63, 64–65
  election of 1948 and, 113–14
  election of 1956 and, 127–28, 130–31, 139,
    148–49, 174
  election of 1960 and, 164
  election of 1966 and, 171–72
  election of 1976 and, 212–13, 228–29
  Hurricane Katrina (2005) and, 284
  Republican National Committee and, 25, 106,
    123–24, 164, 168, 171–72, 173, 175, 177,
    202, 204–5, 209, 211–17, 220, 228–29, 247–
    48, 253–54, 280, 282–85, 302–3, 304–5,
    307–8, 319, 327
Blackwell, J. Kenneth, 302–3
Bliss, Ray C.
  Black voters and, 171–72, 173, 177, 202, 319
  party branding efforts and, 203, 204f
  publicity programs and, 169–72, 170t
  Republican Coordinating Committee
    and, 172–73
  selection as RNC chair (1964) of, 169
  urban voters and, 165
Boehner, John, 307–8
Bond, Richard, 255–57, 258–59, 263
Bone, Hugh A., 6
Borah, William, 80–81
Bork, Robert, 210
Boyda, Nancy, 292
Boyle Jr., William M., 115–16, 122
branding of political parties
  Barbour and, 258–59, 261f, 261–62
  Bliss and, 203, 204f
  Brock and, 209–10, 211f, 211, 217, 251f, 251
  Butler and, 145f, 145–46, 147–48, 153f, 160,
    318, 319
  consistency as a value in, 10–12, 314
  constraints on, 19–26, 314–15, 323–26
  Dean and, 18, 278, 289–91, 292–93, 297–98,
    298f, 312–13, 319, 324
  Democratic Advisory Council and, 141–42,
    147–48, 317
  Dole and, 208–9, 215–16, 228–29, 256–57
  heuristic value of, 9–10, 13, 314
  Hull and, 73f, 73–74
  Internet's impact on, 3, 278, 312–13, 325–26
  intra-party conflicts and, 2, 10–11, 13, 18–19,
    20, 22, 314
  Kirk and, 240, 293
  Manatt and, 234, 237, 238f
  McAuliffe and, 287, 288f, 293, 312
  Miller and, 166f, 166–67, 318–19
  Mitchell and, 134–35, 135f, 145–46, 319

O'Brien and, 182f, 182, 317–18
  partisan media outlets and, 22, 324–26
  party chairs' role in, 18, 19–20
  political polarization in the twenty-first century
    and, 278, 327–28
  presidential incumbency's impact on, 19–21,
    23, 33–44, 37t, 39f, 40t, 41f, 43f, 45t, 46t, 47f,
    48–49, 50t, 51t, 52t, 53f, 54f, 315–23, 324
  presidential primary campaigns' impact on,
    22–23, 25–26, 231, 242–43, 252–53, 276,
    277–78, 293, 312, 315, 323–24
  Priebus and, 306–8, 309f, 312
  Raskob and, 78–80, 79f, 94–95, 95f
  Shaver and, 78–80, 79f, 317–18
  Steele and, 303, 308, 309f
  Strauss and, 193–94, 197, 224–25, 225f,
    228, 317–18
  talk radio's impact on, 3, 22, 278, 312–
    13, 324–25
Brennan, Mary, 173
Brewer, Albert, 189
Brock, Bill
  advisory committees established by, 210
  Black voters and, 177, 211–13, 215–17, 228–
    29, 247–48, 319
  election of 1978 and, 216–17
  election of 1980 and, 220, 231–32
  evangelical Christian voters and, 177, 217–
    20, 229
  party branding efforts by, 209–10, 211f, 211,
    217, 251f, 251
  Republican National Convention (1980)
    and, 216–17
  selection as RNC chair (1977) of, 177, 209
Broder, David S., 196–97, 234, 269
Brown, Edmund G. ("Jerry"), 235–36
Brown, John Y., 190–91
Brown, Ron, 243–47, 266, 293
Brownell, Herbert, 110, 116–17
Brown v. Board of Education, 158
Bryan, Richard H., 268–69
Buchanan, Pat, 208–9, 217, 255–56
Bumpers, Dale, 196
Burch, Dean, 168–69, 172, 317–19
Burgess, Duke, 165–66
Burns, James Macgregor, 76–77
Bush, George H.W.
  abortion policy and, 254
  election of 1988 and, 243, 252–53
  election of 1992 and, 246, 247, 255–56
  as Republican National Committee chair during
    1970s, 203–5, 254
  Republican National Committee during
    presidency of, 253–56, 261f, 261, 274–75,
    320, 321
Bush, George W.
  Afghanistan War and, 281, 303